THEATRE

103

THEATRE

AN INTRODUCTION

MARSH CASSADY

In memory of my wife, Pat Mizer Cassady;
In memory of Rev. Robert Rau—whose humanity
helped me to realize my own;
And, as always, for JDK

Executive Editor: Marisa L. L'Heureux
Project Editor: Sue Schumer
Cover and interior design: Ophelia Chambliss
Production Manager: Rosemary Dolinski

Acknowledgments for excerpts of literary and dramatic works begin on page 396, which is to be considered an extension of this copyright page.

ISBN 0-8442-5868-7 (student text)

ISBN 0-8442-5869-5 (instructor's edition)

Published by NTC Publishing Group,
a division of NTC/Contemporary Publishing Group, Inc.,
4255 West Touhy Avenue,
Lincolnwood (Chicago), Illinois 60646-1975 U.S.A.

Library of Congress Catalog Card Number: 94-68799
Manufactured in the United States of America.

8 9 0 QB 9 8 7 6 5 4 3 2

Contents

Preface

My main concern in writing *Theatre: An Introduction* was to present a readable and interesting text. To my way of thinking, too many textbooks, whatever ground they cover, are academic and boring. Although I have experience in many facets of theatre—acting, directing, design, and university teaching—I consider myself primarily a writer. Thus for me, the major criterion for any book is its readability, and I feel that the readability of this book sets it apart.

Although the text covers traditional ground, I have tried to offer different perspectives in a few somewhat neglected areas. For example, as a writer, one of my major interests is playwriting, which often seems to be ignored or treated summarily in the largest number of introduction to theatre texts. Only so much material is practical to include in a beginning text. However, *Theatre: An Introduction* will acquaint you with facets of theatre that have been neglected in traditional texts. These include alternative theatre and contributions of ethnic and minority groups to theatre. Minority theatre, of its own and in its contributions to the mainstream, is one of the most important factors in the evolution of American theatre.

To my mind, theatre is a collaborative art. Certainly it requires teamwork among the various theatre artists. More than that, theatre is a collaboration of those with a myriad of different lifestyles, religions, ethnic or racial backgrounds, and experiences.

Due in part to this collaboration and the contributions of many people, theatre is constantly evolving. Another reason for change in the theatre experience is new technology. Thus, in the text I touch upon recent developments in theatre and drama, such as multimedia productions featuring the Internet and computer programs developed for set design. Theatre continues to evolve in other ways as well. Women are beginning to gain more of the credit they deserve as playwrights, in particular, and as actors and artists in other phases of theatre, an important point I also discuss in the text.

Of course, an introductory book cannot deal in depth with any one subject. By the very fact of choosing to include or not to include historical facts, for instance, a writer becomes an editor and a censor. An author of a textbook can only hope, if he or she is conscientious, to include that which is most enlightening, most captivating, and most valuable.

What I hope to have accomplished with *Theatre: An Introduction* is to instill in you a strong interest in theatre. In addition, I hope to encourage you to further investigate the wide range of minority contributions to American theatre, important historical developments that are mentioned only in passing due to space and time limitations, individual theatre artists and what their work includes, and the collaborative effort required to bring a production to fruition.

One of the main goals of any introductory text is to spark an interest and appreciation of the subject. This is another reason for including cuttings from books and journals by and about practicing theatre artists. It is why I include in the text a number of excerpts from many different plays, ranging from classic to contemporary, and why I address theatre criticism.

This book is organized in such a way that you immediately become acquainted with the ideas of what theatre and drama are and what they entail. This is the purpose of the first two chapters, which then lead to the history of theatre.

Chapter Three through Chapter Seven cover theatre from ancient times to the present. Years back, when I was taking my first courses in theatre, there was little mention of Eastern theatre, except to say that it did exist. Yet, as I explain in the text, Asian theatre has greatly influenced American theatre, and, therefore, it is important to know its roots as well as those of Western theatre.

Covering the diversity of modern theatre, Chapter Eight addresses the development of the musical, multimedia approaches in play production, alternative theatre, and the contributions of women and minority groups that have made theatre what it is today.

Chapters Nine and Ten discuss dramatic structure, genre, and style, using illustrations and examples to better explain the material. I believe this is important because it is unique or unusual details that provide interest and involvement. Throughout all these chapters are excerpts from plays that characterize movements, styles, and general beliefs.

In Chapter Eleven, you are given a look at theatre architecture and space, the physical theatre. I have included this chapter because I have found that many students have not had the opportunity to experience plays in more than one or two types of environments. Often they have viewed productions only at proscenium theatres.

Chapters Twelve through Fifteen explain how various theatre artists work, including the playwright, the actor, the director, the designers, and supporting artists, as well as the sorts of backgrounds these artists have. I have tried to show you that there are many different approaches in theatre, but I stress that theatre requires a collaborative effort. Although the artists in a production express their own unique creativity, all the elements of a theatrical production must mesh. Seeing that they do is the responsibility of one person, most often the director.

No matter what the job in theatre, the preparation is exacting. A strength of Chapter Fifteen, which deals with designers and supporting artists, is that this preparation is explained, from the designing of light and sound plots to preparing production or prompt books.

The business and house staffs of a theatre, including the technicians, are necessary to the success of any theatre or individual production. For this reason, in Chapter Sixteen I talk about the roles and responsibilities of the producer, the stage manager, and those other business people who work "behind the scenes" in educational, professional, and community theatre.

Finally, the text concludes with an appendix on theatre criticism, not because I imagine a great number of beginning theatre students will become theatre critics, but rather to show you that with the knowledge you have gained, you can apply standards of judgement to any theatrical production, just as professional theatre critics do.

Acknowledgments

I owe a great debt of gratitude to two people who gave immeasurable help in writing *Theatre: An Introduction.* The first is my wife, Pat Cassady (1936-1978), who coauthored with me the text that became the starting point for this book. The second is Jim Kitchen for his help with the research for the history section and for his editorial suggestions.

I would also like to gratefully acknowledge the following reviewers, who provided valuable feedback on the manuscript: Les Hinderyckx, Northwestern University; Joe Karioth, The Florida State University; Nancy Hovasse, University of Illinois at Urbana-Champaign; and Darrell Anderson, University of Dayton.

Special thanks to the theatre and drama departments, faculty, and students of the following universities for photographs of their theatrical productions used in this book: The University of Wisconsin-Madison; North Carolina School of the Arts; The Yale School of Drama; Kent State University; University of California-San Diego; Northwestern University; University of Illinois at Urbana-Champaign; Buena Vista College, Iowa; Midwestern State University, Texas; and Ferrum College, Virginia.

Thanks also to Dennis Staub for helping me locate the elusive book.

—M.C.

Chapter One

What Is Theatre?

Theatre is imagination. It is emotion and intellect. It is art. It has form, but that form moves and changes as constantly as clouds in a stormy sky. Through theatre we gain enlightenment and bring order and change to our environment. Theatre embraces all the world's cultures and perspectives, answers questions, predicts our tomorrows, and mirrors our today. It enhances individuality, yet brings us closer to one another. It enriches our lives and frees our creativity. Like all art forms, it expands our awareness and appreciation of life.

Perhaps the oldest of the arts, theatre closely approximates life. Characters on stage experience emotions we all experience. They become entangled in the same uncomfortable situations, and they react in much the same way we do. Even stage settings can be near replicas of real life.

Modern and Primitive Theatre

Although theatre is one of the oldest of the arts, its earliest form probably bore little resemblance to what most of us think of as theatrical entertainment. More likely, it began as nonverbal reenactments of human beings struggling against their environment, such as in a hunt for prey or a battle.

Figure 1.1

The Theatre of Dionysus at Athens.

Stock Montage, Inc.

As cultures became more refined, theatre became more elaborate. Language developed; plays were recorded. The first of which we have knowledge dates back to around 3000 B.C. in Egypt, although we cannot know whether such "drama" ever was performed. Since the ancient Greeks admired Egyptian culture, Greek theatre—from which most of our present theatre practices evolved—most certainly had roots in Egyptian theatre practices. Religious in nature, the earliest Greek plays consisted of little more than men in robes standing in a semicircle around an altar and chanting hymns of praise to the god of wine and debauchery, Dionysus.

Despite differences, primitive and modern theatre serve similar purposes. Both relieve a sense of "otherness"—the isolation each of us feels in never fully knowing or understanding anyone else. These feelings of separation may be instinctive due to evolution and the awareness of self that developed as a result. Yet "otherness" is not inherent in newborn infants, who perceive their surroundings and different people as a part of themselves, which, it is theorized, was the case with primitive human beings.

As children develop, however, they realize that they are isolated and that others are different entities, often unfamiliar and therefore frightening.

As they developed self-awareness and a feeling of ethnocentricity or community, primitive people felt this same sort of strangeness or alienation because each tribe or settlement (outside their own) was, in effect, a different country. Probably there was little mingling with other tribes, so it was natural to fear them. In theatre, these primitive people attempted to deal with the

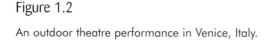

Figure 1.2

An outdoor theatre performance in Venice, Italy.

Superstock

Jo Ann Sieburg-Baker

Figure 1.3

A modern theatre, featuring a thrust stage, at the North Carolina School of the Arts. Of all modern staging types, the thrust most closely resembles ancient Greek staging.

"otherness" of their gods and of neighboring tribes so as to confirm their own tribe's identity and power.

Today various peoples still believe in the inherent superiority of their own groups or cultures, which often accounts for wars and feelings of racial and ethnic prejudice. Yet, when we take time to acquaint ourselves with these others, and to approach them openly, we often find they aren't so different from ourselves. Theatre is one means of discovering information about other people and cultures.

A number of plays deal with the concept of hate through "otherness" or through feelings of racial or ethnic superiority. Examples are Athol Fugard's *Master Harold and the Boys* (as well as other plays about apartheid as it was practiced in South Africa), written in the 1980s; Lorraine Hansberry's *A Raisin in the Sun* (about an African-American family's wanting to move into an all-white neighborhood), written in the 1960s; and Mary Burrill's *Aftermath* (the story of a young man returning from meritorious duty as an American soldier to find that in his absence his father was lynched), published in 1919.

In any theatrical performance, the audience deals with the idea of "otherness." The modern theatregoer attempts to cope with it by seeking to understand it. The audience watches the "others" on stage, witnessing their struggles and conflicts at a safe distance, separated from them by an "invisible wall," which—in most types of performance—neither actor nor audience will cross.

Theatre Compared with Other Art Forms

Any fine art, such as theatre, painting, sculpture, dance, or music, communicates a message. If the art and its creators are honest, the message that is communicated is truth—at least as perceived by the artists involved. Unlike a game of football or basketball, a work of art is more deliberate in its planning and its results. Thus, unless something unexpected happens, a ballet, a painting, or an opera follows a particular plan that realizes a particular effect.

To a greater degree than many other arts, theatre is specific in its communication. A symphony communicates feelings and beauty through sound, using intricate arrangements of melody and harmony. Theatre communicates through **dialogue,** or character conversations, which conveys more exact content. In other words, a musical phrase is less specific than a spoken one. Although it is true that music can stir us to excitement, spoken lines can define a more specific reason for that excitement.

Consider James Goldman's *The Lion in Winter,* in which the sons of Henry II plan to attack and kill him in the dungeon of the castle. Each of the sons is hoping to become king. Queen Eleanor, however, reveals the plot, after which we have the following dialogue:

> **HENRY:** Brave boys; that's what I have. Three warriors. Who had the first crack? How was I divided up? Christ—
>
> **RICHARD:** You drove us to it.
>
> **HENRY:** Why stop now? You're killers, aren't you? I am. I can do it. *(To Geoffrey.)* Take a knife. *(To Richard.)* Come on. What is it? Come for me.

When we hear these lines, we can understand Henry's shock, disbelief, and scorn, as well as his decision to goad the boys into action or to call their bluff. The lines transmit mood and emotional intensity, as well as information.

Theatre is not only more specific than nonverbal art, it is more encompassing than a novel, a poem, or a painting—not necessarily in what it tells, but because it combines so many elements in the telling. It is one of the most unlimited forms of art. Despite a certain framework—the three-act structure, for instance—theatre is limitless in what it can convey.

Finally, theatre is more personally involving and arouses a direct aesthetic response in both audience and artist.

We can distinguish theatre from many of the other arts in that a performance exists for a limited period of time. A particular production can never be witnessed again once the final line has been delivered or the final action has been performed. In this respect, theatre differs from painting or literature or architecture. Works in these arts can be enjoyed again and again in exactly the same state.

Of course, a play can be presented time and time again, but each performance will differ from any other. The director, the designers, and the actors of one production have a different interpretation of the play than do any other artists. One actor's appearance, movement, and voice vary from those of any other actor who takes the same role. Even the look of the play changes as stages differ in size, and **properties** (objects the actors carry or use in the play) and costumes vary from production to production. In fact, the third night of a production's run will not be the same as the first night or the second because the actors, affected by the audience, will continue to grow in their roles. They experiment; they attempt to find out what will work best; they and their performances are affected by the audience.

Theatre is unique in that it directly imitates human experiences by allowing spectators to identify with characters who are represented as real. Members of the audience can put themselves in the characters' places and feel as the characters do. Thus, theatre satisfies our **mimetic instinct** (the human need or desire to imitate, which provides much of our learning); it resembles life as it actually is lived or could be lived.

Theatre also interprets life. That is, the playwright, the actors, the director, and the designers all add their backgrounds and experiences to a production. They judge; they overlook; they point out specific traits to the exclusion of others. They select, and through this choice, add their own personalities or their perceptions of the world, interpreting events and actions in the play from differing viewpoints. Each of the individuals involved contributes something personal to the total production.

Theatre encompasses many other art forms—architecture in the staging and sets, sculpture in three-dimensional forms and the creative use of lights and shadow, dance in the **blocking** (the planned movement of actors in the play), painting in the setting and makeup, literature in the words, and music in songs and the flow of the language.

Theatre as Imitation and Ritual

How did such a complex art form arise? Theatre probably had its beginnings in two basic human traits: *mimetic instinct* and the need for *ritual.*

The Mimetic Instinct

Just as primitive people portrayed what was important in their lives, modern theatre artists most often begin by communicating what they have learned from the world around them. In other words, they imitate. Usually the imitation is only a starting point, and the playwright, actors, and designers allow their imaginations free rein.

Figure 1.4

A scene from South African writer Athol Fugard's *Master Harold and the Boys,* a play that explores apartheid. Performing in this Yale Repertory Theatre production of the play were Danny Glover (left), Zakes Mokae (middle), and Zeljko Ivanek (right).

Psychologists state that each of our new experiences is built upon something we already know. We relate a new situation to our awareness of the past and thus build memories and experiences. We have certain expectations, which are only slightly altered by new surroundings or new people. We use our past, then, as a point of departure in learning or in creativity.

Essentially, theatre artists use the same technique, but they need not be bound by what is—only by what could be.

Theatre artists explore and, through their art, present a wide range of thoughts and feelings. Theatre can be a vehicle of learning for both artist and audience. It can broaden cultural and humanistic horizons. It can give us confidence by showing us we are like others, and it can help us explore our individual selves.

Everyday Ritual

Just as primitive people wore special clothing and masks in enacting rituals for entertainment and to please the gods, so do we. Today we participate in

Figure 1.5

Blocking, planned movement during a play, focused attention on Paul Muni (with Bible in hand) in this scene from the 1955 stage production of *Inherit the Wind,* with Ed Begley, Tony Randall, and Louis Hector.

parades; we dress up more formally to attend religious services, we belong to business and social organizations, wear name badges and use passwords for security. At sporting events, we have the rituals of the singing of the national anthem, the introduction of the players, and the entertainment at halftime. Although loosely constructed, these rituals follow a pattern.

This type of behavior is closely allied to theatre. For example, a show is rehearsed and presented more than once. Organized ritual is rehearsed through repetition and performed over and over. Although audience participation in theatre rituals generally is less direct, rituals such as that of communion in the Christian church do involve the audience. The drinking of wine and eating of unleavened bread involve both actors and audience—the clergy and the congregation.

Pretending

Children play a game in which those on one side try to find and "shoot dead" those on the other side before they themselves are "killed." In playing this game, the children assume roles (as actors), follow certain loosely drawn rules (the format of the play), and treat themselves or the players as the audience. When one side has "eliminated" the other, the game ends. Like the portrayal of the hunt in primitive times, this game is similar to theatre. It includes performers, a play, a space, and an audience. And, like many children's games of "pretend," theatre involves imitation, communication, and entertainment.

We are forced to pretend or "make believe" in social situations. We "enjoy" a party, "like" somebody's new outfit, or pretend to be interested in subjects that hold little interest for us. Often, we do these things to avoid hurting someone's feelings or, less nobly, to help us reach a later goal. If we are "interested" in a professor's theories about World War II, then maybe he or she will look upon us more favorably when grades are due. Regardless of our motives for pretending, however, playing "make believe" places us in actors' roles.

Imitation

Like pretending, imitation helps us achieve certain goals. A baby cries, and the mother rushes to the crib to change its position or to feed it. Later the child imitates the first cry, and the mother comes once more. The baby has learned that imitating a certain action elicits a certain response.

Most important, as children, we gain much of our knowledge by imitating others. For instance, we learn to speak by imitating those around us. We see how others behave in social situations and imitate them. The basic instinct for imitation continues throughout our lives. We watch someone seated near us at a formal dinner to see which piece of silverware to use. We do what we think is expected of us, based on what we did or saw others do in similar situations. In other words, we use the same instinct in everyday living that the actor and dramatist use in creating characters for a play.

Role Playing

Imitation often takes the form of **role playing,** in which we assume roles to gain a certain response. Usually, in everyday situations, there are no memorized lines or formally rehearsed parts. Yet, when first assumed, the role of parent or grandparent may seem alien and thus difficult. Yet each time we play the role, we gain practice for the next time. We use a certain vocabulary in particular situations, and later, under similar circumstances, we refine and improve this vocabulary. In playing the role of job applicant, for instance, we may rehearse answers to anticipated questions. Role playing in everyday life and acting in a stage production are both forms of theatre, although the latter generally is much more polished.

At various times or in different sets of circumstances we allow different aspects of our personalities to surface. We follow different, relatively established patterns of behavior from situation to situation.

Because the image of ourselves that we want to project to others varies, we are not always the "same" people. We speak in different ways to the dean of our school or to our boss from the way we speak to friends. Further, we don't play just one role. At school, a professor may play the role of theatre instructor. He or she may be, for instance, a parent, a co-worker and friend, a shopper, and a competitor on a bowling team. Different actions and conversational styles go along with the changes in role. Even our clothing contributes to the roles we play. Imagine wearing gym shorts and a T-shirt to graduation ceremonies.

We find the theatrical all around us. Children "show off" to gain attention. We tend to dramatize certain situations to gain sympathy. We tell a long tale about the minor traffic accident in which we were involved. We are theatrical in creating caricatures of people with whom we have had an argument. Our voices become unpleasant and exaggerated, maybe with a hint of truth, when we relate what the other person said and how we were wronged.

You: Well, you know what Mark's always been like.

Friend: What do you mean?

You: Oh, come on. Remember when he had the party and didn't invite either of us.

Friend: I guess so.

You: You guess so. *(Your voice becomes mocking and sarcastic, in supposed imitation of MARK.)* "Oh, well, I thought you were going to be out of town," he said.

Friend: Both of us were out of town, weren't we?

You: But that isn't the point!

Friend: Oh?

You: He's so damned mealy-mouthed! *(Your voice becomes mocking again, in supposed imitation of MARK.)* "Oh, I didn't want to hurt your feelings," he said, "but my God, you know how small my apartment is." Small, my foot.

Friend: Why are you so angry?

You: Me, angry? Not at a jerk like that. I wouldn't give him the satisfaction.

Theatre in Evolution

Clearly, life and theatre have close ties. An important similarity is that neither stands still. Theatre has always been in a state of change. Romanticism was a revolt against the rigid rules of earlier neoclassicism. Realism and naturalism were revolts against the artificial sentimentalism that romanticism became.

During the 1960s there was a move in theatre (and in society, as well) toward freedom of expression and dress. Forbidden topics became the subjects for plays. Nudity, often for its own sake, became the usual rather than the exceptional. Language had few taboos. We began to see such productions as the rock musical *Hair* (by Gerome Ragni, James Radi, and Galt MacDermot), a protest against the "establishment," and *Oh! Calcutta!,* an erotic production by Kenneth Tynan.

Many such productions depended on shock value to attract patrons. When the shock faded, the theatre again experienced change. Part of this change was the nostalgia movement of the early seventies, with the revivals of early musicals, such as *No, No, Nanette* (1925) by Harbach, Mandel, Youmans, and Caesar, and straight plays, such as Eugene O'Neill's *A Moon for the Misbegotten* (first produced in 1946). Nostalgia was strong in *Grease* (by Jim Jacobs and Warren Casey), which tried to recapture the fifties. Theatre was rebelling against current plays, but as yet had developed no widely accepted ideas that were entirely new. Meanwhile, since many taboos had been broken, playwrights had freedom to explore previously unapproachable themes.

Each change in theatre is important. It not only mirrors the times; it leads the way to emerging attitudes. The total abandonment of inhibitions in some of the plays in the sixties and seventies opened the way for such plays as David Storey's *The Changing Room,* acted partially in the nude—not for the sake of nudity, but to present realistically the environment of a locker room. The play emphasizes the refusal of human beings to accept a defeatist attitude toward life, symbolized by the sport of rugby.

Universality

Just as many plays from earlier periods have little meaning for us now, many now being written are certain to mean little to future generations. For a play to have lasting value, except as a museum piece or as a reflection of the time and place in which it was written, it must possess **universality;** that is, it must be relevant for all people at all times. Obviously, this is an overstatement, as nothing will have meaning for every individual. If someone were to present a Shakespearean drama to a primitive tribe, the production would not convey much. Nevertheless, some plays have themes that move audiences many years after the playwrights have written them.

A play with universality deals with common feelings and beliefs. It enables us to empathize with a character in a play or with the circumstances of the characters. Thornton Wilder's *Our Town* deals with life, love, death, and the hereafter, as experienced by the people of a small town around the turn of the century. The play concentrates on George, son of the town's physician, and Emily, daughter of the newspaper editor. The character of the Stage Manager acts as narrator. The two young people are seen going to high school together, falling in love over ice cream sodas at the drugstore, getting married, and

Figure 1.6

A scene from *Our Town* as produced at Long Wharf Theatre in New Haven, Connecticut.

suffering as Emily dies in childbirth. In a touching third act, the two young people are reunited briefly after Emily has found out how painful a return to life can be, because the living take all of life for granted.

Every action which has ever taken place—every thought, every emotion—has taken place only once, at one moment in time and place. "I love you," "I rejoice," "I suffer," have been said and felt many billions of times, and never twice the same. Every person who has ever lived has lived an unbroken succession of unique occasions. Yet the more one is aware of this individuality in experience (innumerable! innumerable!) the more one becomes attentive to what these disparate moments have in common, to repetitive patterns. As an artist (or listener or beholder) which "Truth" do you prefer—that of the isolated occasion, or that which includes and resumes the innumerable? Which truth is more worth telling? Every age differs in this. Is the Venus de Milo "one woman"? Is the play *Macbeth* the story of "one destiny"? The theatre is admirably fitted to tell both truths.[1]

DEATH OF A SALESMAN

Arthur Miller

Willy Loman, a traveling salesman, has always felt that social success or "being well-liked" is the key to financial success. When the play opens, Willy is sixty-three and no longer able to sell. He is at the point of hallucinating and talking to himself; for him the past and the present intermingle. Through flashbacks (scenes from the past) we learn how Willy's world has fallen apart. He always viewed himself as the ideal father and husband. His image shatters when Biff, the older of his two sons, finds him in a hotel room with a woman. Willy had led Biff to believe that social popularity and success on the football field were more important than education, and he pampered both sons. The younger son, Happy, has patterned his life after Willy's and views success as his father does. After Willy finally asks his boss for an in-town selling job and is fired instead, Biff forces him to realize that both of them are failures. Because his insurance is paid up, Willy feels he still can be a success by killing himself and leaving the insurance money to his family. He goes to the garage to start his car, and his wife, Linda, foresees what will happen. Even though she loves him for what he is, she is powerless to stop him.

We have little trouble identifying with the characters, because their experiences of growing up, living together as families, and dealing with death are similar to our own. Wilder reinforces the universal belief that each of us should learn to appreciate and notice others.

Many plays that have survived from earlier periods contain universal themes simply because our drives and motives are the same as they were thousands of years ago. *Agamemnon* (458 B.C.), by the Greek playwright Aeschylus,

---

[1] Thornton Wilder, *Three Plays by Thornton Wilder* (New York: Harper and Row, 1957; reprinted by Bantam, 1958), pp. ix–x.

involves unfaithfulness. Clytemnestra takes a lover while her husband Agamemnon is away at war. He returns home with the captured princess Cassandra, and Clytemnestra murders both of them. Unfaithfulness is treated in many modern plays. In Arthur Miller's *Death of a Salesman,* Biff discovers his father, Willy, in a hotel room with a woman. In Muriel Resnik's comedy *Any Wednesday,* a business executive maintains an apartment, supposedly for business purposes, but actually to house his mistress.

Theatre is an imitation of what we ourselves experience. It imitates but heightens life's experiences. It offers new insights into our feelings. It has relevance for us both as individuals and as part of the human race. We understand our own motives more fully when we see them portrayed on the stage. Certainly, most of us never will become murderers, yet we recognize that under certain circumstances—attacks against us or our families, for instance—we may be capable of killing another human being. We can understand and sympathize with Hamlet, for instance, when he expresses the desire to avenge his father's death.

When *Hamlet* opens, Claudius has become the ruler of Denmark by killing Hamlet's father and marrying his mother. This scene from Act I shows how strongly Hamlet despises his father's murderer.

Now might I do it pat, now he is praying;
And now I'll do't. And so he goes to heaven;
And so am I revenged. That would be scann'd:
A villain kills my father; and for that,
I, his sole son, do this same villain send
To heaven.
O, this is hire and salary, not revenge.
He took my father grossly, full of bread;
With all his crimes broad blown, as flush as May;
And how his audit stands who knows save heaven?
But in other circumstance and course of thought,
'Tis heavy with him: and am I then revenged,
To take him in the purging of his soul,
When he is fit and season'd for his passage?
No!
Up, sword; and know thou a more horrid hent:
When he is drunk asleep, or in his rage,
Or in the incestuous pleasure of his bed;
At gaming, swearing, or about some act
That has no relish of salvation it 't;
Then trip him, that his heels may kick at heaven.
And that his soul may be as damn'd and black
As hell, whereto it goes.

HAMLET, PRINCE OF DENMARK

William Shakespeare

Because "the times are out of joint," sin has corrupted the royal court. Claudius, Hamlet's uncle, has secretly murdered Hamlet's father and married his mother, Gertrude. Sworn by his father's ghost to vengeance, Hamlet must first make certain that Claudius indeed is guilty. He does so by hiring a band of players (actors) to reenact the murder. Claudius betrays himself during the performance. Hamlet suspects Polonius of being a part of the conspiracy. He now suspects Polonius's daughter, Ophelia, as well—even though formerly Hamlet had courted her. Ophelia is deeply in love with Hamlet.

Inadvertently, Hamlet kills Polonius, after which he is exiled and Ophelia goes mad. Laertes, Polonius's son and a former friend of Hamlet, challenges Hamlet to a fencing match. He puts poison on his sword point with the approval of the king. Gertrude dies after consuming a poisoned drink that Claudius had prepared for Hamlet. Hamlet kills Claudius; Laertes kills Hamlet. But Laertes himself dies by the poisoned rapier.

Comedy, as well as other genres of drama, imitates life. Yet the imitation involves a heightening of the ordinary, often in the form of **stock characters** (exaggerated character types). Playwrights choose certain personality traits and heighten them. In Neil Simon's *The Odd Couple,* Felix, a man who is both finicky and a hypochondriac, moves into an apartment with his friend Oscar, who is very sloppy. This sets up immediate conflict.

The Role of the Audience

There is an unknown quality in every theatre presentation: the direct contact between artist and spectator. Even with the same script, setting, and performers, a play differs from night to night. Not only do the performers' attitudes and actions change, the audience changes as well. Each group of theatregoers brings new expectations and perspectives. The size of an audience affects the flow of communication to a certain degree, but even two audiences of the same size may react much differently to a production. In a theatre production there is a constant flow between the audience and the actors. The script is communicated by

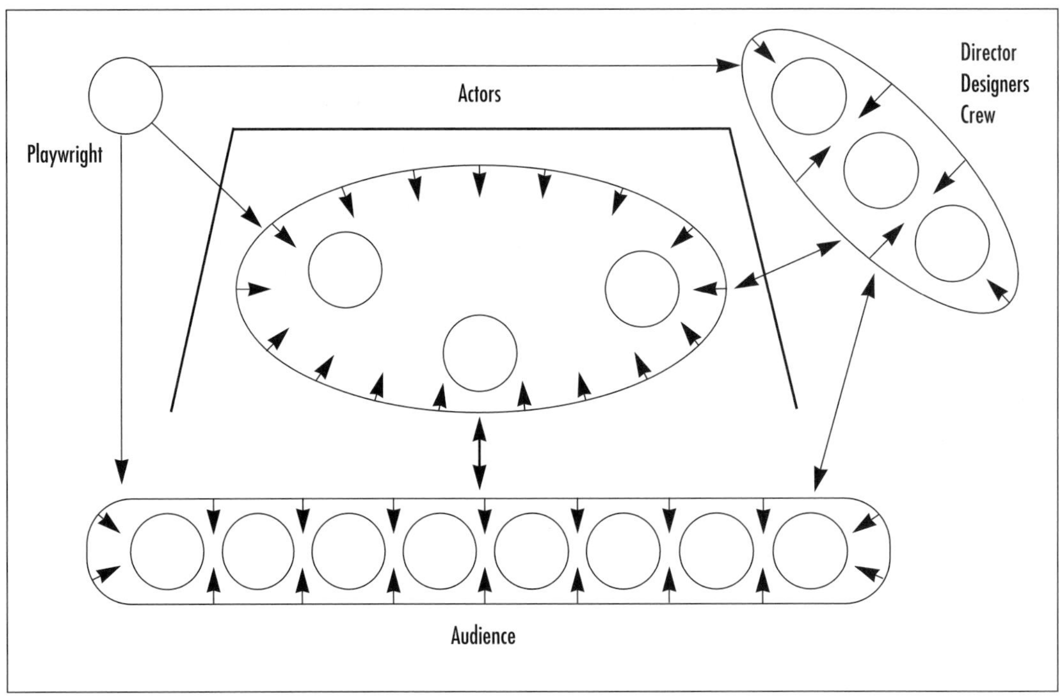

Figure 1.7

A Communication Model for Theatre

the playwright to the other theatre artists and the audience. The theatre artists add their interpretations to the script. During the actual presentation most flow and feedback is between the performers and the spectators.

This direct flow of feeling between audience and artist sets theatre and other live arts apart from film and television. Eric Bentley observes that film has many of the same qualities as theatre, including a theatre building, actors, and an audience. But "we cannot be caught up in a flow of living feeling that passes from actor to the audience and back again to the actor."[2] Similarly, when asked if a performance depends on the audience's reaction, Julie Andrews said: "It's almost the biggest part of the challenge. Nobody knows you were good last night except the people who were there."[3]

[2] Eric Bentley, *The Theatre of Commitment and Other Essays* (New York: Atheneum, 1967), pp. 59–60. Reprinted by permission of the author.

[3] Roy Newquist, *Showcase* (New York: William Morrow & Co., Inc., 1966), p. 41.

An audience affects not only the performers but also itself. Whether we call what happens "reinforcement" or "mob psychology," as part of a group we partially lose our own identities and inhibitions. We somehow sense what the group wants and what direction it will take, although our own purpose or response may not be fully defined before we join with others. Generally, as part of a theatre audience, we are willing to experience more of a release of our emotions than we will by ourselves or with one or two others.

It is difficult to appreciate a theatre performance if there are few members in an audience, or even if they are isolated from one another. If there are several rows of empty seats directly in front of the stage, the members of the audience will tend to retain some of their individual inhibitions. For the audience to merge, the members must experience physical closeness.

Gradually, a bonding occurs. That is why, for example, we often hear a burst of laughter at a line that strikes the audience as funny. The members trust each other, and so most responses encompass the group and are immediate.

Of course, different types of plays will attract different audiences. What draws audiences in New York City may leave empty seats in the South or Midwest. Not only do moral and sociological outlooks differ from one area to another, but a larger city has a larger potential audience of any particular type from which to draw than does a small community.

Thus, the theatre audience has half a contract to fulfill. Their responsibility includes becoming acquainted with theatre in order to understand it as an art form. Only by attending and experiencing a variety of plays—from current tragicomedy to Elizabethan tragedy—can an audience member learn to judge the worth of a production. The more effectively we can judge a production, the more it enriches our lives.

Why Audiences Attend the Theatre

There are many reasons for attending the theatre, but people most often attend to be entertained. Theatre offers a chance to escape into a make-believe existence and to forget everyday cares. As dramatist Bertold Brecht once said, the theatre "needs no other passport than fun."[4]

The theatre also offers us the opportunity to learn of recent, present, and imminent change. Theatre, like other arts, not only mirrors the society in which it is produced, but often judges the social, economic, and political climate in which it is presented. Norwegian playwright Henrik Ibsen stated that the artist must be a few years ahead of the average person in thinking. Artists

[4] Bertold Brecht, "A Short Organum for the Theatre," John Willet, trans., in *Playwrights on Playwriting,* Toby Cole, ed. (New York: Hill and Wang, 1960), p. 74.

must anticipate what changes will occur in their society. Art gauges the undercurrents of society and predicts the future.

For example, in a series of loosely related scenes protesting established society and its attitudes, productions such as *Hair* pointed out changing attitudes about patriotism, the Vietnam conflict, and sex. Theatre productions most often do not cause change in themselves. Rather, they show what is likely to occur or is already afoot.

Further, audiences attend the theatre to confront social problems. Since World War II, theatre has changed in content and style as it has tried to alert us to the needs of society. Frank D. Gilroy's *The Subject Was Roses* (1964) shows the discouragement and disillusionment faced by a young man home from World War II. This production foreshadowed the increasing discontent over the Vietnam conflict, seen, for instance, in David Rabe's *Sticks and Bones* (1972), a violent antiwar play that attacks the silliness and hypocrisy of middle-class America. Whereas Gilroy's play uses realistic subject matter, characterization, and dialogue, Rabe's play uses strong new devices: a phantom Vietnamese girl, present only in the memory of a returning Vietnam veteran; characters patterned after the Nelson family on the old (1950s) *Ozzie and Harriet* television show; and dialogue that often is purposely inane or "corny."

In past ages, the theatre presented problems about isolated individuals or groups far removed from the experiences of the audience, such as the nobility in Greek tragedy. Most of the audience members could empathize with the characters, but also could feel secure in the knowledge that the productions presented someone else's particular troubles.

In our own time, theatre has tried to come closer to its audience's problems and needs, even placing the dilemmas squarely in the laps of the audience. David Henry Hwang's *FOB* shows how difficult it is for people of a different culture to adapt to living in the United States. Lucy Gannon's *Keeping Tom Nice* is about a family's trying to deal with a severely disabled son/brother who is unable to communicate. Lanford Wilson's *Burn This* is about the accidental death of a young gay man and the effect on the lives of others, including his parents (who didn't know he was gay) and his boorish brother.

Earlier plays, such as Ibsen's social dramas, did not neglect universality or **immediacy** (the quality of a work of art that makes it important or relevant to the time in which it is presented to the public), but more recent theatre has tried consciously to dramatize the concerns of its audience. One group to attempt this was the Living Theatre. In its production of *Paradise Now* (1968), the group openly confronted audiences and demanded responses to such issues as war and "establishment" rules. The Open Theatre, under the guidance of Joseph Chaikin, presented such plays as *America Hurrah* (composed of three one-acts), which ridiculed the treatment individuals often receive in impersonal job interviews and protested the disregard we often show for others' property.

In the eighties and nineties came plays that honestly explored the base and basic feelings of humankind. These include Terrence McNally's *Frankie and Johnny in the Clair de Lune,* the story of the love between two lonely middle-aged people, a short-order cook and a waitress, and David Rabe's *Hurlyburly,* about two divorced casting agents caught up in a frenzy of cocaine and booze and abusing the women in their lives.

A fourth reason audiences go to the theatre is to learn about individuals and their personalities. Shakespeare's *Othello,* for instance, deals with jealousy—an emotion we all experience at one time or another. By contrast, the characters of Henrik Ibsen often face the immediate concerns of their own time. In *Ghosts,* for example, Mrs. Alving is a woman who, because divorce was frowned upon at the time, stayed with an unworthy husband, now dead. Written in 1881, the play shows the mental anguish a person may have to suffer in choosing the "safe" route. She continues to suffer when she learns that her son Oswald has a venereal disease, inherited from his father—something that she tries to keep hidden.

Another reason audiences are drawn to the theatre is to learn from the past. A play can acquaint us with the past in order to provide new interpretations of the present. Such is the case with Peter Shaffer's *The Royal Hunt of the Sun,* which deals with Pizarro's conquest of the Incas of Peru. Although it presents historical events, the play also portrays a loss of faith. Pizarro has lost faith in Christianity and wants to believe in the immortality of the Indian emperor, Atahuallpa.The emperor believes that because the Sun is his father, he will be resurrected if he is put to death. Of course, when Pizarro kills him, the emperor is not resurrected. August Wilson often deals with a more recent past in such plays as *Joe Turner's Come and Gone* and *Ma Rainey's Black Bottom* because, he says, he wants to write about issues that have confronted and will continue to confront black people.

Attending the theatre can also serve to reaffirm the audience's beliefs about an issue. A playwright has a better chance of reaching his or her audience by beginning with a common premise—something that most potential theatregoers already believe. For example, if an audience did not feel at the beginning of a production that war is inhumane, a play with an antiwar theme, such as Laurence Stallings and Maxwell Anderson's *What Price Glory?* (1924), would have little chance of success. According to theatre critic John Gassner, the play "did more than any other dramatic piece to promote the cause of realism and freedom on the American stage . . . . In its day . . . [it] was also considered the last word in pacifism because the authors described fighting as grimy business . . . and refrained from attributing exalted sentiments to its warriors."[5]

---

[5] John Gassner, editor. *Twenty-Five Best Plays of the Modern American Theatre: Early Series* (New York: Crown Publishers, 1949), p. 58.

Plays sometimes are simply observations of life. The absurdist movement, which reached its height in the 1950s, stated only that life is absurd, thus reaffirming a belief many people shared, though they hadn't necessarily thought much about it.

Often an audience is willing to be led in a certain direction, but doesn't want a decision forced upon it. *West Side Story* pleads for understanding among individuals of different cultural backgrounds by showing how prejudice can destroy. One of its messages is that understanding, caring, and love should begin on an individual basis.

WEST SIDE STORY

Script by Arthur Laurents, lyrics by Stephen Sondheim, music by Leonard Bernstein; based on an original idea of Jerome Robbins, 1957.

Modeled after Shakespeare's *Romeo and Juliet,* the musical tells the tragic love story of Maria and Tony. Leader of the Jets until he turned the position over to Riff, Tony is a New Yorker. The Jets, a white street gang, are determined to keep out Puerto Ricans from their area of Manhattan. The Sharks are Puerto Ricans, determined to dominate their block. The gangs meet at a dance in a neighborhood gym. Tony, still supporting the Jets, goes to the dance and meets Maria, the sister of Bernardo, leader of the Sharks. The two young people fall in love and plan to meet at the bridal shop where Maria works. At the same time the two gangs plan a rumble. Tony persuades them to have just one person from each gang meet to fight the following day. Then Bernardo learns of Tony's and Maria's love and threatens Tony. A major fight ensues, and Tony's friend Riff is killed. Tony, enraged over his friend's death, stabs Bernardo to death with Riff's knife. Then Tony is killed by Chino, Maria's intended husband.

An audience attends the theatre simply to feel—to experience emotion. The playwright, the designers, and the actors all work together to try to elicit certain responses. A serious play allows empathy or identification more often than does a comedy. Yet almost any subject can be treated humorously or seriously. For instance, compare how seriously the idea of greed is treated in Lillian Hellman's *The Little Foxes* and in Molière's *The Miser.*

THE LITTLE FOXES

Lillian Hellman

The members of the Hubbard family, united against the outside world, often hate one another. They attempt to raise money to establish a cotton mill in a nearby town. When the play opens, Regina's husband Horace, president of the local bank, is in Johns Hopkins, a Baltimore hospital, being treated for a heart ailment. When letters to him fail to bring the money necessary for the Hubbards' venture, Regina sends her daughter Alexandra to bring Horace back home.

Weakened by the trip, Horace refuses to provide the money Regina and her brothers need, so Benjamin and Oscar steal securities belonging to Horace and cut Regina out of her share in the entrepreneurial venture. She becomes enraged.

The shock of realizing what his wife is really like causes Horace to have a heart attack. By giving him medication, Regina could save his life. She refuses, and he dies. Regina confronts her brothers with the theft and demands seventy-five percent of the business not to expose them.

THE MISER

Molière

Harpagon, a widower and father of an adult son and daughter, lets his miserliness rule his life, which in turn frustrates his two children and makes him the dupe of everyone who recognizes his all-consuming weakness. The two children plot to select their own marriage partners rather than the ones Harpagon chose out of greed.

Harpagon's own son Cléante, Harpagon's rival for the affections of Marianne, forces his father to choose between her and his cash box. Of course, he chooses the money.

Chapter Two

What Is Drama?

Even though certain elements have characterized theatre since its beginning, no one can seem to agree on what constitutes **drama,** or the written play. According to French theatre critic Ferdinand Brunetiére, there should be no rules—only conventions that vary from person to person, piece to piece, and time to time.

Nearly all we can assume for certain is that a play is the basic plan for communicating with an audience. A script, whether written in detail or only a bare outline, gives the performer a jumping-off place.

Usually, a script begins with a writer, who records, refines, and finally shares the work with other theatre artists. Most often dramatists begin the work alone, in touch only with their imaginations and creativity. Each has a different perspective, a different way of beginning. Even documentary plays are both more and less than the history they portray. The playwright, by choosing and eliminating, is editing and adding a perspective.

What constitutes a good idea for a play? The only judgment of value relates to how well the playwright succeeds in transferring a vision to paper and how well the written script translates into a production. And even this is subjective, as seen in the following sets of reviews:

> Taking a 1946 potboiler by J. B. Priestly, *An Inspector Calls,* [Stephen Daldry] has transformed it into a steadily engrossing drama and, more significantly, one of the most astonishing spectacles on Broadway right now. . . .
>
> Against all odds, something that was functional and boxy has been made dark and gleaming and elegant.
>
> —*The New York Times,* April 28, 1994.

> Rarely has glitzy irrelevance been parlayed more craftily into undeserved success than by Steven Daldry's ludicrously overheated and pompous staging of . . . *An Inspector Calls.*
>
> The brilliant special effects out-Disney Disney, yet this remains a pedestrian if dramatically overly emphatic staging with a naive and spurious look of thoughtful, deconstructed originality.
>
> —*New York Post,* April 28, 1994.

> *Passion* is a great, great show. . . . It's great, because with fifteen musicals behind him, our theatre's most provocative composer and lyricist [Stephen Sondheim] is still reinventing the form while honoring it, still writing shows that tell haunting tales while delighting the ear and eye.

> [T]o this listener Sondheim's newest show stands unchallenged as the most emotionally engaging new musical Broadway has had in years.
>
> —*Variety,* May 24, 1994.

> There have been musicals about which the complaint was that all the songs sounded too familiar; this one goes a step further: all the songs sound the same. The score is a glutinous mass. . . .
>
> Watching *Passion* is like watching the mating dance of a pair of snakes.
>
> —*New York Post,* May 23, 1994.

A general belief is that, unlike other forms of literature, a play is not a complete piece of art simply because someone wrote and revised it. Except for "closet drama"—expressly written to be read and not performed—a play requires the collaboration of the other theatre artists to bring it fully to life. Tennessee Williams calls the script "hardly more than an architect's blueprint of a house not yet built. . . . The color, the grace and levitation, the structural pattern in motion, the quick interplay of live beings, suspended like fitful lightning in a cloud, these things are the play, not words on paper, nor thoughts and ideas of an author. . . ."[1]

Playwright Terrence McNally feels much the same. "Reading a play," he says, "is like looking at a map. The journey is the rehearsal process. The destination is the production. I'm too impatient to get to Oz to be a good play reader. I want to be there."[2]

Of course, if we read a play and are able to visualize a setting and actors, the script can appeal to us emotionally and aesthetically. Playwright Jeffrey Sweet says that "there is no necessary correlation between" how well a script reads and how well it plays.[3] To be fully appreciated, the script needs the atmosphere of a theatre and the technical aspects of a performance. When the set designer adds a visual interpretation, when the actors analyze and impersonate the characters, and when the director integrates the total production, only then does a script fully communicate the playwright's intention.

---

[1] Tennessee Williams, Afterword to *Camino Real, Where I Live: Selected Essays* (New York: New Directions, 1978, reprinted from the first published version of *Camino Real,* New Directions, 1953), p. 69.

[2] Terrence McNally, "Introduction," *Fifteen Short Plays* (Lyme, N.H.: Smith and Kraus, Inc., 1994), p. ix.

[3] Jeffrey Sweet, *The Dramatist's Toolkit: The Craft of the Working Playwright* (Portsmouth, N.H.: Heinemann, 1994), pp. 1–2.

On the other hand, dramatist Edward Albee contends that: "Plays—good ones, at any rate—are literature, and the pervasive notion that a play comes to full life only on stage speaks either of an inability to realize a production through reading or a flawed play."[4]

A Theory of Drama

According to the Greek philosopher Aristotle in *The Poetics* (c. 330–320 B.C.), the earliest treatise we have on the theory of drama, a tragedy should have a beginning, a middle, and an end, that is, it should be complete in itself. It should contain everything necessary to an audience's understanding of it. Further, the incidents should exhibit a cause-and-effect relationship. In other words, a dramatic question should be asked early on, and the rest of the play should answer this question.

Although Aristotle was discussing tragedy, what he says can be applied to drama as a whole. A play, then, is based in life, but is vastly different, since life has no real beginnings and endings except birth and death. Most often, these are not the stuff of drama. Most of us are born quietly and die quietly. At times we may struggle toward a goal, but after we achieve it or fail to, our lives continue mundanely and anticlimactically.

Since the sixteenth century, when Aristotle's writings on drama became widely known, his work has continued to influence dramatic theorists and playwrights. Yet there are those who disagree with his views. If a writer too closely follows Aristotle's definition, those critics say the resulting play will be artificial. Most concur, however, that an audience needs a sense of ending.

The Elements of Drama

A playwright, like a painter, generally works within a certain structure. The painter can choose colors, brushstrokes, and composition, but has to apply pigment to a surface. No matter how big or how small a canvas, the surface still is a limiting space. The successful artist does not view the canvas as restrictive, however. Similarly, drama and, hence, theatre has a basic structure, within which exists freedom to experiment, to establish new methods, and to present new concepts.

Aristotle described six elements as essential for tragedy: *plot, character, thought, dialogue, melody,* and *spectacle.*

[4] Edward Albee, "Introduction," *Selected Plays by Edward Albee* (Garden City, N.Y.: Nelson Doubleday, Inc., "Introduction" © 1987 by Edward Albee), p. vii.

1. **Plot,** the most important element of a play according to Aristotle, is the framework. Within it occurs the scope of the action.
2. **Character** is the major ingredient for the advancement of the action. The characters most often are the controlling force in a play; through their speech and behavior, the ongoing action is revealed. In similar circumstances, each reacts individually. Each also is typical. Characters need individuality to come across as believable, yet similarity to others in order to arouse feelings of **empathy** or identification.

   A play should affect the audience personally through an appeal to the emotions. It has to provide situations, characters, and events with which audiences can identify and through which they can learn. Each of these has to be different enough to maintain interest but familiar enough to illustrate a general truth.
3. **Thought** (or intellect) refers to the playwright's ideas. Like the characters, the play itself should be both specific and general—the story of an individual, but with universal appeal.
4. **Dialogue** (or diction) refers to the speech of each character. It should suit the characters and help establish the tone of the play, as well as the changing tempos of the scenes.
5. **Melody** refers to the rhythm and flow of the language, which should reflect the emotional content of the situation.
6. **Spectacle,** the least important element according to Aristotle, is the scenery and background. It is the element over which the playwright has the least control.

Because theatre is not life, but an *approximation of life,* it is made up of **symbols.** Nothing in it is real. Yet, if the production has been well planned and presented, we identify with the characters and their situation. We grieve over the death of a character, even though we know that nobody actually has died.

Aesthetic Distance

On the other hand, there should be a balance between empathy and **aesthetic distance**—the detachment that allows us to appreciate the beauty of a work. In some cases, of course, the performers encourage audience participation. In children's theatre, the actors may want the spectators to warn the hero of impending doom or to boo the villain. There have been experiments of bringing audience members to the stage or going into the seating area to talk with them in an attempt to break down the barriers. Sometimes this works; often, however, it fails because it disturbs the balance between involvement and detachment. No matter how affecting the characters or the situation, an audience has to participate on two opposite levels. Otherwise, they view the action as life and try to intervene.

Theatre Conventions

Theatre is built upon **conventions**—devices the actors, the playwright, the designers, or the director use to expedite the production. An audience willingly accepts and expects such devices as a type of shorthand.

As nineteenth-century poet and critic Samuel Taylor Coleridge said, literature in general involves "the willing suspension of disbelief." Those involved in the production of a play attempt to create an illusion of reality through the use of expected devices or conventions, and the audience completes the illusion by accepting as real what it sees and hears.

Although these conventions serve a number of purposes, many relate to the need to be selective. They imply rather than becoming explicit. In old-fashioned melodramas, for instance, we know immediately who the villain is because he dresses in black and twists the ends of his moustache.

Acting Conventions

An audience willingly accepts any number of acting conventions, from performers' projecting their voices to be heard throughout the seating area to

Figure 2.1

In a proscenium theatre, such as this one, the Royal Opera House in Covent Garden, London, the audience sees the performance only from the front.

The Granger Collection

rarely turning their backs on the audience in a **proscenium** (picture-frame) theatre. In a large theatre, actors use broader gestures than people normally do in everyday life. They exaggerate so the audience has no trouble interpreting their physical actions.

Writing Conventions

Most playwriting conventions heighten and condense. These devices include the *soliloquy,* the *aside,* the *monologue,* and the *flashback,* all of which are ways of presenting **exposition** or background information (a convention in itself) and characters' emotions.

A **soliloquy** shows a character thinking aloud, revealing innermost thoughts, in much the same way we talk to ourselves sometimes when we're alone. Soliloquies present thoughts and emotions succinctly. Without conventions such as this, we would have to observe the characters in many more circumstances to understand them. A good example of a soliloquy is Hamlet's "To be or not to be" speech.

The **aside,** popular in late nineteenth- and early twentieth-century melodramas, allows a character to talk only to the audience so that the other characters on stage "cannot hear" what is said. In many instances, during an aside the other characters "freeze."

A **monologue** is a long speech delivered either to the audience or to other characters. In *Our Town,* the stage manager often speaks directly to the theatregoers. In Eugene O'Neill's *Long Day's Journey into Night,* Edmund has a long speech in which he tells his father his feelings about the sea:

> You've just told me some high spots in your memories. Want to hear mine? They're all connected with the sea. Here's one. When I was on the Squarehead square rigger, bound for Buenos Aires. Full moon in the Trades. The old hooker driving fourteen knots. I lay on the bowsprit, facing astern, with the water foaming into spume under me, the masts with every sail white in the moonlight, towering high above me. I became drunk with the beauty and singing rhythm of it, and for a moment I lost myself—actually lost my life. I was set free! I dissolved in the sea, became white sails and flying spray, became beauty and rhythm, became moonlight and the ship and the high dim-starred sky! I belonged without past or future, within peace and unity and a wild joy, within something greater than my own life, or the life of Man, to Life itself! To God, if you want to put it that way. Then another time, on the American Line, when I was lookout on the crow's nest in the dawn watch. A calm sea, that time. Only a lazy ground swell and a slow drowsy roll of the ship. The passengers asleep and none of the crew in sight. No sound of man. Black smoke pouring from the funnels behind and

beneath me. Dreaming, not keeping lookout, feeling alone, and above, and apart, watching the dawn creep like a painted dream over the sky and sea which slept together. Then the moment of ecstatic freedom came. The peace, the end of the quest, the last harbor, the joy of belonging to a fulfillment beyond man's lousy, pitiful, greedy fear and hopes and dreams! And several other times in my life, when I was swimming far out, or lying alone on a beach, I have had the same experience. Became the sun, the hot sand, green seaweed anchored to a rock, swaying in the tide. Like a saint's song of beatitude. Like the veil of things as they seem drawn back by an unseen hand. For a second you see—and seeing the secret, are the secret. For a second there is meaning! Then the hand lets the veil fall and you are alone, lost in the fog again, and you stumble on toward nowhere, for no good reason.

Figure 2.2

A scene from a Kent State University Theatre production of Eugene O'Neill's *Long Day's Journey into Night.*

James Gleason

(He grins wryly.) It was a great mistake, my being born a man. I would have been much more successful as a seagull or a fish. As it is, I will always be a stranger who never feels at home, who does not really want and is not really wanted, who can never belong, who must always be a little in love with death!

A **flashback** is a scene that occurred in the past, before the play's opening scene. Often the audience members are asked to imagine that they can see what a character is thinking as the remembered scene appears on stage. Miller's *Death of a Salesman* contains a number of flashbacks. In one, as **protagonist,** or central character, Willy Loman talks with his wife, he remembers with guilt an affair he had. In his imagination, he moves into this scene, which occurs in a hotel bedroom.

An audience knows that events progress faster on the stage than they do in real life. *Dramatic time,* as opposed to chronological time, means that on stage people express their thoughts more explicitly and concisely than people do in everyday life. The term **dramatic time** refers to the amount of time represented by a play; an hour onstage may represent any amount of actual time, although more time usually is represented as having passed than the actual two hours or so it takes to present a play. Dialogue usually is free of the extraneous and distracting details that are common in ordinary conversations.

In Sophocles' *Oedipus Rex,* for example, we learn all the events that preceded the action of the play from Oedipus's infancy to marrying his mother; yet the action takes place in less than a day's time.

OEDIPUS REX

Sophocles, c. 425 B.C.

The people of Thebes, stricken by a terrible plague, gather in prayer. King Oedipus assures them he is doing what he can to find what is causing it. He has sent his brother-in-law Creon to the oracle at Delphi to find out what to do. Creon returns and says that once the murderer of the former king, Laius, is found and exiled, the plague will end. Oedipus consults the prophet Teiresias, who tells him that Oedipus himself is the man who killed Laius. Oedipus protests, and Teiresias further warns that the king is unclean because he is guilty of incest. Alone with his wife, Jocasta, Oedipus tells her he fears that he may indeed be his father's murderer because once he did kill a man who tried to force him off a roadway. He says that he once had a prophecy from Delphi that he would murder his father and marry his mother. Jocasta comforts him, saying that Laius was murdered by a band of

Roy Anderson

Figure 2.3

The setting of the play *Front Page,* written in 1928 by Charles McArthur in collaboration with Ben Hecht, is—for the most part—a newspaper office. This scene is from a production of the play at Ferrum College's Little Theatre, Virginia.

robbers. As proof, she summons an old herdsman, the last survivor of the fight in which Laius died. Instead of confirming Jocasta's story, the herdsman admits that Oedipus is the murderer. He also recognizes Oedipus as Jocasta's son, whom he had saved as a baby. Upon hearing the news, Jocasta kills herself and Oedipus puts out his eyes. He appears blinded before the citizens of Thebes and asks to be exiled in fulfillment of the curse placed on the killer of Laius.

An audience will accept almost any character or event if the proper framework is developed. In *R.U.R.* Karel Čapek portrays a society in which robots exist. In *Motel* van Itallie uses papier-mâché characters who are grotesque caricatures of human beings. Shakespeare introduced ghosts and witches into his plays. Andrew Lloyd Webber uses characters whom the audience is asked to accept as cats.

Theatregoers are willing to accept such devices once a framework or a world has been established in which they can exist. Only when the author deviates from that framework does a play become unbelievable. For instance, if van Itallie suddenly introduced flesh-and-blood characters into *Motel,* the perspective would be skewed, and the play would become unbelievable.

Production Conventions

Modern audiences accept many conventions connected with the physical production. The entire concept of a **setting** is a convention. The living room onstage is made up of a series of **flats** (painted canvas frames) positioned to bring about a certain effect. The audience knows, of course, that nobody's living room is arranged like the one on stage. In a real house, furniture is closer together to conserve space. In contrast, a room onstage is much larger than those in most homes.

Often properties, or **props,** only represent objects. The diamond ring is costume jewelry, the letter a blank sheet of paper. The lighting is not sunlight or moonlight. Stage lights cast fewer shadows than lamps in living rooms. Actors wear heavy makeup, certainly more than the average person on the sidewalk.

Yet all these things are agreed upon and accepted beforehand, as part of the unspoken audience-theatre contract.

Chapter Three

The Beginnings

Theatre, or at least a form of reenactment, most likely began with a ritualistic "worship" long before the advent of recorded history. In all probability, early human beings became aware that outside forces controlled their food supply, weather conditions, and the movement of animals. To appease these forces the people developed prayers, hymns of praise, and reenactments of rituals that seemed to bring success in the hunt or in battle. Often, rituals were concerned with the changing of the seasons. Fertility rites ensured the return of the growing season. Sometimes a "warrior" representing Winter battled with another representing Spring. In the enactment, of course, Winter died.

At first, an entire tribe or clan would perform the rituals. After a time, only those thought to be more effective enacted them, and so became the religious leaders or priests. The people reasoned that if the ritual was to be effective, perhaps it needed to be done not only in the same way, but in the same location, at the holy place.

Figure 3.1

An undated engraving of a native ritual practiced by the Sinhalese people of what is now Sri Lanka. Celebrated at the time of the Sinhalese new year, this ritual is called Hobson Jobson. Elements of theatre—masks and costumes, dance and music—are obvious as part of this ceremony.

Many cultures developed rituals that were similar, though they had no contact with each other. The most common similarity was dance, frequently combined with poetry to serve as the "text."

Often the dancers used body and facial paints and special costuming so that they would not be recognized, but instead would be something outside themselves.

Sometimes the dancers made themselves up as animals, with masks covering their heads or bodies. In *Through the Fires,* historian Mel Fuller talks about the Wolf priests who at night donned shirts of wolf leather and went into the forest to dance, beat drums, and chant invocations to the Wolf God, associated with healing and magic in battle.[1]

Rituals also were used to re-create past deeds and thus preserve the history and beliefs of the tribe. Only when humor or comedy was introduced was theatre likely to develop. Such was the case with the Peruvian Indians, who developed both tragedy and comedy. The former dealt with noblemen or honored significant military battles, while the latter focused on everyday life. Both dramatic forms were composed in blank verse.

Egypt

In places such as Crete or Mesopotamia, no advances were made in theatre; instead, what "drama" was presented dealt with mythology and religion. One of the oldest "mystery" plays (drama dealing with the gods or religion), presented in Mesopotamia, told of the sacred marriage between gods and men. This presentation occurred in the temples of Sumer, with a blending of music, pantomime, and incantation. Further evidence of theatrical presentations, though not actually theatre, are seen in a humorous dialogue, *Master and Slave,* which resembles later mime plays and *commedia dell'arte* performances.

Other drama forms may have been presented, as well. They include medicinal drama, in which priests celebrated their skills, and a creation piece that possibly was staged periodically in Memphis (Egypt) during the ascendance of Ptah, the guardian god of the kingdom.

The so-called Pyramid Texts, written on the walls of tombs and dating back to 3000 B.C., give record of theatrical coronation ceremonies and jubilees. The texts dealt with the resurrection of the dead and with Isis's casting of a spell to protect her small son Horus from the deadly effects of a scorpion's sting. Although the Pyramid Texts encompassed several types of ritualistic drama, there is no evidence they ever were performed. None of the texts remain and the only information we have about them comes from one of the participants, I-kher-ne-fert, who wrote of producing the drama and playing the leading role.

[1] Mel Fuller, *Through the Fires: The Wizard's Way* (unpublished manuscript), written 1993.

It is likely that religious rituals were performed at the temple sacred to the particular god or myth and that the cast was made up of religious leaders, with a chorus chosen from those who lived nearby. The presentations apparently were given during the daylight hours, and the actors wore costumes reflecting the roles they played, such as an animal mask representative of a particular god. The acting probably was formal, with stereotypical movements and a declamatory speaking style to complement the usual chanting of the priests. These rituals probably included musical accompaniment as well.

India

We know little about the origin and early history of Indian Sanskrit (classical) drama. By the time those pieces that survive were written, the form already was well developed. Most of what we do know comes from the *Natyasastra,* written by Bharata some time between 200 B.C. and 200 A.D. According to legend, the god Indra asked Brahma to invent an art form that could be both seen and heard and that everyone could understand. As a result, Brahma took one component from each of the four *Vedas,* the sacred books of Indian wisdom. From *Rig Veda* came the spoken word; from *Sama Veda* came song; from the *Yajur Veda* came mime; and from the *Atharva Veda* came emotion. Brahma combined all these into the *Natya Veda*—the fifth book of wisdom—which he then taught to the sage Bharata, who recorded it in the *Natyasastra,* or Science of Dramaturgy. In other words, the book discusses the arts that came together to make up theatre.

Drama was based on the concept of two types of emotions, deep mainsprings such as love, and fleeting emotions such as anger. Through witnessing a blending of the two in facial expression and movement, the audience feels a sense of joy or aesthetic pleasure.

As in other primitive societies, dance probably was the precursor of theatrical presentation in ancient India, a country that glorified dance with images of deities, nymphs, and musicians—all in provocative poses—carved into temple walls, gateways, and columns. Dancing pleased the gods and was a way to pay homage to them. Dancing girls, under the authority of priests, performed on the temple grounds, which often spread out to include entire hillsides. Itinerant dancers from outside the temples were mimes and actors as well. They performed in palaces and towns for celebrations and entertainment.

The theatre buildings had precise measurements—ninety-six by forty-eight feet, divided exactly in half. The front section was for the audience and the back section for the stage and for the performers. There were four pillars, each of a single color—white, red, yellow and blue—to indicate where the various castes were to sit. There was no scenery; the prologue established the location, the time, and the situation. Then each successive scene used descriptive passages and pantomime in stylized movements and gestures to establish the location.

Actors relied on established gestures and movements for various parts of the body. For example, there were thirteen specific gestures for the head, nine for the neck, and thirty-two for the feet. Performances had to be exact, which meant the actors had to be able to concentrate right down to the tips of their fingers. Acting and dance were integrated into a single process, an expressive body art encompassing music and speech.

The earliest Sanskrit drama of which we are aware can be traced to 320 A.D. Rather than centering on character development or philosophical issues, it dealt with fundamental moods, or *rasas,* to which all the other dramatic elements were subordinate. This makes it impossible to classify plays according to Western genres. Rather, they relate to such *rasas* as the furious, the peaceful, or the heroic.

A particular play could contain any of these moods that were compatible. So instead of having unity of tone, as in Greek drama, there were many tones of mood. Also, unlike Greek plays, Sanskrit plays were never tragedies. Neither Greek nor Sanskrit drama, however, showed violence onstage.

In Sanskrit plays, right and wrong were clearly defined, and good always triumphed over evil. The plays had clearly defined characters such as the hero's confidante, usually a dwarf, who was bald and greedy, thus providing comic relief in an otherwise serious story. The plays consisted of one to ten acts, each covering no more than twenty-four hours, with no more than a year's time between acts.

Early Theatre in Other Regions of Asia

Like India, China had a specific type of theatre space—a rectangular hall with a balcony on three sides and an acting platform that jutted out into the audience. The actors, who wore colorful costumes, entered from the sides of a curtain in back.

In the ninth century, Emperor Tan Ming Huang established the first school of scenic art and music where he himself trained a hundred singing girls. During the Sung Dynasty (960–1279) song, dance, and dialogue were melded into a story. As in India, a complex system of gestures and movements was used to express various emotional states. An important difference between Chinese and Western theatre, however, was that the spectators came and went as they wished. They could do so because the plays were based on traditional and familiar stories.

Drama in Japan evolved from ritual dances, increasing in importance after the seventh century A.D. From these beginnings came *No,* or doll theatre—sometimes referred to as Noh, and *Kabuki.* Originally, there were two types of No theatre. The first type, *dengaku-no* or *ennen-no,* was performed by monks as entertainment after Buddhist ceremonies and probably derived from rural folk dances. The second type, the *saragku-no* , was written and performed by a father and son, Kanami

Reuters/Bettmann, Photographer: Frederic Neeman

Figure 3.2

A scene from a modern-day Kabuki theatre performance.

Kiyotsugu (1333–84) and Zeami Motokiyo (1364–1444). About a hundred of the approximately 240 still in existence were written by the son, Zeami.

While No performers were associated with a temple, Kabuki actors were placed in the same class as prostitutes, prohibited from performing where the higher classes of people lived. Developed in the seventeenth century when women were barred from acting, Kabuki involved female impersonation. Each Kabuki company had resident playwrights responsible for suiting the writing to individual actors and incorporating current happenings into the material.

Until the nineteenth century the West generally was unaware of Asian theatre.

Bettmann

Figure 3.3

Actors in a classical Greek drama, from a rendering of a painting by J. L. Gerome.

Greek Theatre

Since societal and theatrical advancement go hand in hand, it probably is not surprising that Athens, which evolved into an advanced commercial, political, and cultural center, should also develop the world's most advanced theatre up to that time. No one knows, of course, how long it took for drama and theatre to develop in Greece, but it must have been centuries before the appearance of the playwrights whose work we know today.

The theatre from which the rest of Western theatre developed was a blending of ritual and imitation that began sometime before the sixth century B.C.

in Greece, with dithyrambs, or hymns to Dionysus. They were sung around an altar by a chorus of fifty men, five from each of ten tribes of Attica. Dionysus was the god of wine and harvest, and the hymns related episodes from his life. According to legend, Dionysus—son of Zeus, the greatest of Greek gods, and of the mortal Semele—was killed, dismembered, and then resurrected (similar to the story of Osiris, suggesting Egyptian influence). The Dionysian legend then was related to the cycle of life: birth, maturation, death, and rebirth, in turn suggesting spring, summer, fall, winter, and the return of spring. As happened in many primitive societies, the Greeks worshiped a god whom they felt was responsible for the yearly cycle and the return of the planting and growing seasons.

The Greeks had many festivals, one for each principal deity, each worshiped in a particular way, but often with sacrifices, orgies, games, and dances. The most popular was the festival held to honor Dionysus. Since he was the god of wine, it was natural that the celebrations in his honor were unrestrained.

The Development of Drama

Theatre's development from the Dionysian hymns to the appearance of full-scale drama was gradual. First, there was only a chorus speaking or singing, and later, an individual actor speaking by himself. According to legend, the first person to do this was named Thespis (from which comes *thespian,* a synonym for actor), who thus is given the distinction of being the first playwright, the first actor, and the first director in the history of Western theatre. There is record that Thespis initially performed in 534 B.C., because it was in that year that he is credited with winning the prize at the first tragedy contest in Greece. And even though the introduction of an actor added dialogue to the dithyrambs, still there was no conflict. The actor played different roles by changing masks, and the chorus itself remained the unifying force of the plays, serving both as a narrator and a character.

As the festivals continued, the dithyramb developed and changed. After a time, the chorus dressed as satyrs—creatures that were half goat and half man. The worship then became known as the "goat song," or *tragoidia,* from which comes the word *tragedy.* It was not until the work of the playwright Aeschylus, however, that the Dionysian presentations could be called drama and theatre. Even then, theatre's ritualistic roots still were discernible, since plays dealt with legendary heroes and gods. It wasn't until the writings of Euripides that the characters were treated more realistically.

Out of the ecclesiastical part of the celebration came both tragedy and the satyr play. Only one complete satyr play survives—*The Cyclops* by Euripides, as well as part of a play by Sophocles. Because of this, we know little about satyr plays, except that they were a ribald form of comedy in which appeared the folkloric figure of Silenus, a water spirit, always accompanied by the satyrs. Part goat and part human, the satyrs had tails and pointed ears.

We know that tragedy and satyr plays grew out of religious celebration, but the origin of comedy is not known. It may have developed from dances and songs improvised by Dionysian revelers or from farces enacted at various places in Greece and Italy. Another theory is that a group of young men (*komos*) began to join the processions to the altar of Dionysus, improvising songs and witticisms to the crowd, which answered back, with both groups becoming increasingly insulting.

Throughout all Greek drama, the chorus continued to serve as the unifying force. Although its size fluctuated, it acted as a character, or sometimes as two characters discussing events with each other, or even as the narrator. Sometimes the chorus played the role of a messenger. The members usually entered just after the opening of the play and remained onstage until the end.

Unlike most of today's plays, Greek drama was not divided into acts, but continued without any break from beginning to end. Certain divisions—the episodes—were separated from each other by the intervention of the chorus. But there was no intermission, and the earlier tragedies were not much longer than many current one-acts.

Theatre Festivals and Theatrical Production

The three festivals at which Greek drama developed were the City Dionysia, held in Athens at the end of March each year; the Lenaia, held in Athens each January; and the Rural Dionysia, held each year in December. All of the plays still in existence were written for the City Dionysia. Each of these festivals had a master of revels, called the *archon.* He selected the plays and the order in which they would be presented. He also chose wealthy citizens to bear the expense of room and board for the chorus members. These citizens, called the **choregoi**, paid for training the chorus, for the costumes, for the musicians, and for any additional expenses. While the *archon* was elected, the *choregoi* were appointed to what was considered a prestigious position. Sometimes there was a strong rivalry among the *choregoi* to see who could spend the most money.

The playwright, who sometimes had a strong rivalry going with other writers, applied to the *archon* for rights to present plays. If selected, he was given a chorus and was expected to present music as well as drama. Many playwrights directed their plays and appeared in them. The actors (the Greek word for them is *hypokrites,* which at first meant simply "answerer") were paid by the state. There is indication that admission to the festivals was free, and everyone was expected to attend.

The most important of the festivals was the City Dionysia. During the time it was held, some believe all prisoners were freed and no legal proceedings were allowed to continue. The festival, frequently attended by dignitaries of other states, began with a processional and pageant in which the statue of Dionysus was taken from the temple at the foot of the Acropolis, carried outside the city of Athens, and then carried back with great celebration. After the processional, ten dithyrambs were presented, five composed of choruses of boys and five composed of choruses of men. For the next few days, plays were presented. Three writers of tragedy were chosen every year, and each was expected to present a trilogy plus a satyr play—all taking place the same day. Another day was set aside for comedy. No one is certain, however, of the exact order of events beyond the opening and closing.

At first, awards were presented for the best tragedies and, later, for the best tragic actor and comedy. The festival ended with the presentation of the prizes and a meeting of governmental leaders to discuss affairs of state.

Greece's golden age of drama was the fifth century B.C., when all the most important developments in playwriting and production occurred.

Plays and Playwrights

From its beginning, comedy formed a complete whole, performed separately from other plays. On the other hand, tragedy was presented in trilogies, that is, a cycle of legends, each telling a story complete in itself, but connected both chronologically and through subject matter. The tragedies and satyr plays were presented during the mornings, comedies during the afternoons.

Aeschylus

The first important dramatist of whom we have record is Aeschylus (525–456 B.C.), who wrote eighty to ninety plays, seven of which still are extant. Aeschylus relied largely on the chorus, still composed of fifty members. Primarily, he used traditional themes based on myths and Olympian law. Although his plays had a plot line, they were mostly choral. Aeschylus introduced a second actor into his plays, not to provide dramatic conflict, but for the sake of variety.

Aeschylus's best work is considered to be the *Orestian Trilogy* (458 B.C.), in which all three plays—*Agamemnon*, *The Libation Bearers*, and *Eumenides*—deal with revenge.

Sophocles

The next major writer of tragedy was Sophocles (496–406 B.C.), who wrote well over a hundred plays. He is credited with introducing a third actor and with reducing the size of the chorus from fifty to twelve. The lyricism of the chorus still is important in his tragedies, as is its effect on the direction the action takes.

There was now a definite form to tragedy, which was divided into specific sections: the *prologos*, an introductory scene; the *parados*, a lyric entrance by the chorus; the *episodes*, dramatic scenes (usually there were five); the *stasimon*, a choral ode; and the *exodus*, where the chorus delivers its final dialogue as it leaves the playing area. The episodes were divided by choral odes.

Sophocles was more interested in the interplay between characters than in the telling of religious myths. His plots are much more realistic than those of Aeschylus, and he is concerned with human beings as the determiners of their own fate, rather than as subject to the gods. His characters are complex, strong, and believable, and the central character always has a tragic flaw that brings about his or her downfall. Sophocles' plays, better developed than those of Aeschylus, have a skillful and believable climax.

Euripides

The third major writer of Greek tragedy was Euripides (480–406 B.C.), who is credited with ninety-two plays, of which seventeen tragedies and a satyr play survive. Concerned largely with the human being as an individual, Euripides dealt with the inner conflict of good and evil—that is, human beings against conscience—and questioned many of the ideals of Greek society and religion. He was admired for his ideas and the presentation of realistic characters, but criticized for the structure of his plays, which often were melodramatic and contrived.

The chorus is of much less importance in Euripides' plays, serving largely as a mouthpiece for the playwright rather than as a part of the action.

Euripides' most widely performed play is *The Trojan Women.* Produced in 415 B.C., a few months after Athenian forces had massacred all the males on the neutral island of Melos, the play takes a strong antiwar stand. Although the women and the city itself already have suffered tragedy as the drama opens, the intensity mounts throughout. Adding more power to the idea of "man's inhumanity to man" is Hecuba's vengeance in begging Menelaus to kill his wife, Helen.

THE TROJAN WOMEN

Euripides

Translated by Richmond Lattimore

The city of Troy is burning and in ruins, its men dead. The women and children are to become slaves to the victorious Greeks, commanded by Menelaus and Agamemnon.

The play tells of the suffering and despair of the women, including Queen Hecuba, who has become a slave to Odysseus, the man she most despises. Now she learns that one of her daughters, Polyxena, and her grandson Astyanax have been murdered. Another daughter, Cassandra, has been made Agamemnon's mistress.

Cassandra, half crazed, rejoices in her fate because it has angered the goddess Athene, who thus will wreck the Greek fleet in a storm.

Andromache, mother of Astyanax, is forced to set sail with her new master, leaving Hecuba to bury the baby. The queen encounters Menelaus and Helen, his beautiful spouse, who caused the war by deserting Menelaus for Hecuba's son Paris. Hecuba pleads with Menelaus to execute Helen, which he agrees to do.

As Hecuba prepares to bury the small body of her grandson, the Greeks burn Troy and, amidst the wailing, Trojan women set sail for home.

(*Cassandra is taken away by Talthybios and his soldiers. Hecuba collapses*)

CHORUS: Handmaids of aged Hecuba, can you not see
how your mistress, powerless to cry out, lies prone? Oh, take
her hand and help her to her feet, you wretched maids.
Will you let an aged helpless woman lie so long?

HECUBA: No. Let me lie where I have fallen. Kind acts, my maids,
must be unkind, unwanted. All that I endure
and have endured and shall, deserves to strike me down.
O gods! What wretched things to call on—gods!—for help
although the decorous action is to invoke their aid when all our
hands lay hold on is unhappiness.
No. It is my pleasure first to tell good fortune's tale,
to cast its count more sadly against disasters now.
I was a princess, who was once a prince's bride,
mother by him of sons preeminent, beyond
the mere numbers of them, lords of the Phrygian domain,
such sons for pride to point to as no woman of Troy,
no Hellene, none in the outlander's wide world might match.
And then I saw them fall before the spears of Greece, and cut
this hair for them, and laid it on their graves.
I mourned their father, Priam. None told me the tale
of his death. I saw it, with these eyes. I stood to watch
his throat cut, next the altar of the protecting god. I saw my
city taken. And the girls I nursed,
choice flowers to wear the pride of any husband's eyes,
matured to be dragged by hands of strangers from my arms.
There is no hope left that they will ever see me more, no hope
that I shall ever look on them again.
There is one more stone to key this arch of wretchedness:
I must be carried away to Hellas now, an old
slave woman, where all those tasks that wrack old age shall be
given me by my masters. I must work the bolt
that bars their doorway, I whose son was Hektor once;
or bake their bread; lay down these withered limbs to sleep
on the bare ground, whose bed was royal once; abuse this skin
once delicate the slattern's way, exposed through robes whose
rags will mock my luxury of long since.

Unhappy, O unhappy. And all this came to pass and shall be, for
the way one woman chose a man. Cassandra, O daughter, whose
excitements were the god's,
you have paid for your consecration now; at what a price!
And you, my poor Polyxena, where are you now?
Not here, nor any boy or girl of mine, who were
so many once, is near me in my unhappiness.
And you would lift me from the ground? What hope? What use?
Guide these feet long ago so delicate in Troy,
a slave's feet now, to the straw sacks laid on the ground
and the piled stones; let me lay down my head and die
in an exhaustion of tears. Of all who walk in bliss call not one
happy yet, until the man is dead.

(***HECUBA**, after being led to the back of the stage, flings herself to the ground once more*)

Comedy: Old and New

Throughout the history of classical Greece, tragedy dealt with the gods and heroes, while comedy related to current events and people. Greek comedy was developed after tragedy and was considered inferior, yet it was important to Greek citizens, who stressed the concept of "a well-balanced man in a well-balanced state."

Although comedies were presented at the City Dionysia, they were given more support at the Lenaia. Choruses of twenty-four members were used, and often there were more individual actors than appeared in tragedies.

The plots of Greek comedies were more complicated than those of tragedies, but were more episodic. Unlike tragic heroes, comic characters were ordinary people. In essence, tragedy dealt with what humankind should be, while comedy dealt with what it actually is.

There are two categories of comedy, Old and New. Old Comedy (454–404 B.C.) is characterized by its emphasis on an idea rather than on a cause-to-effect relationship of events. The episodes often seem unrelated. However, they do build in comic intensity. Often broad satires on well-known people and events, comedies parodied the same subjects treated seriously in tragedy.

Old Comedy also made use of a chorus, from whom the play took its name, such as *The Wasps* or *The Frogs*.

The major writer of Old Comedy was Aristophanes (c. 448–380 B.C.). In *The Clouds* (423 B.C.) Socrates (and philosophers in general) becomes the scapegoat of Aristophanes' biting wit. The story concerns Strepsiades, who decides to seek Socrates' advice about how he can avoid paying back money he owes as a result of his unscrupulous son running up huge debts. The dialogue is filled with pseudo-intellectual babbling about science and logic, which Aristophanes sees as a "narrow-minded effort to stifle the breadth, complexity, beauty, and joy of experience, for it substitutes clever thinking for full wholesome living."[2] When the play was produced, according to legend:

> Socrates . . . stood up so that the spectators could compare him with the image on the stage. But in 399 B.C., when he showed himself to a court of 501 Athenians, he could not convince them that he was not the dishonest and irreverent creature whom they had seen in Aristophanes' comedy.[3]

THE CLOUDS

Aristophanes
Translated by Benjamin Bickley Rogers

SOCRATES: What is it that you want? first tell me that.

STREPSIADES: You have heard a million times what 'tis I want:
My debts! my debts! I want to shirk my debts.

SOCRATES: Come, come, pull up the clothes: refine your thoughts
With subtle wit: look at the case on all sides:
Mind you divide correctly.

STREPSIADES: Ugh! O me.

SOCRATES: Hush: if you meet with any difficulty
Leave it a moment: then return again
To the same thought: then lift and weigh it well.

STREPSIADES: O, here, dear Socrates!

SOCRATES: Well, my old friend.

STREPSIADES: I've found a notion how to shirk my debt:

SOCRATES: Well then, propound it.

---

[2] Sylvan Barnet, Morton Berman, and William Burro, eds. *Eight Great Comedies* (New York: New American Library, 1958), p. 15.

[3] Barnet, p. 16.

STREPSIADES: What do you think of this?
Suppose I hire some grand Thessalian witch
To Conjure down the Moon, and then I take it
And clap it into some round helmet-box,
And keep it fast there, like a looking-glass,—

SOCRATES: But what's the use of that?

STREPSIADES: The use quotha:
Why if the Moon should never rise again,
I'd never pay one farthing.

SOCRATES: No! why not?

STREPSIADES: Why, don't we pay our interest by the month?

SOCRATES: Good! now I'll proffer you another problem.
Suppose an action: damages, five talents:
Now tell me how you can evade that same.

STREPSIADES: How! how! can't say at all: but I'll go seek.

SOCRATES: Don't wrap your mind for ever round yourself,
But let your thoughts range freely through the air,
Like chafers with a thread about their feet.

STREPSIADES: I've found a bright evasion of the action:
Confess yourself, tis glorious.

SOCRATES: But what is it?

STREPSIADES: I say, haven't you seen in druggists' shops
That stone, that splendidly transparent stone,
By which they kindle fire?

SOCRATES: The burning glass?

STREPSIADES: That's it: well then, I'd get me one of these,
And as the clerk was entering down my case,
I'd stand, like this, some distance towards the sun,
And burn out every line.

SOCRATES: By the Three Graces,
A clever dodge!

STREPSIADES: O me, how pleased I am
To have a debt like that clean blotted out.

SOCRATES: Come, then, make haste and snap up this.

STREPSIADES: Well, what?

SOCRATES: How to prevent an adversary's suit
Supposing you were sure to lose it; tell me.

STREPSIADES: O, nothing easier.

SOCRATES: How, pray?

Strepsiades: Why thus,
While there was yet one trial intervening,
Ere mine was cited, I'd go hang myself.

Socrates: Absurd!

Strepsiades: No, by the Gods, it isn't though:
They could not prosecute me were I dead.

New Comedy, popular in the time of Alexander the Great, is associated with Menander (c. 342–292 B.C.), the most celebrated writer of this form. He wrote more than one hundred plays, with the first performance of his work in 321 B.C. Although he won only eight prizes, after his death he became known as one of the most popular writers of ancient Greece.

New Comedy dealt with middle-class citizens because the government, perhaps due to the theatregoers' changing tastes, no longer allowed playwrights to poke fun at leaders or other well-known people. As a result, the characters are more types than individuals. To make them interesting, the writer had to place them in situations where their follies could be exposed and ridiculed.

The chorus was omitted entirely from later comedy, perhaps due to heavy taxation and the absence of financial support. However, New Comedy included both a prologue (which Euripides had used for his plays) and an epilogue. In the former, usually a supernatural being or sometimes an allegorical figure such as "Air" came onstage to explain the subject matter of the play. At the conclusion, the author appeared before the audience with a collection box, soliciting approval for himself and his play.

The Physical Theatre

Plays were presented outdoors, on a flat place, or **orchestra**, at the base of a hill. At first, this was an open space with no walls or ceiling. The auditorium, or **theatron**, was the hillside itself where the audience stood to watch the plays. In time, permanent seats were constructed of stone. (See page 2.) The theatre of Dionysus, the most famous Greek theatre, seated about 14,000 spectators. By this time, however, Greek theatre already was beginning to decline.

An altar to Dionysus, called the *themele*, was located in the middle of each site. Some time during the fifth century B.C., a **skene** building, or scene house, was added, which, of course, eliminated part of the audience area that up to this time had been a circle. The skene's original purpose was to provide a place where the actors might dress and where they could wait before going onstage, but it eventually came to be used as a background for the dramatic action.

Despite the changes, the auditorium and the acting areas in Greek theatre remained separate. Between them was the orchestra. Providing entrance into that area, principally for the chorus—though sometimes used by actors and audience—were the entrances called **parodoi**.

The scene house later became a two-story building with various openings on both stories. The second story was used for the appearance of the gods, while the doors below were for the protagonist and the other characters. One of the openings, the *thyromata,* framed action that occurred within the building. It is believed that the *thyromata* may have been the predecessor of our proscenium, or picture-frame, stage. Actors used doors in the *proskenion* to make entrances and exits.

Since most of the action in Greek drama takes place outside, little scenery was used. Some believe, however, that painted flats occasionally were leaned against the exterior walls of the scene house. Another later form of scenery was the *periaktoi*—tall prisms with three sides on which different scenes were painted. The prisms, mounted on poles at each side of the stage, could be rotated to show the appropriate scenes. The paintings probably were simple, only suggesting changes rather than supplying realistic backgrounds.

After the fourth century much more elaborate stone theatres were built all over the country, yet the drama itself never came close to matching the quality of that of the fifth century.

Stage Machinery

One type of stage machinery used in ancient Greece was called the *mechane,* or machine. While the construction and actual workings are unknown, we do know that this device was a crane of some sort that lowered the gods when the play called for them to intervene in characters' lives. The *mechane* also is called the **deus ex machina**, or god from the machine, which in our time has come to mean a less-than-desirable literary device in which a playwright has fate solve the protagonist's problem, rather than having the character solve it. Gods also sometimes appeared on the roof of the *proskenion,* stepping from the upper story of the skene. The *proskenion* was a facade for the first story of the *skene* building.

Another piece of stage machinery was the **ekkyklema**, a cart or platform that rolled out of the *thyromata.* It may have been used to carry the bodies of actors portraying warriors killed in battle since, so far as is known, the Greeks did not show violence onstage.

Masks and Costumes

The actors in the Greek theatre were highly respected. They were trusted as diplomats, were exempt from military service, and were considered servants of Dionysus. The Greek actor also was highly trained and skillful, because he was expected to assume many different roles. For each role he wore a different mask.

Every type of character that appeared in a Greek play had a specific mask, making it easy for the audience to recognize a servant, a young woman, or an old man just by the mask the actor wore. This was particularly important because all the performers were men. The tragic actor also wore a high boot, or *cothurnus*, to give him added stature, and possibly a *chiton*, an ankle-length embroidered robe.

There are no recorded accounts, but in all probability the Greek style of acting was artificial by modern standards. The delivery of the lines probably would have sounded unnatural to our ears, since the masks included cone-shaped pieces in front of the mouth. Some historians believe these may have served as miniature megaphones, though others disagree.

Costumes for comedy were less cumbersome, since the comic actor also was required to be nimble. Usually he wore slippers, flesh-colored tights, a short tunic, and in Aristophanes' plays, a large leather phallus. For satyr plays, the actors wore a tail as well as a phallus.

Finally, perhaps the most important contribution of the Greek theatre to that of our own era was the writings of Aristotle. Though much of his work is lost and so cannot be interpreted exactly, Aristotle's approach continues to influence the writing of drama even today.

Roman Theatre

During the First Punic War (264–241 B.C.) the Romans became exposed to the drama of Greece and began importing Greek plays. In 240 B.C., Livius Andronicus produced at the Roman games the first Greek play that had been translated into Latin. Others followed. The performances began in the morning, and each play was finished by noon.

Thus, Roman drama stemmed directly from Greek drama and theatrical practice. Roman citizens saw imported plays, as well as mimes that were performed by Greek citizens who had settled in Sicily. Loosely improvised plays, with suggestive action and dialogue, sensational elements, and stereotyped characters, mimes first appeared in Rome in the third century B.C.. Like later forms of drama, these plays were presented as part of the Roman games—the **ludi romani**.

Although the Romans regarded the Greek culture as decadent, Roman playwrights imitated Greek plays, particularly those written by Menander. Perhaps they felt that since the audience would be certain to know that the plays were adapted from the Greek, the decadence could be presented on stage without offending the authorities in charge of the festivals. By 150 B.C., the popularity of this sort of fare faded and it was presented only occasionally.

Despite the many similarities between Greek and Roman theatre, some differences existed as well. Whereas the Greeks viewed drama as reflecting moral values and important issues, the Romans regarded it strictly as entertainment. In addition, the Greeks made more use of a chorus both for speaking and singing, while music in the Roman theatre was associated with single actors and was more equally distributed throughout the play.

The presentation of plays was not associated with the worship of any particular god. In fact, there was no real connection between plays and religion, although shrines to various gods often were part of the theatre buildings and sacrifices were made to them during the festivals. At first, drama was presented during festivals held only four times a year, but later was included for occasions such as military victories or funerals of noted citizens. In addition to the plays, the festivals featured chariot races, gladiatorial displays, enactments of sea battles, boxing, and public crucifixions. Slaves were forced to participate in gladiatorial battles to the death, often with the promise of freedom if they fought well and were victorious. Jugglers, acrobats, trained animal acts, and pantomimes in which dancing played the most important part also were presented at the festivals.

Acting Companies

At first the actors in the *ludi romani* were amateurs, but later professional companies were formed. A magistrate was in charge of the festivals, which were financed in much the same way as they had been in Greece. The magistrate

Figure 3.4

A 19th-century engraving of a performance of an ancient Roman comedy.

The Granger Collection

received aid from the state, but might contribute some of his own money. He then contracted with an acting company and a manager for the plays, which it is believed were bought outright from the writers and may have been viewed beforehand to check for appropriateness rather than for artistic quality. Several acting companies participated in each festival, and admission was free. In addition to receiving money for acting, the companies that were judged the best (that is, received the most applause) were given prizes.

Actors sometimes engaged their own companies for various festivals. Later companies were controlled by a manager and consisted of slaves who might be flogged or even put to death at the slightest provocation. According to one theory, actors in general began to lose prestige, though some historians dispute this idea. Yet there also are records of wealthy citizens being actors. Roscius, as Rome's most famous actor, was made a knight. He died in 62 B.C. In the first century, some actors became celebrities with large followings.

Roman actors, known as *histriones*, usually specialized in playing certain types of characters, although it is recorded that Roscius played in both comedy and tragedy. Both comic and tragic actors wore masks made of linen with attached wigs, so they covered the actor's entire head. Mime actors, considered inferior to those playing in comedy and tragedy, did not wear masks, and their gestures were more animated than those of comic and tragic actors.

The acting style of Rome was more improvisational in nature than that of Greece. The movements were broad and exaggerated, because in large theatres many spectators could not discern small movements. Costumes for tragedy were similar to those worn by Greek actors. Costumes for comedy were Greek if the play was based on Greek life, or Roman if it dealt with everyday Roman life. Female roles were played by men, except in the mimes, and certain colors in costuming represented specific occupations.

Theatre Buildings

Initially, Roman theatres were temporary structures made of wood, with only a platform and a scene (Greek *skene*) building. Not until 55 B.C. was the first permanent theatre erected, at Pompeii. Others followed at various locations in the empire—each more elaborate than those preceding it. There were stone columns and arches and intricate statues and friezes. Often, the buildings were covered to protect the artistry as well as the actors.

Rather than being constructed on a hillside as were Greek theatres, those in Rome stood on a level spot with stadium-type seating. The auditorium and orchestra area were semicircular, and the stages were deeper from front to back. The orchestra area was not used for scenes, but usually for the seating of distinguished members of the audience. The Roman theatre buildings were more of an architectural whole than were the theatres of Greece because they existed inside high walls. In this respect, they resembled later indoor theatres in Europe, particularly since an awning often was stretched over the top. In some of the later theatres, the orchestra area was enclosed by a wall for gladiatorial contests, or flooded for the enactment of sea battles or water ballets. In some of the theatres there was a front curtain, which could be dropped either into the orchestra area or into slots. In addition, the stages had trapdoors for the shifting of properties. Usually, the stage was raised, making it easier for the audience to see the actors.

Scenery for the comedies would show houses on a street. Some historians believe that a back curtain was used both as scenery and to mask the backstage area, while others think that the scenery was three-dimensional. *Periaktoi* were used to indicate changes in location, since the same street scene was used for all comedy and a palace scene was used for all tragedy.

Forms of Drama

Several types of mimes were presented in Rome, but more important historically was the Atellan farce, which is believed to have originated in the town of Atella, possibly in the marketplace. One of the oldest forms of Roman comedy, it was characterized by improvisation and stock characters, who included the braggart, the gluttonous fool, and the old miser—the model for Shakespeare's Shylock in *The Merchant of Venice* and Molière's Harpagon in *The Miser*. The plots consisted of ludicrous situations involving such things as drunkenness and trickery. Unlike the mime, the Atellan farce used no women in the cast. Early mimes were entirely improvised, but those that came later, during the first century B.C., were written. During the latter stages of their popularity they became indecent and obscene.

Playwrights

The first Roman dramatist of whom there is a record was Gnaeus Naevius (270–201 B.C.). The two most popular playwrights were Plautus and Terence.

Plautus

Titus Maccius Plautus, Rome's first major playwright (254 to 184 B.C.), wrote a large number of comedies, twenty-one of which still exist. Although he borrowed his plots from Menander, he adapted and changed them. Two of his best-known works are *The Menaechmi* and *Amphitruo*, both of which deal with the complications of mistaken identity. Shakespeare based his *Comedy of Errors* on *The Menaechmi.*

Plautus's plays differed from Greek comedies in that they did not satirize the government, since that practice was frowned upon by the leaders of Rome. Instead, they pointed up the idiosyncrasies of individual characters, often dealing with misunderstood motives and deceptions. A prologue outlined the plot, and the plays, though coarse, remained popular long after his death due to their broad humor, improbable situations, and lively spirit.

Terence

Second in popularity was Publius Terentius Afer, known as Terence (about 195–159 B.C.). His style was too literary to have a wide appeal. His dialogue, however, was written in the style of everyday conversation, and his plays showed a sympathetic treatment of character. A slave who had lived in Athens, Terence wrote six plays, all of which survive. *The Brothers* is one of his better known works. He based his writings on Menander, but attempted to improve the form and structure, often combining several Greek plays into one drama of his own. Each of the plays had a double plot and was more polished and more skillfully written than those of Plautus. In effect, Plautus wrote comedies of situation, while Terence wrote romantic comedies.

Seneca

The only Roman tragedies still in existence were written by Lucius Annaeus Seneca (4 B.C.–65 A.D.). Although his plays were adaptations of Greek tragedies, they differed markedly from their sources. Because they were written to be recited rather than produced, they contained much violence that would have been nearly impossible to present on the stage. They were characterized by elaborate speeches, soliloquies, asides, and sensationalism in general. Almost all the rules for tragedy formulated in medieval Italy were based on the writings of Seneca.

After the fourth century A.D., largely because of the influence of the Christian church, the theatre existed only in a very limited way until the tenth century, when it once more began to gain popularity.

Chapter Four

The Medieval Theatre

"The theatres," Augustine said in 400 A.D. "are falling nearly everywhere, the theatres, those sinks of uncleanness and public places of debauchery. And why are they falling? They are falling because of the reformation of the age, because the lewd and sacrilegious practices for which they are built are out of fashion." That the theatres were falling is an indisputable fact; that the age had reformed is far less certain. Barbarian attacks on Italy had contributed much to theatre's devastation.[1] After the fall of the western Roman Empire, overrun by invaders in 476, little in the way of drama or theatrical entertainment was presented for several hundred years. Yet, a fondness remained. Minstrels (itinerant troubadours), acrobats, singers, jugglers, and animal trainers traveled through the countryside, stopping to perform in towns and villages.

There were mimes and pantomimes, pagan rites, and festivals. But the Christian church was a powerful institution, growing more so year by year, gaining in strength since before the fall of Rome. The church was against theatre, declaring it was sacrilegious, evil, and immoral, so it was difficult for drama to exist. Those few actors who continued to perform were even forbidden the sacrament of communion.

Apparently, however, this didn't seem to matter a great deal to the occasional performers who continued to present their fare, nor did it bother their audiences. This is apparent from the order given repeatedly by the church to stop presenting *and* attending all theatrical performances!

The Beginnings

Ironically, when drama was reborn it appeared as a part of the church service in much of western Europe. It was during this time, the tenth century, that Hrosvitha, a noblewoman who lived in a convent in what is now Germany, became the first person in more than 1100 years to write plays. Although she sometimes used humor to teach moral lessons, her play *Paphnutius* is a more straightforward account of the conversion of a courtesan by a hermit who first approaches her as a would-be customer. The play is a forerunner of a type of drama, the miracle play, which became common during the Middle Ages.

In the ninth century, the cross and the Resurrection of Christ became increasingly important symbols of the church. At about the same time, the liturgy was expanded to include Latin sequences, or hymns. The person responsible for this was the St. Gall monk Notker Balbulus, the Stammerer (840–912). A colleague of his named Tutilo (c. 850–915) then changed the

[1] Sylvan Barnet, Morton Berman, and William Burto, eds., *The Genius of the Early American Theater* (New York: New American Library, 1962), p. 10.

liturgical insertions into dialogue delivered by priests. One priest impersonated an angel and three others impersonated the three women visiting Christ's tomb. Thus liturgical drama came into existence one Easter morning in the form of a playlet—a **trope** designed to teach and to provide visual examples of the biblical story of Jesus' crucifixion and rising from the dead:

> **ANGEL:** *Quem queritis in sepulchro, o Christicole?*
> [Whom seek ye in the sepulcher, O women of Christ?]
>
> **MARYS:** *Jesum Nazerenum crucifixum, o caelicolae.*
> [Jesus of Nazareth, who is crucified, o heavenly one.]
>
> **ANGEL:** *Non est hic, surrexit sicut praedixerat. Ite, nuntiate quia surrexit de speculchro.*
> [He is not here; He is risen, as was foretold. Go, proclaim that he has risen from the sepulcher!]

This trope was the source of the *passion play* still performed today.

As occurred in Greece, Egypt, and in other emerging civilizations, drama stemmed from ritual. Some would argue that since it was sung, the presentation actually was music rather than drama. Regardless, theatre once more took root and began to grow.

The *tropes* (from the Latin *tropus,* melody) continued to be a part of the mass at the church's major yearly events, such as Easter, Advent, and Christmas, and thus became a tradition throughout western Europe. The widespread use of such playlets is not surprising when we consider that the church, rather than national governments, still ruled the actions of the people. Thus, drama was similar from Holland to France to Italy to England, with only local customs and tastes dictating slight differences.

Gradually, the playlets were expanded until they became more elaborate and were included extensively in church services. In one trope Mary Magdalene, at Christ's tomb, mistakes Christ for a gardener. In another drama the Marys buy perfume from a stall that has been set up outside Christ's tomb, and so on.

At first, lines were delivered in Latin. Later, each line was repeated—as in the previous example—in the language of the country. Beginning in the eleventh century the Latin was dropped, and the lines were spoken in the local language.

The Staging of Liturgical Drama

In the beginning, the tropes were presented only by clergymen in the larger churches and cathedrals. The staging or scenery consisted of "mansions," or **sedes**, and an acting area, or **platea**. A *sede* represented a specific place, such as Christ's tomb, which was most often at the altar of the church. After the dramatizations became more lengthy and elaborate, additional *tropes* showed events leading up to and following the Resurrection.

Now there were several different *sedes*—one for each locale—placed at various points around the interior of the sanctuary. Since each mansion was small, the *platea* could be a central area or the entire open space. The action would start at one mansion or *sede* (the specific location) and move into the *platea* (the nonspecific or central location). The congregation was expected to imagine the action still was taking place at a particular mansion. When the play switched to another mansion, the same general central area was used, and the audience now recognized the action as taking place at a new locale.

As the presentations grew longer, the staging became more elaborate. At first, chairs or the altar indicated the different mansions. Later, more elaborate *sedes* were built, such as a realistic sepulcher for Christ's tomb, large enough for several people to enter. Although it didn't matter how the mansions were placed, usually it was more convenient for the audience if they appeared in a straight or slightly curved line.

As time went on, the presentations grew longer and longer, with more and more mansions added. The dialogue departed from that recorded in the Bible, becoming more secular and even including occasional humor. In addition, more people were participating, and the costuming and scenery were becoming increasingly spectacular.

Moving Outside the Church

By the thirteenth century, the presentations had become too elaborate and disruptive to be presented within the confines of the church building, and the churches were overcrowded with spectators. Thus, the drama, usually still acted by clergymen, came to be presented on the west side of the church. Here, in many cases, was a porch—a ready-made stage of sorts—opening onto the town square, where local residents could stand and watch.

Many church officials began to have doubts about whether the plays should be presented at all; they were becoming more and more what the leaders had earlier feared. One edict about their presentation followed another, so that gradually laymen began acting in them, and by the fourteenth and fifteenth centuries, all the responsibilities of the production were assumed by secular groups. By this time, the dialogue was spoken entirely in the local language.

One of the most popular forms that developed was the Corpus Christi (Body of Christ) play, presented from about 1350 to about 1550 on the Thursday following Pentecost, that is, some time between late May and late June. This drama emphasized transubstantiation, or the mystery of communion bread and wine becoming Christ's body and blood. (The Corpus Christi holiday had been established in 1311.) The productions grew to include dozens of scenes, encompassing all of creation, and were presented in towns

Stock Montage, Inc.

Figure 4.1

A passion play, c. 15th century, medieval Europe.

and villages all across England. There is no record of authorship of these or any other liturgical or religious dramas of the medieval period, though certain individual styles are recognizable in multiple plays.

The Producing Groups and the Productions

The secular play-producing groups were largely trade guilds or special societies, the latter formed just for this purpose. In France, one such group was the *Confrérie de la Passion*, established in 1402 by Charles VI at the Hôpital de la Trinité, thus becoming the first permanent company to have a particular theatre to call its home. Although the church no longer participated to any great extent in the productions, its approval still was necessary. Each guild had a patron saint, its own priest, and a chapel. Sometimes several small guilds joined together to produce a single play.

Later, the drama moved from the west door of the church to other locations. Various types of structures were used. Some plays, for example, were produced on a platform pushed against a building, while others were presented in old Roman amphitheatres or in town squares.

Production and Spectacle

In England, there were two major means of production. One was to present plays in "rounds" or ancient amphitheatres, and the other was to use **pageant wagons** as stages. A pageant wagon carried two or more mansions, and some historians believe that at times several were placed next to each other. The acting may have taken place entirely on the wagons or on the ground in front of them. The wagons were designed to be moved from place to place, with each site marked by flags indicating where they were to stop. Some wagons symbolized particular locations, such as the mouth of hell belching fire. One was shaped like a ship for a play about Noah.

Typically, the mansions were positioned to represent the planes of heaven, earth, and hell. Heaven usually was at one end of the playing area and hell at the other, with a series of mansions between. The more mansions there were, the longer and more elaborate the presentation. It is recorded, for instance, that in 1501 at Mons, France, a play was given with sixty-seven mansions. It took forty-eight days to rehearse, and one performance lasted four days.

The scenes were really short episodes that had no connection with each other except that they dealt with biblical subject matter. Each episode was complete in itself, and the overall presentation had no continuing plot.

Of great concern were special effects. There are records of professionals being hired to invent all sorts of startling "secrets" (as they were called) including Christ's walking on the water and smoke and fire billowing from the mouth of hell. There were earthquakes and clouds. Thunder roared. Actors and objects were raised and lowered by means of ropes and pulleys, allowing the audience to watch as monsters and animals flew freely through hell. There is even record of an effigy being filled with bones and animal entrails to provide a realistic scene. Fountains sprang up, water turned into wine, and the miracle of the loaves and fishes was enacted. (Actually, even before the drama moved out of the church, many of these special effects were used, and the mansions were constructed to resemble the places they represented.)

Unlike the drama of Greece, medieval religious drama involved much violence, including sword fights and battles. The list of battle regalia and other properties was often long and costly.

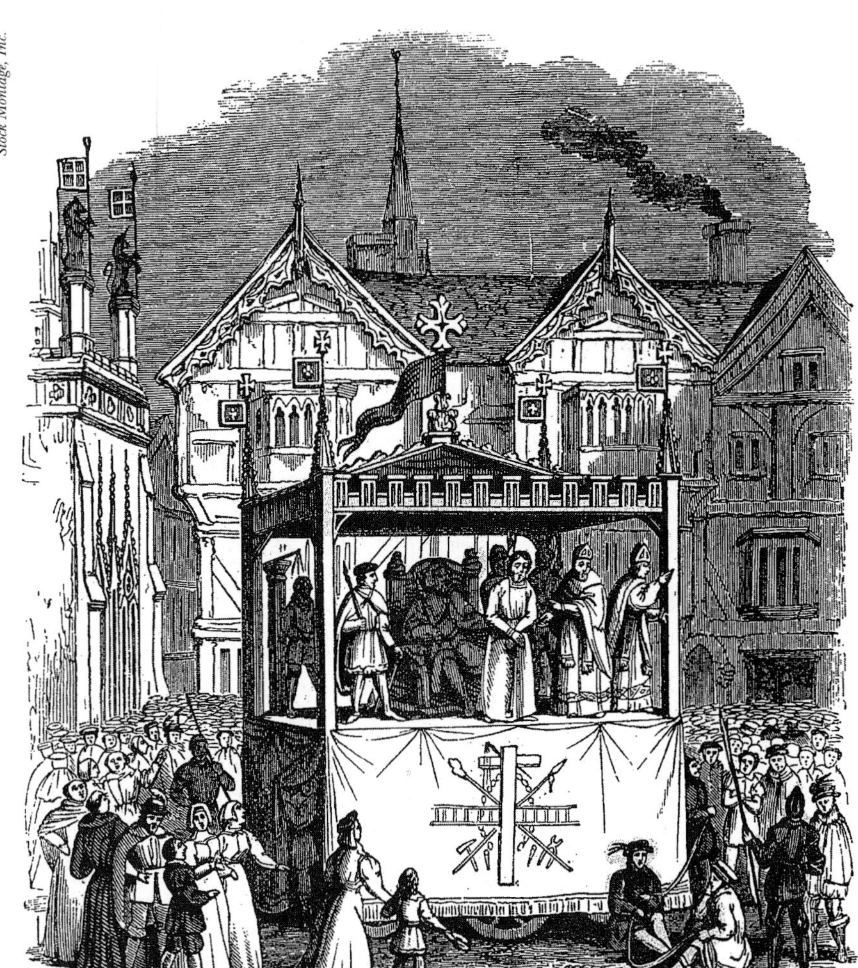

Figure 4.2

A mystery play on a pageant wagon, one of the Chester Cycle plays, c. 1400.

Most of the actors dressed in contemporary costumes they supplied themselves, but angels wore white robes with wings, and God was dressed as an official of the church. Satan, wearing wings, horns, claws, and a tail, was designed to be both humorous and awe-inspiring. In fact, beginning in the sixteenth century, the plays included many comic elements. Unfortunately, not many of the texts of these works survive, however. Of the hundreds given in England, only those from Chester, York, Coventry, and Wakefield exist in complete form.

Cycle Plays

At the end of the fourteenth century, all the plays that had been presented throughout the church year were combined into a single presentation, or cycle. The Wakefield Cycle contained thirty-two episodes, while the York Cycle comprised forty-eight. Elaborate productions such as these continued until the middle of the sixteenth century, all the while changing in content as old sections were deleted and new ones were added.

Further, more and more humor, often centered on wives, crept into the presentations. For example, in each of two plays about the flooding of the earth, Noah has a shrewish wife. Another example of a play that contains humor is *The Second Shepherd's Play*, part of the Wakefield Cycle. (Its title is in reference to the fact that of the thirty-two plays that make up the cycle, this is the *second* dealing with the Nativity.) Mak complains about his wife and how he can ill afford to support his family. He then casts a spell on three shepherds so that they fall asleep. Then he steals one of their sheep. Among his complaints, which sets up what happens later, are that his wife . . .

Lies wallowing—by the rood—by the fire, lo!
And a house full of brood. She drinks well, too
There's no other good that she will do!
But she
Eats as fast as may be,
And every year that we see
She brings forth a baby—
And, some years, two.
Were I even more prosperous and richer by some,
I were eaten out of house and even of home.
Yet is she a foul souse, if ye come near;
There is none that goes or anywhere roams
'Worse than she. . . .

Mak then proposes the idea of passing off the stolen sheep as a newborn baby. His wife agrees to go along with the deception.

The play presents a parallel between the tale of Mak, his wife, and their newborn "baby" and the nativity story of Joseph, Mary, and their newborn "lamb." First, each of the two births is preceded by song, with Mak singing out of tune and the angels singing sweetly. The shepherds also offer gifts to both of the newborns. The humor was not intended to be sacrilegious, but rather to point up humankind's follies. Thus side-by-side exist a realistic world of bad weather, lack of money, and less-than-ideal family relationships—often treated humorously—and a world of faith, innocence, and awe at the birth of Jesus.

THE SECOND SHEPHERD'S PLAY

Anonymous

First Shepherd: Gave ye the child anything?

Second Shepherd: I swear not one farthing.

Third Shepherd: Quickly back will I fling;
Abide ye me here. (*He runs back.*)
Mak, take it to no grief if I come to thy son.

Mak: Nay, thou dost me great mischief, and foul hast thou done.

Third Shepherd: The child will it not grieve, that daystar one?
Mak, with your leave, let me give your son
But sixpence.

Mak: Nay, go way! He sleeps.

Third Shepherd: Methinks he peeps.

Mak: When he wakens he weeps.
I pray you, go hence!

(*The others return.*)

Third Shepherd: Give me leave him to kiss, and lift up the clout.[2] (*He lifts up the cover.*)
What the devil is this? He has a long snout!

First Shepherd: He is shapèd amiss. Let's not wait about.

Second Shepherd: "Ill-spun weft," iwis, "aye comes foul out."[3]
A son! (*Recognizes the sheep.*) He is like to our sheep!

Third Shepherd: How, Gib, may I peep?

First Shepherd: "How nature will creep
Where it cannot run!"

Second Shepherd: This was a quaint gaud and a far cast;[4]
It was a high fraud.

Third Shepherd: Yea, sirs, was't.
Let's burn this bawd and bind her fast.
A false scold hangs at the last;
So shalt thou.
Will ye see how they swaddle
His four feet in the middle?

---

2 cloth

3 "An ill-spun weft always comes out foul," meaning that the parents' deformity appears in the child.

4 a clever prank and a sly trick

Saw I never in a cradle
A horned lad ere now.

Mak: Peace, bid I. What! Leave off your care!
I am he that begat, and yond woman him bare.

First Shepherd: How named is your brat? "Mak?" Lo, God, Mak's heir.

Second Shepherd: Let be all that. Now God curse his fare,
This boy.

Wife: A pretty child is he
As sits on a woman's knee;
A dillydown, pardie,
To give a man joy.

Third Shepherd: I know him by the ear-mark; that is a good token.

Mak: I tell you, sirs, hark!—his nose was broken.
I was told by a clerk a spell had been spoken.

First Shepherd: This is a false work; my vengeance is woken.
Get weapon!

Wife: He was taken by an elf,
I saw it myself;
When the clock struck twelve
Was he misshapen.

Second Shepherd: Ye two are most deft, but we're not misled.

First Shepherd: Since they stand by their theft, let's see them both dead.

Mak: If I trespass eft,[5] strike off my head.
With you will I be left.

Third Shepherd: Sirs, let them dread:
For this trespass
We will neither curse nor fight,
Strike nor smite;
But hold him tight,
And cast him in canvas.

(*They toss MAK in a sheet and return to the field.*)

---

[5] again

On the other hand, *Abraham and Isaac* is serious and completely reverential in tone, with the intent of showing what Christian behavior should be like. The play could be part of a lost cycle, though this is only speculation. Abraham knows, when forced to choose between God and his own family, that, as a pious man, he really has no choice. When the time comes to sacrifice his son Isaac, he hesitates briefly, yet is resolved to continue as commanded by God.

ABRAHAM AND ISAAC

Anonymous

Abraham: Rise up my child, and fast come hither,
My gentle bairn that art so wise,
For we two, child, must go together
And unto my Lord make sacrifice.

Isaac: I am full ready, my father, lo!
Even at your hands I stand right here;
And whatsoever ye bid me do,
It shall be done with glad cheer,
Full well and fine.

Abraham: Ah, Isaac, my own son so dear,
God's blessing I give them, and mine.

Hold this faggot upon thy back
And here myself fire shall bring.

Isaac: Father, all this here will I pack:
I am full fain to do your bidding.

Abraham: (*Aside*) Ah, Lord, my heart breaketh in twain,
This child's words, they be so tender.

(*They reach the mount.*)

Ah, Isaac, son, anon lay it down;
No longer upon thy back it hold,
For I must make ready bon[6]
To honor my Lord God as I should.

Isaac: Lo, my dear father, there it is.
To cheer you always I draw me near.
But, father, I marvel sore of this,
Why make ye this heavy cheer.[7]
And also, father, evermore dread I:
Where is your quick[8] beast that ye should kill?
Both fire and wood we have ready,
But quick beast have we none on this hill.
A quick beast, I wot[9] well, must be dead[10]
Your sacrifice for to make.

---

6 quickly
7 look
8 live
9 know
10 slaughtered

Abraham: Dread thee nought, my child, I thee rede,[11]
Our Lord will send me unto this stead[12]
Some manner a beast for to take,
Through his sweet sand.

Isaac: Yea, father, but my heart beginneth to quake
To see that sharp sword in your hand.

Why bear ye your sword drawn so?
Of your count'nance I have much wonder.

Abraham: (*Aside*) Ah, Father of heaven, so I am woe.
This child here breaks my heart asunder.

Isaac: Tell me, my dear father, ere that ye cease,
Bear ye your sword drawn for me?

Abraham: Ah, Isaac sweet son, peace, peace.
For, iwis, thou break my heart in three.

---

[11] advise
[12] site

The guilds or town councils hired directors who were in charge of the technical aspects of the production as well as the acting. A director also was responsible for collecting admission fees and welcoming the audience. Until laymen began appearing extensively in the plays, the actors chanted their lines. Later, their speech became more natural.

For the most part, actors were amateurs. Some received minimal pay, and sometimes those playing leading roles were paid large sums of money. All were given food and drink during the rehearsal and performance periods. At first, all the performers were men, though later women and children appeared in some of the plays. For example, in 1498 at Metz, one young woman (a nonprofessional) delivered 2300 lines as St. Catherine. The actors typically were local citizens of the working class.

The three most important forms of drama to evolve from the church presentations were mystery plays, miracle plays, and morality plays. The mystery play dealt with the life of Christ and depicted scenes from the Creation to the Second Coming. This is the form that began in the church, but later moved outdoors. Miracle plays (also called saint plays) dealt with the lives of saints and martyrs, but could include topical scenes involving family troubles. These dramas emphasized such things as miraculous power and divine intervention in people's lives. In some parts of Europe, such as Coventry, the miracle plays lasted until the late sixteenth century. At this time, however, morality plays were gaining in importance.

Morality Plays

The morality plays, which developed later than the mystery and miracle plays, were most popular between the beginning of the fifteenth century and the mid-sixteenth century. The subject matter concerned moral instruction—particularly man's attempt to save his soul. All the characters were allegorical. The central figure usually was called Everyman, and such characters as Virtue and Vice fought over his soul. The first morality play of which there is record was the *Play of the Lord's Prayer,* presented in York, England, in 1384. Another is *The Castle of Perseverance,* presented in about 1425. The latter shows the battle between a Bad Angel and a Good Angel for the soul of Humanum Genus.

Often, morality plays dealt with a person's entire life, presenting humorous or mischievous characters in the form of the Devil and Vice. Most had humerous scenes satirizing current social and political conditions, somewhat similar to Old Comedy in Greece. Scenes such as these were not the main point of the drama, however, but existed to capture and direct the audience's attention to the crux of the play—the need to live a virtuous life.

Morality plays were more popular in England than anywhere else, although they also were presented on the continent of Europe. Unlike the cycle plays, morality plays generally were performed by professional actors. They are important in that they were a step toward secularization of drama. Further, they had a great influence on Elizabethan playwrights such as Christopher Marlowe, who relied heavily upon the morality play for his *The Tragical History of Doctor Faustus,* in which the title character makes a pact with the devil.

An example of the morality play is *Everyman,* although it is different from most in that it is shorter and contains no humor. On the other hand, the characters have more depth than in most plays of this sort. Written during the last years of the fifteenth century, *Everyman* is believed to have been adapted from the Dutch play *Elckerlijk,* written in 1495 by Peter Dorlandus, although it isn't known who did the translating and adapting into English.

During the sixteenth century morality plays became more secularized, at first arguing for either the Catholic point of view or the Protestant. Eventually, some became entirely secular, relating to current concerns.

Secular Drama

Along with the church plays, several forms of secular drama developed during the Middle Ages. The most important was the farce, typically presented in France, Germany, and England. Usually bawdy and risqué, this form was concerned with man's depravity, and was not more than a few hundred lines in length. One writer of medieval farce was Hans Sachs of Germany, who is credited with writing more than two hundred plays. A second secular form was the interlude, a comic play performed by professional traveling players for wealthy citizens at celebrations. The interlude, so named because it was presented between courses at banquets, became popular at the end of the fifteenth century. The least important of the secular forms was the folk play, presented by amateur actors who went from house to house enacting stories of heroes or legendary figures.

For a number of reasons, medieval drama began to decline during the sixteenth century. First, the social structure of Europe was changing and the plays no longer could be presented effectively as community undertakings. Second, there was an increased interest in classical learning, and new forms of drama combining both medieval and classical influences were beginning to develop. Third, there is evidence that many of the actors began to travel as professionals or semiprofessionals. Fourth, and perhaps most important, there was dissension in the church. Queen Elizabeth I of England forbade religious plays in 1559, and the church itself forbade such plays in continental Europe. By the beginning of the seventeenth century medieval drama was at an end except in Spain, where the style continued well past the middle of the eighteenth century.

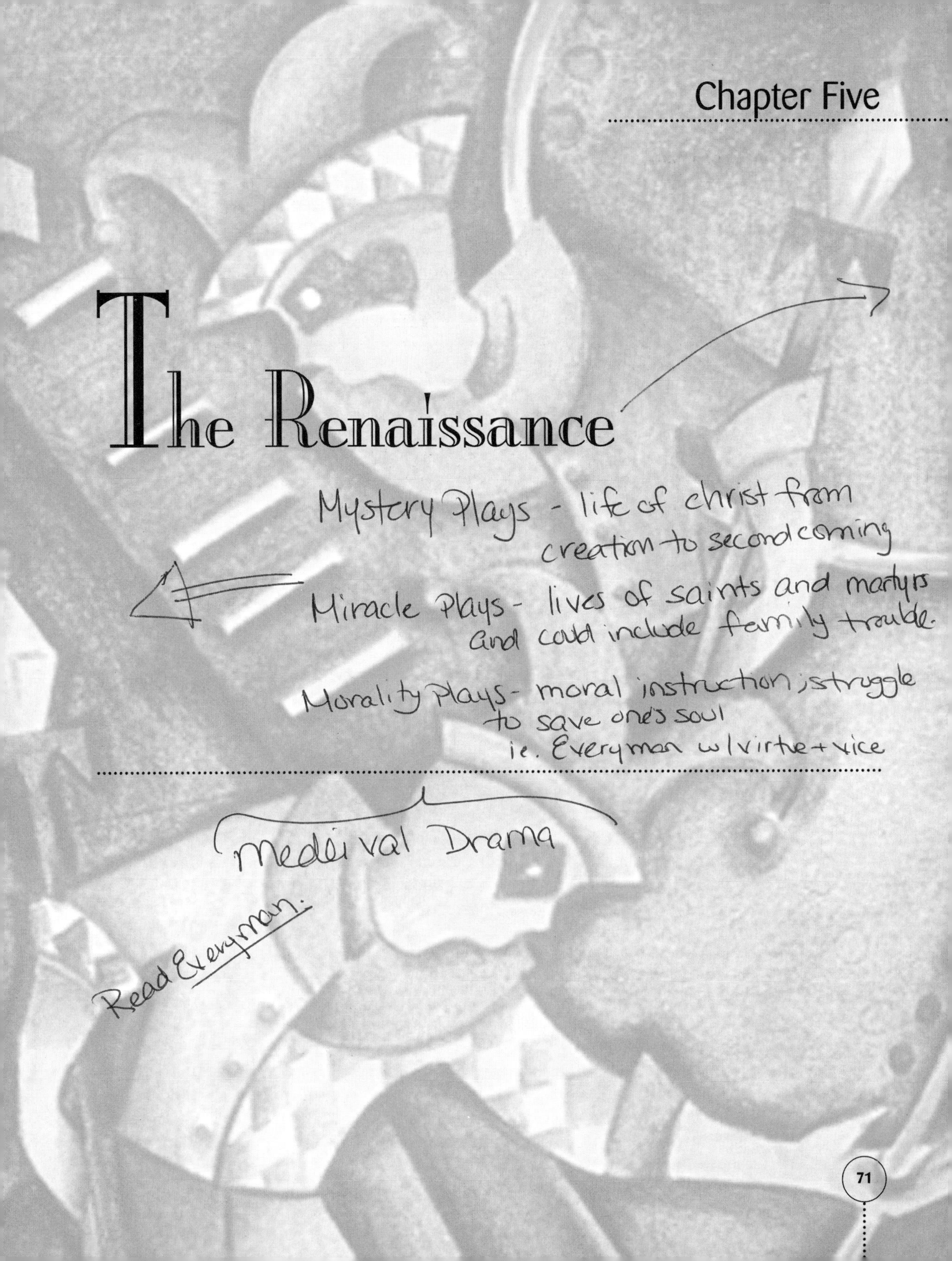

The Renaissance

Mystery Plays - life of christ from creation to second coming

Miracle Plays - lives of saints and martyrs and could include family trouble.

Morality Plays - moral instruction; struggle to save one's soul
ie. Everyman w/ virtue + vice

Medeival Drama

Read Everyman.

Renaissance, or reawakening, aptly describes what occurred throughout western Europe during the fifteenth century. There was renewed interest in classical learning and in looking toward humanity, rather than solely the church, for the salvation of the human race.

In the Middle Ages, theatre already had experienced a rebirth, a change related to religion that spawned the great sprawling dramas that spread across wide areas of staging and geography. Now it was as if blinders were removed from humankind's eyes.

With England's breaking away from the papacy under Henry VIII, secular drama became much more important. But just as the church in the previous age had decreed that drama be religious in nature, during the late 1500s, conversely, Queen Elizabeth (Henry's daughter) declared religion an unfit subject for drama and decreed it could not be used.

Emerging from Darkness

The Renaissance brought great changes. Although the causes and effects are complex, three events generally are considered important in the rebirth of learning. First is the fall of Constantinople to the Turks in 1453, causing Christian monks to abandon this seaport in northwest Turkey, site of ancient Byzantium and the former capital of the Eastern Roman Empire.

Facing an end to their way of life and even to those lives themselves, Christian monks and scholars fled by the scores, taking with them in their exodus all the precious ancient manuscripts they could carry. For the first time ever, many ancient Greek writings became available to those in the West—particularly in Italy. A collection of independent states with courts and academies where the arts were patronized, Italy became the major focus for the new interest in classical learning and the new sense of humanism. The middle class had already begun its rise and guilds and academies were becoming the lifeblood of culture.

Another event that led to change was the invention and spread of the printing press. This became particularly important in 1467 when Pope Paul II established Rome's first press, which then issued works in Greek. The third occurred in 1429 when Nicholas of Cusa, a young graduate in law, discovered twelve Senecan tragedies, hitherto known only by name.

From the early 1500s, when small bands of professional actors performed in the homes of noblemen or in booths in the town square, to the early 1600s, when Shakespeare's company was playing at the Globe, the changes were spectacular. In Italy in the early 1500s actors played on stages with draw curtains; by late in the century, "Florentine spectators were being enchanted by productions in which richly painted scenes continually changed, by seeming magic, before their wondering eyes. Thus within the course of a single century the theatre was brought from ancient medieval world into a world perceptibly modern."[1]

The change in theatre, however, was gradual, and took different paths in various parts of Europe. In fact, theatre took two nearly opposing directions—one that looked backward, the other forward. The first grew out of attempts by writers and architects to reach what they considered to be the perfection of the classic form. For writers, this meant imitating Greek and Roman plays; for architects, it meant changing and adapting recently discovered principles of perspective to scenery, framing it behind a proscenium arch.

The second approach, which grew out of the free-form style of medieval drama and staging, established a looser form that relied on sensational effects and romantic adventures.

The Italian Renaissance

Because Latin was understood by scholars of the time and because classical learning was greatly admired, the works of the Roman playwrights Plautus, Seneca, and Terence influenced the beginnings of drama in Italy. In particular, the works of Terence were well regarded for his purity of language. Among the first plays of the Renaissance were adaptations of translations of these three writers' works. Of these playwrights, Seneca was most admired, and thus it was largely due to his influence that rigid rules were formulated for the writing of drama.

The resulting inflexible framework became known as neoclassicism. This structure dictated that all plays must be written in five acts; that tragedies had to teach a moral lesson; and that all drama, in fact, should be viewed as a vehicle for instruction. Furthermore, the depicted events had to be those that could occur in everyday life. Tragedy was to deal with nobility, and comedy with the middle and lower classes. Furthermore, there could be no mixing of comic and tragic elements.

In addition to the Roman dramatists, other influences affected the formulation of neoclassic rules. Most important were Aristotle's *Poetics* and Horace's *Art of Poetry*, which was written during the first century B.C. One of the most binding and ridiculous rules was that every drama had to adhere strictly to the three unities of time, place, and action. That is:

a. a play had to occur in the space of one day;

b. the setting, once established, could not change;

c. there could be no subplots.

---

[1] Allardyce Nicol, *The Development of the Theatre*, 5th ed. (New York: Harcourt, Brace & World, Inc., 1966), p. 69.

Culver Pictures

Figure 5.1

An engraving from *Baltasar de Beaujoyeulx Balet Comique de la Royne,* Paris, 1582, showing the interior scene of a French theatre, the first representation of the stage in France in Elizabethan times.

The exclusion of subplots actually is the only one of the unities insisted upon by Aristotle.

Such rules were stifling, allowing for little creativity, so that during the entire period of the Italian Renaissance very little good drama appeared.

One of the first writers of comedy was Lodovico Ariosto, who lived from 1474 to 1533. Until this time plays had been written in Latin. His *La Cassaria,* produced in 1508, marks the true beginning of Italian drama in that it was the first play to be performed using the language of the time.

Another playwright was Niccolò Machiavelli, perhaps better known for his writings on political philosophy. His play *La Mandragola,* written between 1513 and 1520 and often considered the masterpiece of Italian Renaissance drama, followed the classic format, but was much more original, as well as highly cynical in its subject matter, which relied on medieval farce.

For the most part, neoclassic plays were too strictly structured to provide much entertainment. Thus, several new forms of drama began to develop. The *pastoral,* for example, was widely popular during the sixteenth century. The characters were shepherds and shepherdesses, nymphs and fauns, and the plots involved romantic love. One of the best known is Giambattista Guarini's *The Faithful Shepherd* (1590), which influenced the later development of romantic literature in France and England. It is filled with idealistic language and lofty ideas.

Another drama form, the *intermezzi,* was originally a series of short scenes or plays with singing and dancing that was presented between the acts of a neoclassic tragedy. The subject matter often was drawn from mythology and the stage effects were elaborate, making the form a favorite of theatregoers. At first, the *intermezzi* presented at a single performance were unrelated. Later, they were tied together, usually with the neoclassic tragedy with which they appeared.

By the seventeenth century, opera, first written and produced in the 1590s, replaced the *intermezzi* in popularity. Begun as an attempt to add music, dance, and choral singing to tragedies, in much the same way (the Italians believed) as had been done in ancient Greece, opera became so popular so quickly that by 1650 it had spread through much of Europe.

Theatre Design and Architecture

The Italian Renaissance contributed most to theatre, not through drama, but through its staging. There was a strong movement toward the presentation of spectacles and spectacular effects, influenced by Vitruvius, who, near the beginning of the first century A.D., had written a book about constructing buildings. *De architectura* was rediscovered in 1414 and translated into Italian in 1521. This led Sebastiano Serlio in 1545 to write *Architettura,* in which he showed how a theatre should be planned and how scenery was to be erected and used. He assumed that theatres would be constructed in existing buildings and recommended following the Roman style, with seating arrangements at one end of a hall and a stage at the other.

Serlio described three settings that could be used for all plays: tragic, comic, and pastoral. Both the comic and tragic settings were street scenes, while the pastoral setting was a wooded area. All three used false perspective. The floor of the stage was to be painted in squares, which became smaller and smaller toward the back. The stage floor itself was to be **raked**, that is, it sloped upward from front to back. It is from Serlio's description that we have the terms **upstage** and **downstage**. The reason for raking the stage, or sloping it up toward the back, and for painting squares of decreasing size was to give the impression of distance. Such use of false perspective became a distinctive characteristic of all theatres constructed in Italy during the Renaissance. Even today there are a few theatres with raked stages.

The use of perspective scenery marked the start of a movement away from the formal or fixed stages of the Greek and Roman theatre to much more flexible settings where changes from one location to another could be shown by shifting the scenery.

New Theatre Structures and Scenery

After a time, the idea of adapting existing halls was abandoned in favor of erecting permanent theatre buildings based on Roman models. The oldest still in existence is the Teatro Olimpico, constructed for the Olympic Academy in Vicenza and first used in 1585. Begun in 1580 by Andrea Palladio, who died before it was erected, it was finished by his pupil Vincenzo Scamozzi, who added his own ideas. Scamozzi followed the Roman plan, but added false perspective in the raked floors and the three-dimensional background, which shows openings for streets. The aisleways, or streets, gradually decrease in size, giving the effect of great distance. The seating area was elliptical, providing excellent sightlines from any seat in the house.

The Teatro Farnese, built at Parma in 1618, was the first to use a proscenium arch, or framing device. With a proscenium opening, settings consisted of a backdrop, borders across the top of the stage, and wings. Still, however, the action could not be portrayed realistically because of the false or forced perspective. If actors walked too far upstage, they dwarfed the buildings, ruining the effect. However, the proscenium arch was important in providing a definite separation of audience and action.

Although scenery still provided background rather than an environment, various methods could be used to show changes in location. One was based on Serlio's work and involved a modified use of the Greek *periaktoi.* These "Serlion wings" were two flats fastened together in a V shape. Later a third side was added. Each three-sided wing was placed slightly more toward the center of the stage than the one in front of it. The side facing the audience could be painted to give the effect of walls or any specific location. To change the scene, the wing could be rotated to expose another view to the audience.

Another means of changing scenes was developed by Nicola Sabbattini. He used the two-sided, V-shaped wings—one very close behind the other—in groups. One of the sides faced the audience. The other was angled upstage to support the wing so it could stand alone. Since the wings were in groups, it was a simple task to pull away the front wing of each group to reveal a new scene behind. From these two approaches the wing and drop system was further refined, spreading throughout Europe and to the United States.

Stage machinery provided almost miraculous effects. Buildings rose and descended through trapdoors, and mechanical animals and chariots, called "glories" and constructed of wooden frames covered with canvas, flew over the stage, manipulated by ropes and pulleys. Professional artists, among the best of their day, were hired to paint the scenery. Candles provided lighting, with special effects achieved by placing them behind colored bottles.

Commedia dell'arte

In addition to the drama presented in buildings, another form developed in Renaissance Italy—the *commedia dell'arte,* believed to have evolved either from ancient pantomimes or from the plays of Plautus and Terence. Definitely an actors' theatre, it involved improvising from outlines called *scenarios,* thus making it adaptable to changing locations and situations. Performed by professional troupes, *commedia dell'arte* attracted audiences from the mid-fifteenth to the mid-sixteenth centuries.

Although the actors built lines and actions from basic outlines, they were free to add whatever they wished. Since the troupes moved from village to village, the performers adapted their material to specific places by referring to current events and residents of each locale.

Stock characters, similar to those in Roman comedy, were divided into three groups: the lovers, who played straight characters; the professional types; and the servants. The latter two types were always comic. Some were Pantalone, the old miser; Il Capitano, the braggart soldier; and Il Dottore, the academician or "Ph.D.," who used a sort of gibberish in substituting incorrect words and phrases for the proper ones. The comic servants as a group were called **zanni** (from which our word *zany* derives) and included Pulcinella, a hunchback with a hooked nose similar to the character of Punch in Punch and Judy shows, and Arlecchino, who performed comedy similar to that of the modern-day Three Stooges.

Once actors were accepted as members of a troupe, they played the same character the rest of their lives, so a "young lover" might remain a romantic figure up until retirement. At the core of each troupe was a family, with the children trained from an early age to take the places of the elderly. Most

The Granger Collection

Figure 5.2

Stock characters of *commedia dell'arte,* from a French woodcut, 17th century.

troupes performed in the marketplace, although those with the best reputations, such as the Gelosi or the Accesi, sometimes were invited to play in court theatres for the nobility. Generally, however, a wagon with a piece of cloth as background served as the stage.

A major part of the show consisted of **lazzi**—verbal or visual business—in which a character went into a certain comedy routine whenever he or she wished. By using prearranged signals, the others let the person know when they felt the routine should end and the troupe should get on with the performance. The *commedia dell'arte* had a strong influence on later forms of drama, as did other Italian theatre practices.

Spanish Theatre

During the time that neoclassicism was gaining a foothold in Italy, drama and the theatre also were developing in Spain. Although influenced to a certain degree by neoclassicism, Spain, because of its independence and isolation from the rest of Europe, developed a drama of greater literary value than that of Italy. Since a great number of plays were written between 1580 and 1680, this era became known as Spain's Golden Age.

Native Spanish drama began to develop between 1500 and 1550. The first playwright of note was Juan del Encina (1468–1537), whose plays were similar to Italian pastorals. The first popular dramatist was Lope de Rueda, who toured with his own company and whose comedies showed the influence of the *commedia dell'arte.* Rueda is credited with inventing the *paso,* or comic sketch, presented as an interlude.

Spanish drama, which developed later than that of other countries, was produced by guilds and later by city councils. The most popular drama, the *auto sacramental,* was akin to the medieval mystery play and miracle play in subject matter, yet similar to the morality play in the use of allegorical characters. The first actors in these plays were amateurs. Three productions were presented each year until 1592, when the number increased to four. This continued until 1647, after which there were only two productions annually. Some plays were repeated from year to year, while others were new. All ended with dancing. The early dramas were presented in the church, but after a time the actors traveled through the city in pageant wagons called *carros,* which carried their scenery. The productions included songs, comic sketches, and juggling. Interludes of comedy and obscenity sometimes accompanied even the religious plays.

Some of the early plays dealt with religious themes, but contained references to contemporary events. Later plays dealt only with contemporary life. Unlike other European countries, Spain's religious drama continued until 1765, when it finally was forbidden. The only writer of religious drama in the city of Madrid between 1647 and 1681 was Pedro Calderón de la Barca, whose plays totaled more than two hundred. He took many of his ideas from other sources, but made the writings more poetic and spiritual.

Secular drama was written and produced by the beginning of the sixteenth century. Spain's best known and most prolific playwright was Lope de Vega (1562–1635), believed to have written more than 1800 plays—quite a feat in the days of the quill pen! His drama was characterized by a mixing of form, vigorous action, and suspense, with most of his characters drawn from history or mythology. Because he wrote so quickly, his plays often were potboilers, that is, written quickly for profit. Still, he had a good command of language and probably could have become a much better writer if he'd spent more time on each play.

By the end of Spain's Golden Age, more than 30,000 plays had been written, a large percentage of which dealt with the themes of love and honor. Produced largely between 1623 and 1654, they were presented either in court theatres or **corrales**. The latter, typical of northern Spain, were open courtyards formed by the outer walls of houses. Spectators filled the balconies and rooms of the houses, sat on benches in the courtyard, or, for a small admission fee, stood behind the last row of seats. The stage itself was wide and uncurtained, with a large apron extending into the courtyard. A balcony above the general playing area also could be used for scenes. Though there

The Granger Collection

Figure 5.3

Lope de Vega.

existed some crudely painted scenery, most of the changes of locale were indicated through dialogue.

The first theatres were temporary structures. Then, in 1579 in Madrid, the first of the country's many permanent theatre buildings was erected.

The number of acting companies increased with the number of permanent theatres. In 1603, the government sought to restrict their number to eight, but the attempt at regulation failed. Some of the companies were sharing troupes, dividing expenses and profits equally, while others were organized under a manager. Unlike companies in the rest of Europe, some troupes included women, even though actresses were not licensed to appear in plays until 1587.

Each company contained sixteen to twenty members and generally bought plays outright from the authors. Although opposed by the church and considered undesirable members of society, generally actors were tolerated. By 1700 Spain's power began to decline. Fifty years later, the Golden Age was past.

The Theatre of Elizabethan England

Although there were traveling players in England before the Elizabethan era (1558–1603), their performances were infrequent and scattered. In the fifteenth century traveling players were defined by law as vagabonds and rogues. Then during the reign of Elizabeth, they were legally recognized by a 1572 law that required a license from two justices of the peace or the patronage of a nobleman in order to perform. Two years later, a Master of Revels was appointed to license acting companies.

Patronage by a nobleman did not guarantee success, however, since no financial support was involved. It meant only that he protected the troupe, which in turn was expected to present entertainments for him. In general, despite legal recognition, actors were little more than tolerated by the middle class, which distrusted the theatre. It was, in fact, the nobility who helped to establish the theatre as a respectable form of entertainment for everyone, not just the upper classes. Yet, it took time before the general public ceased to regard theatre as only a means of camouflaging more undesirable activities. Even after the government's recognition of acting as a profession, there was strong opposition from local leaders in smaller towns. Sometimes actors were paid *not* to perform. Still, theatre was firmly established in England by the 1580s.

Theatre's development under Elizabeth was influenced by several factors. Because of the religious discontent brought about by the conflict between Catholics and Protestants, the queen sought to unite the country by making the citizens aware of their cultural heritage. This spirit of nationalism in turn affected theatre in that dramatists now often chose patriotic themes for their plays.

Origins

The English theatre had several early origins. First were the schools, where plays were read, and sometimes performed, in Latin. Students then wrote in imitation of the models. Although influenced by the classical style of writing, they dealt with English locations and subject matter.

A second origin of theatre was in the Inns of Court, schools and places of residence for lawyers. Because the residents were from the upper class and attending such schools was the expected thing to do, they were exposed to classical learning and influenced by the plays of ancient Rome.

Corbis-Bettmann

Figure 5.4

An Elizabethan stage.

A third origin was in professional acting companies whose plays were a mixture of various classical and medieval practices. Even so, playwrights were not bound by the unities of time, place, and action, as can be seen in Shakespeare's plays, which have subplots, switch time and place, and sometimes mix comic and tragic elements.

Playwrights

One of the earliest English playwrights was John Heywood (1497–1578). A musician at the court of Henry VIII, he is known principally for developing the **interlude**, a short sketch similar to the morality play, but with English characters. The first truly British tragedy and the first play to be written in England in blank verse was *Gorboduc* by Thomas Sackville and Thomas Norton. Produced in 1561, it used traditional allegorical characters and a chorus.

English drama did not achieve greatness until such plays as Thomas Kyd's *The Spanish Tragedy* (c. 1587) set an example for such other gripping "revenge" tragedies as Shakespeare's *Hamlet.* Wholly different was the work of England's first writer of sophisticated comedy, John Lyly, who was noted for his use of mythological themes and pastoral settings.

The three greatest writers of Elizabethan drama were Ben Jonson, Christopher Marlowe, and William Shakespeare. Jonson's first comedy, *Every Man in His Humor* (1598), presented the eccentricities of the English middle class. *Every Man Out of His Humor* (1599) satirized all that Jonson detested in society. Thus he used comedy to denounce middle-class vices and foolish actions with the purpose of correcting England's social ills. His most widely read play, *Volpone, or the Fox* (1606), is a bitter satire of human greed. Volpone, with the help of his "parasite" Mosca, tricks three men into promising him their wealth in the hope of inheriting his estates and fortune. One of them even pledges his wife to Volpone. In the end, she is saved after Volpone is exposed to the justice of a Venetian court.

Christopher Marlowe often is called the father of English tragedy. His *Tamburlaine the Great* (c. 1587), written in blank verse, ushered in the first great age of drama in England. He wrote only four plays and was considered a greater poet than a dramatist. Although his early death prevented the full development of his powers, he helped to free Elizabethan drama from the restrictions of medieval forms.

His *The Tragical History of Doctor Faustus* owes much of its inspiration to the medieval morality play. Based on a German legend, the plot concerns a man, Faustus, who summons up Mephistopheles and sells his soul in return for twenty-four years in which all his wishes will be fulfilled. Scene 16 occurs as the agreed-upon time is ending.

THE TRAGICAL HISTORY OF DOCTOR FAUSTUS

Christopher Marlowe
From Scene 16

FAUSTUS: Ah, Faustus.
Now hast thou but one bare hour to live,
And then thou must be damn'd perpetually!
Stand still, you ever-moving spheres of heaven,

That time may cease, and midnight never come;
Fair Nature's eye, rise, rise again, and make
Perpetual day; or let this hour be but
A year, a month, a week, a natural day,
That Faustus may repent and save his soul!
O lente, lente, currite noctis equi![2]
The stars move still, time runs, the clock will strike,
The devil will come, and Faustus must be damn'd.
O, I'll leap up to my God!—Who pulls me down?
See, see, where Christ's blood streams in the firmament!
One drop would save my soul, half a drop: ah, my Christ!—
Ah, rend not my heart for naming of my Christ!
Yet will I call on him: O, spare me, Lucifer!—
Where is it now? 'tis gone: and see, where God
Stretcheth out his arm, and bends his ireful brows!
Mountains and hills, come, come, and fall on me,
And hide me from the heavy wrath of God!
No, no!
Then will I headlong run into the earth:
Earth, gape! O, no, it will not harbour me!
You stars that reign'd at my nativity,
Whose influence hath allotted death and hell,
Now draw up Faustus, like a foggy mist,
Into the entrails of yon labouring clouds,
That, when you vomit forth into the air,
My limbs may issue from your smoky mouths,
So that my soul may but ascend to heaven!
(*The clock strikes the half-hour*)
Ah, half the hour is past! 'twill all be past anon.
O God,
If thou wilt not have mercy on my soul,
Yet for Christ's sake, whose blood hath ransom'd me,
Impose some end to my incessant pain;
Let Faustus live in hell a thousand years,
A hundred thousand, and at last be sav'd!
O, no end is limited to damned souls!
Why wert thou not a creature wanting soul?
Or why is this immortal that thou hast?
Ah, Pythagoras' metempsychosis,[3] were that true,

---

[2] "Oh, run slowly, slowly, horses of the night." From Ovid's *Amores.*
[3] transmigration of souls

This soul should fly from me, and I be chang'd
Unto some brutish beast! all beasts are happy,
For, when they die,
Their souls are soon dissolv'd in elements;
But mine must live still to be plagu'd in hell.
Curs'd be the parents that engendered me!
No, Faustus, curse thyself, curse Lucifer
That hath depriv'd thee of the joys of heaven.
(*The clock strikes twelve*)
O, it strikes, it strikes! Now, body, turn to air,
Or Lucifer will bear thee quick to hell!
(*Thunder and lightning*)
O soul, be chang'd into little water-drops,
And fall into the ocean, ne'er be found!
(*Enter Devils*)
My God, my God, look not so fierce on me!
Adders and serpents, let me breathe a while!
Ugly hell, gape not! come not, Lucifer!
I'll burn my books!—Ah, Mephistopheles!
(*Exeunt Devils with Faustus*)

The greatest Elizabethan dramatist was William Shakespeare. Not much is known about his early life other than that he was born in 1564 and was the son of John and Mary Shakespeare. Records show he was married to Anne Hathaway in 1582. By the 1590s he was a dramatist and actor in London. In 1595 he was a shareholder or part owner in the Lord Chamberlain's Men, later called the King's Men upon the ascension of James I to the throne, at the Globe Theatre. He began writing around 1590 and wrote thirty-eight plays, some as collaborations, before he died in 1616. Although he borrowed many of his plots from other sources, the plays he based on these plots nevertheless were highly original and entertaining. He wrote in various genres, though his tragedies as a whole constitute his best work. (See Color Gallery Plates 9–12 for scenes of *Romeo and Juliet*.)

The Theatres

During the Elizabethan era there were two types of theatres, public (outdoor) and private (indoor), although the private theatres were open to anyone who could afford the price of admission. The public theatres operated during the summer and the private theatres during the winter. The first private theatre was built in 1576 in Blackfriars, a residential section of

London. The indoor theatres, which played to more exclusive audiences, accommodated only one-fourth to one-half as many spectators as did the public theatres. Audience members sat in the pit (the main floor of the auditorium), in galleries, or in private boxes. Usually the stage was three to four feet above the level of the pit, and there was no proscenium arch or front curtain.

All the popular public theatres, such as the Swan, the Fortune, and the Globe, had to be located outside the City of London, which at that time was disease-ridden. The theatres varied in size, but usually held two thousand to three thousand spectators. The playhouses were constructed in various shapes, from circles to squares. The Globe, where Shakespeare's plays were performed, long was believed to have been eight-sided. Excavations in 1989 indicate, however, that this may not have been the case. It is impossible to be certain about the shape and dimensions because other buildings now cover much of the site.

It is conjectured that in the public theatre the pit was a large unroofed open space where the groundlings, or those paying the lowest admission fee, stood to watch the plays. Around the pit (or yard, as it sometimes was called) were galleries, which formed the outer portion of the building and contained boxes for spectators who paid a higher admission fee. The stage projected into the pit, so that spectators could view the action from three sides. Spectators even sat on the stage itself, forcing the actors to move around them.

Action could take place on three levels. At the rear of the stage was an area called the "inner below"—a large room to conceal or reveal characters and locations. There also was an upper stage where, for example, the balcony scene in *Romeo and Juliet* could have been performed. A third level was for musicians. It is generally believed that scenery was not used in the public theatres, and there was no artificial lighting since the plays were presented in the afternoon. Night scenes were suggested by having the actors carry lanterns or candles. The stages contained trapdoors, as used in the gravediggers' scene in *Hamlet.*

Acting Companies

Acting companies at the public theatres consisted of ten to twenty men and three to five boy apprentices. The boys played female parts until they reached maturity, then were taken in as permanent members of the company. Each actor specialized in a certain type of role, but almost all wore contemporary costumes unless they played unusual roles such as foreigners or supernatural beings. About half the members were shareholders, while the boys were apprenticed to learn the trade of acting.

Each playwright wrote for a specific company. Some were salaried, while others sold their plays outright. The playwright thus often wrote for particular actors and frequently helped with the rehearsals of the plays. The companies all had a repertoire of plays they had rehearsed, and hence could change the bill frequently.

After the death of Elizabeth, the English theatre lost popularity for a time; then, nearly sixty years later, it again began to emerge as a lively form of entertainment.

OTHELLO, THE MOOR OF VENICE

William Shakespeare

Othello is one of Shakespeare's greatest tragedies. It's somewhat flawed in that it's difficult to believe that a man with as much military experience as Othello—a black general in the service of Venice—would be so gullible, or even that his ensign Iago would be so perverse, without adequate reason. Othello's naiveté, coupled with his passion and his descents into anger and rage, bring about his downfall.

Yet, perhaps it isn't fair to fault Shakespeare for such flaws because he had to write quickly—a play or two a year. It's amazing he could accomplish so much in a world of quill pens and ink, in an era when travel was slow and European civilization was just emerging from an age of little progress and a general lack of learning. It's also amazing when we consider that, in addition to being a playwright, Shakespeare was a theatre shareholder and an actor. He had a vast store of knowledge of human nature that he put to use in his plays, as well as a masterful command of language and poetic imagery.

Othello is an affecting play, in part, no doubt, because the protagonist so well fits Aristotle's definition of the tragic hero—a man of great virtue, but with a tragic flaw. One thing that makes the character of Othello interesting is his contradictory nature—on the surface a simple man, trusting and believing in human nature's basic good, yet a man with deep currents.

Othello is used to taking orders from the high command, perhaps divorcing his feelings from these orders to accomplish what he must. Certainly, this carries into his own life, into the direct way he has of approaching solutions to his problems. Although descended from royalty, he is the opposite of a sophisticate, and his marriage is outside his realm of experience. A general rather than a ladies' man, he has lived his life in camps and campaigns and knows little of women.

Iago, on the other hand, is cynical, distrustful, and willing to see the worst in humanity. An encounter between men such as Othello

UPI/Corbis-Bettmann

Figure 5.5

A scene from the 1930 London production of *Othello,* starring American actor Paul Robeson (center) in the title role.

and Iago is bound to result in conflict, if for no other reason than that Iago, by nature, will bait and try to best others.

Someone like Iago undoubtedly would have difficulty understanding Othello's simplicity in outlook. So, too, would Othello—used to the straightforward life where things *are* what they seem—be incredulous were he able to catch a glimpse of Iago's soul. Most likely in a child's world Iago would be the taunter, the one on the playground who gets two others to fight for his own amusement. He is a manipulator, filled with the sense of his own power over those less devious than he. He's amoral or sociopathic in not caring whom he destroys, including his wife Emilia.

Iago has somewhat of a reason to manipulate, to gain what satisfaction he will. Yet the situation certainly does not call for such extreme revenge. Indeed, his manipulation goes beyond that, becoming a game. He agitates, incites, and pits one man against another. Then he steps back in gleeful anticipation of what will occur.

Othello and Desdemona are ill-matched in background, though at first she probably didn't realize the extent of their differences or else felt they didn't matter. He obviously felt the same way. Often viewed as the "perfect young woman of breeding," in fact, she is not. She knew what she wanted, went after it aggressively as only she knew how, and gained it, for there is this account of the courtship:

OTH: Her father loved me, oft invited me,
Still[4] questioned me the story of my life
From year, to year, the battles, sieges, fortunes,
That I have passed.
I ran it through, even from my boyish days
To the very moment that he bade me tell it.
Wherein I spake of most disastrous chances,[5]
Of moving accidents[6] by flood and field,
Of hairbreadth 'scapes i' the imminent deadly breach,[7]
Of being taken by the insolent foe
And sold to slavery, of my redemption thence,
and portance[8] in my travels' history.
Wherein of the antres vast and deserts idle,[9]
Rough quarries, rocks, and hills whose heads touch heaven,
It was my hint[10] to speak—such was the process.
And of the cannibals that each other eat,
The anthropophagi,[11] and men whose heads
Do grow beneath their shoulders. This to hear
Would Desdemona seriously incline.
But still the house affairs would draw her thence,
Which ever as she could with haste dispatch,
She'd come again, and with a greedy ear
Devour up my discourse. Which I observing,

4 always
5 accidents
6 occurrences
7 assault on a city
8 bearing
9 vast caves and worthless deserts
10 occasion
11 cannibals

Took once a pliant[12] hour and found good means
To draw from her a prayer of earnest heart
That I would all my pilgrimage dilate,[13]
Whereof by parcels[14] she had something heard,
But not intentively. I did consent,
And often did beguile her[15] of her tears
When I did speak of some distressful stroke
That my youth suffered. My story being done,
She gave me for my pains a world of sighs.
She swore, in faith, 'twas strange, 'twas passing strange,
'Twas pitiful, 'twas wondrous pitiful.
She wished she had not heard it, yet she wished
That Heaven had made her[16] such a man. She thanked me,
And bade me, if I had a friend that loved her,
I should but teach him how to tell my story
And that would woo her. Upon this hint I spake.
She loved me for the dangers I had passed,
And I loved her that she did pity them.
This only is the witchcraft I have used.

Toward the end, Desdemona isn't so different from Othello in her bewilderment and her simplicity, in being unable to accept or understand her husband's doubt of her and his jealousy. She *is* as Othello believes all others to be—one who can be trusted, who would never deceive or lie or cheat. Doing such for her own gains simply would never enter her mind.

Othello unwittingly evokes the spirt of evil in Iago, a young Venetian and Othello's ensign, when he passes over him in choosing Michael Cassio as his lieutenant. This gives Iago the perfect excuse to indulge his evil nature in bringing about Othello's downfall. He takes great satisfaction in hiding his intentions behind a frank and open mien, so that to others he appears the "honest Iago." Othello, an unsuspicious man, plays easily into Iago's hands.

Othello has long spun tales of his adventurous past, his battles, and his campaigns for the pleasure of the Venetian senator Brabantio and his daughter Desdemona. Because of "the dangers" he "has pass'd," she has grown to love him and he to love her. So they marry in secret.

Iago tells Brabantio of the elopement. Embittered at Othello's "spells and medicine" in stealing away his daughter, Brabantio appeals to the

12 suitable
13 tell at length
14 parts or portions
15 draw from her
16 for her

Duke of Venice to intervene. Instead, he is told that Othello is being sent to Cyprus to stave off an invasion by a Turkish fleet.

Desdemona not only refuses to give up Othello, but insists on accompanying him to Cyprus:

Des: That I did love the Moor to live with him,
My downright violence and storm of fortunes
May trumpet to the world. My heart's subdued
Even to the very quality of my lord.[17]
I saw Othello's visage in his mind,
And to his honors and his valiant parts
Did I my soul and fortunes consecrate.
So that, dear lords, if I be left behind,
A moth of peace,[18] and he go to the war,
The rites which I love him are bereft me,
And I a heavy interim shall support
By his dear absence. Let me go with him.

Shortly thereafter, Brabantio sows what turn out to be the first seeds of doubt about Desdemona in Othello's mind—words Iago calls up in his perversity in manipulating Othello:

Bra: Look to her, Moor, if thou hast eyes to see;
She has deceived her father, and may thee.

Roderigo, a former suitor whom Desdemona has rejected, tells Iago that he wishes to drown himself, since, "It is silliness to live when to live is torment." Iago tells him that Desdemona soon will be "sated" with Othello's body and "find the error of her choice." He persuades Roderigo to accompany him in escorting Desdemona to Cyprus, the idea already in his mind to use Roderigo as a pawn.

A storm off the coast of Cyprus delays those arriving from Venice, but also drives away the Turkish fleet, leaving Othello, the new governor, to order a celebration. To see that it doesn't get out of hand, he names Cassio officer of the guard. Cassio and Desdemona's chance greeting gives Iago the idea of plotting to make Othello believe that Desdemona and Cassio have made love. Thus he gets Cassio drunk, pushes Roderigo into picking a quarrel with him and wakes up Othello, who, of course, reduces Cassio in rank. As part of the plot, Iago convinces Cassio to beg Desdemona to intercede on his behalf.

Thus Desdemona promises:

---

17 That I . . . lord: My love for the Moor is publicly shown in the way I have violently taken my fortunes in my hands; my heart has become a soldier like my husband.

18 a useless creature that lives in luxury

Do not doubt[19] that. Before Emilia here
I give thee warrant of thy place.[20] Assure thee,
If I do vow a friendship, I'll perform it
To the last article. My lord shall never rest.
I'll watch him tame[21] and talk him out of patients,
His bed shall seem a school, his board a shrift.[22]
I'll intermingle every thing he does
With Cassio's suit. Therefore be merry, Cassio,
For thy solicitor shall rather die
Than give thy cause away.

At this point Othello and Iago enter, and Cassio leaves, not wanting to be discovered talking with Desdemona:

IAGO: Ha! I like not that.

OTH: What dost thou say?

IAGO: Nothing, my lord. Or if—I know not what.

OTH: Was not that Cassio parted from my wife?

IAGO: Cassio, my lord! No, sure, I cannot think it,
That he would steal away so guilty-like,
Seeing you coming.

OTH: I do believe 'twas he.

DES: How now, my lord!
I have been talking with a suitor here,
A man that languishes in your displeasure.

OTH: Who is 't you mean?

DES: Why, your Lieutenant, Cassio. Good, my lord.
If I have any grace or power to move you,
His present reconciliation take.[23]
For if he be not one that truly loves you,
That errs in ignorance and not in cunning,[24]
I'll have no judgment in an honest face.
I prithee call him back.

---

19 fear
20 I guarantee you will be restored to your position.
21 as wild hawks are tamed by not letting them sleep
22 place of confession and absolution
23 accept his apology and forgive him
24 not knowingly

She continues to plead with Othello to restore Cassio to his former rank. After she leaves, Iago furthers his treachery. Pretending reluctance even to hint at impropriety, he says, "I speak not yet of proof. Look to your wife. Observe her well with Cassio. Wear your eye thus, not jealous nor secure."

Othello tells Iago, "I do not think but Desdemona's honest." And then a few lines later: "And yet, how nature erring from itself—"

Othello has begun to doubt and so demands proof of Desdemona's unfaithfulness. Iago has repeatedly asked his wife, Desdemona's lady in waiting, to steal a handkerchief that Othello gave to Desdemona early in their courtship. Emilia has refused to do so. But then Desdemona loses the handkerchief. Emilia finds it and gives it to her husband.

Iago: I will in Cassio's lodging lose this napkin,
And let him find it. Trifles light as air
Are to the jealous confirmations strong
As proofs of Holy Writ. This may do something.
The Moor already changes with my poison.

In a moment, Othello enters:

Oth: Ha! Ha! False to me?

Iago: Why, how now, General! No more of that.

Oth: Avaunt![25] Be gone! Thou hast set me on the rack.[26]
I swear 'tis better to be much abused
Than but to know 't a little.

Iago: How now, my lord!

Oth: What sense had I of her stol'n hours of lust?
O saw 't now, thought it not, it harmed not me.
I slept the next night well, was free and merry.
I found not Casiso's kisses on her lips.
He that is robbed, not wanting[27] what is stol'n,
Let him not know 't and he's not robbed at all.

Iago: I am sorry to hear this.

Oth: I had been happy if the general camp,
Pioneers[28] and all, had tasted her sweet body,
So I had nothing known. Oh, now forever
Farewell the tranquil mind! Farewell content!

---

25 Be off!
26 in torment
27 missing
28 pioneers, meaning the lowest type of soldier

Othello tells Iago:

If thou dost slander her and torture me,
Never pray more, abandon all remorse.[29]
On horror's head horrors accumulate,
Do deeds to make Heaven weep, all earth amazed,
For nothing canst thou to damnation add
Greater than that.

After pretending hurt at Othello's words, Iago tells him:

I do not like the office.
But sith I am entered in this cause so far.
Pricked[30] to 't by foolish honesty and love,
I will go on. I lay with Cassio lately,
And being troubled with a raging tooth,
I could not sleep.
There are a kind of men so loose of soul
That in their sleeps will mutter their affairs.
One of this kind is Cassio.
In sleep I heard him say "Sweet Desdemona,
Let us be wary, let us hide our loves."
And then, sir, would he gripe[31] and wring my hand,
Cry, "O sweet creature!" and then kiss me hard,
As if he plucked up kisses by the roots
That grew upon my lips. Then laid his leg
Over my thigh, and sighed and kissed, and then
Cried "Cursed fate that gave thee to the Moor!"

OTH: O, monstrous! Monstrous!

Iago protests that it is but a dream:

IAGO: Nay, but be wise. Yet we see nothing done.
She may be honest yet. Tell me but this:
Have you not sometimes seen a handkerchief
Spotted[32] with strawberries, in your wife's hand?

OTH: I gave her such a one, 'twas my first gift.

IAGO: I know not that. But such a handkerchief—
I am sure it was your wife's—did I today
See Cassio wipe his beard with.

---

29 pity
30 spurred
31 grip
32 patterned

Later Othello demands that Desdemona show him the handkerchief. When she cannot, he's convinced of her guilt and swears an oath of vengeance upon her and Cassio.

To convince Othello still further of his wife's guilt, Iago arranges for him to overhear Cassio deriding Bianca, yet apparently alluding to Desdemona. Utterly convinced now, Othello takes Iago's suggestion that he strangle Desdemona and Iago murder Cassio. In the meantime, Lodovico arrives with letters from the duke recalling Othello to Venice and appointing Cassio his successor in Cyprus. Desdemona tells Lodovico "an unkind breech" has "fall'n between" Cassio and Othello:

A most unhappy one. I would do much
To atone[33] them, for the love I bear Cassio.

Oth: Fire and brimstone!

Des: My lord?

Oth: Are you wise?[34]

Des: What, is he angry?

Lod: Maybe the letter moved him,
For, as I think, they do command him home,
Deputing Cassio in his government.[35]

Des: By my troth, I am glad on 't.

Oth: Indeed!

Des: My lord?

Oth: I am glad to see you mad.

Des: Why, sweet Othello?

Oth: Devil! (*Striking her*)

Des: I have not deserved this.

Lod: My lord, this would not be believed in Venice.
Though I should swear I saw 't. 'Tis very much.[36]
Make her amends, she weeps.

Oth: O devil, devil!
If the earth could teem with a woman's tears,
Each drop she falls would prove a crocodile.
Out of my sight.

Des: I will not stay to offend you. (*Going*)

---

33 reconcile
34 Are you wise in saying you love Cassio?
35 in his place as governor
36 This is too much.

Emilia speaks of Desdemona's innocence, yet Othello refuses to believe her. Later, he openly accuses Desdemona of being a "strumpet," a "whore." After he leaves, Emilia returns with Iago.

DES: O good Iago,
What shall I do to win my lord again?
Good friend, go to him, for, by this light of Heaven,
I know not how I lost him. Here I kneel.
If e'er my will did trespass 'gainst his love
Either in discourse of thought or actual deed,
Or that mine eyes, mine ears, or any sense
Delighted them in any other form,
Or that I do not yet, and never did,
And ever will, though he do shake me off
To beggarly divorcement, love him dearly,
Comfort forswear[37] me! Unkindness may do much,
And his unkindness may defeat[38] my life,
But never taint my love. I cannot say "whore,"
It doth abhor me now I speak the word
To do the act this might the addition[39] earn
Not the world's mass of vanity[40] could make me.

Shortly afterward, Iago convinces Roderigo to waylay and kill Cassio. In the final scene of Act IV, Desdemona, apparently sensing something of what will happen, sings to herself a song of a "poor soul" "sighing by a sycamore tree." Then she dismisses Emilia, telling her that not "for the whole world" would she "abuse" her husband in the manner he accused her.

As Act V opens, Iago has placed Roderigo in a position to await Cassio in order to kill him. He then reveals the depths of his amorality.

IAGO: I have rubbed this young quat[41] almost to the sense.[42]
And he grows angry. Now, whether he kill Cassio,
Or Cassio him, or each do kill the other,
Every way makes my gain. Live Roderigo,
He calls me to a restitution large[43]
Of gold and jewels that I bobbed[44] from him
As gifts to Desdemona.

---

[37] repudiate
[38] destroy
[39] title
[40] riches
[41] pimple
[42] to the quick
[43] full
[44] cheated

It must not be. If Cassio do remain,
He hath a daily beauty in his life
That makes me ugly,[45] and besides, the Moor
May unfold me to him. There stand I in much peril.
No, he must die. Be 't so. I hear him coming.

Roderigo attacks Cassio, who draws his own sword. He stabs Roderigo. Iago then stabs Cassio, whose cry for help brings Lodovico and Gratiano, Brabantio's brother. To keep hidden what he has done, Iago stabs Roderigo as if he is killing Cassio's assailant. When Bianca hears the cries and comes to investigate, Iago, ever seeking ways to divert attention from his own evil deeds, tries to implicate her in the matter.

The wounded Cassio is borne off as Bianca protests her innocence.

The next scene occurs in the castle. Desdemona is asleep as Othello enters.

Des: Who's there? Othello?

Oth: Aye, Desdemona.

Des: Will you come to bed, my lord?

Oth: Have you prayed tonight, Desdemona?

Des: Aye, my lord.

Oth: If you bethink yourself of any crime
Unreconciled as yet to Heaven and grace,
Solicit for it straight.

Des: Alas, my lord, what may you mean by that?

Oth: Well, do it, and be brief. I will walk by.
I would not kill thy unprepared spirit.
No, Heaven forfend! I would not kill thy soul.[46]

Des: Talk you of killing?

Oth: Aye, I do.

Des: Then Heaven have mercy on me!

Oth: Amen, with all my heart!

Des: If you say so, I hope you will not kill me.

Oth: Hum!

Des: And yet I fear you, for you are fatal[47] then
When your eyes roll so. Why I should fear I know not,
Since guiltiness I know not, but yet I feel I fear.

---

45 Iago is admitting that he has not Cassio's social graces.

46 He will not condemn her to hell, which is just the opposite of what Hamlet wants to do to his uncle, the king.

47 deadly

OTH: Think on thy sins.

DES: They are loves I bear to you.

OTH: Aye, and for that thou diest.

DES: That death's unnatural that kills for loving. Alas,
why gnaw you so your nether lip?
Some bloody passion shakes your very frame.
These are portents,[48] but yet I hope, I hope,
They do not point on me.

OTH: Peace, and be still!

DES: I will so. What's the matter?

OTH: That handkerchief which I so loved and gave thee
Thou gavest to Cassio.

DES: No, by my life and soul!
Send for the man, and ask him.

OTH: Sweet soul, take heed,
Take heed of perjury, thou art on thy deathbed.

DES: Aye, but not yet to die.

OTH: Yes, presently.
Therefore confess thee freely of thy sin,
For to deny each article with oath
Cannot remove nor choke the strong conception[49]
That I do groan withal. Thou art to die.

DES: Then Lord have mercy on me!

OTH: I say amen.

DES: And have you mercy too! I never did
Offend you in my life, never loved Cassio
But with such general warranty[50] of Heaven
As I might love. I never gave him token.

OTH: By Heaven, I saw my handkerchief in 's hand.
O perjured woman! Thou dost stone[51] my heart,
And makest me call what I intend to do
A murder, which I thought a sacrifice.
I saw the handkerchief.

DES: He found it, then,
I never gave it him. Send for him hither.
Let him confess a truth.

---

48 signs foretelling disaster
49 thought
50 permission
51 turn to stone

OTH: He has confessed.

DES: What, my lord?

OTH: That he hath used thee.

DES: How? Unlawfully?

OTH: Aye.

DES: He will not say so.

OTH: No, his mouth is stopped.
Honest Iago hath ta'en order for 't.

DES: Oh, my fear interprets! What, is he dead?

OTH: Had all his hairs been lives, my great revenge
Had stomach for them all.

DES: Alas, he is betrayed, and I undone!

OTH: Out, strumpet! Weep'st thou for him to my face?

DES: Oh, banish me, my lord, but kill me not!

OTH: Down, strumpet!

DES: Kill me tomorrow, let me live tonight!

OTH: Nay, if you strive—

DES: But half an hour!

OTH: Being done, there is no pause.

DES: But while I say one prayer!

OTH: It is too late.

(*He stifles her.*)

Emilia enters to find Desdemona dying and again tells Othello she was innocent. Othello replies that it was Emilia's husband who told him of Desdemona and Cassio. Iago admits he told Othello "what I thought, and told no more than what he found himself was apt and true." In the meantime, others, hearing Emilia's cries, rush to the bedroom. One of them is Gratiano, Desdemona's uncle, who says Othello and Desdemona's marriage killed Brabantio.

OTH: 'Tis pitiful, but yet Iago knows
That she with Cassio hath the act of shame
A thousand times committed. Cassio confessed it.
And she did gratify his amorous works
With that recognizance[52] and pledge of love
Which I first gave her, I saw it in his hand.

---

52 token

It was a handkerchief, an antique token
My father gave my mother.

Emil: Oh, Heaven! Oh, heavenly powers!

Iago: 'Zounds! Hold your peace.

Emil: 'Twill out, 'twill out. I peace!
No, I will speak as liberal as the north.[53]
Let Heaven and men and devils, let them all
All, all, cry shame against me, yet I'll speak.

Iago: Be wise, and get you home.

Emil: I will not.

(*Iago offers to stab Emilia*)

Gra: Fie!
Your sword upon a woman!

Emil: O thou dull Moor! That handkerchief thou speak'st of
I found by fortune and did give my husband,
For often with a solemn earnestness,
More than indeed belong to such a trifle,
He begged of me to steal it.

Calling his wife a "villainous whore," Iago stabs and kills her. Now Othello begins to realize that Desdemona indeed was innocent. Further proof of Iago's role in all of this is a letter found on Roderigo's body. Othello attacks and stabs Iago, but fails to kill him.

Lod: You must forsake this room, and go with us.
Your power and your command is taken off,
And Cassio rules in Cyprus. For this slave,
If there be any cunning cruelty
That can torment him much and hold him long
It shall be his. You shall close prisoner rest
Till that the nature of your fault be known
To the Venetian state. Come, bring away.

Oth: Soft you,[54] a word or two before you go.
I have done the state some service, and they know 't.
No more of that, I pray you, in your letters,
When you shall these unlucky deeds relate,
Speak of me as I am, nothing extenuate,
Nor set down aught in malice. Then must you speak
Of one that loved not wisely but too well,

---

53 as freely as the north wind, which is loud and bitter
54 wait awhile

Of one not easily jealous, but, being wrought,
Perplexed in the extreme, of one whose hand,
Like the base Indian, threw a pearl away
Richer than all his tribe—of one whose subdued eyes,
Albeit unusèd to the melting mood,
Drop tears as fast as the Arabian trees
Their medicinal gum. Set you down this,
And say besides that in Aleppo once,
Where a malignant and a turbaned Turk
Beat a Venetian and traduced[55] the state
I took by the throat the circumcisèd dog
And smote him, thus.

"I kissed thee ere I killed thee," Othello says. "No way but this, killing myself, to die upon a kiss."

---

55 insulted

Chapter Six

17th- and 18th-Century Theatre

Great change took place in the theatres of Europe during the second half of the seventeenth and on through the eighteenth centuries. Italy, with its spectacular staging, still dominated the technical aspects of production, with its influence spreading to France, England, Spain, Germany, Poland, Hungary, and Scandinavia. Most often, the spectacle was used for opera or for a new drama form called the **masque**, which used elaborate costumes and staging to tell allegorical stories of well-known people or events. This form of drama allowed the ornate style of baroque to be witnessed at its lavish best.

By the mid-seventeenth century, Europe was developing more of a sense of nationalism, with governments becoming centralized within each nation rather than the rulers' owing allegiance to the pope. With the spirit of nationalism, however, came civil strife in France and Spain and England. It was also a time when royalty became actively involved in building theatres, often for costly and spectacular productions.

Neoclassicism spread, particularly to France early in the century, where it was refined and developed with rigid rules and the establishment of the French Academy for writers.

In England, the Puritans gained control, beheaded Charles I, and banned theatre. Thirteen years later, Charles II was restored to the throne and lifted the ban. The **Restoration**, which lasted for the next forty-two years, was a time of dazzling comedy addressing the foibles of the upper classes.

After the death of Charles II in 1685 (which some historians insist ended the Restoration period), his brother James II ruled for three years. He was replaced on the throne by his daughter Mary and her husband William of Orange. Because William and Mary were Protestants, their rule brought change, including a Bill of Rights and more power to Parliament.

The Renaissance move toward humanism gave impetus to scientific advancements. Earth was no longer considered to be the center of the planetary system. Nature, defined as the workings of the universe, was viewed as machinelike, relying neither on God nor humanity as essential to its operation. Sir Isaac Newton's *Principia* further enforced this view of the universe. This thinking led to secularization, the philosophy of rational thought as the basis of the workings of the human mind. This took two directions: the development of a mechanized society and an interest in the workings of the human mind.

At the beginning of the eighteenth century, with the advancement of trade and industry, more money was available to the middle class, who in their leisure turned to cultural pursuits. A result was the development of sentimental, though mundane, theatre, concerned with everyday problems of the middle class. This was a change from Restoration theatre, which had been focused on the nobility and the upper class.

Style and manners became important, particularly in France, where there grew to be a strict division between the way of life of the mainstream and the artificiality of court life. Cardinal Richelieu, though not the country's ruler, exerted great power in his insistence on the neoclassic ideal and the return of humankind to a belief in reason and rules. Likewise, in England, perhaps because government was moving toward control by Parliament, the upper and middle classes were approaching a common code of conduct.

The State of European Theatre

In Russia, theatre was just beginning to exist outside the court, except for a weak medieval drama that continued well into the seventeenth century. Foreign troupes appeared sporadically, but there was no drama of significance.

Elsewhere, Spain's *corrales* fell out of favor as the Italian influence spread. At the same time, theatre began to develop in Holland and Scandinavia. In Germany, the medieval style persisted into the seventeenth century, when two forms evolved: the court theatre, where mostly foreign plays were produced and foreign companies and performers appeared, and a type of low comedy for the common theatre. Germany as yet had developed no outstanding drama of its own.

With the beginning of the eighteenth century and the Age of Enlightenment, a new wave of intellectual activity spread across western Europe, bringing further change to theatre. The idea of "sensationalism," that knowledge comes only from sense perceptions, as advanced by philosopher John Locke, already had taken hold in England and now began to spread to the rest of Europe.

Nature (as instinct), rather than reason, was seen as civilization's ruling force. Such ideas were further refined and developed in France under Voltaire, Diderot, and Rousseau. The world was becoming more and more industrialized, in large part as a result of the invention of the stream engine, which provided a sure and steady source of power. Mass production made manufactured goods much more widely available, so that wealth shifted away from agriculture toward commerce.

After mid-century, the theatre began attracting large numbers of spectators. Old theatres were remodeled and new ones erected. Growing cities became more able to support theatrical activity.

In England came a surge of new plays. Germany began to produce her own playwrights. In France, neoclassicism persisted in certain theatres, based largely now on Greek models rather than Roman, while opera dropped the use of stock characters and began to use original music and sentimentality in its plots. There was a resurgence of humorous comedy and a renewed interest in the plays of Shakespeare. Acting styles changed from an emphasis on declamation to an emphasis on movement and variety.

English Theatre

At the beginning of the seventeenth century the theatre of England was not very much different from that of the Elizabethan era. Not only did public theatres continue to exist when James I assumed the throne (1603), but all the acting companies came under royal patronage. Shakespeare's own company was now known as the King's Men.

The new king, however, was not content with visiting the public theatres, and so he established a court theatre where an older form of entertainment was revived and presented. The masque had been popular during the reign of Henry VIII, but rarely was presented during Elizabeth's reign. Masques featured spectacular staging and costumes. Sets were designed by court architect Inigo Jones, who had spent time in Italy studying the methods used for the **intermezzi**—a series of brief plays with singing and dancing, presented between the acts of a neoclassic tragedy.

Presented once a year at the court of James I, twice a year after Charles I assumed the throne (1625), and at Inns of Court, masques featured singing and dancing. Written for the most part by Ben Jonson, they told allegorical stories honoring well-known persons or occasions. Jonson, however, felt that the story itself was secondary to the presentation of fine poetry.

Soon the government was overthrown by the Puritans under Oliver Cromwell and Charles was beheaded, establishing conditions similar to those existing in the Middle Ages, when the church viewed theatre as sinful and degrading. In 1642 the theatres were closed and all theatrical entertainment was forbidden. Yet, as in the medieval period, some entertainments continued, particularly at inns and noblemen's houses. At fairs could be seen presentations called **drolls**, comic excerpts from familiar plays. In 1656, playwright and producer William D'Avenant received Cromwell's permission to stage an opera that would not offend the Puritans. Titled *The Siege of Rhodes*, it was performed in a house owned by the Earl of Rutland. This was the first time music and drama had been combined in operatic form in England. With these exceptions, England was without theatre until 1660, when Charles II was restored to the throne.

The Restoration

The first theatres of the period were established in tennis courts, after which the king opened two indoor theatres. Patents, or permissions for operation, were issued to D'Avenant, who headed a company called the Duke's Men, and to Thomas Killigrew, who headed the King's Men. As in Queen Elizabeth's time, the presentation of plays was strictly regulated by the government. All plays had to be licensed by a censor, the Lord Chamberlain, who could cut out any material he deemed undesirable.

New theatre buildings were somewhat similar to those of Italy, yet also akin to those where the court masques had been presented. They had proscenium arches and proscenium doors through which the actors could enter and exit. These opened on each of the two walls at the sides of the proscenium arch. An apron stage projected into the audience, providing the advantage of intimacy between spectator and performer, but the disadvantage of actors performing in front of rather than amidst the scenery. The audience sat (rather than stood) in the pit and in boxes and galleries, as well as onstage. Scenery was painted in perspective on wings and backdrops, which by 1800 depicted specific locations.

Actresses appeared for the first time on the English stage and by the mid-1660s were an accepted part of the theatre. Yet, for a time both men and women played female roles.

The eighteenth century ushered in the era of "actors' theatre," so that performers outranked playwrights in importance. Dramatists now received no salary, nor did they share in the profits of a play. They received only a benefit performance every third night of a production, receiving all the day's receipts, minus expenses. Since plays usually ran for just a few nights, a playwright was fortunate indeed to receive a second benefit.

Once a play closed its run, the producing company owned it outright. Now not only were actors more important than playwrights, their social status

Figure 6.1

A scene from a Yale Repertory Theatre production of *The Beaux' Strategem,* a popular Restoration comedy written by George Farquhar.

increased as well. Actresses sometimes married nobility and performers—male and female—were laid to rest in Westminster Abbey. Still, the general population often viewed actors with at least some suspicion.

As had been the custom earlier, actors continued to play certain types of roles and to receive their training through experience. Theatres still followed the repertory system. That is, once an actor was cast in a role, it was his property as long as he stayed with the company. A stage manager saw to the staging of the older plays, while the playwright directed new plays. The acting style was less exaggerated, though certainly would be considered artificial by contemporary standards.

The most important form of drama during the Restoration was **comedy of manners** (also called Restoration comedy), which satirized the social customs of the time. The underlying theme was that humankind is less than perfect, but that this is to be expected, since nothing can bring about change in basic human nature. The plays most often satirized those persons who were self-deceived or who made an attempt to deceive others.

Next to comedy of manners ranked **heroic tragedy**. Written in rhymed couplets, it nearly always dealt with themes of love and honor. Among the playwrights was John Dryden, a poet and essayist whose best-known work was *All for Love,* based on Shakespeare's *Antony and Cleopatra* but recast in a neoclassic framework. He borrowed plots for his tragedies from other writers, but invented his own comic plots.

Most notable among the playwrights was William Congreve, important historically for refining and developing comedy of manners to a high style of art. His best play was *The Way of the World* (1700). Intellectual in approach, with a complicated plot and names descriptive of the characters' personalities, it deals with the intrigues of love—specifically the wooing of Millamant by Mirabell. Congreve uses a sparkling wit and writing style.

THE WAY OF THE WORLD

William Congreve

Mirabell and Fainall are opponents, first at cards and second over the matter of inheritances. Both are sharp-witted at repartee, but there the similarities end. Mirabell is a generous man, while Fainall is ruthless.

Mirabell and the stunning Mrs. Millamant (every female, married or single, was addressed as Mrs.) are in love, yet Mirabell has alienated Lady Wishfort, Mrs. Millamant's aunt, by pretending romantic interest in her to conceal what he feels for her niece.

Mrs. Wishfort, who controls Mrs. Millamant's fortune, has determined that she will marry Sir Wilfull. Yet when Fainall and his paramour Mrs. Marwood try to blackmail Lady Wishfort by threatening to expose the reputation of her daughter Mrs. Fainall (Mirabell's former mistress), Lady Wishfort seeks Mirabell's help.

He already has acted to protect Mrs. Fainall's fortune, ruining Fainall's scheme. Sir Wilfull says he would rather travel than wed, so Lady Wishfort agrees to Mirabell and Millamant's marriage.

The following scene, occurring in Act IV, Scene 1, is the highlight of the play.

Mirabell: "*Like Daphne she, as lovely and as coy.*"[1] Do you lock yourself up from me, to make my search more curious? Or is this pretty artifice contrived to signify that here the chase must end, and my pursuit be crowned, for you can fly no further?

Millamant: Vanity! No—I'll fly and be followed to the last moment. Though I am upon the very verge of matrimony, I expect you should solicit me as much as if I were wavering at the gate of a monastery, with one foot over the threshold. I'll be solicited to the very last, nay, and afterwards.

Mirabell: What, after the last?

Millamant: Oh, I should think I was poor and had nothing to bestow, if I were reduced to an inglorious ease, and freed from the agreeable fatigues of solicitation.

Mirabell: But do not you know, that when favors are conferred upon instant and tedious solicitation, that they diminish in their value, and that both the giver loses the grace, and the receiver lessens his pleasure?

Millamant: It may be in things of common application, but never sure in love. Oh, I hate a lover that can dare to think he draws a moment's air independent of the bounty of his mistress. There is not so impudent a thing in nature as the saucy look of an assured man, confident of success. The pedantic arrogance of a very husband has not so pragmatical an air. Ah! I will never marry, unless I am first made sure of my will and pleasure.

Mirabell: Would you have 'em both before marriage? Or will you be contented with the first now, and stay for the other till after grace?

Millamant: Ah, don't be impertinent.—My dear liberty, shall I leave thee? My faithful solitude, my darling contemplation, must I bid you then adieu? Ay-h, adieu—my morning thoughts, agreeable wakings, indolent slumbers, all ye *douceurs,* ye *sommeils du matin,* I adieu?—I can't do't, 'tis more than impossible. Positively Mirabell, I'll lie abed in a morning as long as I please.

---

[1] Mirabell is reciting a poem by Edmund Waller (1606–1687) as he enters.

Mirabell: Then I'll get up in a morning as early as I please.

Millamant: Ah! Idle creature, get up when you will.—And d'ye hear, I won't be called names after I'm married; positively I won't be called names.

Mirabell: Names?

Millamant: Ay, as wife, spouse, my dear, joy, jewel, love, sweetheart, and the rest of the nauseous cant, in which men and their wives are so fulsomely familiar—I shall never bear that.—Good Mirabell, don't let us be familiar or fond, nor kiss before folks, like my Lady Fadler and Sir Francis; nor go to Hyde Park together the first Sunday in a new chariot, to provoke eyes and whispers, and then never to be seen together again, as if we were proud of one another the first week, and ashamed of one another for ever after. Let us never visit together, nor go to a play together, but let us be very strange and well bred. Let us be as strange as if we had been married a great while, and as well bred as if we were not married at all.

Mirabell: Have you any more conditions to offer? Hitherto your demands are pretty reasonable.

Millamant: Trifles,—as liberty to pay and receive visits to and from whom I please; to write and receive letters, without interrogatories or wry faces on your part. To wear what I please, and choose conversation with regard only to my own taste; to have no obligation upon me to converse with wits that I don't like, because they are your acquaintance; or to be intimate with fools, because they may be your relations. Come to dinner when I please, dine in my dressing-room when I'm out of humor, without giving a reason. To have my closet inviolate; to be sole empress of my tea-table, which you must never presume to approach without first asking leave. And lastly, wherever I am, you shall always knock at the door before you come in. These articles subscribed, if I continue to endure you a little longer, I may by degrees dwindle into a wife.

Mirabell: Your bill of fare is something advanced in this latter account. Well, have I liberty to offer conditions—that when you are dwindled into a wife I may not be beyond measure enlarged into a husband?

Millamant: You have free leave; propose your utmost; speak and spare not.

Mirabell: I thank you. *Imprimis* then, I covenant that your acquaintance be general; that you admit no sworn confidant or intimate of your own sex; no she-friend to screen her affairs under your countenance and tempt you to make trial of a mutual secrecy. No decoy-duck to wheedle you a fop-scrambling to the play in a mask—then bring you home in a pretended fright, when you think you shall be found out—and rail at me for missing the play and disappointing the frolic which you had, to pick me up and prove my constancy.

Millamant: Detestable *imprimis*! I go to the play in a mask!

Mirabell: *Item,* I article, that you continue to like your own face as long as I shall; and while it passes current with me, that you endeavor not to new-coin it. To which end, together with all vizards for the day, I prohibit all masks for the night, made of oiled-skins and I know not what—hog's bones, hare's gall, pig-water, and the marrow of a roasted cat. In short, I forbid all commerce with the gentlewoman in What-d'ye-call-it Court. *Item,* I shut my doors against all bawds with baskets, and pennyworths of muslin, china, fans, atlases, etc.—*Item,* when you shall be breeding—

Millamant: Ah! name it not.

Mirabell: Which may be presumed, with a blessing on our endeavors—

Millamant: Odious endeavors!

Mirabell: I denounce against all strait lacing, squeezing for a shape, till you mold my boy's head like a sugar-loaf, and instead of a man-child, make me the father of a crooked billet. Lastly, to the dominion of the tea-table I submit,—but with proviso, that you exceed not in your province; but restrain yourself to native and simple tea-table drinks, as tea, chocolate, and coffee, as likewise to genuine and authorized tea-table talk—such as mending of fashions, spoiling reputations, railing at absent friends, and so forth—but that on no account you encroach upon the men's prerogative, and presume to drink healths, or toast fellows; for prevention of which I banish all foreign forces, all auxiliaries to the tea-table, as orange-brandy, all aniseed, cinnamon, citron, and Barbadoes waters, together with ratafia and the most noble spirit, clary,—but for cowslip wine, poppy water, and all dormitives, those I allow. These provisos admitted, in other things I may prove a tractable and complying husband.

Millamant: Oh, horrid provisos! Filthy strong waters! I toast fellows, other men! I hate your odious provisos.

Mirabell: Then we are agreed. Shall I kiss your hand upon the contract?

By the end of the Restoration period, England was becoming industrialized. The middle class, with more money and leisure time, began attending the theatre regularly. New playwrights, such as George Farquhar, were helping to bring about change. An actor who turned to writing after accidentally wounding a fellow performer onstage, Farquhar had his first play produced at age 21. Had he not died at the age of thirty, he might have become a truly important dramatist. Farquhar's work resembled comedy of manners, but was more riotous than witty. This is most evident in *The Recruiting Officer* (1706) and *The Beaux' Stratagem* (1707).

Theatre in the Time of Queen Anne

Queen Anne, who assumed the throne at the beginning of the eighteenth century, was interested neither in art nor theatre. But the theatre went on, reflecting the changes in the social and economic structure of England. The emergence of the middle class as the main theatre audience led to romanticism and melodrama. The new audiences now wanted sensationalism in their plays, though at the same time they felt that plays should teach a moral lesson. Thus, in much of eighteenth-century drama perseverance was rewarded, and dishonesty and laziness resulted in defeat. Shakespeare became more popular than he had been during his own time.

The type of drama most prevalent was **sentimental comedy,** characterized by false emotions and sentimentality over the misfortunes of others. The major characters bore their ills with a smile, and always were rewarded in the end. The plays were referred to as comedies—not because they were funny, but because they ended happily. The situations often were too bad to be believed, and the characters were too noble. The prevailing viewpoint was that humanity is basically good and has only to heed an inner conscience to reap just rewards.

A similar form was bourgeois tragedy. Written in much the same style, the plays ended unhappily when the leading characters yielded to temptation. The playwright with the greatest influence in this form was George Lillo (1693–1739). His *The London Merchant* (1731) shows how a good man can be led astray through love of an undesirable woman. Produced frequently, it influenced the writing of sentimental drama in France.

THE LONDON MERCHANT

George Lillo

A young London merchant named George Barnwell falls prey to the lure of the villainous seductress Millwood. At her urging, he robs his master and kills his uncle. Remorseful, he is arrested and sentenced to death. The characters are wooden stereotypes and the dialogue sounds like a parody. It would be extremely difficult for today's audiences to take the play seriously.

From Act V, Scene 5

BARNWELL: Trueman—my friend, whom I so wisht to see! Yet now he's here I dare not look upon him.

(*Weeps*)

TRUEMAN: Oh Barnwell! Barnwell!

BARNWELL: Mercy, Mercy, gracious Heaven! For death, but not for this, was I prepared.

TRUEMAN: What have I suffer'd since I saw you last! What pain has absence given me!—But oh! to see thee thus!

BARNWELL: I know it is dreadful! I feel the anguish of thy generous soul—but I was born to murder all who love me.

(*Both weep*)

TRUEMAN: I came not to reproach you; I thought to bring you comfort. But I'm deceiv'd, for I have none to give. I came to share thy sorrow, but cannot bear my own.

BARNWELL: My sense of guilt indeed you cannot know—'tis what the good and innocent, like you, can ne'er conceive. But other griefs at present I have none, but what I feel for you. In your sorrow I read you love me still. But yet methinks 'tis strange, when I consider what I am.

TRUEMAN: No more of that! I can remember nothing but thy virtues, thy honest, tender friendship, our former happy state, and present misery.—O, had you trusted me when first the fair seducer tempted you, all might have been prevented.

BARNWELL: Alas, thou know'st not what a wretch I've been! Breach of friendship was my first and least offence. So far was I lost to goodness, so devoted to the author of my ruin, that, had she insisted on my murdering thee, I think I shou'd have done it.

TRUEMAN: Prithee, aggravate thy faults no more!

BARNWELL: I think I shou'd! Thus, good and generous as you are, I shou'd have murder'd you!

Another form was **burlesque farce,** which made fun of the other dramas of the day. The prime example is Henry Fielding's *The Tragedy of Tragedies, or, the Life and Death of Tom Thumb the Great.*

Pantomime, as performed by John Rich, was most popular of all. Featuring dances and mimicry to the accompaniment of music, it presented both comic and serious scenes with elaborate scenery and effects. Also popular was **ballad**

Figure 6.2

Today's mime—using neither speech nor props—is personified by Marcel Marceau as "BIP." Pantomime as dramatic form originated in ancient Rome and was very popular in the 18th century.

opera such as John Gay's *The Beggar's Opera* (1728), which burlesqued Italian opera and satirized the current political situation. All the characters are criminals of one sort or another, yet all live by a binding code of honor. Like the characters of sentimental comedy, they believe that only through hard—though illegal—work can a person succeed.

A major dramatist was Oliver Goldsmith (1730–1774). His *She Stoops to Conquer* was an attempt to return to comedy that was truly funny, rather than sentimental. He based his plays largely on those of Elizabethan writers. Another playwright was Richard Brinsley Sheridan, who wrote *The Rivals* and *The School for Scandal,* returning to comedy of manners.

Possibly the most famous theatrical figure of the time was David Garrick (1717–1779). As manager of the Drury Lane Theatre, he was credited with introducing a natural style of acting to the English stage. He believed in closely supervised rehearsals in which he took charge of directing the actors, something not done before this time. Garrick brought French scene designer

Philippe-Jacques de Loutherbourg to England to design three-dimensional settings. Moreover, Garrick insisted that the audience could no longer sit on the stage. He also was responsible for concealing stage lighting from the audience.

By the end of the eighteenth century, there was a definite movement toward realism in sets and staging. This move opened the way for the modern era of the theatre.

French Theatre

Because civil wars divided the country from the 1560s to the 1620s, French theatre developed later than the theatre of England. A number of companies did play in Paris earlier, and the *Confrérie de la Passion* presented religious plays. In 1548, this same company opened a new theatre, the Hôtel de Bourgogne. Shortly thereafter, religious plays were forbidden, and the building was rented to traveling companies. Near the end of the sixteenth century, the Hôtel de Bourgogne was leased to the King's Players, headed by France's first important theatre manager, Valleran LeComte. Thus, performances were not regularly presented until the early part of the seventeenth century.

The most important early French playwright, attached to the King's Players, was Alexandre Hardy (1572–1632), believed to have written more than five hundred plays. Most were tragicomedies characterized by continuous action. Although lacking in depth, Hardy's plays were immensely popular.

French staging differed from that in England in that the indoor stages resembled those advocated by Serlio and still followed the medieval custom of mansions and an unlocalized acting area, the middle of the stage. At the Hôtel de Bourgogne, this area was only about twenty-five feet wide.

Cardinal Richelieu and the French Academy

Cardinal Richelieu, who came to power in 1625, looked to Italy as a model for improving France's cultural image. In 1641, as part of his effort to raise awareness of the arts, he had a theatre built in the Palais Cardinal. (After his death it was renamed the Palais Royal.) Built in the manner of Italian theatres, it later became home to the company led by Molière. Previously, only the Hôtel de Bourgogne and another theatre, the Théâtre du Marais, had been operating in Paris. The latter had been constructed from a tennis court in 1634.

In 1629 Cardinal Richelieu established the French Academy, where various playwrights gathered to write, adhering to the rules of neoclassicism even more rigidly than had their counterparts in Italy. They felt that comedy's aim was to ridicule, while tragedy's purpose was to show the results of humankind's misdeeds and errors. They were particularly concerned with the three unities and with purity of form. They believed an important element of drama should be verisimilitude—the appearance of truth.

Culver Pictures, Inc.

Figure 6.3

The French stage—a representation of *Mirame,* a tragedy written by Cardinal Richelieu, c. mid-1600s.

The two most important writers of the French Academy were Pierre Corneille and Jean Racine. Corneille began writing in the late 1620s, and in 1636 he wrote his most successful play, *Le Cid* (the word *cid* is comparable to *lord*). It was a tragicomedy, so-called because it deals with a serious theme but ends happily. It became one of the most popular plays of the century. Staged with multiple settings, it harkened back to medieval drama. The play spurred great debate and disagreement in a country whose arts were ruled by the tenets of neoclassicism, particularly since Corneille had been a part of Richelieu's group. Yet Corneille, who did not follow the unities of time, place, and action, apparently believed the play to be neoclassic, but closer to the rules adapted in Spain.

The worst attack on the play came from critic/dramatist Georges de Scudéry, who felt the piece was badly flawed because the heroine Chimène agrees to marry Rodrigue, even though he had killed her father in a duel. This, he felt, was immoral and inappropriate. In addition, the play covered too much ground to logically be included in a single day's action. Thus, the Academy agreed that *Le Cid* lacked verisimilitude on the basis of Chimène's choice of husband.

Racine (1639–1699) was the greatest writer of French classical tragedy. His best-known play, *Phèdre,* deals with the internal conflict of a single character—a woman who wanted to do right but was prevented from it by circumstances and emotions.

After Richelieu's death in 1642, Cardinal Mazarin of Italy became prime minister, and the French theatre was further influenced by Italian styles. The new prime minister was particularly partial to opera. After the Théâtre du Marais burned in 1644 and was rebuilt, it was devoted to scenic spectacles and remained in use until 1673.

Molière and Other Playwrights

Jean-Baptiste Poquelin (1622–1673), known as Molière, often has been called the French Shakespeare. Born in 1622, the son of the private upholsterer of Louis XIV, Molière grew up close to the court, received the education of a nobleman, and later studied law. At the age of twenty-one he helped found the Théatre Illustre, which failed after two years. As a result, Molière was thrown into debtor's prison. Upon his release, he and his troupe toured the provinces for the next dozen years, at which time he became the group's principal playwright. When the company was invited to Paris in 1658, Louis XIV saw one of Molière's plays and granted him the right to perform at a small theatre, the Petit Bourbon, and later at the Palais Royal.

Credited with introducing literary comedy into France, Molière based his plots in part on a variety of sources, including Greek, Roman, Italian, and Spanish drama, although he adapted the material for specific actors in his company. His plays deal with types, based on Roman comedy and the *commedia dell'arte,* but he gave them individual characteristics. He always played his own leading roles, and many of his plays contained elements of autobiography. In *The School for Husbands,* an early satire, he ridiculed himself for his marriage at the age of forty to Armande Béjart, who was eighteen.

One of his most humorous plays is *The Miser,* which owes its stock characters and comic routines to the *commedia dell'arte* and its misunderstandings and lack of communication to Roman comedy. The protagonist Harpagon is ruled by greed, which affects every aspect of his life. Yet he is a human being, an individual, "vivified by a few details—he has a cough, he is subject to flattery, he wishes to wed a pretty girl—but always he is the essence of avarice."[2] (See the synopsis in Chapter 1.)

---

[2] Sylvan Barnet, Morton Berman, and William Burto, eds., *Eight Great Comedies* (New York: New American Library, 1985), p. 175.

Stock Montage, Inc.

Figure 6.4

Molière.

Often considered Molière's masterpiece, however, is *The Misanthrope,* a different sort of writing that comes closer to comedy of manners. The central character is Alceste, whose "intense revulsion and protest . . . suggest a modern social consciousness that threatens to burst the confines of neoclassic humor." Audiences found it too serious "to be considered unalloyed comedy."[3]

Alceste has become so bitter about society's superficiality and hypocrisy that he wants to withdraw from the world. A succession of scenes reveal his justification in criticizing gossips, fops, and pretentious poets. At the same time, the play reveals his own intolerance, his refusal to compromise, and his obsessions with humankind's faults.

Alceste loves Célimène, who is very much a part of the society he despises. Further, she enjoys pitting one man against another for the winning of her

[3] John Gassner, ed. *A Treasury of the Theatre, Volume One: World Drama From Aeschyulus to Ostrovsky,* revised and expanded edition (New York: Simon and Schuster, 1967), pp. 389–90.

affections. Later, he discovers proof of Célimène's games and is willing to forgive her if she will agree to marry him and retire from the world. When she refuses, he goes off alone, more violently determined to flee the ills of society.

Acting Companies

The French acting companies during the seventeenth century were organized on the sharing plan—women participating equally with men. Plays were accepted or rejected by a vote of the company. When a play was selected, the playwright usually was given a percentage of the gate receipts for a certain number of performances. After that, the company owned the play. Less commonly, plays were bought outright.

The playwright selected the cast and assisted with rehearsals. New members of a company learned their roles from the persons whom they were replacing. Actors would specialize either in comedy or in tragedy, with men customarily playing old women's roles. Spectators sat on the stage, and because the stages were small, there was little room for actors to move about. Usually a long play and a short one were presented on the same bill.

After Molière's death, the state of the French theatre declined. Corneille gave up writing in 1674, and Racine wrote no new plays for public presentation after 1677. Thus, the Golden Age of French drama came to a close. The only outstanding French playwright of the eighteenth century was Voltaire (1694–1778), who, after spending time in England, decided that French drama was too hampered by rules. He thus attempted to bring greater realism to the acting. Like Garrick in England, he was responsible for moving the spectators off the stage and back into the auditorium.

France was now recognized by the rest of Europe as the political and cultural center of Europe. The great plays that had been written during the seventeenth century became the models for other countries. Yet, several other types of drama were popular in the eighteenth century, including sentimental comedy, as written by Pierre-Claude La Chaussée. An important theatrical figure of the time was Denis Diderot, who advocated the writing of domestic tragedy. He was greatly concerned with audience reaction and felt that the more emotion was aroused in the spectators, the better the illusion of reality. He was in favor of naturalness of presentation, but believed the actor should not permit himself to feel anything in his role, conveying an emotion only by external signs. The playwright who most closely followed the style advocated by Diderot was Pierre-Augustin de Beaumarchais, whose two best plays are *The Barber of Seville* (1775) and *The Marriage of Figaro* (1784).

The eighteenth century in France was a period of actor supremacy. The most noted actress of the time was Adrienne Lecouvreur. An actor of note was Joseph Talma, who startled audiences by wearing a Roman toga with his bare legs and arms showing. This faithfulness to history was unheard of at the time, but did much to further exact costuming practices.

Although many important advances in drama were made in France and England during the seventeenth and eighteenth centuries, interesting theatrical activities were likewise occurring in other countries. In Italy the most popular dramatic form still was the opera, and continued advances were being made in operatic staging and design. In Russia, the first public theatre was opened during the eighteenth century, but no good drama was written there until the nineteenth century. The countries of northern Europe also began to develop theatres and drama, but made no important progress. Theatre in America, too, began during the eighteenth century, but was really only an imitation of the English theatre. The first plays in the colonies were performed by English actors, but during the Revolutionary War all theatrical activity was suspended.

German Theatre

The most sweeping changes in theatre were occurring in Germany, which, until the eighteenth century, had been a collection of small states and duchies. A generally poor country, it relied for theatre on performances by traveling companies and court productions that featured unbelievable action and violence. Caroline Neuber, an actress who headed her own troupe beginning in 1727, raised the level of acting and drama by insisting on careful rehearsals, high personal morals, and the presentation of plays with higher literary standards than were common. Her work, with that of intellectual Johann Gottsched, is considered the turning point in the history of the German theatre; from that time on, drama was more respected.

During the eighteenth century, as the government became centralized and a national awareness and pride began to emerge, there was a trend toward romanticism, one form of which was *Sturm und Drang* (storm and stress), born largely as a result of the writings of Johann Friedrich Schiller (1759–1805). The movement was characterized by a reverence for Shakespeare, a return to nature, and a disregard for the dramatic unities as practiced in France. Romanticism emphasized freedom from the bonds of society, a clear division between good and evil, and a return to man's basic emotions. Schiller's *The Robbers,* which he wrote at age nineteen, was in great part responsible for the beginnings of German romanticism. Its story condemns the social laws of the day and advocates that men should turn away from the law in order to be free.

Another eighteenth-century German writer, Gotthold Ephraim Lessing (1729–1781), was one of the first to recognize the artistry of Shakespeare and to attack French neoclassicism, even though his plays followed the true classic model. He favored domestic tragedy and used a cause/effect structure. His dramatic poem *Nathan der Weise* (*Nathan the Wise*), written in 1779, deals with religious tolerance and is based on the theme that any religion that is concerned with humanitarianism is good.

Figure 6.5

A scene from a performance (c.1880) of *Faust,* French composer Gounod's opera based on the Goethe play. Faust has just found his love, Marguerite, awaiting her execution.

Johann Wolfgang von Goethe (1749–1832) is best known for his play *Faust*—like Marlowe's *Dr. Faustus,* based on the legend of a man who makes a pact with the devil. The first part of *Faust* was published in 1808. The play is considered the ultimate example of romanticism, although both Goethe and Schiller denied being romanticists.

By the end of the eighteenth century, romanticism was well established in Germany. In some of the other European countries, the movement did not reach maturity until the nineteenth century.

Chapter Seven

19th- and 20th-Century Theatre

With the Industrial Revolution in full swing and a change from the country to the city as the controller of a nation's wealth, it is little wonder that emphasis shifted gradually from romanticism and sentiment to more realistic presentations in which neither base nor benevolent human feeling exists as a controlling force. Thus, as the nineteenth century ended and the twentieth century began, theatrical styles shifted from one "ism" to another almost as quickly as colored glass in a kaleidoscope.

The move began with sentimental comedy and bourgeois tragedy. Although both were divorced from true human feelings, they tried to depict real problems. Unfortunately, the style was florid and overblown. Before long the pendulum swung in the opposite direction, and it became a playwright's task simply to record life and report it. Yet a swing too far either way lasts for only a time before the pendulum falls again toward moderation.

Throughout the past two hundred years, changes have come more quickly than at any other time in theatrical history, and innovations have often disappeared just as fast. Never before have so many dramatic forms and styles existed within such a short period of time. Much of the rapid growth occurred due to the change of railroads, which allowed theatrical companies to travel to many locations where professional theatre had never before been seen on a regular basis.

Romanticism

Even before the storm and stress movement developed in Germany, many of the concepts of romanticism had already appeared in English theatre. It was easier for romanticism to gain a foothold in England because neoclassicism had never been so widely adopted there as in other countries. The lure of romanticism showed that there was a growing distrust of reason and a growing conviction that one had only to follow his or her instincts to do what was right. Hence, humankind could discover truth by examining nature. The subject matter of nineteenth-century romantic plays often dealt with humankind's need to be free from the restraining forces of society.

Despite romanticism's roots in England, few such plays were written there. The most successful playwright was James Sheridan Knowles (1784–1862) with *Virginius* (1820) and *The Hunchback* (1832), written in a pseudo-Elizabethan style of blank verse.

Romanticism was receding in both England and Germany before it gained acceptance in France. It finally became established through the writings of Victor Hugo, whose *Hernani* was produced in 1830. In his preface to his play *Cromwell,* he set forth the doctrine of romanticism and called for abandoning the unities and a strict separation of genres.

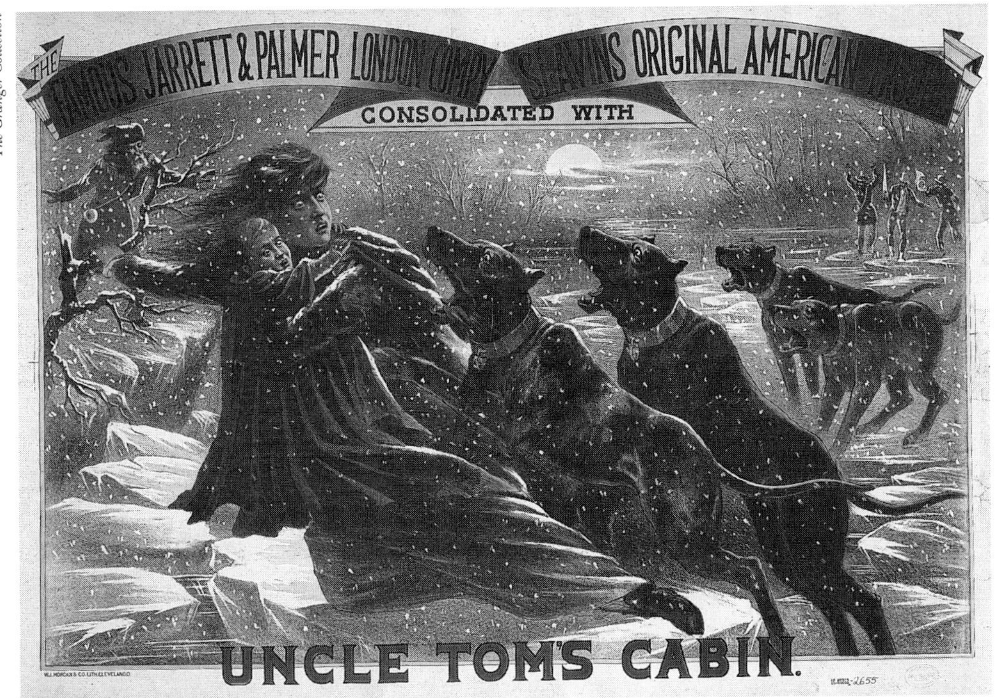

The Granger Collection

Figure 7.1

An 1881 American poster for a theatrical production of the melodrama *Uncle Tom's Cabin.*

Melodrama

Melodrama, characterized by a simple and suspenseful plot and a strong emotional appeal, became highly popular during the nineteenth century. The name *melodrama* goes back to the time when musical accompaniments were used to heighten the changes in mood and pace, a device borrowed from opera and then modified.

The first two major European writers of melodrama were August Kotzebue of Germany and Guilbert de Pixérécourt of France. Melodrama was related to both tragedies and sentimental comedies, which advocated virtue above all else as the solution to humankind's woes. Vice, on the other hand, would ultimately be punished. The genre also was influenced by both Jean-Jacques Rousseau and Immanuel Kant. "Rousseau offered ideas relating to the noble savage, the natural goodness of man and the equation of evil with inequality; Kant emphasized the individual's right to freedom."[1]

Thus developed a spectrum of nineteenth-century "common" heroes—such as the cowboy, the American Indian, Davy Crockett (the frontiersman), and, in England, Jack Tar (the sailor). Of course, this also led to stereotyping and to later objections by such groups as Native Americans and blacks. For instance, in America the most widely produced nineteenth-century play was *Uncle Tom's Cabin,* based on the Harriet Beecher Stowe novel. There were several dramatized versions, but the most successful was an adaptation by George Aikin, which ran for more than two hundred performances at New York's National Theatre. Until the early part of the twentieth century, touring companies presented "Tom" shows five or more times a year in dozens of communities.

Much of melodrama's popularity was due to spectacle—drawing on new advances in staging and such diverse media as the circus and fantasy novels. For instance, in addition to writing melodrama, Pixérécourt managed theatres in Paris, where he added a number of sensational effects to the plays. These included a large orchestra to accompany the dialogue, explosions, and a volcano.

Melodrama also was popular in England because it offered a way for music halls to "link songs, dances and spectacular tableaux into sequences illustrating a popular theme with a well-defined beginning, middle and end." "These shows came to be called burlettas. All that was required to give this embryonic type of popular entertainment a shape and quality of its own was a suitable injection of moral, philosophic and literary animation."[2]

Throughout the century theatre increased in popularity, attracting far more spectators than ever before. Many new theatres were erected so as to offer specialized types of entertainment, ranging from variety and burlesque to serious dramas. Both in England and America, Shakespeare drew large audiences, especially with the acting of performers such as Edwin Booth (particularly in *Hamlet*) and Charlotte Cushman (playing male roles in America), and, in England, Edmund Kean.

Settings were now being built for individual plays, and they had to be historically accurate, following the trend begun in Germany just after the turn of the century. In England, Charles Kemble's production of Shakespeare's *King John* in 1823 was the first play in which the costuming was historically correct. It was followed in 1824 by a production of *Henry IV, Part I,* which was scenically accurate. By mid-century, nearly every production reflected the backgrounds and costumes of its period.

---

1 Glynne Wickham, *A History of the Theatre,* 2nd ed. (London: Phaidon Press Limited, 1992), pp. 184–85.

2 Wickham, p. 184.

Theatre Companies

Until the 1830s, in both Europe and America the most popular type of acting troupe was the **repertory company**, which presented a repertoire of shows for a season. This was followed by the **star system** in which actors who had gained prominence began traveling to various communities with their own companies. Many cities found it difficult to keep a good resident troupe. In America, this system was aided by the rapid expansion of the railroads. The star system then gradually gave way to **combination companies** that traveled for a season to a "combination" of theatres along a route. Generally they presented a single play, although some had a repertoire of several plays. By the beginning of the twentieth century, however, almost all actors were hired only for specific roles in specific plays.

In America, an outgrowth of these changes was the Theatrical Syndicate, formed in 1896 to book touring shows in various communities. The syndicate demanded that local theatre owners work with it exclusively. Since it handled most of the major touring companies, theatre managers were afraid to try to run a season independently. Those who did usually found that the syndicate bought rival theatres in town to try to put the resistant managers out of business. The syndicate's monopoly on theatrical booking was not broken until 1915.

In England, acting was becoming a socially accepted profession. Henry Irving (1838–1905), the first actor to be knighted, was renowned for his presentations of romantic plays and melodramas. Other actors and actresses of the time were John Philip Kemble; his sister, Mrs. Sarah Siddons; and Ellen Terry, who often acted with Irving.

The playwrights of the nineteenth century were protected by copyright laws that prevented their works from being pirated. At first the laws were inadequate, in that they protected writers only within their own country. By the beginning of the twentieth century, however, international copyright laws were passed.

Realism

New dramatic forms slowly replaced the old. Following romanticism and melodrama came their direct opposite—realism, which developed as a result of oppressive political and economic conditions. Playwrights who favored realism felt that Western society was unacceptable and must be changed, thus their task was to reveal social ills and injustices. They emphasized the importance of what could be observed through the senses, for only thus could real truth be known. Playwrights believed that if audiences didn't like the social conditions depicted on the stage, they'd be driven to change them, rather than simply attacking the playwright.

The Granger Collection

Figure 7.2

The Gaity Theater in Hankow, China; wood engraving, English, 1873. The row of gas lights at the front of the stage illuminates the action, which can now take place farther upstage, within the set.

Advances in Staging

Perhaps the most significant change in staging in the nineteenth century was the development of gas lights. This innovation made it possible to go from general illumination which spilled into the audience areas, to specific lighting. Now the designer could control the amount, the intensity, and the direction of the light onstage. By 1840, most theatres had gas lights. By 1880, electricity was in general use and lighting could be even more effectively controlled from a central location—the dimmer board. The use of gas and electricity allowed actors to move from the forestage—that is, from in front of the scenery—upstage and within a setting that provided an environment.

The Industrial Revolution placed theatre within the reach of the common person, who demanded more realistic settings and the abandonment of stock or standard sets that previously had been adapted for use in any number of plays.

The development of the realistic movement, which began in France around 1850, was aided by technical advances that made for more believable settings. The **box set**, which was built of flats to represent an indoor location, was developed by 1840 and was in general use by the end of the century. There was a trend toward making stage floors flat, rather than raking them for purposes of perspective.

To facilitate quick changes of scene, elevator and revolving stages were used, as were wagons on which entire sets would be rolled on and off. The ultimate theatre of the period was Steele MacKaye's Madison Square Theatre in New York.

FROM THE SCIENTIFIC AMERICAN

April 5, 1884

[The Madison Square Theatre consists] of two theatrical stages, one above another, to be moved up and down as an elevator car is operated in a high building, and so that either one of them can easily and quickly be at any time brought to the proper level for acting thereon in front of the auditorium. . . .

This immense contrivance is suspended at each corner by two steel cables, each of which would be capable of sustaining far more than the whole load, and these cables pass upward over sheaves or pulleys set at different angles, thence downward to a saddle, to which all are connected. Connected to this saddle is a hoisting cable, attached to a hoisting drum, by the rotation of which the stages are raised and lowered. Practically, only forty seconds are required to raise or lower a stage into position, and four men at the winch are as much as is ever required. This movement is thus easily effected, without sound, jar or vibration. . . .

While the play is proceeding before the audience, another scene is . . . arranged by the assistants on the upper stage, to be followed, when this is lowered, by similar preparations for the succeeding scene, should this be necessary, on the stage that will then be twenty-five feet below.

Forms of Drama

The Well-Made Play

Realistic dramas had been seen at times before the beginning of the nineteenth century, but did not gain popularity until the plays of Eugène Scribe

(1791–1861). Critics referred to his work and that of his followers as **well-made plays**. In this sort of drama, a cause or problem is introduced early, and the effects are progressively explored. Not only does the well-made play have a plot that builds to a climax, it has (as developed by Scribe) a clear exposition of background material that lays the groundwork for everything that occurs. There is great suspense and logical—though unexpected—reversals in the action. The play concludes logically.

One of the most popular early authors of the well-made play was Alexandre Dumas fils, who lived from 1824 to 1895. His best-known play is *The Lady of the Camellias*, based on his novel of the same name, known simply as *Camille*. The play, written in 1849, was romantic in style, but was a move toward realism in that it dealt with a social problem and attempted to teach a moral lesson.

The Thesis Play

The **thesis play**, a subgenre of the well-made play, attempted to teach a moral lesson. Many nineteenth-century thesis plays now appear dated, since many of the problems they point up no longer exist.

The man who brought the thesis play to its highest development was the Norwegian playwright Henrik Ibsen (1828–1906), sometimes called the father of modern drama. Although he began writing in 1850, his early plays were romantic. Not until the 1870s did he shift to a realistic vein and deal with socially significant themes. More than any other playwright of his time, he established realism as an integral part of drama. Among Ibsen's dramatic reforms was a discontinuation of the use of soliloquies and asides. In addition, the thesis play provided a thorough exposition of prior events, presented logically and interestingly. Every element of the production was to contribute to the overall effect, with each character an individual affected both by heredity (or personality) and environment (including experience). His plays deal with a variety of social issues, including women's rights—*A Doll's House*—and conscience versus financial success—*The Pillars of Society* and *An Enemy of the People.*

The Slice-of-Life Drama

Naturalism carried realistic drama to its ultimate end. As developed by the novelist Émile Zola, naturalism meant that playwrights should constantly seek the truth through objectivity—that is, their own ideas must not be allowed to intrude upon the facts presented in their writings. Playwrights should be recorders of events, not interpreters. They should select the beginnings and endings of their drama at random. Any attempt to concoct a plot results in a distortion of the truth, since life itself has no real beginnings or endings. This **slice-of-life** technique insists that the dramatist reproduce actual life on the stage. In some naturalistic productions actors made no attempt to project their voices and turned their backs to the audience at will.

Nineteenth-century naturalism has been criticized for depicting the seamiest sides of life. Still, Zola's ideas spread quickly over Europe and influenced writers and producers everywhere.

The Playwrights

In England, the most important playwright of the late nineteenth and early twentieth century was Irish-born George Bernard Shaw (1856–1950), whose witty plays emphasize social themes and feature believable characters. In his intellectual plays, such as *Saint Joan, Misalliance, Androcles and the Lion,* and *Arms and the Man,* he preached his own social beliefs. The latter, for instance, is a satire on romantic ideas about war. The following excerpts contrast the views held by the two women with the opinion of the man (Captain Bluntschli). The second scene picks up after The Man has hidden in Raina's room.

Figure 7.3

George Bernard Shaw (right) rehearsing *Androcles and the Lion*, 1913.

The Granger Collection

ARMS AND THE MAN

George Bernard Shaw
From Act I

CATHERINE (*entering hastily, full of good news*): Raina! (*She pronounces it Rah-eena, with the stress on the ee.*) Raina! (*She goes to the bed, expecting to find RAINA there.*) Why, where—? (*RAINA looks into the room.*) Heavens, child, are you out in the night air instead of in your bed? You'll catch your death. Louka told me you were asleep.

RAINA (*dreamily*): I sent her away. I wanted to be alone. The stars are so beautiful! What is the matter?

CATHERINE: Such news! There has been a battle.

RAINA (*her eyes dilating*): Ah! (*She throws the cloak on the ottoman and comes eagerly to CATHERINE in her nightgown, a pretty garment but evidently the only one she had on.*)

CATHERINE: A great battle at Slivnitza. A victory! And it was won by Sergius.

RAINA (*with a cry of delight*): Ah! (*They embrace rapturously.*) Oh, mother! (*Then, with sudden anxiety*) Is father safe?

CATHERINE: Of course! he sends me the news. Sergius is the hero of the hour, the idol of the regiment.

RAINA: Tell me, tell me. How was it? (*Ecstatically*) Oh, mother! mother! mother! (*She pulls her mother down on the ottoman; and they kiss one another frantically.*)

CATHERINE (*with surging enthusiasm*): You can't guess how splendid it is. A cavalry charge! think of that! He defied our Russian commanders—acted without orders—led a charge on his own responsibility—headed it himself—was the first man to sweep through their guns. Can't you see it Raina? Our gallant splendid Bulgarians with their swords and eyes flashing, thundering down like an avalanche and scattering the wretched Servians and their dandified Austrian officers like chaff. And you! you kept Sergius waiting a year before you would be betrothed to him. Oh, if you have a drop of Bulgarian blood in your veins, you will worship him when he comes back.

* * *

THE MAN: A narrow shave; but a miss is as good as a mile. Dear young lady: your servant to the death. I wish for your sake I had joined the Bulgarian army instead of the other one. I am not a native Serb.

RAINA (*haughtily*): No: you are one of the Austrians who set the Serbs on to rob us of our national liberty, and who officer their army for them. We hate them!

The Man: Austrian! not I. Don't hate me, dear young lady. I am a Swiss, fighting merely as a professional soldier. I joined the Serbs because they came first on the road from Switzerland. Be generous: you've beaten us hollow.

Raina: Have I not been generous?

The Man: Noble! Heroic! But I'm not saved yet. This particular rush will soon pass through; but the pursuit will go on all night by fits and starts. I must take my chance to get off in a quiet interval. (*Pleasantly*) You don't mind my waiting just a minute or two, do you?

Raina (*putting on her most genteel society manner*): Oh, no: I'm sorry you will have to go into danger again. *(Pointing to the ottoman)* Won't you sit—(*She breaks off with an irrepressible cry of alarm as she catches sight of the pistol. The man, all nervous shies like a frightened horse.)*

The Man (*irritably*): Don't frighten me like that. What is it?

Raina: Your revolver! It was staring that officer in the face all the time. What an escape

The Man (*vexed at being unnecessarily terrified*): Oh, is that all?

Raina (*staring at him rather superciliously as she conceives a poorer and poorer opinion of him, and feels proportionately more and more at her ease.* I am sorry I frightened you. (*She takes up the pistol and hands it to him.*) Pray take it to protect yourself against me.

The Man (*grinning wearily at the sarcasm as he takes the pistol*): No use, dear young lady; there's nothing in it. It's not loaded. (*He makes a grimace at it, and drops it despairingly into his revolver case.*)

Raina: Load it by all means.

The Man: I've no ammunition. What use are cartridges in battle? I always carry chocolate instead; and I finished the last cake of that hours ago.

Raina (*outraged in her most cherished ideals of manhood*): Chocolate! Do you stuff your pockets with sweets—like a schoolboy—even in the field?

The Man (*grinning hungrily*): Yes: isn't it contemptible? I wish I had some now.

Other important English playwrights were W. S. Gilbert (1836–1911) and Arthur Sullivan (1842–1900). Through their operettas satirizing the upper classes, they hoped to bring about changes in the social structure. Among their best-known works are *H.M.S. Pinafore, The Mikado,* and *The Pirates of Penzance.*

Another satirist of the time was Oscar Wilde (1856–1900), who wrote *The Importance of Being Earnest* and *Lady Windermere's Fan.* He, too, was a witty and entertaining writer who satirized the prudery of his day.

In Ireland, Sean O'Casey (1880–1964), with his satiric tragedies, became known as the playwright of the Irish slums. O'Casey's work includes *Juno and the Paycock* and *The Plough and the Stars.*

One of Ireland's greatest dramatists was John Millington Synge who, on the recommendation of William Butler Yeats, spent several years observing the Irish peasants. As a result of his observations, he proceeded to write six plays that are considered the best among any written in Ireland. They include *The Playboy of the Western World, In the Shadow of the Glen,* and *Riders to the Sea.* The latter usually is considered to be his best. It is the tragic story of the sea claiming the lives of all the men in a family. Yet none of the catastrophe is shown onstage—only the reaction to it.

In Russia, Anton Chekhov (1860–1904) wrote plays based on contemporary Russian life, presenting sympathetic characters who are defeated by circumstances. Among his best works are *Uncle Vanya* and *The Cherry Orchard.* Another noted Russian playwright, Maxim Gorky (1868–1936), wrote of derelicts living in a basement in *The Lower Depths.*

In Chekhov's *Uncle Vanya,* the title character has lost all will to manage the estate ever since the arrival of old Serebrakoff and his young wife, Helena. The brother of Serebrakoff's first wife, Uncle Vanya (Voitski), had scrimped to send Serebrakoff as much money as possible. Now he is disillusioned by the retired professor's egotistical and demanding ways and by the fact that he apparently does not love Helena, though she loves him.

UNCLE VANYA

Anton Chekhov

From Act I

Translated by Marian Fell

VOITSKI: There goes our learned scholar on a hot, sultry day like this, in his overcoat and galoshes and carrying an umbrella!

ASTROFF: He is trying to take good care of his health.

VOITSKI: How lovely she is! How lovely! I have never in my life seen a more beautiful woman.

TELEGIN: Do you know, Marina, that as I walk in the fields or in the shady garden, as I look at this table here, my heart swells with unbounded happiness. The weather is enchanting, the birds are singing, we are all living in peace and contentment—what more could the soul desire? (*Takes a glass of tea.*)

Figure 7.4

A Yale Repertory Theatre production of Anton Chekhov's *Uncle Vanya*.

Voitski (*dreaming*): Such eyes—a glorious woman!

Astroff: Come, Ivan, tell us something.

Voitski (*indolently*): What shall I tell you?

Astroff: Haven't you any news for us?

Voitski: No, it is all stale. I am just the same as usual, or perhaps worse, because I have become lazy. I don't do anything now but croak like an old raven. My mother, the old magpie, is still chattering about the emancipation of woman, with one eye on her grave and the other on her learned books, in which she is always looking for the dawn of a new life.

Astroff: And the professor?

Voitski: The professor sits in his library from morning till night, as usual—

"Straining the mind, wrinkling the brow,
We write, write, write,
Without respite
Or hope of praise in the future or now."

Poor paper! He ought to write his autobiography; he would make a really splendid subject for a book! Imagine it, the life of a retired professor, as stale as a piece of hardtack, tortured by gout, headaches, and rheumatism, his liver bursting with jealousy and envy, living on the estate of his first wife, although he hates it, because he can't afford to live in town. He is everlastingly whining about his hard lot, though, as a matter of fact, he is extraordinarily lucky. He is the son of a common deacon and has attained the professor's chair, become the son-in-law of a senator, is called "your Excellency," and so on. But I'll tell you something; the man has been writing on art for twenty-five years, and he doesn't know the very first thing about it. For twenty-five years he has been chewing on other men's thoughts about realism, naturalism, and all such foolishness; for twenty-five years he has been reading and writing things that clever men have long known and stupid ones are not interested in; for twenty-five years he has been making his imaginary mountains out of molehills. And just think of the man's self-conceit and presumption all this time! For twenty-five years he has been masquerading in false clothes and has now retired, absolutely unknown to any living soul; and yet see him! stalking across the earth like a demi-god!

Astroff: I believe you envy him.

Voitski: Yes, I do. Look at the success he has had with women! Don Juan himself was not more favored. His first wife, who was my sister, was a beautiful, gentle being, as pure as the blue heaven there above us, noble, great-hearted, with more admirers than he has pupils, and she loved him as only beings of angelic purity can love those who are as pure and beautiful as themselves. His mother-in-law, my mother, adores him to this day, and he still inspires a sort of worshipful awe in her. His second wife is, as you see, a brilliant beauty; she married him in his old age and has surrendered all the glory of her beauty and freedom to him. Why? What for?

Astroff: Is she faithful to him?

Voitski: Yes, unfortunately she is.

Astroff: Why "unfortunately"?

Voitski: Because such fidelity is false and unnatural, root and branch. It sounds well, but there is no logic in it. It is thought immoral for a woman to deceive an old husband whom she hates, but quite moral for her to strangle her poor youth in her breast and banish every vital desire from her heart.

TELEGIN (*in a tearful voice*): Vanya, I don't like to hear you talk so. Listen, Vanya; every one who betrays husband or wife is faithless, and could also betray his country.

VOITSKI (*crossly*): Turn off the tap, Waffles.

TELEGIN: No, allow me, Vanya. My wife ran away with a lover on the day after our wedding, because my exterior was unprepossessing. I have never failed in my duty since then. I love her and am true to her to this day. I help her all I can and have given my fortune to educate the daughter of herself and her lover. I have forfeited my happiness, but I have kept my pride. And she? Her youth has fled, her beauty has faded according to the laws of nature, and her lover is dead. What has she kept?

In America, David Belasco (1853–1931) was giving productions of melodramas in naturalistic settings. Hired by Charles Kean during his tour of the West Coast in 1868, Belasco played the young Duke of York in *Richard III,* where he became acquainted with realism as advocated by Kean. Later, he adapted stage realism to his own works, such as *Madame Butterfly* (1900) and *The Girl of the Golden West* (1905), which were melodramas.

The Rise of the Director

The trend toward a style of drama that would be strongly representative of life began in the mid-nineteenth century and continued into the mid-twentieth. Thus, due to the need for more careful rehearsals and a more thorough coordination of all the elements, the director gradually became the most important figure of the theatre.

In a small duchy, now Thuringia, Germany, Georg II, the Duke of Saxe-Meiningen (1826–1914), refined in his Meiningen Court Theatre the concept of **ensemble acting,** in which no one actor is more important than any other, and the effect of the total production is more important than any of its parts. The duke believed that the director should be the dominant artist in the theatre, with complete authority over his actors; the stage picture should be worked out meticulously; and there should be accuracy in historical detail. The company became one of the most admired in Europe.

Since plays were subject to censorship in much of Europe, a number of independent theatres were established. That is, they were open only to members and so were exempt from government censorship. The first, organized in

Paris in 1887 by André Antoine (1858–1943), was the Théâtre Libre, which produced all types of plays but was largely concerned with naturalism. Antoine believed that the actors' environment determined their movements. He went so far as to bring in people off the streets to act in his plays, so they would appear natural. Once he even hung carcasses of beef onstage to make a butcher shop scene realistic.

Two years later, Otto Brahm (1856–1912) established the Freie Bühne (Free Theatre) in Germany and gave a hearing to new writers, thus contributing to the establishment of modern drama in Germany.

In 1891, J. T. Grein, along with William Archer and George Moore, founded the Independent Theatre Society in London. Its initial production was Ibsen's *Ghosts*. Perhaps most important, the Independent Theatre was responsible for George Bernard Shaw's turning to playwriting.

In Russia, Konstantin Stanislavsky (1863–1938), who was an actor, director and producer, developed a system of acting based on human emotions and experiences that required each actor to feel and understand his or her role.

The Eclectic Approach

Recent theatre is eclectic in its combination of many forms. This approach was given impetus by the work of director Max Reinhardt (1873–1943), who believed each play required a different style of presentation and that the director must control the style. Reinhardt, perhaps more than anyone else, made various movements in the theatre acceptable to audiences. Another person who used a variety of styles was Vsevolod Meyerhold of Russia (1874–1942), who favored a return to such forms as the *commedia dell'arte,* Japanese drama, and Greek theatre. To Meyerhold, the actors were no more important than any other elements of a production.

Many new forms of staging and directing were widely accepted in Europe before they gained a foothold in America. In particular, Robert Edmond Jones (1887–1954) and Lee Simonson (1888–1967) were important in bringing European ideas of design to America.

The new stagecraft was first presented to American audiences by little theatre groups such as the Provincetown Players, which produced many of Eugene O'Neill's plays, and the Group Theatre, which worked with the playwright Clifford Odets and directors Elia Kazan and Harold Clurman. Indeed, the Group Theatre was responsible for developing the talents of many performers who later became America's foremost actors.

Another form that developed along with realism and naturalism was **symbolism**, which began in France and usually took its subject matter from the past. The symbolists did not believe in realistic scenery, preferring backgrounds that gave a general impression of the mood of the play. The idea is that truth, which is elusive and subjective, can be hinted at only through the use of symbols that evoke feelings. The outstanding symbolist playwright was Maurice Maeterlinck (1862–1949).

On the other hand, Adolphe Appia (1862–1928), a Swiss theorist and designer, and Edward Gordon Craig (1872–1966), an English producer, actor, and stage designer, sought to create an environment that was fitting for each play. Working independently, they laid the foundations upon which much of modern theatrical practice was built. Craig's settings were designed to capture the feeling of a work without representing an actual place. Appia emphasized the role of light in creating unity for his productions.

Expressionism was another important trend in playwriting. The entire drama is presented through the eyes of a central character, so that the audience views reality as the character does. Expressionist writers, at the opposite extreme from the realists, feel that the way to truth is through an understanding of humankind's soul. One of the best-known expressionist playwrights was August Strindberg (1849–1912), the first important Swedish playwright. He began writing in a realistic vein, but his later plays, such as *The Ghost Sonata* (1907), were actually forerunners of the new movement. Another expressionist was Georg Kaiser (1878–1945), of Germany. In 1918 he wrote *From Morn to Midnight.* Several important American playwrights, including Eugene O'Neill (1888–1953), wrote expressionistic plays. (O'Neill, considered by many to be America's most outstanding playwright, experimented successfully with a variety of styles.) For instance, *The Hairy Ape,* first presented by the Provincetown Players in 1922, shows what might happen if the rules of the universe are changed and our worst fears become reality.

In the play, Yank, a stoker on an ocean liner, is convinced that he and his co-workers are the only ones who count or "belong," since they run the ship. Then Mildred Douglas, daughter of the shipowner, comes to see the men working. Meeting Yank, whom she calls a hairy ape, so repulses her that she faints. This makes him begin to doubt his humanness, a doubt reinforced when he cannot find acceptance in New York City. He goes to a zoo to claim kinship with an ape, but it crushes him to death.

Similar to the work of European expressionists, the play is highly symbolic in its subject matter and content. Yank is the symbol of man, who has emerged from an animal state but has failed to progress spiritually. Alienated from society, he makes the ultimate discovery that he does not belong in the world either as a man or as a worker. Despite the symbolism and expressionism in the play, much of the dialogue is realistic.

Surrealism developed in the theatre at about the same time as expressionism and encompasses a number of other styles, such as theatre of cruelty and theatre of the absurd. Actually, its roots can be traced back at least to the beginning of the twentieth century in painting and novels. The word *surrealist,* for instance, was used to describe Alfred Jarry's *Le Surmâle,* a 1902 novel. The movement involves breaking down the barriers between the inner and outer, or conscious and subconscious, worlds, as illustrated, for instance, in the dreamlike paintings of Marc Chagall.

One of the earliest dramatists to write in this style was Luigi Pirandello (1867–1936) with *Right You Are—If You Think You Are* and *Six Characters in Search of an Author.* One of the ideas behind surrealism is that we can never define the true self—because of the many things we are and the many roles we play, which may be altogether different from the inner person.

Epic Theatre

Bertolt (also spelled Bertold) Brecht, a German writer and director, developed his concept of "making strange," or distancing, in what is called **epic theatre** or the **theatre of alienation**. He wanted the audience to identify with the social and political issues of plays rather than with the characters. Two of his plays are *Mother Courage and Her Children* (1937) and *The Good Woman of Setzuan* (1943).

Still another important new form was **absurdism**, which asserts that nothing is good or bad as such—only what human beings attribute to something can

Figure 7.5

A scene from a Yale School of Drama production of Bertolt Brecht's *The Good Woman of Setzuan*, the story of Shen Te, a good-hearted prostitute.

make it either moral or immoral. Truth is to be found in disorder and chaos, because everything is equally illogical. Among the forerunners of absurdism were the French writers Jean-Paul Sartre and Albert Camus. Later came Romanian-born Eugène Ionesco, whose first play *The Bald Soprano* (1950) opened in Paris to rave reviews. The play consists of non sequiturs, and at the end the characters are shouting nonsense syllables at each other.

Irish born Samuel Beckett's *Waiting for Godot* is often considered to be the archetypal absurdist drama. Produced in Paris in 1952, *Godot* helped focus the world's attention on the theatre of the absurd. In the play, the two characters seem to be expecting something to happen that will save them in some way, symbolized by their waiting for someone or something called Godot.

WAITING FOR GODOT

Samuel Beckett
Translated from the French by Marsh Cassady
From Act II:

VLADIMIR: You again! (***ESTRAGON*** *halts but does not raise his head.* ***VLADIMIR*** *goes toward him.*) Come here till I embrace you.

ESTRAGON: Don't touch me!

*(**VLADIMIR** holds back, pained.)*

VLADIMIR: Do you want me to go away? (*Pause.*) Gogo!

(*Pause.* ***VLADIMIR*** *observes him attentively.*) Did they beat you? (*Pause.*) Gogol (***ESTRAGON*** *remains silent, head bowed.*) Where did you spend the night?

ESTRAGON: Don't touch me! Don't question me! Don't speak to me! Stay with me!

VLADIMIR: Did I ever leave you?

ESTRAGON: You let me go.

VLADIMIR: Look at me. (***ESTRAGON*** *does not raise his head. Violently.*) Will you look at me!

*(**ESTRAGON** raises his head. They look long at each other, then suddenly embrace, clapping each other on the back. End of the embrace.* ***ESTRAGON,*** *no longer supported, almost falls.)*

ESTRAGON: What a day!

VLADIMIR: Who beat you? Tell me.

ESTRAGON: Another day done with.

VLADIMIR: Not yet.

ESTRAGON: For me it's over and done with, no matter what happens. (*Silence.*) I heard you singing.

VLADIMIR: That's right, I remember.

ESTRAGON: That finished me. I said to myself, He's all alone, he thinks I'm gone for ever, and he sings.

VLADIMIR: One is not master of one's moods. All day I've felt in great form. (*Pause.*) I didn't get up in the night, not once!

ESTRAGON: (*sadly*), You see, you piss better when I'm not there.

VLADIMIR: I missed you . . . and at the same time I was happy. Isn't that a queer thing?

ESTRAGON: (*shocked*). Happy?

VLADIMIR: Perhaps it's not quite the right word.

ESTRAGON: And now?

VLADIMIR: Now? . . . (*joyous*) There you are again . . . (*Indifferent*) There we are again . . . (*gloomy*) There I am again.

Amid such a diversity of dramatic forms, the eclectic approach became a necessity. The distinctions between forms blurred over time.

Coming to prominence in the 1960s was Edward Albee with such plays as *The Zoo Story* (1958), *Who's Afraid of Virginia Woolf?* (1962, winner of the Drama Critics Circle Award), and *Three Tall Women* (1994), the latter of which won Albee his third Pulitzer.

Two other playwrights who first became known in the 1960s were John Guare and Sam Shepard, both of whom had work produced at Off-Broadway's Caffe Cino. Guare's early work was somewhat satirical. In the 1990s, with *Six Degrees of Separation,* his work became much more so in exploring social and cultural issues. Shepard's drama, though more lyrical and poetic, always seems to involve a degree of violence. In *Fool for Love,* May and Eddie have a dangerous overpowering and devouring attraction and need for each other, or else they reject each other completely.

Influences on American Theatre

Theatre in the United States began to come into its own in the early part of the twentieth century. Its forerunners were several specific but diverse types of entertainment: the minstrel show, with its jokes and songs and variety; the circus, which developed on a larger scale than in Europe; the showboat, which provided entertainment for isolated communities; variety shows and vaudeville; and musicals. The Broadway district in New York City became the center of American theatre.

Concepts that developed in Europe also influenced American theatre. An example is the **theatre of cruelty** as advocated by Antonin Artaud (1896–1949). In the twenties and thirties he advocated capturing a sense of danger in relation to the theatre as an expression of the loss of the spiritual aspect of life. To Artaud, the director became the important theatre artist, more important than the playwright, in using sound, lights, color, objects, and actors. The "cruelty" was not against the performers, but rather in compelling the audience to face itself.

Another influence was Jerzy Grotowski's Polish Laboratory Theatre, which sought to rid the theatre of everything that wasn't necessary. Grotowski concluded that the only two essentials were the actor and the audience. His group became a powerful force in influencing the development of theatre throughout the Western world.

One avant-garde group was Julian Beck and Judith Malina's Living Theatre, considered by some to be the beginnings of the Off-Off Broadway movement. From its founding, the group rebelled against the mainstream in all of its facets. There were similar groups, though the Living Theatre was the most radical.

After leaving the Living Theatre, Joseph Chaikin founded The Open Theatre, developing a technique for focusing on the performer, not the role, and on "transformation," in which the actor changed from one character to another in front of the audience. The group began working on ensemble creations shaped by one playwright. For instance, it did van Italie's *The Serpent* and Megan Terry's *Viet Rock.* Also, Richard Schechner began experimenting with **environmental theatre,** or **found space**, that is, performing in any available space and mingling performers and audiences.

The **happenings**, a specialized form popular in the 1960s, combined a variety of media—film, painting, and theatre. Seemingly unrelated occurrences came together in an almost uncontrolled format. One of the early advocates of this form was John Cage, who wanted each person at his happenings to be aware of what was occurring and to judge it independently. Later, people laid more groundwork for the happenings, even preparing outlines. Here, too, there was little or no separation of audience and performer; the spectator was to become an integral part of the happening. The purpose was to break down any separation of life and art.

From this grew today's multimedia presentations by **performance artists,** who use a combination of forms and disciplines. Although performance art started out largely as unplanned and unstructured, a recent trend has been toward *one-person shows* that consist of acting, oral interpretation and storytelling, pantomime, and dance.

Many performance artists present shows that follow a particular theme, often taking a stand against or for a particular social issue, such as the impact of AIDS, while others exist largely for entertainment. In general, **alternative theatre,** including women's, minority, and ethnic theatre, came into its own after the 1960s. Productions dealing with gay and lesbian themes have been particularly successful in the 1980s and 1990s.

Broadway, however, tends to stay with the more established dramatic forms. During recent years, revivals of older plays have been highly successful. The 1927 Jerome Kern and Oscar Hammerstein II musical *Show Boat* won five Tony awards in 1994, and fourteen of the twenty-four productions eligible for Tony nominations that year were revivals. A major reason is that Broadway doesn't want to take chances, preferring the shows that previously have been successful. This is implied in the fact that only one new Broadway musical opened in 1994. It was *Sunset Boulevard* by Andrew Lloyd Webber, whose musicals, on the basis of his past record—*Evita, Cats, Joseph and His Amazing Technicolor Dream Coat,* and *The Phantom of the Opera*—are almost certain to be successful.

Postmodernism is a trend of recent years in which older plays are reinterpreted without the necessity of analyzing what the playwright intended, and, in fact, with little analysis at all. There is no particular application of logic or cause-and-effect. It involves redefining something that already exists. Whereas modernism, which came into being with the various "isms," embraced the present and the future, postmodernism looks to the past, redefining it in new and unexpected ways. It combines styles, rather than coordinating a production into a single style.

Modern theatre trends and movements in American theatre are discussed in more detail in the next chapter.

Chapter Eight

The Diversity of Modern Theatre

Oscar Wilde - Importance of Being Earnest
Samuel Beckett - Waiting for Godot

Theatre today is diverse in background and experience. It is possible to see plays that draw on dozens of different cultures, from different historical perspectives, from dozens of different ethnic and racial origins and various geographic areas—and plays that deal with diversity of sexual orientation.

In the United States alone a myriad of dramatic forms, styles, and characters has developed. Examples are the Yankee character, the protest drama, and the musical. In fact, the latter often has been called America's most influential contribution to world theatre. Alternative drama forms have also developed, along with a rich variety in ethnic and minority theatre.

This chapter will discuss this diversity of modern theatre and drama.

Musical Theatre

Musicals are the most popular form of theatrical entertainment in the United States. Although we tend to think of the form as a relatively recent development in theatre, music has been a part of dramatic presentations in every area in which theatre has existed.

The Development of the Musical

A number of circumstances contributed to the establishment of musical theatre, or "musical comedy," as it first developed in the United States. The Puritans and Quakers strongly objected to drama in general, on moral grounds. Yet their objections usually were withdrawn when music was involved. Thus, during the early 1800s company managers often billed the productions as concerts and/or "moral entertainments." Even when music was not included in the original script, it often was added.

Musical theatre in the United States has its basis in a number of sources in the 1800s, including the extravaganza, the burlesque show, the minstrel show, and vaudeville and variety shows. The **extravaganza** consisted of spectacular scenic effects, singing, and dancing, and often was based on mythology. **Burlesque,** as originally presented, was a musical parody or satire of a play or other entertainment. The **minstrel show** consisted of white men with blackened faces presenting comedy, music, and dance. Vaudeville and variety shows similarly presented a series of unrelated acts in one program.

Music also accompanied melodramas, which accounted for about a third of America's theatrical fare in the mid-nineteenth century. Actually, the performances often were more like dancing than acting.

Another popular form, **ballet pantomime,** included singing and dancing along with a plot. By the 1860s, variety, which developed at the same time as burlesque, had a reputation, often undeserved, as entertainment fit only for men, so Tony Pastor, a New York variety performer and manager, opened Tony Pastor's Opera House to present "family entertainment." Bit by bit, variety shows, now called vaudeville, began to spread, becoming most popular from 1890 to 1910.

Ballad Opera, Comic Operas, and Operettas

Ballad opera, as created by John Gay with *The Beggar's Opera,* used ballads to create a satire of various elements of society. Imported from England, it was the most popular early form of musical in America. Replacing it was comic opera, with music composed specifically for each production. In America, opera reflected national concerns and usually tended toward burlesque and parody.

After the Civil War, opéra bouffe, satiric comic operas like those of Jacques Offenbach, was popular. Next to arrive in the U.S. were operettas. Although Gilbert and Sullivan's opera epitomizes the form, there were many other writers/composers as well. An example is Victor Herbert, whose works, such as *Babes in Toyland* (1903) and *Naughty Marietta* (1910), still are produced. There are frequent revivals of Gilbert and Sullivan operettas today.

James Gleason

Figure 8.1

A scene from a Kent State University Theatre production of *H.M.S. Pinafore*, a Gilbert and Sullivan operetta.

Ethnic humor also contributed to the development of musicals. One of the first was *Fritz, Our Cousin German* (1870), written by Charles Gayle and portrayed by Joseph Kline Emmet. Even though this was not a musical, Emmet began to insert his own songs, which became the highlights of the show.

Black musicals, which grew directly out of black minstrel shows—with white actors in blackface—flourished in New York at the turn of the century. During the second decade of the twentieth century, musicals began to include plots and individual characters. One of the earliest was *Very Good Eddie* (music by Jerome Kern, lyrics by Schuyler Green, and book by Guy Bolton). By 1920, such composers as Irving Berlin, Cole Porter, and George Gershwin were writing musicals.

The Departure from Musical Comedy

Show Boat, which opened in 1927, with book and lyrics by Oscar Hammerstein II and score by Jerome Kern, most often is credited with being the major turning point in American musical theatre in that it treated serious subjects such as adultery, racial issues, and murder. It also attempted to make the songs appropriate to the action and characters, becoming the first American musical to integrate all the elements into a believable play. *I'd Rather Be Right* (1937), with music and lyrics by Richard Rodgers and Lorenz Hart and book by George S. Kaufman and Moss Hart, was awarded a Pulitzer Prize as best play of the year.

More than to anyone else, the era of musicals of the 1950s and 1960s belong to Rodgers and Hammerstein, whose show *Oklahoma!* (1943) became the standard against which others were judged—as discussed below.

> The glitter of an opening chorus was replaced by the simplicity of one character sitting alone on stage. The songs (and the choruses when used) grew out of the plot and were appropriate to it. Agnes de Mille's dream-sequence dances moved the story forward, so much so that no musical with serious pretensions could do without a dream ballet for years to come. . . . Now dance had to be integrated structurally into the story—and the 1950s would find Jack Cole, Bob Fosse, Jerome Robbins, Gower Champion, and Michael Kidd discovering musicals as a congenial form in which to work.
>
> More than anything, however, the sentimentality and the simplicity of the lyrics and emotions and stories of Hammerstein combined with the absolutely appropriate music of Rodgers to form not merely . . . [a] "seamless web" . . . but also the sort of story which could travel all over America and find an audience.[1]

[1] Julian Mates. *The American Musical Stage Before 1800* (New Brunswick, N.J.: Rutgers University Press, 1962), p. 190.

Bettmann

Figure 8.2

A scene from the original 1948 production of Cole Porter's *Kiss Me, Kate*, a Broadway musical hit based on Shakespeare's *Taming of the Shrew*. Here Petruchio sings "I've Come to Wive It Wealthily in Padua."

Many musicals, such as Kurt Weill's *The Threepenny Opera* (1954) and Harvey Schmidt's *The Fantasticks* (1960), became hits Off-Broadway. The musical continued to change and to encompass new subject matter, for example, the tale of the homosexual couple in *La Cage aux Folles* (1983). Stephen Sondheim, with a long list of musicals, used such plays as *Company* (1970) to bring out a particular theme rather than encompassing a strong plot. His *Sunday in the Park with George* was lacking in dance and described by *The New York Times* reviewer Frank Rich as "the first truly modernist" musical theatre, forming "a bridge between the musical and . . . more daring playwriting."

Figure 8.3

A scene from the musical *Jacques Brel Is Alive and Well and Living in Paris*, with lyrics by Eric Blau and Mort Sherman, a University of San Diego, Theatre production.

Jesus Christ Superstar (1971), by the British team of Tim Rice and Andrew Lloyd Webber, was unique in that it first was a best-selling record and later toured in concert before becoming a Broadway show. Soon, other British imports—all expensive extravaganzas—were dominating Broadway. These included *Cats* and *Phantom of the Opera* by Webber and *Les Misérables* and *Miss Saigon* by Claude-Michel Schönberg. Actually closer to opera, these works contain little or no dialogue.

The tide turned somewhat in 1989 with Tommy Tune's staging of *Grand Hotel*, set in pre-Nazi Germany, and *City of Angels*, both of which do not depend on star performers because the shows themselves are the stars.

Women in Theatre: Yesterday and Today

Looking back at past centuries, women were often denied the right to participate in theatre, except in limited ways. In ancient Greece and Rome, for example, women could only be jugglers, dancers, and singers. In many ways, women were practically unrepresented in theatre up until the seventeenth century. Until the 1940s, women were usually in the roles of actors or costume designers.

The next two sections deal with the history of women as playwrights and as actors. Since the role of the director started developing in the early 1900s, women have gradually made advances as directors in the New York theatre as well as in repertory and children's theatre—especially in the last three decades.

Women as Playwrights

The first woman playwright of whom we have record is Hrosvitha of Gandersheim, a tenth-century German noblewoman who lived voluntarily in a Benedictine convent, whose work often contained elements of farce. For instance, the title character in her play *Dulcitus* hopes to ravish three Christian maidens he thinks are being held in the kitchen. He spends the night fondling pots and pans, thinking them the three virgins.

It was another six centuries before any other woman of whom we have record wrote plays. Isabella Andreini was a member of the *commedia dell'arte*'s Gelosi troupe. She was an actor and mother of seven children, and she and her husband developed scenarios for the troupe.

Aphra Behn, 1640–1689, was the first English woman to be a professional novelist and playwright, composing at least seventeen plays. Her first real

Corbis-Bettmann

Figure 8.4

Aphra Behn.

success was *The Rover; or the Banished Cavalier* (1671). Well-crafted, her comedies often deal with the miseries of marriages made for money. Although condemned by many for their bawdiness, Behn's plays were typical of the age, and were no more risqué than those written by men.

In all probability, the first woman playwright in America was Mercy Otis Warren, who wrote during the 1700s. However, her play *The Group* was little more than a political tract satirizing British officials and American Tories. America's first important female playwright (and also an important actress) was Anna Cora Mowatt Ritchie, author of *Fashion* (1845), a social satire and the first long-running play written by an American. The title refers to people who wanted to be fashionable by imitating everything European, and especially everything French.

FASHION

Anna Cora Mowatt Ritchie
From Act III, Scene I

TIF: Your extravagance will ruin me, Mrs. Tiffany!

MRS. TIF: And your stinginess will ruin me, Mr. Tiffany! It is totally and toot a fate impossible to convince you of the necessity of keeping up appearances. There is a certain display which every woman of fashion is forced to make!

TIF: And pray who made you a woman of fashion?

MRS. TIF: What a vulgar question! All women of fashion, Mr. Tiffany—

TIF: In this land are self-constituted, like you, Madam—and fashion is the cloak for more sins than charity ever covered! It was for fashion's sake that you insisted upon my purchasing this expensive house—it was for fashion's sake that you ran me in debt at every exorbitant upholsterer's and extravagant furniture warehouse in the city—it was for fashion's sake that you built that ruinous conservatory—hired more servants than they have persons to wait upon—and dressed your footman like a harlequin!

MRS. TIF: Mr. Tiffany, you are thoroughly plebeian, and insufferably American, in your grovelling ideas! And, pray, what was the occasion of these very mal-ap-pro-pos remarks? Merely because I requested a paltry fifty dollars to purchase a new style of head-dress—a bijou of an article just introduced in France.

TIF: Time was, Mrs. Tiffany, when you manufactured your own French headdresses—took off their first gloss at the public balls, and then sold them to your shortest-sighted customers. And all you knew about France, or French either, was what you spelt out at the bottom of your fashion plates—but now you have grown so fashionable, forsooth, that you have forgotten how to speak your mother tongue!

MRS. TIF: Mr. Tiffany, Mr. Tiffany! Nothing is more positively vulgarian—more unaristocratic than any allusions to the past!

TIF: Why I thought, my dear, that aristocrats lived principally upon the past—and traded in the market of fashion with the bones of their ancestors for capital?

MRS. TIF: Mr. Tiffany, such vulgar remarks are only suitable to the counting house, in my drawing room you should—

TIF: Vary my sentiments with my locality, as you change your manners with your dress!

Other commercially successful women dramatists include Anne Nichols, who wrote *Abie's Irish Rose* (1922), one of the longest-running plays in history; and Rachel Crothers, whose social comedies often dealt with problems of women. An example is *A Man's World* (1909), which deals with the double standard of judging men's and women's actions.

By World War I, the Little Theatre movement was acclaimed as the alternative to commercial theatre. One of the most successful was the Provincetown Players, whose members included Edna Ferber, Edna St. Vincent Millay, and novelist/journalist Susan Glaspell, whose best-known play is *Trifles* (1916). In this one-act work, Glaspell used the technique of leaving the main female character offstage. The character, Minnie Wright, murdered her husband, and is a symbol of all women trapped in loveless relationships and roles with no options.

Although most plays in the early part of the twentieth century were realistic, Sophie Treadwell's *Machinal* (1928) is expressionistic in its story of an ordinary woman who lives in a mechanized world, in which she has no control. *Machinal* is based on the Snyder-Gray trial, which resulted in the first woman being electrocuted in the United States. The characters in the play remain,

Figure 8.5

A scene from *Machinal* by Sophie Treadwell, as performed in 1996 at the University of Illinois, Department of Theatre. First produced in 1928, *Machinal* is viewed by many as an early feminist drama.

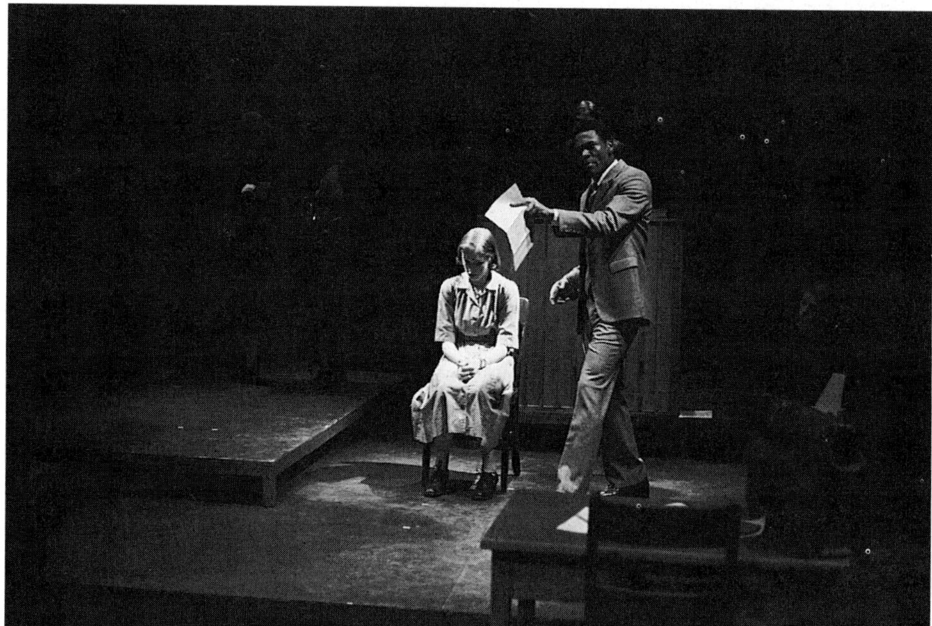

Donald Clegg

for the most part, nameless, which leads the audience to feel alienated from the story unfolding before them. The play's theme is that life is impersonal even in the face of heartbreak, frustration, and injustice.

One of the most prominent women playwrights is Lillian Hellman (1906–1984), whose first success came in 1935 with a production of *The Children's Hour,* in which a child destroys her teachers' lives by intimating that they are lesbians. With the success of *The Little Foxes* (1939), Hellman became recognized as one of America's leading playwrights.

THE LITTLE FOXES

Lillian Hellman

REGINA: (*laughs awkwardly*): Well. Here we are. It's been a long time. (*Horace smiles*) Five months. You know, Horace. I wanted to come and be with you in the hospital, but I didn't know where my duty was. Here, or with you. But you know how much I wanted to come.

HORACE: That's kind of you, Regina. There was no need to come.

Springer/Corbis-Bettmann

Figure 8.6

Tallulah Bankhead played Regina in the original 1939 stage production of Lillian Hellman's *The Little Foxes.*

Regina: Oh, but there was. Five months lying there all by yourself, no kinfolks, no friends. Don't try to tell me you didn't have a bad time of it.

Horace: I didn't have a bad time. (*As she shakes her head, he becomes insistent*) No, I didn't, Regina. Oh, at first when I—when I heard the news about myself—but after I got used to that, I liked it there.

Regina: You liked it? Isn't that strange. You liked it so well you didn't want to come home?

Horace: That's not the way to put it. (*Then, kindly, as he sees her turn her head away*) But there I was and I got kind of used to it, kind of to like lying there and thinking. I never had much time to think before. And time's become valuable to me.

Regina: It sounds almost like a holiday.

Horace: (*laughs*): It was, sort of. The first holiday I've had since I was a little kid.

Regina: And here I was thinking you were in pain and—

Horace (*quietly*): I was in pain.

Regina: And instead you were having a holiday! A holiday of thinking. Couldn't you have done that here?

Horace: I wanted to do it before I came here. I was thinking about us.

Regina: About us? About you and me? Thinking about you and me after all these years. You shall tell me everything you thought—someday.

Horace (*there is silence for a minute*): Regina. (*She turns to him*) Why did you send Zan to Baltimore?

Regina: Why? Because I wanted you home. You can't make anything suspicious out of that, can you?

Horace: I didn't mean to make anything suspicious about it. (*Hesitantly, taking her hand*) Zan said you wanted me to come home. I was so pleased at that and touched. It made me feel good.

Regina: (*taking away her hand*): Touched that I should want you home?

In the 1960s, with the development of Off-Off-Broadway, plays written by women were produced in greater number. In the past few decades, several women playwrights—including Marsha Norman, Beth Henley, and Wendy Wasserstein—have won Pulitzer Prizes. Shirley Lauro won critical acclaim for *A Piece of My Heart* in 1988. In addition to Henley's play winning the 1988

Michel Daniel

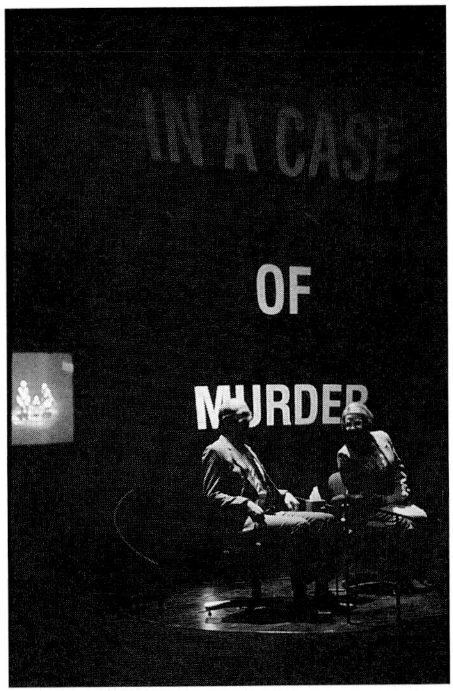

Figure 8.7

A scene from a 1995 production of the short play *Tone Clusters*, authored by Joyce Carol Oates and directed by Risa Brainin. Produced at the Guthrie Theater in Minneapolis, the play featured John Carroll Lynch as Frank and Suzanne Warman as Emily.

Pulitzer Prize, *Crimes of the Heart* also won the Drama Critics Circle Award for its tale of three sisters who still feel isolation and despair stemming from the suicide of their mother sixteen years earlier—when abandoned by her husband. Marsha Norman's Pulitzer Prize was awarded in 1983 for *'Night Mother,* and Wendy Wasserstein's, in 1989 for *The Heidi Chronicles.* In Norman's play, thirty-eight-year-old Jessie announces to her mother her intentions of committing suicide that evening. The ninety-minute play, timed by an onstage clock, leads relentlessly toward that end. In *The Heidi Chronicles,* Wasserstein portrays the past twenty years of the women's movement as seen in thirteen episodes from the life of title character Heidi Holland, an academic and "mildly" feminist art historian of the 1980s.

A number of American women writers have gained prominence for their plays in recent years, including Rita Dove for her verse drama *The Darker Face of Earth* (1993), Teresa Rebek for *The Family of Mann* (1994), and Paula Vogel for *Desdemona* (1994).

Women as Actors

During the Italian Renaissance, the Christian church still excluded women from the theatre, but they continued as strolling singers and dancers, sometimes appearing in short farces. Women of nobility also acted in all-female productions presented in their homes. A Roman named Flaminia, well established by 1565, is the first professional actress of whom there is record. An important *commedia dell'arte* actress was Vittoria Piisimi, who appeared with the Gelosi troupe. In 1562 she started her own *commedia* company, making her the first actress/manager of whom there is record. Her replacement was Isabella Andreini, who performed with the Gelosi troupe until she died in 1604 at age 42.

During the medieval period in France, women appeared in mystery plays. Usually these actresses had no speaking roles, yet there is record in 1468 of an eighteen-year-old female having memorized 2,300 lines to play St. Catherine. Then, in 1535, Françoise Beautier played the Virgin Mary. Ten years later Marie Farrit received an acting contract, making her France's first professional actress.

By Molière's time in France, women performed regularly onstage. The two best-known are actresses Madeleine Béjart, a tragedienne, and Armande Béjart (who married Molière).

The first English actress of whom we have record is Mrs. Coleman, who in 1656 played Ianthe in Sir William D'Avenant's production of John Webb's *The Siege of Rhodes.* Within the next few years came the first generation of great women actresses, including Nell Gwyn and Mary Betterton. In Germany, Caroline Neuber (1697–1760) acted in a variety of genres, although she was most successful in comedy. With her husband Johann, she formed what became the most successful traveling company in the country. And in America, the first actresses to be widely acclaimed were Charlotte Cushman (1816–1876) and Anna Cora Mowatt Ritchie (1819–1870). Trained for opera, Cushman, within a year of appearing on the stage, ruined her singing voice. She then became an actress, making her debut at age nineteen as Lady Macbeth at the Bowery Theatre in New York.

During the latter part of the nineteenth century and the early part of the twentieth, Minnie Maddern Fiske was one of America's leading actresses, as well as a playwright, manager, and producer. She also is noteworthy in that, almost single-handedly, she fought the Theatrical Syndicate, which sought to monopolize professional theatre throughout the United States.

During the 1930s the two preeminent actresses in American theatre were Katherine Cornell and Helen Hayes, often referred to as the first ladies of the American stage. Jessica Tandy was highly regarded for her work on the stage from the 1940s through the 1980s, with such plays as *A Streetcar Named Desire* (1948), *The Gin Run* (1977), and *Driving Miss Daisy* (1986); she won an Oscar for the 1989 film version of *Daisy.* Tandy worked in partnership with actor-husband Hume Cronyn in many productions. Prominent American stage actresses in recent years include Marsha Mason, Rita Moreno, Kathy Bates, Mary Alice, Mary Beth Hurt, Bernadette Peters, Pamela Reed, Glenn Close, Meryl Streep, and Swoosie Kurtz, many with film as well as stage successes.

Figure 8.8

A scene from the 1947 stage performance of Tennessee Williams's *A Streetcar Named Desire* with award-winning actor Jessica Tandy as a distraught Blanche, Edna Thomas as the woman with flowers, and Karl Malden as Mitch.

Ethnic and Minority Theatre in the United States

From the beginning, American theatre was influenced by European standards, with nearly all of the early actors and plays imported from England. To a lesser degree, other countries also contributed through traveling companies and stars. Yet for much of America's history, ethnic and minority theatre has existed along with the mainstream.

A combination of causes led to the establishment of ethnic theatre. First, it helped minorities retain their identities and cope with their separation from the language and culture of mainstream America. In many cases, minority theatres came into being to re-create reminders of homelands and cultures long left behind.

Ethnic theatre came to America from all around the globe. There was French theatre beginning in 1803, when the United States purchased Louisiana from France. Immigrants from Europe and Asia established theatres soon after their arrival. Mexicans who lived in land territories acquired by the United States made their drama part of the fabric of American theatre. At about the same time, German theatres were established in New York, New Orleans, and the Midwest. Chinese theatre began to appear in San Francisco, and a few decades later Japanese entertainers had established themselves in Seattle. The following is an excerpt from *Hogan's Goat,* a play about the immigrant experience.

HOGAN'S GOAT

William Alfred

From Act One, Scene 1

STANTON:

Are you the only exile of us all?
You slept your crossing through in a rosewood berth
With the swells a hundred feet below your portholes,
And ate off china on a linen cloth,
With the air around you fresh as the first of May.
I slept six deep in a bunk short as a coffin
Between a poisoned pup of a seasick boy
And a slaughtered pig of a snorer from Kildare,
Who wrestled elephants the wild nights through,
And sweated sour milk. I wolfed my meals,
Green water, and salt beef, and wooden biscuits,
On my hunkers like an ape, in a four-foot aisle
As choked as the one door of a burning school.
I crossed in mid-December: seven weeks
Of driving rain that kept the hatches battened
In a hold so low of beam a man my height
Could never lift his head. And I couldn't wash.
Water was low; the place was like an icehouse;
And girls were thick as field mice in a haystack
In the bunk across. I would have died of shame,
When I stood in the landing shed of this "promised land,"
As naked as the day I first saw light,
Defiled with my own waste like a dying cat,
And a lousy red beard on me like a tinker's,
While a bitch of a doctor, with his nails too long,
Dared tell me: "In Amurrica, we bathe!"
I'd have died with shame, had I sailed here to die.

I swallowed pride and rage, and made a vow
The time would come when I could spit both out
In the face of the likes of him. I made a vow
I'd fight my way to power if it killed me,
Not only for myself, but for our kind,
For the men behind me, laughing out of fear,
At their own shame as well as mine, for the women,
Behind the board partition, frightened dumb
With worry they'd be sent back home to starve
Because they'd dirty feet. I was born again.
It came to me as brutal as the cold
That makes us flinch the day the midwife takes
Our wet heels in her fist, and punches breath
Into our dangling carcasses: Get power!
Without it, there can be no decency,
No virtue and no grace. I have kept my vow.
The mayor's chair is mine but for the running.
Will you have me lose it for your convent scruples?

Ethnic Theatre as Protest

An important reason for the development of ethnic theatre was as a means of protest. Chinese-American playwright David Henry Hwang, says he wrote *M. Butterfly* in the late 1980s "as a plea to all sides to cut through our respective layers of cultural and sexual mis-perception, to deal with one another truthfully for our mutual good, from the common and equal ground we share as human beings."[2]

Ethnic and minority theatre allowed its participants to move beyond stereotyping and to establish their own theatres. In presenting or writing their own plays they could escape the stereotypical and degrading images offered by society in general.

The Influence of Minority Theatre

Minority theatre, in turn, had a great influence on mainstream America, not only in the theatre artists it created, but in bringing various cultures and issues to the attention of the American theatregoing public.

---

2 David Henry Hwang, "Afterword," *M. Butterfly* (New York: New American Library, 1989), p. 99.

In addition, the civil rights movement of the 1960s brought about an increase in political activism and ethnic and racial pride, beginning with African Americans but quickly embracing Hispanic Americans, Asian Americans, and Native Americans. From the 1960s on, there was an explosion of ethnic theatre into the mainstream.

> The black, the Indian, the Chicano, the Chinese and, in another area, the homosexual, had found their own lives reflected, if at all, only as stereotype, as comic caricature or simple villain. They were effectively excluded from national myths which turned on white supremacy. In the central plot of American history—that of the invention of a nation—they had been presented as either mere observers or dangerous impediments. The culture hero was on the whole Anglo-Saxon and male. . . .[3]

Native American Theatre

Native American drama is important not so much because of its effect on mainstream theatre, but rather because the dramatic activities of American Indians were widespread, including all the many tribes and nations on the North American continent.

There has been little Native American drama presented commercially because it is not the sort likely to succeed on a stage dominated by European or Western theatrical practice. Rather, Native American drama is tied more to storytelling, dancing, communal celebrations, and rites, often intended for participation by an entire group rather than for viewing by an audience.

Central to most American Indian rituals are two beliefs that "have few direct counterparts for Euro-Americans"—nonlinear time "that may be viewed cyclically from one perspective and eternally from another" and "the concept of a dimensionless sacred place, the center of the universe and the locative counterpart of the ever-present time." The concepts really are the same, "for each point in time or space is infinitely large, extending outward from the sacred event to include all creation, yet located around the event in a way that precisely fixes the position and assumes the security of all participants."[4]

The first collection of plays of Native American life written by a Native American, Hanay Geiogamah, was published in 1980. Geiogamah's work was first presented Off-Broadway by the Native American Theatre Ensemble, which he founded.

---

[3] C. W. E. Bigsby, *A Critical Introduction to Twentieth-Century American Drama* (New York: Cambridge University Press, 1985), p. 374.

[4] Jeffrey Huntsman, "Introduction," *New Native American Drama: Three Plays by Hanay Geigomah* (Norman, Okla.: University of Oklahoma Press, 1980), pp. 359–60.

Michael Daniel

Figure 8.9

Today's theatre experience includes non-Western dramas, such as the Guthrie Theatre's 1993 production of *Naga Mandala* by Indian playwright Girish Karnad. Pictured: Nirupama Nityanandan and Stan Egi.

Asian-American Theatre

In 1965, a number of actors of Chinese, Japanese, and Korean heritage met in Los Angeles to form the first Asian-American theatre group, the East West Players. They began by dramatizing the writings of such novelists as Yukio Mishima, and by performing mainstream works with Asian-American actors. Then, in 1973, a group including Frank Chin, Janis Chan, and Jeffrey Chin founded the Asian American Theatre Workshop in San Francisco. Here, Frank Chin's *Chickencoop Chinaman* was developed to become the first major play written by an Asian American.

Soon, other plays, such as Genny Lim's *Paper Angels*, gained widespread recognition. Increasingly, playwrights such as David Henry Hwang, Velina Hasu Houston, Elizabeth Wong, and Philip Gotanda are being produced for mainstream audiences. The most widely recognized is Hwang, whose first play—*FOB*—was first presented in his dormitory at Stanford University in 1979 and went on to be produced professionally in Connecticut and at Joseph Papp's Public Theatre in New York. His second work, *The Dance and the Railroad* (1981), was produced at the New Federal Theater. Subsequent works have been premiered by the New York Shakespeare Festival. He won a Tony for best play of 1988 for *M. Butterfly*, based on a true story in which a man, a French diplomat, has an ongoing affair with Song Liling, a beautiful Chinese diva, who—he finds out after twenty years—is really a spy as well as a *man*.

M. BUTTERFLY

David Henry Hwang

From Act Three, Scene One [in a courthouse]

JUDGE: Did Monsieur Gallimard know you were a man?

SONG: Well, he never saw me completely naked. Ever.

JUDGE: But surely, he must've . . . how can I put this?

SONG: Put it however you like. I'm not shy. He must've felt around?

JUDGE: Mmmm.

SONG: Not really. I did all the work. He just laid back. Of course we did enjoy more . . . complete union, and I suppose he *might* have wondered why I was always on my stomach, but . . . . But what you're thinking is, "Of course a wrist must've brushed . . . a hand hit . . . over twenty years!" Yeah. Well, Your Honor, it was my job to make him think I was a woman. And chew on this: it wasn't all that hard. See, my mother was a prostitute along the Bundt before the Revolution. And, uh, I think it's fair to say she learned a few things about Western men. So I borrowed her knowledge. In service to my country.

JUDGE: Would you care to enlighten the court with this secret knowledge? I'm sure we're all very curious.

SONG: I'm sure you are. (*Pause*) Okay, Rule One is: Men always believe what they want to hear. So a girl can tell the most obnoxious lies and the guys will believe them every time—"This is my first time"—"That's the biggest I've ever seen"—or *both*, which, if you really think about it, is not possible in a single lifetime. You've maybe heard those phrases a few times in your own life, yes, Your Honor?

JUDGE: It's not my life, Monsieur Song, which is on trial today.

SONG: Okay, okay, just trying to lighten up the proceedings. Tough room.

JUDGE: Go on

SONG: Rule Two: As soon as a Western man comes into contact with the East—he's already confused. The West has sort of an international rape mentality towards the East. Do you know rape mentality?

JUDGE: Give us your definition, please.

SONG: Basically, "Her mouth says no, but her eyes say yes."

The West thinks of itself as masculine—big guns, big industry, big money—so the East is feminine—weak, delicate, poor . . . but good at art, and full of inscrutable wisdom—the feminine mystique.

Her mouth says no, but her eyes say yes. The West believes the East, deep down, wants to be dominated—because a woman can't think for herself.

JUDGE: What does this have to do with my question?

SONG: You expect Oriental countries to submit to your guns, and you expect Oriental women to be submissive to your men. That's why you say they make the best wives.

JUDGE: But why would that make it possible for you to fool Monsieur Gallimard? Please—get to the point.

SONG: One, because when he finally met his fantasy woman, he wanted more than anything to believe that she was, in fact, a woman. And second, I am an Oriental. And being an Oriental, I could never be completely a man.

Pause.

JUDGE: Your armchair political theory is tenuous, Monsieur Song.

SONG: You think so? That's why you'll lose in all your dealings with the East.

JUDGE: Just answer my question: did he know you were a man?

Pause.

SONG: You know, Your Honor, I never asked.

An Overview of Jewish Theatre

In ancient times, Jewish religious leaders viewed theatre as immoral, in that it defied the biblical injunction against men dressing as women. Even so, Jews were influenced by classical Greek culture, and there is record of Jewish actors in the Roman Empire. In the second century A.D., the Jewish poet Ezekiel of Alexandria wrote, in imitation of Euripides, a play about the Exodus.

As occurred in Christianity, plays began to be inserted as questions and responses in the worship service. From this evolved Purim plays, depicting the Old Testament story of Esther and Haman. Other religious plays developed and gradually moved outside the synagogue. Yet Jewish theatre developed more slowly than other European theatre. First, Jews were forbidden to share in the neoclassic movements. Second, they had no real home to call their own. Third, Yiddish was not a uniform language, and many felt it was slang—unfit for more formal purposes, while Hebrew was considered suitable only for reading and study.

Yet, plays sometimes were written in Hebrew. In 1918 in Moscow, Nahum Zemach founded a professional Hebrew theatre. Called Habimah (The Stage), it became one of three studios associated with the Moscow Art Theatre under Stanislavski. Among its early productions were S. Anski's *The Dybbuk*, David Pinski's *The Eternal Jew*—based on a Talmudic legend, and H. Leivik's *The Golem*.

Yiddish Theatre

However, during the late nineteenth and early twentieth centuries, these plays—usually heavily moralistic and didactic—could not compete. The emerging Yiddish theatre appealed to the common person through popular art, including song and dance.

The beginnings of the modern Yiddish theatre generally are traced to an 1876 production in Romania, where Abraham Goldfaden founded the first Yiddish theatre company. Its premiere production, a two-act musical, was so successful that Goldfaden began writing other plays, little more than scenarios, presented much like *commedia dell'arte* productions. Altogether, he wrote about 400 of them, borrowing plots from many European dramatists.

The style included horseplay, burlesque, caricatures of various Jewish people, earthy jokes and buffoonery, and lilting tunes. The producer of the first Yiddish play in America was Boris Thomashefsky (1862 or 1864–1939). By 1917, there were four Yiddish theatres in Manhattan, four in Philadelphia, two in Brooklyn, and others in the East and Midwest.

The most prolific writers were Moyshe Hurwitz and Jacob Lateiner, whose musicals, farces, and melodramas had broad appeal. The writers borrowed heavily from other sources, sentimentalized, and took liberties with Jewish history.

In the 1890s Jacob Gordin introduced realism into Yiddish theatre. Opposed to improvisation, he wrote complete scripts, adapting many of the great European plays. A recurring theme in his work was the breakdown of the Jewish family due to stress caused by relocation to new surroundings.

Jewish actors, trained for the Russian stage, began working with writer Peretz (or Perez) Hirshbein to form the Hirshbein Troupe, with the purpose of producing plays of literary value. The group toured Europe, presenting plays by Sholem Asch, David Pinski, Sholem Aleichem, and Gordin. From this beginning came the Vilna Troupe (1916). Directed by David Herman, the company toured America and Europe, gaining high regard for its artistic quality. Its best-known work was S. Anski's *The Dybbuk* (1920).

One of the most instrumental in establishing Yiddish theatre in New York was Maurice Schwartz. He recruited well-known actors, including Jacob Ben-Ami, who had been associated with the Hirshbein Troupe. In addition to recognized classics and plays of literary merit, Schwartz produced typical Yiddish plays, using a broad style of acting.

Jewish Activist Theatre

During the Depression, a new sort of Jewish theatre emerged. The best-known group was Artef, a Yiddish acronym for Workers' Theater Group. The group was begun in 1926 to provide theatre classes to workers, and its objective, according to director Joseph Mestel, was to establish a theatre dedicated to left-wing ideology, yet rooted in the Jewish heritage.

Repertory companies played a significant role in Jewish theatre across the United States. The most visible and most important certainly was the Jewish Repertory Theatre, begun in 1974 as an Off-Off Broadway company.

Contemporary Jewish Drama

Jewish theatre of today is a combination of styles, including revivals of Jewish plays, new settings for examination of family values, nostalgia, the recasting of early Yiddish plays, and plays about the Holocaust. In recent years, there has been a blossoming of theatre companies across the United States and in Canada.

Successful in keeping alive the Jewish identity is Herb Gardner's *Conversations with my Father* (1994), a play whose central theme relates to coming to terms with one's identity. In the play, Eddie Ross (originally Itzik Roth) responds to anti-Semitism in Europe and New York City by changing his name and railing against Jews, all the while using a dialect full of Yiddish words and inflections. Conversely, his son Charlie, a grown man narrating the play, is struggling to connect to his own Jewishness, as well as with his father's.

CONVERSATIONS WITH MY FATHER

Herb Gardner
From Act I

EDDIE (*shouting*): Gloria! (*Remains with his back to Stroller, continues briskly cleaning glasses.*) Gloria, the kid! Change the kid! (*The Kid is instantly quieter, comforted by the sound of his father's voice even though he's shouting.*) Gloria, the kid! Time to change him! (*Then, louder.*) For another kid! (*Turns towards stairway.*) Gloria, why don't you *answer* me?!

GUSTA'S VOICE (*from upstairs, a strong Russian accent*): Because I only been Gloria two and a half weeks . . . and I was Gusta for thirty-eight years; I'm waiting to recognize.

EDDIE: I thought you liked the name.

GUSTA'S VOICE: I liked it till I heard it hollered. Meanwhile, your wife, Gloria, she's got a rusty sink to clean.

EDDIE: Hey, what about the *kid* here? I gotta get the bar open!

GUSTA'S VOICE (*graciously*): A shaynim dank, mit eyn toches ken men nit zayn oyf tsvey simches.

CHARLIE (*to Audience*): Roughly, that's "Thank you, but with one rear-end I can't go to two parties."

EDDIE: English! English! Say it in *English,* for Chrissakes!

GUSTA'S VOICE: You can't say it in English, Eddie, it don't do the job.

CHARLIE: She's right, of course, English don't do the job. Sure, you can say "Rise and shine!," but is that as good as "Shlof gicher, me darf der kishen," which means "Sleep faster, we need your pillow"? Does "You can't take it with you" serve the moment better than "Tachtrich macht me on keshenes," which means "They don't put pockets in shrouds"? Can there be a greater scoundrel than a paskudnyak, a more screwed-up life than one that is ongepatshket? Why go into battle with a punch, a jab, a sock and a swing when you could be armed with a klop, a frosk, a zetz and a chamalia? Can poor, undernourished English turn an answer into a question, a proposition into a conclusion, a sigh into an opera? No. No, it just don't do the job, Pop.

Hispanic-American Theatre

Spanish-speaking theatre was established in what would become the United States long before English-speaking theatre arrived. And although the first English settlers in America thought theatre at worst sinful and at best a waste of time, it was a big part of the culture of Hispanics.

The first recorded performance of a Spanish-language play occurred in a mission in 1567 near what would become Miami. Yet Spanish language plays became established early on only in the Southwest. The real history of Hispanic theatre began with improvised plays presented in 1598 by members of Juan de Oñate's expedition, which was on its way to New Mexico to establish a colony. The plays were presented near what is now El Paso, predating English performances by about a hundred years.

These first presentations sowed the seeds for further theatrical activity in the form of secular plays and religious folk drama. Much of early theatre comprises *pastorelas*—"shepherds' plays," presented during the Christmas season.

Professional Hispanic-American Theatre: The Beginnings

Professional theatre began in the early 1800s when Mexican and Spanish actors appeared in the port cities of California and northern Mexico. By 1850, troupes such as Gerardo López del Castillo's Compañía Española had established a theatrical circuit that ran from Mazatlán to San Francisco, including stops in San Diego and Los Angeles. The group also traveled inland, going as far east as Tucson. During the 1860s, the company became a resident theatre in San Francisco, presenting Spanish, Mexican, and Cuban melodramas. López del Castillo became president of the Junta Patriótica Méxicana de San Francisco, and his company gave benefit performances for Juarez' liberation forces, as well as for widows and orphans of the Franco-Mexican War. This set a precedent that has continued ever since—the use of theatre as a social and political force in the Hispanic community.

By the last decade of the century, Hispanic professional theatre was becoming established farther east, especially in Texas. With thousands of immigrants entering the United States as a result of the Mexican Revolution of 1917, there was a greater demand for theatrical entertainment in the Southwest and Midwest. By the 1920s virtually all cities in the Southwest were seeing Spanish-language performances, with actors and entertainers traveling well-established circuits.

In the last decade of the nineteenth century, theatre was becoming established in Tampa, Florida, catering to the wishes of immigrants who had entered the country due to the turmoil created by the Cuban War of Independence.

The first professional Hispanic company to be based in New York was *La Compañía del teatro español*, which produced a series of eight plays during the 1921–22 theatrical season.

The Development of Contemporary Hispanic-American Theatre

In 1965 Mexican-American Luis Valdez founded the Teatro Campesino (Farmworkers' Theatre) under the wing of César Chávez's farm labor union. Composed of striking farmworkers, the group did plays that could be presented for others in similar situations in almost any sort of location, in theatre buildings or fields.

In the 1970s Valdez was severely criticized for turning away from **agitprop** (propaganda in the form of drama designed to stir viewers to political action); yet, he realized "that to speak only to the politically committed leads, at best, to a revolt in which power changes hands, rather than to a revolution in which the system changes. To achieve the latter, he had

El Teatro Campesino

Figure 8.10

Luis Valdez.

to create a drama with which the lower-class *campesino* (farmworker) or descendant of *campesinos* could identify, and which the upper-class Anglo would strive to emulate."[5] This is what he did with *Zoot Suit,* which played in Los Angeles and later on Broadway before becoming a successful film. It was based on a murder case in which seventeen Mexican-American youths were convicted of murdering another young man, and on the "Zoot Suit Riots," in which a group of sailors attacked and stripped Hispanic men of their "zoot suits"—colorful suits with tight cuffs, pleats, and wide-legged trousers pegged at the ankles. The play's message was that the violence and convictions both occurred due to racial prejudice and the search for a scapegoat on whom to vent fears and frustrations resulting from U.S. involvement in World War II.

---

[5] Richard G. Scharine, *From Class to Caste in American Drama: Political and Social Themes Since the 1930s* (New York: Greenwood Press, 1991), pp. 188–89.

ZOOT SUIT

Luis Valdez
From Act II
Scene 7. Alice

ALICE: Henry, I just found out you did ninety days in solitary. I'm furious at the rest of the guys for keeping it from me. I talked to Warden Duffy, and he said you struck a guard. Did something happen I should know about? I wouldn't ask if it wasn't so important, but a clean record . . .(*HENRY rips up the letter he has been reading and scatters the others. Alarmed.*) Henry? (*HENRY pauses, his instant fury spent and under control HE sounds almost weary, but the anger is still there.*)

HENRY: You still don't understand, Alice.

ALICE: (*Softly, compassionate.*) But I do! I'm not accusing you of anything. I don't care what happened or why they sent you there. I'm sure you had your reasons. But you know the public is watching you.

HENRY: (*Frustrated, a deep question.*) Why do you do this, Alice?

ALICE: What?

HENRY: The appeal, the case, all the shit you do. You think the public gives a goddamn?

ALICE: (*With conviction.*) Yes! We are going to get you out of here, Henry Reyna. We are going to win!

HENRY: (*Probing.*) What if we lose?

ALICE: (*Surprised but moving on.*) We're not going to lose.

HENRY: (*Forcefully, insistent, meaning more than HE is saying.*) What if we do? What if we get another crooked judge, and he nixes the appeal?

ALICE: Then we'll appeal again. We'll take it to the Supreme Court. (*A forced laugh.*) Hell, we'll take it all the way to President Roosevelt!

HENRY: (*Backing her up—emotionally.*) What if we still lose?

ALICE: (*Bracing herself against his aggression.*) We can't.

HENRY: Why can't we?

ALICE: (*Giving a political response in spite of herself.*) Because we've got too much support. You should see the kinds of people responding to us. Unions, Mexicans, Negroes, Oakies. It's fantastic.

HENRY: (*Driving harder.*) Why can't we lose, Alice?

ALICE: I'm telling you.

HENRY: No, you're not.

ALICE: (*Starting to feel vulnerable.*) I don't know what to tell you.

HENRY: Yes, you do!

ALICE: (*Frightened.*) Henry . . . ?

HENRY: Tell me why we can't lose, Alice!

ALICE: (*Forced to fight back, with characteristic passion.*) Stop it, Henry! Please stop it! I won't have you treat me this way. I never have been able to accept one person pushing another around . . . pushing me around! Can't you see that's why I'm here? Because I can't stand it happening to you. Because I'm a Jew, goddammit! I have been there . . . I have been there! If you lose, I lose. (*Pause. The emotional tension is immense. ALICE fights to hold back tears. SHE turns away.*)

Although *Zoot Suit* was the first Mexican-American show to arrive on Broadway, soon other Latino plays followed. There also was an enormous increase in the number of Hispanic-American theatre companies and productions in New York. Some of the most successful have been the national touring El Teatro Repertorio Español; Miriam Colón's Puerto Rican Traveling Theatre in the Broadway district; and several Off-Broadway houses.

One of the most highly regarded playwrights is Carlos Morton, whose best-known play is *The Many Deaths of Danny Rosales* (1983), a quasi-documentary, based in part on the 1975 shooting death of Richard Morales, at the hands of the Castroville, Texas, sheriff. Other successful writers have been Puerto Ricans Miguel Piñero, winner of an Obie and New York Drama Critics Circle Award for *Short Eyes*, and Iván Acosta, author of *El Super.*

One of the most successful Cuban-American playwrights is María Irene Fornés, who first had work produced in the 1950s and received critical acclaim in 1977 for *Fefu and Her Friends.*

African-American Theatre

Pioneers

William Wells Brown (1815?–1884), an escaped slave, often is considered the first African-American dramatist, though his two plays, *Experience, or How to Give a Northern Man a Backbone* and *The Escape, or A Leap to Freedom*, both satires, were written to be read but not produced. Another early black American play was *The Brown Overcoat* by Victor Séjour.

While the mainstream American stage continued to portray blacks as shuffling and empty-headed, James (or perhaps John) Hewlett played leading roles in Shakespearean plays at the African Grove Theatre, thus becoming America's first black tragedian. The African Grove Theatre actually was but one in a series of "theatres" founded in Harlem by a man named Brown. His play, *The Drama of King Shotaway*, preceded those written by William Wells Brown, but in all probability was a mishmash of scenes.

Although Hewlett may have been the first black American tragedian, the one who gained renown in Shakespearean roles was Ira Aldridge (1807–1867). As a teenager he played Rollo in Richard Sheridan's *Pizarro*, presented privately with an all-black cast. However, he was prevented from playing major roles in mainstream theatres. Disillusioned, he moved to England and acted for years in the provinces. In 1852 he began touring Europe and Russia, where he was highly praised for his skills. Equally at home in comedy, he often played Mungo in Bickerstaffe's comic operetta *The Padlock*, and Othello on the same bill.

In 1897, black American actor/dramatist Bob Cole organized the first black stock company in New York, and a year later produced Willy Johnson's *A Trip to Coontown*. Jesse Shipp and Alex Rogers wrote a number of shows for the musical comedy team of Bert Williams and George Walker, who formed their own African-American production company. Williams and Walker's biggest hit was *Bandana Land* (1908), about a group of blacks who buy land in a white section of town, throw wild parties to disturb the whites, and then sell the land back at twice what they paid.

In 1921, Miller and Lyles, in collaboration with Noble Sissle and Eubie Blake, wrote *Shuffle Along*, which departed from the usual loosely structured revue in blending story and music. In the cast was dancer and singer Josephine Baker, who became a sensation in Paris in the late 1920s.

Williams was to appear in Abraham Erlanger's *Follies* in a role that Erlanger had written especially for him. However, the all-white cast objected to appearing onstage with a black man and threatened to strike. As a compromise, Williams was to appear onstage alone to deliver his monologues. "Williams' artistry did the rest. He literally stopped the show. And, of course, the cast very quickly changed its collective thinking and wanted Williams integrated into the show!"[6]

The Harlem Renaissance

The 1920s brought an interest in philosophy and the arts—music, painting, writing, and theatre—that was centered in Harlem. New theatres and theatrical companies sprang into existence both there and elsewhere. Emerging writers created new forms of drama by, for, and about African-American life.

---

[6] Loften Mitchell, *Voices of the Black Theatre* (Clifton, N.J.: James T. White & Company, 1975), p. 25.

African-American plays, many of them one-acts, were presented at the Harlem Experimental Theatre, the New Negro Theatre, Karamu House in Cleveland, and Langston Hughes's Harlem Suitcase Theatre.

With the establishment of black community theatres, dramatists were free to write different plays for black audiences than for white ones. When writing for whites, they had little choice but to imitate the white imitations of black life and gradually try to change the stereotypes. Now, however, they could write more true-to-life or even idealized characters for African-American audiences. A playwright (and poet) who wrote for the two different audiences was Langston Hughes, one of the most important black writers of the time. His first play was *The Gold Piece* (1921). Fourteen years later his *Mulatto* ran for more than a year on Broadway.

The Federal Negro Theatre presented plays at the Lafayette Theatre in Harlem under the direction of John Houseman, a Broadway producer and president of the Phoenix Theatre. The position had been offered to Rose McClendon, who turned it down in favor of performing. McClendon (1885–1936), who acted in the 1920s and 1930s was considered the foremost African-American actress of her generation, attracting critical attention playing opposite Charles Gilpin in a touring production of *Roseanne* (1924).

In 1950, actress and director Alice Childress wrote *Florence* as a result of what she saw as "Mama" stereotypes for black women. She often is credited with opening the New York stage to black women with *Gold Through the Trees* (1952). This was the first play by a black woman to be produced Off-Broadway, and none yet had appeared on Broadway.

There was generally little work for black actors in American theatre. The bleak outlook was aided somewhat by the Committee for the Negro Arts, begun in the latter part of 1951 to support Harlem theatres, and the Black Theatre Alliance, begun in 1971. These groups were responsible for a number of productions.

The most important play to change the scope of African-American theatre was Lorraine Hansberry's *A Raisin in the Sun* (1958) advancing a move toward realism in depicting black Americans. (See Color Gallery Plates 13–16.)

Ossie Davis, an alumnus of the Negro Art Theatre and the Rose McClendon Players, wrote *Purlie Victorious*, which opened on Broadway in 1961 with Davis and his actress wife, Ruby Dee, thus becoming the first new black professional production of the decade. The play ridicules all the usual stereotypes of southern blacks *and* whites.

Langston Hughes's *Tambourines to Glory* (1963) is a morality play about two women attempting to establish a storefront church in Harlem. They are assisted and finally controlled by the devil. In the same year, Adrienne Kennedy's *Funnyhouse of a Negro*—a surrealistic, symbolic play about a mulatto's hatred for her black father—opened Off-Broadway to generally good reviews. Since then Kennedy has written a number of other plays, such as *A Rat's Mass*, somewhat similar in style in that it is poetic, mythological, and highly personalized.

Civil Rights

The civil rights movement in the United States was beginning to have a great effect on black American theatre as evidenced by LeRoi Jones's *Dutchman*, which received an Obie Award, and James Baldwin's *Blues for Mr. Charlie.* Such plays as this set the standard in the 1960s for militant protests against oppression. Baldwin's *Blues for Mr. Charlie* is about an angry young black man—Richard Henry—who returns home to the deep South after drugs have ended his musical career. He is murdered by a white man, who is then acquitted.

Soon LeRoi Jones, who changed his name to the Muslim name Amiri Baraka, received funds from an antipoverty program to help establish his Black Arts Theatre in Harlem, which produced a number of his plays.

During the 1960s and 1970s as the Black Theatre Movement took hold, more and more African Americans became involved Off-Broadway. The Negro Ensemble Company was formed in 1967 by a group of theatre artists who had worked together in *Day of Absence* and *Happy Ending*, both of which satirized black-white relationships.

The NEC also staged Charles Fuller's *A Soldier's Play*, beginning in late 1981. Fuller was awarded a Pulitzer Prize for the play, thus becoming only the second African American to be so honored. *A Soldier's Play* is about a black captain's investigation of a black sergeant's murder on a Louisiana army base during the Second World War and explores the theme of racism and hatred in the military, but also questions how blacks should conduct themselves in a predominantly white society.

A SOLDIER'S PLAY

Charles Fuller

From Act I

DAVENPORT: Call me Davenport—Captain, United States Army, attached to the 343rd Military Police Corps Unit, Fort Neal, Louisiana. I'm a lawyer the segregated Armed Services couldn't find a place for. My job in this war? Policing colored troops. (*slight pause*) One morning during mid-April 1944, a colored tech/sergeant, Vernon C. Waters, assigned to the 221st Chemical Smoke Generating Company, stationed here before transfer to Europe, was brutally shot to death in a wooded section off the New Post Road and the junction of Highway 51—just two hundred yards from the colored N.C.O. club—by a person or persons unknown. (*pauses a little*) Naturally, the unofficial consensus was the local Ku Klux Klan, and for that reason,

I was told at the time, Colonel Barton Nivens ordered the Military Police to surround the enlisted men's quarters—then instructed all his company commanders to initiate a thorough search of all personal property for unauthorized knives, guns—weapons of any kind. (*slight pause*) You see, ninety percent of the Colonel's command—all of the enlisted men stationed here are Negroes, and the Colonel felt—and I suppose justly—that once word of the Sergeant's death spread among his troops, there might be some retaliation against the white citizens of Tynin. (*shrugs*) What he did worked—there was no retaliation, and no racial incidents. (*pause*) The week after the killing took place, several correspondents from the Negro press wrote lead articles about it. But the headlines faded—(*smiles*) The NAACP got me involved in this. Rumor has it, Thurgood Marshall ordered an immediate investigation of the killing, and the army, pressured by Secretary of War Stimson, rather randomly ordered Colonel Nivens to initiate a preliminary inquiry into the Sergeant's death. Now, the Colonel didn't want to rehash the murder, but he complied with the army's order by instructing Provost Marshal, my C.O., Major Hines, to conduct a few question-and-answer sessions among the men of Sergeant Waters's platoon and file a report. The matter was to be given the lowest priority. (*pause*) The case was mine, five minutes later. It was four to five weeks after his death—the month of May. (*He pauses as the light builds in Captain Taylor's office. Taylor is facing Davenport, expressionless. Davenport is a bit puzzled.*) Captain?

TAYLOR: Forgive me for occasionally staring, Davenport, you're the first colored officer I've ever met. I'd heard you had arrived a month ago, and you're a bit startling. (*quickly*) I mean you no offense. (*Starts back to his desk and sits on the edge of it, as Davenport starts into the office a bit cautiously*) We'll be getting some of you as replacements, but we don't expect them until next month. Sit down, Davenport. (*Davenport sits.*) You came out of Fort Benning in '43?

DAVENPORT: Yes.

TAYLOR: And they assigned a lawyer to the Military Police? I'm Infantry and I've been with the Engineers, Field Artillery, and Signal Corps—this is some army. Where'd you graduate law school?

DAVENPORT: Howard University.

TAYLOR: Your daddy a rich minister or something? (***Davenport** shakes his head no.*) I graduated the Point—(*pause*) We didn't have any Negroes at the Point. I never saw a Negro until I was twelve or thirteen.

Paul Penders

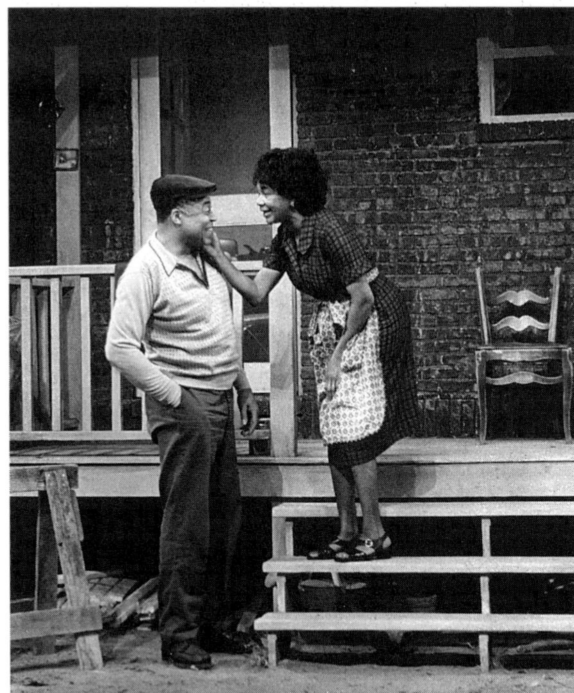

Figure 8.11

James Earl Jones and Mary Alice appeared as Rose and Troy Maxson in the 1984 Yale Repertory Theatre production of August Wilson's *Fences*. Jones won a Tony Award in 1991 for his portrayal of Troy Maxson on Broadway.

Also in the 1960s and 1970s there was a move away from Broadway toward professional, nonprofit theatres throughout the United States. Now most of the plays eventually seen on Broadway are developed in these theatres, which work with many black writers. An example is George C. Wolfe, whose play, *The Colored Museum,* originated at Crossroads Theatre Company in New Jersey. Wolfe also is important as a director of such shows as Tony Kushner's *Angels in America* and Smith's *Twilight: Los Angeles.*

August Wilson, whose work includes *Joe Turner's Come and Gone,* also was first produced outside New York. His plays were given staged readings at the National Playwrights Conference of the Eugene O'Neill Theater Center in Waterford, Connecticut, before having full productions at the Yale Repertory Theatre.

The man responsible for first recognizing Wilson's potential was Lloyd Richards, who had directed *A Raisin in the Sun.* From there "Richards had become one of the most important figures in American theatre, as Artistic Director of the Playwrights Conference and of the Yale Repertory Theater, and Dean of the Yale Drama School."[7] He worked with such playwrights as Lee Blessing, John Guare, Christopher Durang, Wendy Wasserstein, Lanford Wilson, and David Henry Hwang.

In 1974, Joseph A. Walker's *The River,* produced by the Negro Ensemble Company, won a Tony Award for best play, and *Raisin,* based on *A Raisin in the Sun,* was named best musical. The following year *The Wiz,* a black musical version of *The Wizard of Oz,* won several Tonys. In the 1980s, a number of musicals by and/or about African Americans appeared on Broadway. They included *Dreamgirls and the Tap Dance Kid.*

Off-Broadway had notable successes with shows by and/or about blacks through the 1980s. Plays were in constant development in minority-oriented institutional theatres such as The Negro Ensemble Company and AMAS, a multiracial theatre founded in 1969 by black artist Rosetta le Noire. AMAS presented Vy Higginson's *Mama, I Want to Sing,* which later moved Off-Broadway.

Gay and Lesbian Theatre

Two events in the late 1960s led to a proliferation and widespread acceptance of gay drama and performance pieces. The first was the Stonewall riots, in which gays rebelled against the police raid on the Stonewall, a bar in New York's Greenwich Village. This is considered a major turning point in the gay rights movement. The second event was the production of Mart Crowley's *Boys in the Band,* the first highly successful gay play to appear before mainstream audiences. A revival of the play opened Off-Broadway in 1996.

Although there were gay plays (male and female) and gay characters in drama well before this time, as of the 1970s many more now began to appear onstage and in print, most by gay men. In his 1978 anthology, *Gay Plays: The First Collection,* William M. Hoffman attributed the dearth of lesbian plays in part to the fact that until well into the twentieth century only a small percentage of playwrights were women.

---

[7] Holly Hill, "Black Theatre into the Mainstream," in Bruce King, ed., *Contemporary American Theatre* (New York: St. Martin's Press, 1991), p. 88.

Beginnings

The first major gay character presented on stage, so far as we know, was in Christopher Marlowe's *Edward II* (1591), in which Edward is enamored of Piers Gaveston. In 1895 Alphonse Daudet and Adolph Belot's *Sappho*—a play about the lesbian poet—was presented in New York, apparently without any objection. However, a revival of the same play was closed down five years later.

In England, a quarter of a century later, *The Prisoners of War* by J. R. Ackerley somehow escaped the Lord Chamberlain's censorship to become the first twentieth-century play dealing with homosexual desire to be presented either in London or New York. It ran for only twenty-six performances but was successfully revived in 1993. Set during World War I, it portrays British and Canadian prisoners of war interned in Switzerland due to severe injuries. The plot concerns Captain James Conrad's unrequited love for the young Lieutenant Grayle. It differs from many later plays in that Conrad is unashamed of his feelings. "I know all my weaknesses," he says, "and I cherish them. I value them more than my strength."

When homosexuality was treated onstage, most often the playwright gave a negative view of gay men and women, portraying them as having empty, one-dimensional lives. Often, they were shown as pitiable characters who were weak and ineffective. Generally, playwrights portrayed gay men as effeminate and simpering. These dramatists, writing from a heterosexual point of view, saw homosexuality as a deviation from the norm.

The tendency in plays and in society in general was to disparage minorities, including homosexuals. Even homosexual playwrights, such as William Inge, portrayed gays in a negative light. *Where's Daddy?* (1966) takes the Freudian viewpoint that homosexuals are in an arrested stage of development. Thus, homosexuality was being viewed not as immoral, but rather as a psychological problem. This attitude can be seen in plays such as Peter Shaffer's *Five Finger Exercise* (1958) and *Equus* (1973). In the former, the central character Clive has a gruff, unyielding father and an overaffectionate mother (a Freudian stereotype for the breeding of homosexuality in a child), while in the latter a seventeen-year-old boy has blinded six horses after they have witnessed his unsuccessful attempts at having sex with the stable owner's daughter.

Gay characters, however, were appearing more and more often in contemporary plays, despite the fact that until 1967 New York state law still outlawed the presentation of homosexuality onstage. Perhaps much of the credit for changing this can be attributed to Tennessee Williams. Although he rarely openly dealt with homosexual characters or situations, he did present a somewhat sympathetic view of homosexuality in one of Blanche's speeches in *A Streetcar Named Desire* (1947).

In 1967, Britain decriminalized homosexual acts by consenting adults, leading to more freedom in the treatment of homosexuality in plays. Soon afterward, a number of gay theatre companies organized. The most important was the Gay Sweatshop, led by Drew Griffiths and Gerald Chapman.

Gay Theatre Off-Broadway

The Off-Broadway movement began with poetry readings and performances of scenes. Joe Cino's Caffe Cino, which opened in 1958, quickly became the most important theatre for gay plays. The Caffe Cino also nurtured a group of young, untried playwrights, such as Doric Wilson, H. M. Koutoukas, Lanford Wilson, and Robert Patrick, who wrote specifically gay plays. One of the most significant was Wilson's *The Madness of Lady Bright* (1964), which is about an aging drag queen who gradually goes to pieces alone in his room. With 164 performances, it was one of Off-Broadway's first big hits. Also significant was Robert Patrick's *The Haunted Host* (1964), about a writer exercising the ghost of an unhappy affair.

Even though both these plays deal with self-hatred, as does *The Boys in the Band*, the latter often is cited as traitorous to the gay movement, perhaps because it was viewed by heterosexual audiences, whereas Wilson's and Patrick's plays were not.

Soon other Off-Broadway theatres came into existence. One was the Judson Poets Theater, run by Al Carmines. *Home Movies*, the work of lesbian writer Rosalyn Drexler, was presented there in 1964. Another Off-Broadway theatre that did gay plays was Ellen Stewart's La Mama Experimental Theater Club. The Glines, a theatre that remained active for six years, produced a number of original scripts, such as *Last Summer at Bluefish Cove* by Jane Chambers.

Chambers probably is the best-known lesbian playwright of the 1970s. Whereas other lesbians most often wrote experimental plays, Chambers's work was naturalistic. In *A Late Snow*, she presents believable and intelligent women snowbound in an isolated mountain cabin. The play centers on Ellie, who is there with her first, last, current, and future lovers. While working through their relationships, the women realize the importance of forgiving and starting over.

A LATE SNOW

Jane Chambers
From Act II

PAT: You never faced the bills together, you never faced joblessness together, you never built a house together, a life together. You never faced death together. It wasn't real. We were real.

ELLIE: We didn't work.

PAT: Why? I don't know why. I love you.

ELLIE: You don't love you.

PAT: All right. I never wanted to be a woman. It's a crappy thing to be. You can't do anything! I saw my father raking in the money, playing big business, flying to Europe, to the Caribbean, buying booze and women in every part of the globe while my mother ran the diaper brigade for eight kids. She never got farther than the corner A&P. Her conversation was limited to baby talk and what she heard on the radio. My father met Al Capone—met him! While my mother was scrubbing underwear on a washboard. Here's your choice, kiddies. Which one would you rather be?

ELLIE: Your father was a crook. What's good about that?

PAT: Is a crook. A successful one. The main man in Boston. My mother's dead of a heart attack.

ELLIE: I didn't know.

PAT: Last year.

ELLIE: I didn't know.

PAT: It doesn't matter. She's been dead for forty years. We finally buried her. But he goes on. And so do I. And I don't know why anymore. . . . Give us a chance, Ellie.

ELLIE: It's too late.

PAT: Can't you remember how it was? We built a home together: we made love on that beach at midnight and sailed that broken-down boat under the stars until dawn. We were safe from the world.

ELLIE: For a while.

PAT: Then you started teaching. You were gone so much, seeing new people. That's why I went out with other women, Ellie. To make you know how much you loved me.

ELLIE: The wind chimes stopped. And we didn't know how to make it work. Too much has happened. We can't go back.

PAT: Let me come home, Ellie.

ELLIE: I'm sorry. This isn't your home anymore.

Homosexuality in Mainstream Drama

Soon gay theatre was being produced not only in New York, but in cities across the country. Among the first mainstream successes that were about gays or had gay characters were James Kirkwood and Nicholas Dante's *A Chorus Line* and David Rabe's *Streamers.*

Often, mainstream plays have a theme of reconnecting with family. In Lanford Wilson's *The Fifth of July* (1978), Kenny and Jed, who are lovers, are completely accepted by family and friends. Another gay writer who appeals to the mainstream is Terrence McNally, who has written both gay and nongay plays, such as *The Lisbon Traviata, Frankie and Johnny in the Clair de Lune,* and the more recent *Love! Valour! Compassion!*

It was not until the end of the 1970s, however, that gay theatre really came into its own. The two men responsible for reaching a universal audience with gay material were Harvey Fierstein and Martin Sherman, each influential in a different way. Fierstein succeeded with his three one-act plays *The International Stud* (1978), *Fugue in a Nursery* (1979), and *Widows and Children First!* (1979). These were combined to make up *Torch Song Trilogy* (1981), which went from Off-Off-Broaday to Off-Broadway to Broadway to win the 1983 Tony Award for best play. Sherman caught the public's attention with *Bent*—the first commercial production to focus on the persecution of gays.

A major leap forward in gay theatre was taken with the production of Tony Kushner's 1993 Tony Award–winning epic drama series *Angels in America: A Gay Fantasia on National Themes.* According to drama critic John M. Clum, *Angels in America,* a drama about the gay community and public policy in the age of AIDS, marks a turning point in the history of gay drama, in the history of American drama, and in American literary culture as well. *Angels in America* is the only play that has won two Tonys, one for *Part I: The Millennium Approaches* and one for *Part II: Perestroika.* (See Color Gallery Plates 19–21 for scenes of *Angels in America.*)

Within the last two decades of the twentieth century, a largely gay-written type of drama has dealt with AIDS. Among the best-known plays of this type are Larry Kramer's *The Normal Heart* and William Hoffman's *As Is.* Lesbian writer Paula Vogel's *The Baltimore Waltz,* which never specifically mentions AIDS, is one of the most successful. The plot concerns an elementary school teacher, Anna, who tours Europe (in her imagination) with her brother while suffering "Acquired Toilet Disease." The travels end in a Baltimore hospital where her brother dies.

In *Sharing the Delirium: Second Generation AIDS Plays and Performances,* Therese Jones distinguishes between early AIDS plays and those written more recently. Those of the first generation, she feels, are more traditional and sentimental. "Assimilationist in aim . . . they are, above all, poignant expressions of loss." She says that in the newer works "multiplicitious comedies, multimedia performances, and revisioned folk dramas defiantly postulate an alternative discourse which opposes hierarchical structures, asserts subjectivity, and challenges cultural suppression of sexuality. . . . Unlike first generation plays, humor is not incidental but essential in second generation theatre, an entire spectrum of comedic drama: satire, farce, romance, slapstick, and burlesque."[8]

---

[8] Therese Jones, "Introduction," *Sharing the Delirium: Second Generation AIDS Plays and Performances* (Portsmouth, N.H.: Heinemann, 1994), pp. x–xi.

The Multimedia Approach to Theatre

Theatre never has been a pure art form. From the beginnings, it incorporated music and dance and eventually choral readings and instrumental music. Later came recorded sounds.

Influences from Other Forms

As you have learned already, the immediate presence of performer and audience member affects both. According to critic Eric Bentley, "In the movie theatre, we can watch a story and we can admire many things that actors do, but we cannot be caught up in a flow of living feeling that passes from actor to the audience and back again to the actor."[9]

Yet for today's audiences a film, a videotape, or a TV show has advantages that live theatre does not. It can appear more realistic. A setting for a TV show can more closely resemble a real room than a theatre setting can (even though the room may be constructed inside a large studio). Film or TV can take the spectator inside or outside or to far-off locations instantaneously.

Multimedia Design

New techniques are developing day-by-day. Starting in the 1960s, theatre designers devised sets that raced in on grooves on the stage floor, twirled around a time or two perhaps and stopped, providing almost a show in itself. Around the same time, closed-circuit television images appeared on various screens around or on the stage. The term "live" theatre took on new meaning, with special or multimedia effects often becoming an integral part of the drama itself.

Recent innovations now appear nearly simultaneously with the technology that allows their creation. Performances include such devices as video-conferencing and rear screen projections of pages from the World Wide Web.

For instance, a 1995 revival of *Red Horse Animation* by the avant-garde theatre company Mabou Mimes, directed by Lee Breuer and designed by Karen TenEyck, presented digitalized photographs (from the World Wide Web) projected one after another on a scrim at the rear of the stage. Critic Chris Haines comments, "As an interactive technology [in the Mabou Mimes production], the Web-page backdrop functions as a breathing set piece that changes and responds to the actors' movements, manipulated by a technician backstage, who will determine the pace of the 'virtual set changes' with the click of a mouse."[10]

---

9 Eric Bentley, *The Theatre of Commitment and Other Essays* (New York: Atheneum. 1967), pp. 59–60.

10 Chris Haines, "Mabou Mimes Lives on in Cyberspace," *American Theatre* (January 1996), pp. 64–65.

Figure 8.12

A scene from the Steppenwolf Theatre Company (Chicago) world premiere production of *Libra*, from the novel by Don DeLillo, adapted and directed by founding ensemble member John Malkovich. This multimedia production featured Alexis Arquette as Lee Harvey Oswald, shown here. Projection designer John Boesche used the rear projection screen on the stage to display images from thirty computer-controlled slide projectors and three video projectors. Nine additional video monitors were mounted on a downstage truss that could be flown in to any height on the set.

Another instance of complex multimedia usage occurred at the 1996 American Musical Theatre Festival (AMTF), where the purpose was to take "a proactive stance against the 'technophobia' that can pervade the theatre community."[11] One of the goals was to attract younger audiences—the same sort who most likely watch television for hours or sit in front of a computer.

Recent approaches to multimedia entertainment allow these same viewers to form interactive links with performers. An example is a New York performance by the theatre group Ladysmith Black Mambazo and the "Rainbow Connection," an outreach program of the AMTF:

> Ladysmith's founder and director Joseph Shabalala appeared on a large screen, where he could interact with performers on the stage, answer questions from the student audience, and sing along with children in a Spanish-language elementary school in Chicago. Dancers from the Rainbow Connection performed live on stage in front of the screen. When the Chicago students were projected onto the screen singing Shabalala's "Nomathemba" (Zulu for "hope"), the Rainbow Connection performed a simultaneous dance routine. Seeing the dancers on their own monitor, the children in Chicago imitated them in an impromptu cross-continental call and response.[12]

Many of the technologies now in use have been available for years. A significant reason for increased usage of such devices as closed-circuit television, video, film, laser, and other forms of screen projection, is cost. It is much less expensive to project images of settings than to build the settings by conventional means.

Actually, screen projections have been used since the 1920s by such people as Erwin Piscator of Germany and Vsevolod Meyerhold of Russia. The U.S. Federal Theatre Project of the 1930s is well-known for its documentary film/theatre series *Living Newspapers.* Tennessee Williams wrote directions for using slide projections in the script for *The Glass Menagerie.*

One of the pioneers of multimedia stage settings is designer Josef Svoboda, who was born in Czechoslovakia, trained as an architect, and later appointed head designer at the National Theatre in Prague. With his designs, largely metaphoric rather than realistic, he seeks to integrate all the technical elements into a changing and organic component of a production. One of his goals is to point up and/or deemphasize scenic elements as is done in film.

---

11 Chris Haines, "Erasing the Distance," *American Theatre* (July/August 1996), p. 60.
12 Haines, p. 60.

Trends in Multimedia Performances

Part of the movement toward multimedia theatrical events can be attributed to the happenings of the 1960s and to performance art of the 1970s. Happenings combined such art forms as film, painting, and theatre, coming together in an unplanned and often unrelated format. One of the early advocates of the form was John Cage, who wanted each person at his happenings to be aware of what was occurring and judge it independently. Later, more groundwork was laid; outlines were prepared.

An outgrowth of the happening is performance art. Performance art with the integration of multimedia technology has enhanced storytelling. Today, performance artists are no longer limited to the traditional Eurocentric linear storyline, but now can experiment with expressing ideas and themes in a nonlinear, collage-like strategy with the use of multimedia approaches—video, laser technology, and so on.

One of those responsible for a multimedia approach to performance art was Robert Wilson, an American director with training in both architecture and painting. In such work as *A Letter to Queen Victoria* (1974) and *Einstein on the Beach* (1976), Wilson collaborated with Christopher Knowles, an autistic adolescent, to create Knowles's atypical manner of patterning perceptions. The resulting work, lacking plot and conventional characters, encompassed a stream of visual and auditory images, often involving massive scenic and lighting effects presented in slow motion.

In recent years the trend has been away from the purely and essentially visual to performance pieces that may or may not be fully planned, but most often involve a single artist who may combine such performance areas as acting, oral interpretation, pantomime and dance, together with paintings rapidly changing visual and sound effects using various electronic media.

The performers, more often than not appearing solo, may point up particular themes or social problems. A man who has attracted attention in recent years is Guillermo Gómez-Peña with such works as *New World Border* and *The Temple of Confessions.* In the latter, according to Scott T. Cummings, a "blood-red gallery houses a temple adorned with artifacts, icons, trinkets, memorabilia, printed texts, music, and the recorded voices of previous visitors. . . . At either end of the gallery two 'techno-confessionals' sit like plexiglass altar-booths. . . . The temple-keepers encourage visitors to kneel on the prayer bench, don a pair of headphones, and speak into the microphone, which gives them a private, direct connection to the headphoned priest in the booth."[13]

With increased use of digitized images and computer technology, multimedia presentations in today's theatre are icons of our fast-evolving world.

---

[13] Scott T. Cummings, "Guillermo Gómez-Peña: True Confessions of a Techno-Aztec Performance Artist." *American Theatre* (November 1994), p. 52.

Chapter Nine

Dramatic Structure

Like all art, theatre attempts to present truth as the artists see it, yet truth is elusive and subjective. The playwright, the director, the actors, and the designers collaborate in communicating their own form of reality through dramatic structure and style. As Eric Bentley said: "Would art exist at all if men did not desire to live twice? You have your life; and on the stage you have it again."[1]

The Story Play

When we think of a story, we think of being entertained. Both in theatre and in fiction, stories involve people in situations with which we can identify. The story play is an attempt to "make things right"—to re-create a balance in life. As theatre critic John Gassner says:

> The dramatic approach to reality is, to begin with, a view of life as a condition of disequilibrium, a state of crisis, conflict and change; and dramatic vision encompasses movement toward some new equilibrium, however temporary or tentative, or movement toward a reconciliation that makes survival or sanity possible.[2]

Throughout history the story play, sometimes called the **cause-to-effect play,** has been written and produced more than any other type.

A story play has a plot—a type of structure—that relies on conflict. Yet neither the plot nor the structure itself is the story. The story is much more inclusive, encompassing everything that has happened in the world (or universe) of the play before, during, and after the events of the plot. We know, for instance, that these events spring from the same location, just as a limb grows from a tree. However, the tree is much more than just one of its limbs. We know, for example, that Mary, the mother in O'Neill's *Long Day's Journey into Night,* had a long history of drug abuse caused by a quack physician's prescribing morphine, and that this abuse started long before the action of the play opens. We know that James Tyrone, the father, is a talented actor who for years has been caught up in acting a role in a second-rate play, and that no one has been willing to cast him in any other role. These are "realities" of the story and have a direct bearing on the plot. Yet, regardless of how much they

---

[1] Eric Bentley, *The Life of the Drama* (New York: Atheneum, 1946), p. 9.

[2] John Gassner, "The Dramatic Vision," in *Dramatic Soundings, Evaluations and Retractions Culled from 30 Years of Dramatic Criticism* (New York: Crown Publishers, Inc., 1968), p. 109. Reprinted from *Impromptu,* 1961.

influence the *course* of the action, they are not *part* of the action. A plot is not an isolated entity. It exists in the universe in which the play exists, just as the past and the political, social, and cultural atmospheres of our own world affect us. Although they are not actually part of our actions, they often determine our responses.

Frame of Reference

A play cannot exist as an isolated entity that springs into existence out of nothingness. And when a story play ends, the characters and the setting—in our imaginations, at least—don't suddenly fade into wisps of trailing fog.

There is a framework that prescribes all the conditions of the world and universe (the aforementioned branch and tree) in which the play exists. Most of these conditions are never mentioned because they don't directly affect the action. The audience assumes, when given certain conditions, that others are in effect. If the setting is a typical middle-class home in Pittsburgh and the

Figure 9.1

A scene from *A Thurber Carnival,* a production of the Tuscarawas County Little Theatre (Ohio). James Thurber's work is made up of a series of humorous sketches, which provides unity, while a *story play* is unified around a single plot.

time is the present, the audience can assume that everything else about the world/universe of the play is typical of the world/universe in which we all live.

If the framework is alien, however, more has to be explained. If it takes place in a different culture, a distant time, or in an entirely different world, the playwright has to make sure the audience knows everything about that "universe" that has bearing on the action.

Imagine a scene such as this:

CHILD: Tell me a story, Dad. You promised.

DAD: All right, but then you have to go to sleep.

CHILD: Uh huh.

DAD: Once upon a time in a far-off kingdom lived a handsome prince who decided to seek a bride. In order to find the fairest young woman in the land, ...

Children have no trouble accepting a time and place where a handsome prince decides to invite all the young women of the kingdom to his palace. However, once the disbelief is suspended, the conditions cannot change:

DAD: . . . to find the fairest young woman in the land, he decided to hold a big party at this disco in downtown Philadelphia!

CHILD: No, Daddy! No, that's not the way the story goes. He decided to hold a ball. Don't you know what a ball is?

DAD: Something you shoot baskets with?

CHILD: Daddyyyyy! I want to hear the story about how the prince invited everyone to the ball and how poor Cinderella was treated so mean by her stepsisters and—

Once a framework is established—no matter how magical or extraordinary—a playwright cannot change it and hope to keep an audience's attention. From then on, a play deals with a specific action or actions, a specific time or times, and a specific place or places, all of which remain constant within this absolute framework. The play most often answers certain questions. The answers also must remain constant for the audience to continue to immerse themselves in the universe of the play. The questions are: *What* is happening? *When* is it happening? *Where* is it happening?

This exposition, or background necessary to understanding the play, comes largely through the dialogue. Other ways are through sets, lighting, costuming, and, possibly, makeup (see Chapter 15). However, the exposition should not intrude upon the progress of the play. The audience should receive necessary information without being aware that they are receiving it; it should seem a natural part of the presentation. For instance:

THE IMPORTANCE OF BEING EARNEST

Oscar Wilde
From Act I

ALGERNON: How are you, my dear Earnest? What brings you up to town?

JACK: Oh, pleasure, pleasure! What else should bring one anywhere? Eating as usual, I see, Algy!

ALGERNON: *(Stiffly)* I believe it is customary in good society to take some slight refreshment at five o'clock. Where have you been since last Thursday?

JACK: *(sitting down on the sofa)* In the country.

ALGERNON: What on earth do you do there?

JACK: *(pulling off his gloves)* When one is in town one amuses oneself. When one is in the country one amuses other people. It is excessively boring.

ALGERNON: And who are the people you amuse?

JACK: *(airily)* Oh, neighbours, neighbours.

ALGERNON: Got nice neighbours in your part of Shropshire?

JACK: Perfectly horrid! Never speak to them.

ALGERNON: How immensely you must amuse them! *(Goes over and takes a sandwich)* By the way, Shropshire is your county, is it not?

JACK: Eh? Shropshire? Yes, of course. Hallo! Why all these cups? Why cucumber sandwiches? Why such reckless extravagance in one so young? Who is coming to tea?

ALGERNON: Oh! merely Aunt Augusta and Gwendolen.

JACK: How perfectly delightful!

ALGERNON: Yes, that is all very well; but I am afraid Aunt Augusta won't quite approve of your being here.

JACK: May I ask why?

ALGERNON: My dear fellow, the way you flirt with Gwendolen is perfectly disgraceful. It is almost as bad as the way Gwendolen flirts with you.

JACK: I am in love with Gwendolen. I have come up to town expressly to propose to her.

ALGERNON: I thought you had come up for pleasure? . . . I call that business.

JACK: How utterly unromantic you are!

ALGERNON: I really don't see anything romantic in proposing. It is very romantic to be in love. But there is nothing romantic about a definite proposal. Why, one may be accepted. One usually is, I believe. Then the excitement is all over. The very essence of romance is uncertainty. If ever I get married, I'll certainly try to forget the fact.

Wilde gives the audience information in an entertaining way. First, we can surmise that Jack and Algernon are friends—fairly close, since Jack has apparently dropped in unexpectedly. Second, we learn about the social standing of the two. We know that Algernon is soon going to serve tea to Gwendolen and his aunt. We learn that Jack probably loves Gwendolen and the feelings are reciprocated. We learn something about the men's views. Seeds are planted for future events and conflicts, such as a scene between Aunt Augusta and Jack.

Rather than having Jack merely talk about where he's been, Wilde brings out the information through lighthearted bickering that maintains our interest. Algernon is somewhat accusatory in asking where Jack has been. Then, through his line "What on earth do you do there?" we can infer that he doesn't particularly like the country. All of this reveals not only setting and circumstances, but gives us information about the kind of people Jack and Algernon are. The information is conveyed with humor, which, coupled with the circumstances, indicates that the play will be a drawing room comedy, and so we are not to take the characters and situation seriously. We can see that the theme probably will have something to do with romance or love.

A story play involves a clash of wills or forces within the universe that has been established: Which of the two will win—the protagonist or the antagonist? In many plays it's the "good guy" versus the "bad guy." Yet what if they're all "bad guys," like Regina and her brothers in Lillian Hellman's *The Little Foxes?* Usually, it's the protagonist, or the central character, who we want to win. Most of the time we identify with this person; we empathize and sympathize. Sometimes, as with Regina, this is not the case.

The protagonist most often is an individual, though in rare cases it is a group of people, such as the weavers in Gerhart Hauptmann's play *The Weavers,* based on a revolt by Silesian weavers in 1844. Overall, the weavers as a group are the central character, with individuals shown only for brief periods before being submerged once more into the group. The antagonist, on the other hand, can be another person, a group of people, or a nonindividualized force.

Conflict and Opposition

There are four general types of **conflict** or opposition:

1. protagonist against *another person*
2. protagonist against *self*
3. protagonist against *society*
4. protagonist against *the forces of nature or fate*

An example of the first type of opposition is Anthony Shaffer's *Sleuth,* a two-character melodrama in which the characters constantly try to outwit each other and gain the upper hand. Shaffer's play relies a great deal on deception and one-upmanship. Although a play pitting one person against another may have a simple plot that doesn't go deeply into character, that isn't always the case.

A number of well-known plays use the theme of protagonist against self. In Miller's *Death of a Salesman,* for example, Willy tries to live up to his own definition of success. In Herb Gardner's comedy *A Thousand Clowns,* the central character's conflict centers on whether he will remain a nonconformist and maintain his sense of freedom or get a job and be allowed to continue rearing his nephew. And in Sophocles' *Oedipus Rex,* Oedipus struggles against his own sense of pride to prove that he is not his father's killer.

A protagonist against society or a particular segment of society is one of the most common types of opposition. Dramatist Henrik Ibsen, for instance, often structured his plays around such circumstances—for example *Ghosts,* in which Mrs. Alving is forced by social standards to stay with a dissolute husband. After his death she builds an orphanage to honor him and to hide his true character. In Ibsen's *An Enemy of the People,* Stockman battles an entire town when he wants to close the polluted baths—the villagers' main source of income.

Plays that pit the protagonist against such a force as nature or fate may come across as overly melodramatic unless such conflict is only superficial. Many times, the plot really shows the character against self in reaction to flood or drought. The conflict is a test of the character's mettle. Or the protagonist may be coming up against another obstacle in a different sort of struggle. In the nineteenth-century melodrama *Uncle Tom's Cabin,* Eliza attempts to escape across the ice floes, which, at that moment is the hindrance or problem she's up against. Yet the real force she wants to escape is the institution of slavery.

It is difficult to make nature or fate a convincing antagonist, since often it seems the protagonist is being controlled from outside. Brian Clark's *Whose Life Is This Anyway?* may seem to set a human being against fate, given that the central character is dying. Yet, the character really is battling society's views on the right-to-die issue. And though fate left Helen Keller deaf and blind, her struggle against her own stubbornness forms the basis of the conflict in *The Miracle Worker.*

Point of Attack

The playwright decides the **point of attack**—the place to begin the play. According to theatre critic William Archer:

> If his [the writer's] play be a comedy, and if his object be gently and quietly to interest and entertain, the chances are that he begins by showing us his personages in their normal state, concisely indicates their characters, circumstances and relations, and then lets the crisis develop from the outset before our eyes. If, on the other hand, his play be of a more stirring description, and he wants to seize the spectator's attention firmly from the start, he will probably go straight at his crisis, plunging, perhaps, into the very middle of it, even at the cost of having afterwards to go back in order to put the audience in possession of the antecedent circumstances. In a third type of play . . . the curtain rises on a surface aspect of profound peace, which is presently found to be a thin crust over an absolutely volcanic condition of affairs, the origin of which has to be traced backwards, it may be for many years.[3]

Background (the universe in which the play exists) plus plot (the characters in action) thus equals a story play.

Elements of Plot

Plot involves an **inciting incident, rising action** (which usually involves a series of minor crises), a **turning point,** a **climax,** and the **denouement** or **falling action,** all following a linear pattern, the Aristotelian model. The play begins when the antagonist in some way interferes with the evenness of the protagonist's life. The following shows what occurs, though, of course, most plays would be much more complicated.

1. Inciting incident: Someone unexpectedly knocks you to the ground.
2. Rising action: You try to rise, but the antagonist shoves you back down. You manage to leap to your feet and chase him down the sidewalk. As you

---

[3] William Archer, *Play-Making: A Manual of Craftsmanship* (New York: Dover Publications, Inc., 1960), p. 58.

peer around the corner to see where he's gone, he sneaks up behind you and grabs you around the neck. Your bewilderment turns to anger. You are determined to put an end to this nonsense.

Each incident in a play ends with a minor crisis. These crises build in intensity toward an irrevocable change, a point of no return.

3. Turning point: You spin around, grab the person who's attacked you, and shove him up against the wall. You have him cornered and know beyond any doubt that you are going to defeat him. Then comes the high point of the drama.

4. Climax: As your attacker cowers in fear, you force him to consume a vial of magic potion that makes him a "good guy."

5. Denouement: Even though the antagonist no longer wants to harm you, you're curious about why he's attacked you. He tells you that he envies your skills as a playwright or actor. This made him so jealous that he wanted to beat you up. You're astounded because you never thought you were very good. The play ends happily for both of you when you agree to teach him all you know about writing or acting.

Some plots have many more minor complications or crises than others. A musical with a very simple plot is *The Fantasticks,* off-Broadway's longest-running musical ever. The fathers of Matt and Luisa want their offspring to fall in love and marry, which they do, and so a happy ending seems assured. However, at the beginning of the second (and final) act, Matt and Luisa become dissatisfied, feeling the need to experience life before settling down. The rest of the act shows that they do separate for a time, but eventually they reunite. In contrast, Shaffer's *Sleuth* has many more complications, each resulting in a minor climax in which one of the two characters seems to be winning, only to be outwitted by the other. In effect, the plot can be referred to as a fencing match in which two participants are closely matched.

Figure 9.2

The progression of a story play.

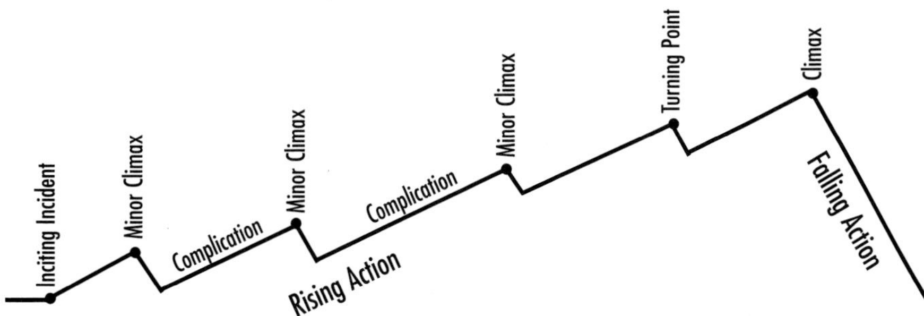

Sometimes, the turning point and the climax are the same, sometimes not. In Joan Schenkar's 1990 satire *The Universal Wolf,* Grandmother decides to kill Little Red Riding Hood, which is the turning point. Before she actually kills her, which is the climax, she sings her to sleep with a lullaby. Only then does she repeatedly stab Little Red Riding Hood with knitting needles. However, if Grandmother had decided she couldn't stand to be around Little Red Riding Hood one second more and had killed her immediately, the turning point and climax would be the same.

A play's climax begins to reveal the answer to the question asked when the problem was introduced; the denouement completes the answer by tying up the loose ends. It explains more fully how and why a thing happened, or sometimes shows the effects of the resolution on the characters. In a comedy, the audience wants to enjoy the protagonist's triumph; in a tragedy, the audience wants to come to terms with their feelings. For example, in the final scene of *Death of a Salesman,* "The Requiem," shows how Willy's suicide affects the other characters.

Plays often include scenes in which there appears to be no direct conflict between the protagonist and the antagonist. Yet if the play is well-written, the conflict is inherent; it relates to what already has been shown. For example, one character may be describing to another what is bothering her, what has caused the central problem and conflict. In so doing, she may begin to glimpse a possible solution or clarify her own thoughts about the situation, foreshadowing and thus building tension and suspense about whether she will succeed in her plan.

Dramatic Action

Everything that occurs in a play has to be relevant to the advancement of the plot, to the protagonist's attempt to reach his or her goal. The device that advances the plot is called the **dramatic action.**

Most important, the dramatic action relates to the struggle between the protagonist and the antagonist, and often results in a direct clash between the two. However, it doesn't necessarily have to involve physical movement. In the soliloquy in which Hamlet decides to kill his uncle, the plot definitely is moving forward, yet no physical activity occurs just then.

Dramatic action can help individualize a character, revealing traits that may be important to action that occurs later in the play. This is another type of foreshadowing, in that it lays the groundwork for what comes later, making it believable and logical. For instance, a character who is irritable in little ways may later direct a burst of temper at someone else. A major plot development may come as a surprise. Yet, once the audience thinks back over past events and what was revealed about the characters in the way they reacted, they should realize that what occurred was within the range of predictability or possibility. Action or conflict is important in revealing character. It shows how the protagonist, and often the antagonist, will react when faced with opposition.

Dramatic action also helps create atmosphere, as shown in the following excerpt.

BRIGHTON BEACH MEMOIRS

Neil Simon

From Act I

EUGENE: One out, a man on second, bottom of the seventh, two balls, no strikes . . . . Ruffing checks the runner on second, gets the sign from Dickey, Ruffing stretches, Ruffing pitches—*(He throws the ball)* Caught the inside corner, steerike one! Atta baby! No hitter up there. *(He retrieves the ball.)* One out, a man on second, bottom of the seventh, two balls, one strike, . . . Ruffing checks the runner on second, gets the sign from Dickey, Ruffing stretches, Ruffing pitches—*(He throws the ball)* Low and outside, ball three. Come on, Red! Make him a hitter! No batter up there. In there all the time, Red.

BLANCHE *(Stops sewing):* Kate, please. My head is splitting.

KATE: I told that boy a hundred and nine times. *(She yells out)* Eugene! Stop banging the wall!

EUGENE *(Calls out):* In a minute, Ma! This is for the World Series! *(Back to his game)* One out, a man on second, bottom of the seventh, three balls, one strike . . . Ruffing stretches, Ruffing pitches—*(He throws the ball)* Oh, no! High and outside, Jojo Moore walks! First and second and Mel Ott lopes up to the plate . . .

BLANCHE *(Stops again):* Can't he do that someplace else?

KATE: I'll break his arm, that's where he'll do it *(She calls out)* Eugene, I'm not going to tell you again. Do you hear me?

EUGENE: It's the last batter, Mom. Mel Ott is up. It's a crucial moment in World Series history.

KATE: Your Aunt Blanche has a splitting headache.

BLANCHE: I don't want him to stop playing. It's just the banging.

LAURIE *(Looks up from her book):* He always does it when I'm studying. I have a big test in history tomorrow.

EUGENE: One pitch, Mom? I think I can get him to pop up. I have my stuff today.

KATE: Your father will give you plenty of stuff when he comes home! You hear?

EUGENE: All right! All right!

KATE: I want you inside now! Put out the water glasses.

Blanche: I can do that.

Kate: Why? Is his arm broken? *(She yells out again)* And I don't want any back talk, you hear? *(She goes back to the kitchen)*

Eugene *(Slams the ball into his glove angrily. Then he cups his hand, making a megaphone out of it and announces to the grandstands):* "Attention, ladeees and gentlemen! Today's game will be delayed because of my Aunt Blanche's headache . . . ."

As Wilde did in *The Importance of Being Earnest,* Simon gives us a lot of information about time and place, and about the characters and their relationships. Just as in Wilde's play, much of the exposition is brought out in the conflict. Dramatic action or conflict, however, must relate in some way to the protagonist—even if he or she isn't present.

Character

Each character in a play has a goal, sometimes referred to as the superobjective. In Beth Henley's one-act play *Am I Blue?* John and Ashbe meet for the first time in a bar, from which they then are evicted for being underage. Ashbe invites John to her apartment in New Orleans, where she offers him hot Kool-Aid and green marshmallows. Her father is out of town and her mother lives in Atlanta.

The superobjective seems to be for the two characters to become friends. However, each has a more fundamental goal—to be accepted socially. Both are misfits, who react differently to their situations. Ashbe refuses to conform, while John will do almost anything to be accepted.

Central Problems

There are many ways in which the action in a play can progress; that is, there are various types of central problems affected by the introduction of the dramatic question or inciting incident. These include:

1. The need for revenge. An example is Hamlet's wanting to get back at his uncle for killing Hamlet's father.

2. Being lured by money, sex, or fame. In Marlowe's *The Tragical History of Dr. Faustus,* the title character sells his soul to the devil and then tries to get out of the bargain.

3. The need to escape from an intolerable situation. In Schenkar's *The Universal Wolf,* Grandmother murders Little Red Riding Hood because she cannot stand the girl's "attitude" or "voice" or "smile."

4. Arriving at a crossroads, and not knowing which choice to make. In Wendy Kesselman's *My Sister in This House,* Lea must choose between pleasing her sister Christine, with whom she works as a maid, or pleasing her mother.

5. Testing the limits of self or others. In *The Miracle Worker,* Helen Keller and her teacher Annie Sullivan push each other nearly to the breaking point.

Many plays also have one or more subplots (those of lesser importance or subordinate to the central action). In *The Little Foxes,* for example, Regina's daughter, Alexandra, gradually comes to realize that she cannot love or even stay with a woman as corrupt or unethical as her mother.

Shakespeare's comedies often have subplots that deal with love or intrigue. In *As You Like It,* the story that frames the play is that of the wicked Duke Frederick wresting power from his brother, who finds refuge in the Forest of Arden. However, the play's major focus is the love story of Rosalind and Orlando, along with two other love stories.

Figure 9.3

A scene with characters Rosalind (disguised as a young man—Ganymede) and Celia from Shakespeare's *As You Like It,* from a Long Wharf Theatre (Connecticut) production.

Scenes as Structure

Often, an act of a play is divided arbitrarily into two or three scenes, comparable to the chapter divisions in a novel. Within each act can be a number of scenes. Act I, Scene 1, may occur in the afternoon, Scene 2 in the evening, and Scene 3 the following morning.

Theatre artists, however, often think of scenes as **motivational units,** in which the protagonist wants to reach a goal. A motivational unit is made up of the minor inciting incidents and minor climaxes that comprise the rising action. Each of these slightly alters the direction the central character takes in attempting to overcome the antagonist.

In the following excerpt from a play that takes place in a concentration camp in Nazi Germany, Horst's goal is to protect Max by telling him how to behave as he and Horst perform the useless task of moving heavy rocks back and forth from one corner of an enclosure to another.

BENT

Martin Sherman
from Act II, Scene 1

MAX: It's supposed to drive us crazy.

HORST: These are heavy!

MAX: You get used to it.

HORST: What do you mean, drive us crazy?

MAX: Just that. It makes no sense. It serves no purpose. I figured it out. They do it to drive us crazy.

HORST: They probably know what they're doing.

MAX: But it doesn't work. I figured it out. It's the best job to have. That's why I got you here.

HORST: What? *(Puts down his rock.)*

MAX: Don't stop. Keep moving. *(**HORST** picks up the rock and moves it.)* A couple more things. That fence.

HORST: Yes.

MAX: It's electric. Don't touch it. You fry.

HORST: I won't touch it.

MAX: And over there—that pit.

HORST: Where?

MAX: There.

HORST: Oh yes. It smells awful.

MAX: Bodies.

HORST: In the pit.

MAX: Yes. Sometimes we have to throw them in.

HORST: Oh. Well, it will break the routine. What do you mean you got me here?

MAX: Don't walk so fast.

HORST: Why?

MAX: You'll tire yourself. Pace it. Nice and slow.

HORST: Okay. This better?

MAX: Yeah.

HORST: What do you mean you got me here?

MAX: I worked a deal.

HORST: I don't want to hear. *(Silence.)* Yes, I do. What the hell is this? You got me here? What right do you have—

MAX: Careful.

HORST: What?

MAX: You're dropping the rock.

HORST: No, I'm not. I'm holding it, I'm holding it. What right do you have—

MAX: You were at the stones?

HORST: Yes.

MAX: Was it harder than this?

HORST: I guess.

MAX: People get sick?

HORST: Yes.

MAX: Die?

Horst: Yes.

MAX: Guards beat you if you didn't work hard enough?

Horst: Yes.

MAX *(proudly):* So?

Horst: So? So what?

MAX: So it was dangerous.

HORST: This isn't?

MAX: No. No one gets sick here. Look at all those guys moving rocks over there. *(Points off.)* They look healthier than most. No one dies. The guards don't beat you, because the work is totally nonessential. All it can do is drive you crazy.

HORST: That's all?

MAX: Yes.

HORST: Then maybe the other was better.

MAX: No, I figured it out! This is the best work in the camp, if you keep your head, if you have someone to talk to.

On the other hand, a **French scene** begins with the entrance and ends with the exit of an important character, since the direction of a scene is almost always certain to change when a new element is introduced.

Within each scene are "beats," or points of emphasis such as occur in poetry or music. With each new "beat" the action somehow intensifies, though it does not really change direction. A beat occurs each time a character gets the upper hand. The beats are easy to follow in this dialogue from Edward Albee's *Who's Afraid of Virginia Woolf?*

MARTHA *(Swinging around):* Look, sweetheart, I can drink you under any goddamn table you want . . . so don't worry about me!

GEORGE: Martha, I gave you the prize years ago . . . . There isn't an abomination award going that you . . . .

MARTHA: I swear . . . if you existed I'd divorce you . . . .

GEORGE: Well, just stay on your feet, that's all . . . . These people are your guests, you know, and . . . .

MARTHA: I can't even see you . . . I haven't been able to see you for years . . . .

GEORGE: . . . if you pass out, or throw up, or something . . . .

MARTHA: . . . I mean, you're a blank, a cipher . . . .

GEORGE: . . . and try to keep your clothes on, too. There aren't many more sickening sights than you with a couple of drinks in you and your skirt up over your head, you know . . . .

MARTHA: . . . a zero . . . .

Selectivity

Because of the nature of drama, the action of a play is compressed and heightened, and inconsequential details are eliminated. Time is condensed. Dialogue is more purposeful and to the point. It would be rare in real life to find people who have such command of thought and language under intense emotion as do George and Martha.

Because a play is selective, you can think of it in terms of an analogy. The actions are universal; they relate to all (or most) of us, or we wouldn't be interested. Although they deal with specific characters doing specific things, they stand for something larger.

WINE IN THE WILDERNESS

Alice Childress

The action occurs during a 1964 race riot in Harlem. Bill Jameson, an artist and self-styled intellectual, is painting a triptych. Two of the panels are finished—the first, an innocent child, and the second, a regal black woman who symbolizes "Wine in the Wilderness" or "Mother Africa." The third will be a lost woman, defeated and with nothing of substance in her life. Two friends, Cynthia and Sonny-man, call to say they have found a perfect model for the final panel. When they bring her (Tommy) to the apartment, she says her own place has been destroyed in a fire resulting from the riot. Later, when Bill wants to paint her in her wig and mismatched clothes, a result of not being allowed back into her apartment, she objects. Of course, not knowing what the painting is to be, she wants to look her best.

He is very patronizing, telling her she's just like most black women, eager to create a matriarchal society that robs men of their masculinity. He plays the intellectual, quizzing her about black people and white sympathizers throughout recent history. In effect, he keeps implying that he's better than she is. He's an intellectual, she a common woman. When she spills an orange drink on herself, he gives her an African wrap. The phone rings, and she hears Bill telling the caller about the magnificent woman in his painting, "the finest" in the world. Tommy, whose real name is Tomorrow Marie, thinks he's talking about her. As a result, she gains self-respect and actually transforms herself into a beautiful woman.

Bill asks her to put on the wig again. She doesn't want to, saying that she knows he doesn't really like wigs. As she is posing, he asks her to tell about herself, which she does. She also tells him some black history he doesn't know—things about which she is not the least bit pretentious. Bill has become enchanted by her transformation, but now can't recapture the image of her he wanted to paint. They are drawn to each other.

The next morning while Bill is showering, an elderly black man (Oldtimer) explains to Tommy the idea behind the triptych. She's furious, feeling she's been taken advantage of. She lashes out at Bill and Cynthia and Sonny-man. She tells Oldtimer he is a fool for letting middle-class people treat him as though he's invisible. They hadn't even known his real name. She then turns back to the three others. She says when whites call Negroes *nigger,* they mean both the educated, like you, and the uneducated like me. "I called you a 'nigger' but I love you." She tells them that they think they are superior to the masses, but they are the masses and just don't know it.

Bill comes to realize that his vision was wrong and that his painting of "Mother Africa" does not actually represent the black women of America. He says he just dreamed this up out of the "junk room of my mind" and that Tommy really is the "Wine in the Wilderness" because she (as well as her family) has survived slavery and race riots and still holds her head high.

Because of this, Bill decides he will do a new triptych of black womanhood.

TOMMY: Better not. I'll kill him! The "black people" this and the "Afro-American" . . . that . . . You ain't got no use for none-a us. Oldtimer, you their fool too. 'Til I got here they didn't even know your damn name. There's something inside-a me that says I ain' suppose to let *nobody* play me cheap. Don't care how much they know! *(She sweeps some of the books to the floor.)*

BILL: Don't you have any forgiveness in you? Would I be beggin' you if I didn't care? Can't you be generous enough . . .

TOMMY: Nigger, I been too damn generous with you already. All-a these people know I wasn't down here all night posin' for no pitcher, nigger!

BILL: Cut that out, Tommy, and you not going anywhere!

TOMMY: You wanna bet? Nigger!

BILL: Okay, you called it, baby, I did act like a low, degraded person . . .

TOMMY: *(Combing out her wig with her fingers while holding it)* Didn't call you no low, degraded person. Nigger! *(To CYNTHIA who is handing her a comb)* "Do you have to wear a wig? Yes! To soften the blow when yall go up side-a my head with a baseball bat. *(Going back to taunting BILL and ignoring CYNTHIA'S comb)* Nigger!

BILL: That's enough-a that. You right and you're wrong too.

TOMMY: Ain't a-one-a us you like that's alive and walkin' by you on the street. You don't like flesh and blood niggers.

BILL: Call me that, baby, but don't call yourself. That what you think of yourself?

TOMMY: If a black somebody is in a history book, or printed on a pitcher, or drawed on a paintin' . . . or if they're a statue . . . dead, and outta the way, and can't talk back, then you dig 'em and full-a so much-a damn admiration and talk 'bout "our" history. But when you run into us livin' and breathin' ones, with the life's blood still pumpin' through us, . . . then you comin' on 'bout we ain' never together. You hate us, that's what! *You hate black me!*

BILL: *(Stung to the heart, confused and saddened by the half truth which applies to himself)* I never hated you, I never will, no matter what you or any of the rest of you do to *make* me hate you. I won't! Hell, woman, why do you say that! Why would I hate you?

TOMMY: Maybe I look too much like the mother that give birth to you. Like the Ma and Pa that worked in the post office to buy you a house and a screen door with a damn duck on it. And you so ungrateful you didn't even like it.

BILL: No, I didn't, baby. I don't like screen doors with ducks on 'em.

TOMMY: You didn't like who was livin' behind them screen doors. Phoney Nigger!

BILL: That's all! Dammit! Don't go there no more!

TOMMY: Hit me, so I can tear this place down and scream bloody murder.

BILL: *(Somewhere between laughter and tears)* Looka here, baby, I'm willin' to say I'm wrong, even in fronta the room fulla people . . .

TOMMY: *(Through clinched teeth)* Nigger.

SONNY-MAN: The sister is upset.

TOMMY: And you stop callin' me "the" sister, . . . if you feelin' so brotherly why don't you say *"my"* sister? Ain't no we-ness in your talk. "The" Afro-American, "the" black man, there's no we-ness in you. Who you think *you* are?

SONNY-MAN: I was talkin' in general er . . . my sister, 'bout the masses.

TOMMY: There he go again. "The" masses. Tryin' to make out like we pitiful and you got it made. You the masses your damn self and don't even know it. *(Another angry look at BILL)* Nigger.

BILL: *(Pulls dictionary from shelf)* Let's get this ignorant "nigger" talk squared away. You can stand some education.

TOMMY: You treat me like a nigger, that's what. I'd rather be called one than treated that way.

BILL: *(Questions TOMMY)* What is a nigger? *(Talks as he is trying to find word)* A nigger is a low, degraded person, *any* low degraded person. I learned that from my teacher in the fifth grade.

TOMMY: Fifth grade is a liar! Don't pull that dictionary crap on me.

BILL: *(Pointing to the book) Webster's New World Dictionary of the American Language, College Edition.*

TOMMY: I don't need to find out what no college white folks say nigger is.

BILL: I'm tellin' you it's a low, degraded person. Listen. *(Reads from the book)* Nigger, n-i-g-g-e-r, . . . A Negro . . . A member of any dark-skinned people . . . Damn. *(Amazed by dictionary description)*

In plays, as in life, people speak through implication and draw conclusions through inference. Most of the time, they don't come out and say exactly what they mean. The following scene is from Franz Werfel's *Goat Song,* which takes place at the close of the eighteenth century. The parents of Stanja, who is betrothed to Mirko, have just dropped her off so she will get used to his farm. In the following, what Mirko really is saying—in the subtext or by implication—is that he does not understand Stanja. This makes him so frustrated that he says he'll beat her after they're married.

MIRKO: Your parents are gone now. Are you sad?

STANJA: No, I am not sad.

MIRKO: Then you don't love your parents?

STANJA: I love them.

MIRKO: Then you must be sad. Doesn't it hurt you when something is over? The axle creaks, the horses draw up, the whip . . . . And then, something is ended.

Stanja: I never ache for what is past.

Mirko: Oh, I often do. I can lie in the meadow hour after hour longing for the games I played there on the grass.

Stanja: That is because you are a man.

(Short pause)

Mirko: Do the house and the farm please you?

Stanja: Why shouldn't they? House, rooms, chimneys, stables, pigsties, and hencoops and dovecotes, same as everywhere.

Mirko: And do I please you?

Stanja: Why shouldn't you please me?

Mirko: Do you know, Stanja, I would have liked it better if you had cried before, when they left you . . . . *(Suddenly turns on her)* You! What if you've loved someone before! Tell me! Have you loved someone else?

Stanja: *(Hesitatingly)* No.

Mirko: *(Slowly, his eyes closed):* I think, when we're married, I will beat you.

Stanja: That's what all husbands do.

A playwright rarely spells everything out. Elizabeth Wong's *Letters to a Student Revolutionary* is about an American girl, Bibi, and a Chinese girl who calls herself Karen. They meet and speak for only a few minutes when Bibi is vacationing in China, yet their correspondence continues for years. The audience never discovers for certain whether Karen, who participated in the Tiananmen Square revolt in which hundreds of students were massacred, dies or not. Wong never states in words that the situation was an atrocity, though that's what she means.

Other Types of Structure

Thematic

Although the story play is the most common, there are other structures, as well. One is **thematic structure,** in which a variety of scenes deal with the same basic issues but are unrelated in continuity and/or characterization. An example is Bertolt Brecht's *Mother Courage and Her Children,* which shows Mother Courage's blind reliance on war to provide a living for her family. The play makes a strong statement for pacifism.

A play that relies on theme for unity often is episodic; it does not build toward a single turning point and climax. For example, Guillermo Reyes's

Culver Pictures

Figure 9.4

A scene from Eugène Ionesco's *The Bald Soprano,* a 1955 Rooftop/Lee Paton production that featured Salome Jens and David Brooks.

Men on the Verge of a His-Panic Breakdown is a series of monologues all dealing with a gay Hispanic immigrant trying to fit in successfully in America.

Circular

A play using **circular structure** starts and ends with a similar set of circumstances. Such plays usually are thematic as well. An example is Eugène Ionesco's 1948 play *The Bald Soprano,* typical of absurdist (theatre of the absurd) drama, which expresses the idea that life is neither good nor bad at face value. Only what we choose as moral or immoral makes life good or bad to us as individuals. The characters speak recognizable words and sentences, but overall they make no sense. Although there is the appearance of struggle and conflict, as this excerpt reveals, the play does not progress toward a resolution:

Mr. Smith: (still reading his paper.) Tsk, it says here that Bobby Watson died.

Mrs. Smith: My God, the poor man! When did he die?

Mr. Smith: Why do you pretend to be astonished? You know very well that he's been dead these past two years. Surely you remember that we attended his funeral a year and a half ago.

Mrs. Smith: Oh yes, of course I do remember. I remembered it right away, but I don't understand why you yourself were so surprised to see it in the paper.

Mr. Smith: It wasn't in the paper. It's been three years since his death was announced. I remembered it through an association of ideas.

Mrs. Smith: What a pity! He was so well preserved.

Mr. Smith: He was the handsomest corpse in Great Britain. He didn't look his age. Poor Bobby, he's been dead for four years and he was still warm. A veritable living corpse. And how cheerful he was.

Mrs. Smith: Poor Bobby.

Mr. Smith: Which poor Bobby do you mean?

Mrs. Smith: It is his wife that I mean. She is called Bobby too. Bobby Watson. Since they both had the same name, you could never tell one from the other when you saw them together. It was only after his death that you could really tell which was which. And there are still people today who confuse her with the deceased and offer their condolences to him. Do you know her?

Mr. Smith: I only met her once, by chance, at Bobby's burial.

Mrs. Smith: I've never seen her. Is she pretty?

Mr. Smith: She has regular features and yet one cannot say that she is pretty. She is too big and stout. Her features are not regular but still one can say that she is very pretty. She is a little too small and too thin. She's a voice teacher.

Samuel Beckett's *Waiting for Godot* also is the same at the end as at the beginning. It opens with Estragon and Vladimir waiting for someone or something called Godot. They complain about life, pretend repentance, and fall asleep to have nightmares. They wake up and quarrel and wonder what to expect of Godot if Godot comes. Pozzo, a pompous taskmaster, comes down the road with Lucky, a near-idiot through being a slave and ever obedient. Now forced to think, Lucky pours out a mixture of theology and politics before he stumbles down the road with Pozzo. In Act II, Estragon and Vladimir trade hats, recite what they think is humorous poetry, play slave and master, and argue about the past. Pozzo and Lucky come back, the former blind and the latter dumb. Neither of them remembers who he is or was. Godot sends word that he won't come today but he certainly will tomorrow. Vladimir and Estragon know they should move on, but neither does, so they just go on waiting.

To an extent, Thornton Wilder's *Our Town* follows a circular pattern in showing that life is a continuing process, overall just about the same at one period of time as at another, though different people may be involved. The play begins with the Stage Manager acting as narrator, telling what is to come. The play ends with his relating what has transpired, showing that it is similar to what will continue to happen.

Ritualistic Structure

One of the first persons to advocate a return to ritual was Antonin Artaud of France. His book, *Theatre and Its Double,* published in 1938, discusses his ideas for using theatre more directly to bring about social change. Playwright Jean Genet (1910–1986) also believed in ritual. In his play *The Maids,* two maids perform charades as the lady of the house and act out her symbolic murder. In Peter Weiss's *Marat/Sade,* the inmates of an asylum act out their crimes in a primitive, symbolic manner in the course of participating in a play on the French Revolution.

Ritual follows a certain pattern or structure over and over again. This gives comfort and a sense of continuity, a feeling that the world is ordered. David Storey emphasizes the idea of ritual for comfort in *The Changing Room,* where the members of the rugby team follow a pattern or ritual in the way they change in and out of uniform and so on.

Experimentalists such as Artaud and British director Peter Brook view ritual as a means of evoking strong emotions. They believe that ritualistic and primitive movements put people in touch with the dark places in their souls and the basic patterns of human nature. Ritual allows the actor, like the primitive priest, to lead the audience to participate in the performance and thus become a part of nature.

Episodic Structure

Episodic structure expands rather than condensing. Although this structure is by no means new, it has been used differently in recent years. An older example is the dramatization of *Uncle Tom's Cabin,* in which George L. Aiken included widely separated scenes for excitement, often switching locations and characters. It contains several loosely connected stories, with most emphasis on the love story of Eliza and George Harris, on Tom's relationship with Little Eva, and on the cruelty Tom suffers at the hands of Simon Legree. Altogether, the melodrama *Uncle Tom's Cabin* contains thirty scenes.

Jean-Claude Van Itallie's *The Serpent: A Ceremony* switches constantly from recent or current times to biblical times, encompassing events from the Garden of Eden to the assassinations of John F. Kennedy and Martin Luther King, Jr., to the here and now of the individual performers, who state their names and tell about themselves. The play begins with a ritualized procession to the rhythm of the actors beating upon their bodies. The characters often are symbols much more than individuals. There is no continuity of action. Time and place switch abruptly, and the actors often improvise.

Miscellaneous Structure

A play may be presented simply to portray a facet of life or a way of life. An example is Paul Zindel's *The Effects of Gamma Rays on Man in the Moon Marigolds,* which has strong characterizations but no real cause-to-effect plot. It deals with the relationships among a mother and two daughters. Another example, though it does have something of a plot, is *Torch Song Trilogy.* It comprises three one-act plays (tied together more closely in the film than the stage version) that explore gay experience in New York a few decades past.

Sometimes, plays without a plot show incidents following each other in chronological order, but not necessarily growing out of the preceding material. Historical or biographical plays often are like this, as well as plays that are tied to a specific action, such as a trial. When the trial ends, so does the play, which may or may not have a plot. An example is Carlos Morton's *The Many Lives of Danny Rosales.*

Chapter Ten

Dramatic Style and Genre

Theatrical Styles

Some playwrights express their themes by means of realistic scenes, while others use symbolic places and characters. But more than that, each writer's style is individual. It would be easy to recognize, for instance, that playwrights David Rabe and David Henry Hwang have totally different styles of writing.

Nowadays we can see plays in many styles:

> A Greek tragic dramatist in the fifth century B.C. wrote in a tradition which prescribed the use of certain poetic meters, limited the number of characters who could appear on stage at one time, made obligatory the provision of odes and dances for a chorus, and directed that the plot must be drawn from heroic legend and the myths of the distant past. Modern dramatists work in no such dramatic tradition, and they have been left entirely free to choose subjects and invent new dramatic styles. The result has been a bewildering number of styles: realism, naturalism, poetic drama, symbolism, expressionism, the epic theatre, the theater of the absurd, and surrealism, to name only the most prominent among them. As a result of this freedom, modern plays have taken nearly every possible shape and size, ranging from imitations of Elizabethan tragedy in blank verse to modified Japanese Noh plays; from sprawling plays which take half a day to perform and seek to encompass all human life . . . to brief one-act "anti-plays" which prove the impossibility of finding any meaning in life except its meaninglessness.[1]

Various styles are associated with specific historical periods. For example, **romanticism,** characterized by freedom and gracefulness, was a direct revolt against the rigid rules of Renaissance **neoclassicism.**

Later, the Industrial Revolution brought about a lessening of the power of the upper class, and the theatre moved toward presenting a more realistic view of life.

Where realistic styles try to present life as it is, nonrealistic styles are more allegorical and abstract.

---

[1] "The Attempted Dance: A Discussion of the Modern Theatre," from *The Modern American Theatre,* Alvin B. Kernan, ed. (New York: Prentice-Hall, Inc., 1967), pp. 5–6. Reprinted from "Introduction" to *Classics of the Modern Theatre,* Alvin B. Kernan, ed. (New York: Harcourt Brace Jovanovich, 1965).

Style is related to the way the playwright views life, and so it is directly related to genre, or the division of plays into categories such as comedy and tragedy.

The writing and scenic styles of a production should complement each other. Some plays require a particular style in production, whereas others can be done in a variety of ways, depending on the director's interpretation of the script. Indeed, in postmodernism, there is a tendency to deny analysis and mingle styles.

Representational and Presentational Styles

Theatrical styles fall into two overall categories, *representational* and *presentational.* The former leans toward the realistic, the latter toward the nonrealistic.

In **representational** theatre the dialogue, setting, characters, and action are represented as true to life. The action onstage shows the audience as clearly as possible the sort of world they can see outside the theatre. Yet, because the actions occur as part of a planned production, representational theatre cannot actually depict life as it is. Actors speak memorized dialogue, the director plans the movement, and the play takes place in a space specifically set up for a production. Even naturalism—the most representational style—has to be selective. Audiences at a production of Jack Kirkland's *Tobacco Road* know that the action takes place on a stage that is covered with a few inches of sawdust or dirt that only represents poor southern land and is not the land itself.

It would be fair then to say that the representational style is a closer approximation of life than the presentational. The former is **stage-centered** and the latter **audience-centered.** Actors in a representational play do not openly acknowledge the audience; in a presentational play they do, sometimes speaking directly to them. Often the stage is bare, or elements of setting suggest location rather than portraying it. Any scenery is likely to be nonrealistic.

Yet no style is pure. Thornton Wilder's *Our Town* is presentational in that it calls for no scenery, and from time to time a character speaks directly to the audience. It is representational in that occasionally the actors move into specific scenes, such as one at a soda fountain. But even in these more realistic scenes, the Stage Manager assumes another role, whereas George and Emily keep the same roles that they have throughout the play.

Musical theatre is presentational in the use of singing and dancing but often representational in the dialogue.

Of course, in representational drama, actors usually play to the audience. Performers on a proscenium stage don't turn their backs on the audience, except sometimes for effect. Furniture isn't placed across the front of the proscenium opening.

Specific Styles

The other styles of theatre are offshoots of the representational and presentational, leaning more strongly to one or the other.

In pure **naturalism,** an attempt is made to include everything found in life. In writing, this means including all the details of conversation and physical movement. In setting, it means placing onstage everything that we would find in an actual location.

Realism, which depends on the playwright's and the designer's perception of reality, attempts to present life as it is, but selectively. Not all details that are found in real life are presented, only those essential for the audience's understanding of the play and the establishment of mood are included.

Realism in writing means that the dialogue sounds lifelike, but doesn't have the hesitations, the changes in direction, the false starts, or the inconsequentiality of everyday conversation. Although they do not acknowledge an audience, actors in a realistic play consider them in projecting their voices and remaining aware of **sightlines** (the line of vision for the audience).

A style that is more audience-centered, though still it has elements of the representational, is **expressionism,** meant to show the protagonist's inner self. An expressionistic script deals with the internal reality of the mind, and the setting shows how the character views life. This means attempting to let the audience see reality as the protagonist does, to present the protagonist's inner feelings externally.

Symbolism tries to present truth by internal or subjective means or allegorically. Symbolic settings may contain unidentified shapes and strong contrasts in light and darkness.

With **impressionism,** the director and designer determine what they want to stress or call attention to regarding the play's theme or message. For example, in the Broadway production of Tennessee Williams's *Cat on a Hot Tin Roof,* Brick and Maggie's bedroom was constructed to resemble a boxing ring because the two characters quarrel so much.

Theatricalism, formalism, and **constructivism** sometimes are called styles, although they really are only treatments of other styles. With theatricalism, the designer breaks down any suggestion of a fourth wall, and viewers are constantly reminded that they are in a theatre. Lighting instruments and backstage areas may be open to view; actors may enter and exit through the audience. Formalism, which overlaps theatricalism and impressionism, uses only what is necessary to the actor and only because it is there. Drapes rather than flats may conceal backstage areas or provide the means for exits and entrances. Constructivism uses only those elements necessary to the action. Only part of the interior of a room may be built, and a ceiling light may hang directly from an overhead railing.

Style in the Modern Theatre

Styles often overlap. Basically realistic plays such as Tennessee Williams's *The Glass Menagerie* contain elements of symbolism and expressionism. As you know, *Death of a Salesman* contains expressionistic scenes in showing the workings of Willy's mind, particularly in his scenes with the woman or with his brother Ben, now dead.

On the other hand, some plays use a single style throughout. The audience members viewing *The Universal Wolf* are constantly reminded that they are in a theatre. Besides Grandmother, the Wolf, and Little Red Riding Hood, there is a fourth character called Reader. The following stage directions open the play:

> The READER sits in the chair waiting to begin the play. PLAYWRIGHT'S NOTE: the Reader will read all the stage directions that the actors can't, won't or don't do (indicated by indented material). The READER will also create the voices of the structuralists, the bird, the post-structuralists, the audience, the stagehands, and LITTLE RED RIDING HOOD's mother. The READER is very lightly miked.[2]

Throughout the play, the Reader announces that various images or people are being projected, though actually they are not. At times the characters follow the directions that the Reader gives. Her script was influenced in great part, Joan Schenkar says, by the absurdist writers, particularly Samuel Beckett.

In contrast, David Mamet's *Glengarry Glen Ross,* which, like Schenkar's play, deals with human nature at its most base, is presented realistically, with the rough language a person might expect to hear in everyday life. *The Universal Wolf,* as Schenkar says, is about "appetite," in which the Grandmother "will not merely survive, but will devour all the other characters."[3] Mamet's play is about men who lie, deceive, and cheat in their hungering after the quick deal, the fast buck. The play depicts five real estate salesmen who compete for "leads"—names of prospective buyers of the worthless land they are selling. The five are ruthless in their attempts at winning an office sales competition after which the loser will be fired. The setting is realistic, an attempt to convince the audience that they actually are viewing a real estate office. Despite the similarity in theme, the two plays are entirely different.

Dramatic Genres

Genre refers to the manner in which playwrights classify their subject matter. Usually the treatment is closely related to the writer's outlook on life. Is it optimistic or pessimistic? Comic or tragic? The outlook, at least in part, determines the purpose.

[2] Joan M. Schenkar, the opening lines of *The Universal Wolf,* © 1990, 1991, by the author.

[3] Rosette C. Lamont, ed. *Women on the Verge: Seven Avant Garde Plays* (New York: Applause, 1993), Introduction, pp. XXXIV–XXXV.

As illustrated in Figure 10.1, there is a relationship among various genres of drama. For instance, tragedy is the direct opposite of comedy, with comedy being the most encompassing genre. Of course, there are miscellaneous dramatic forms that don't fit neatly in the genres specified.

No one views all of life in the same manner. Each may regard some matters as ludicrous, others as sacred, and some unworthy of any kind of treatment. In contemporary theatre it's often difficult to categorize plays, which often are a mixture of genres. Some comedies have tragic elements, some tragedies have comic elements. There are serious plays that do not end in the death or defeat of the protagonist, as does traditional tragedy. An example is *The Glass Menagerie,* in which the four characters are trapped by circumstances and their own limitations.

> Amanda is trapped in the present but longs to return to the past. Laura is trapped by extreme shyness and a physical handicap. Tom is trapped by his family and circumstances. He manages to escape physically but, like Amanda, is still held by the past. Even the gentleman caller, Jim, is trapped by his own inadequacies and his inability to get ahead, though he has dreams of doing so. The characters are all victims of things they cannot control.[4]

Abandoned by her husband, Amanda has reared her two children alone and seen Tom into his first job. Now her goal is to see that Laura marries. Yet the pressure from her mother to do so drives Laura mad. Still, Amanda urges Tom to bring home a co-worker, Jim, whom it turns out Laura knew in high school.

Williams called this a "memory play" for two reasons. Tom is looking back upon his youth, and the play is semiautobiographical in that Williams is talking about his own relations with his mother and sister. The audience feels compassion for them, but there is no point of defeat in the play. The defeat has started long before the play opens.

As theatre critic Walter Kerr says: "The moment we succeed in consciously patterning our theater, in making it do precisely what we think it ought to be doing, we are apt to paralyze it."[5] All we need ask is that a play depict the truth of the human condition as the playwright sees it. Whether this takes the form of comedy, farce, tragedy, melodrama, or a mixture of genres doesn't matter.

Basically, there are two ways of treating subject matter—serious or comic. A serious treatment of theme contributes to empathy, while a comic treatment

---

[4] Cassady, Marshall, and Pat Cassady, *An Introduction to Theatre and Drama* (Skokie, Ill.: National Textbook Company), 1975.

[5] Walter Kerr, *The Theatre in Spite of Itself* (New York: Simon and Schuster, 1963), p. 19. Originally appeared as "Cheers for the Uninhibited U. S. Theatre," in *Life* Magazine, Feb. 7, 1959.

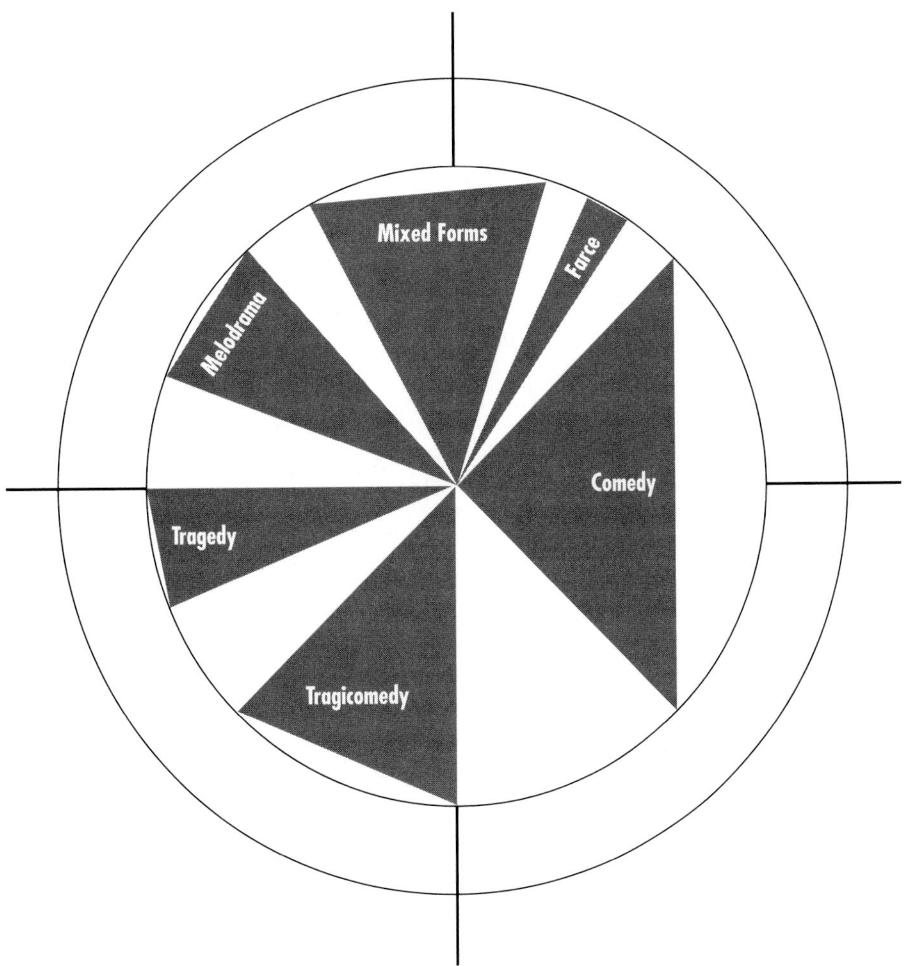

Figure 10.1

The various dramatic genres and their proportional relationships in the spectrum of theatre.

increases aesthetic distance. This means that comedies are more presentational or audience-centered than tragedies. A playwright can reach an audience by making it feel what the character is feeling or by appealing to the intellect. Comedy often is funny because of aesthetic distance. In many comedies, even though we identify with the characters, usually it is to a lesser degree than in a serious play. In real life falling and breaking a leg would not be funny. In a comedy it might be.

As Eric Bentley explains, a good play transcends its framework:

> Plays are generally about the big people, though what they say applies to the little people. And there is a converse to this proposition: that when a great playwright, such as Chekhov, presents the littleness of everyday life, he manages to suggest—as indeed he must—the largeness of everyday life, the size of those fantasies which range from the secret life of Walter Mitty to the chivalric musings of Don Quixote.[6]

Tragedy

The purest form for the serious treatment of a theme is tragedy, which presents a protagonist who struggles against overwhelming odds and is defeated by them.

According to Aristotle, tragedy "is an imitation of an action that is serious, complete, and of a certain magnitude; in language embellished with each kind of artistic ornament, the several kinds being found in separate parts of the play; in the form of action, not narrative; through pity and fear effecting the proper purgation of these emotions."

Many theatre scholars believe that the only true form of tragedy is that which conforms to Aristotle's definition. Thus, tragedy must deal with problems that are highly serious and profound. Tragic characters battle a flaw in themselves or evil in others. They struggle against forces greater than they.

Tragedy is serious in nature. Its purpose, through our responses to the characters and their struggles, is to teach us and to make us feel. We grieve at the protagonist's defeat, which is what Aristotle means by pity. Fear is the anxiety aroused in the play, an anxiety that should carry over to our concern for all human beings.

There should be a **catharsis,** or purging of emotion—a release of all emotional tension. We should be left with a sense of tranquility. When the tragic protagonist pursues a goal to the end, we feel that strength and persistence in ourselves. If the character's actions are affirmative, we too feel the capacity for affirmation. If the character endures great suffering, so can we. Yet we also can feel superior to the tragic hero because we don't have to face the same sort of conflicts. Above all, tragedy maintains our faith in ourselves as a part of the human race. Even when tragic characters die, their heroism continues to live. What the playwright says about life, not death, is important. The issues, the heroic adherence to the dictates of conscience, and the reaffirmation of our belief in humanity are the vital aspects of tragedy.

---

6 Eric Bentley, *The Life of the Drama* (New York: Atheneum, 1964), p. 7.

Truth in Tragedy

Even though we suffer with the protagonist, we find aesthetic beauty in the total conception of the drama. Tragedy is concerned with grandeur of ideas, theme, characters, and action, and grandeur is aesthetically pleasing. Through the tragic character we come to terms with our own deaths. We accept the beauty of trying actively to improve the lot of humanity, rather than passively accepting our doom.

Although the conflict concerns human welfare, universal themes, and general problems, the workings of the protagonist's mind are the most important aspect of a tragedy. It is how the character reacts deep within to exterior events that makes for tragedy. When we hear of the death of another person, we may feel pity. But the more we know about the person's character, the more compassion and sorrow we feel. We can read of a plane crash that kills a hundred people, but unless we know one of those killed, the news usually doesn't affect us strongly. A dramatist allows us to know and thus care about the tragic protagonist.

Even though they are morally good, tragic protagonists are imperfect. We see their weaknesses as well as their strengths. They appear to be human, and so we can relate to their problem.

Figure 10.2

Masks are an age-old tool in theatre, as actors explore comedy, tragedy, and what lies in between.

Claus Meyer/North Carolina School of the Arts

Tragic protagonists must face the consequences of their actions. We know they will be defeated; no fate will intervene. In this respect the genre is true to life. As the characters discover new insights into themselves, we discover new insights into ourselves. We know that there cannot always be happy endings, but we can take satisfaction in our struggles.

Just as in life, the innocent in tragedies often suffer. Ophelia goes mad and commits suicide because Hamlet, the man she loves, kills her father. Society or individuals suffer many times because of the actions of others, even though the suffering seems unjust. Tragedy points out the injustice of life and the suffering of humanity. It shows cruelty and despair; but it also shows the heights to which the human being can rise.

Modern Tragedy

Few tragedies throughout history have reached the Aristotelian ideal; yet that doesn't necessarily make a play invalid. The definition of tragedy depends on a person's viewpoint. If we consider that tragedy occurs when a basically good person commits an irrevocable act because of a particular character flaw, the genre encompasses many more plays than those that follow the strict Aristotelian definition. We feel compassion for Blanche in *A Streetcar Named Desire* and for the foolish Don Quixote in *Man of La Mancha.* We feel sorry for the Young Woman (Helen) in Sophie Treadwell's *Machinal,* trapped and then defeated by a rigid society of which she feels she really is not a part.

Even though tragedy usually no longer deals with characters of noble birth, characters like Tony in *West Side Story* fight for what they believe. They still are basically good. They still pursue the only course of action that is consistent with their own moralities. We can identify with people such as these; we can feel the grandeur of their efforts. They are noble in their motives, if not by birth.

Comedy

The opposite of tragedy is comedy, which usually makes us laugh at ourselves and our institutions, taking them less seriously.

Of all dramatic forms, comedy has the most variety. It can be the subtle *comedy of manners,* which relies on the intellect, or it can be the physical shenanigans of farce. Comedy even has been defined at times as any play that has a happy ending, such as the sentimental comedies of the eighteenth century. Today, however, this definition is not widely accepted. Most often, comedy shows a deviation from the norm of everyday life, although it often deals with mundane problems and the pettiness of day-to-day living.

Comedy makes us laugh, though the dramatist may have another purpose, as well, for writing the play. Some writers want to teach us not to take ourselves so seriously. If we see a fault or frailty as humorous, maybe we can begin to correct it. But similarly, the playwright may want to point up a social injustice by showing how ridiculous it is, thus setting us on the path toward eliminating it. Such was the case with *How the Vote Was Won* (1909) by Cicely Hamilton and

Figure 10.3

A scene from the 1975 Théâtre du Soleil (Paris) production of *L'Age d'Or (The Golden Age)*. The character performing in this scene is dressed in the *commedia* style.

Christopher St. John (both women). Intended both as a comedy and as propaganda to secure voting rights for women in England, the play opens with the following premise.

Winifred: Well, good-bye, Ethel. It's a pity you won't believe me. I wanted to let you and Horace down gently, or I shouldn't be here.

Ethel: But you're always prophesying these dreadful things, Winnie, and nothing ever happens. Do you remember the day when you tried to invade the House of Commons from submarine boats? Oh, Horace did laugh when he saw in the papers that you had all been landed on the Hovis Wharf by mistake! "By accident, on purpose!" Horace said. He couldn't stop laughing all the evening. "What price your sister Winifred," he said. "She asked for a vote, and they gave her bread." He kept on—you can't think how funny he was about it!

Winifred: Oh, but I can! I know my dear brother-in-law's sense of humor is his strong point. Well, we must hope it will bear the strain that is going to be put on it today. Of course, when his female relations invade his house—all with the same story, "I've come to be supported"—he may think it excruciatingly funny. One never knows.

Ethel: Winnie, you're only teasing me. They would never do such a thing. They must know we have only one spare bedroom, and that's to be for a paying guest when we can afford to furnish it.

Winifred: The servants' bedroom will be empty. Don't forget that all the domestic servants have joined the League and are going to strike, too.

Ethel: Not ours, Winnie. Martha is simply devoted to me, and poor little Lily *couldn't* leave. She has no home to go to. She would have to go to the workhouse.

Winifred: Exactly where she will go. All those women who have no male relatives, or are refused help by those they have, have instructions to go to the relieving officer. The number of female paupers who will pour through the workhouse gates tonight all over England will frighten the Guardians into blue fits.

Ethel: Horace says you'll never *frighten* the Government into giving you the vote.

Winifred: It's your husband, your dear Horace, and a million other dear Horaces who are going to do the frightening this time. By tomorrow, perhaps before, Horace will be marching to Westminster shouting out "Votes for Women!"

In most comedies, traits, situations, and characters are exaggerated to show that what we think is important may not be. Particularly in period comedies, but even today, the ending shows a marriage, symbolizing a rebirth of a better set of circumstances. Shakespeare does this in many of his comedies, such as *As You Like It.*

Deviation from the Norm

The humor of comedy often comes from treatment of character or situation. Any subject matter can be used if it can be treated in a humorous light. It is only if the deviation becomes too painful that the comedy ceases to be funny. It would be cruel to treat physical deformities or handicaps as sources of comedy—even though this has been done, for example, on television's *Saturday Night Live.* More often, the things over which we have control, or our views of uncontrollable forces, comprise the subject matter.

Comedy often deals with eccentricities—greed, hypocrisy, laziness, deception, overwhelming ambition, or pomposity. Comic protagonists may become involved in situations outside their knowledge or experience—an office worker posing as a diplomat, a janitor posing as a psychiatrist. The Peter Sellers film *Being There* is funny because everyone comes to view Sellers's character as profound, when actually he is slow-witted. Comedy mocks our desire to be what we are not, or to place too much importance on our goals.

Although comedy usually deals with deviation in a normal society, the theatre of the absurd shows "normal" individuals in an insane, abnormal world. Whether society or the individual is viewed as normal, comedy begins with an idea in which normalcy is somehow reversed.

Unlike tragedy, comedy ends happily; the protagonist wins. Otherwise, the audience would feel uncomfortable for having laughed. It's important that the writer establish a comic frame of reference, or the audience may not know how they are expected to respond. They should know from the beginning that what they are seeing is not to be taken seriously and that they aren't to identify too strongly with either the character or the situation . . . unless it's a matter of laughing with instead of at the character.

Often, comedy does not hold up across the years so well as tragedy. Many comic devices depend on the present, with allusions to current society, trends, and individuals within the play's framework.

Comic Devices

Writers of comedy rely on certain devices or techniques in establishing a comic frame of reference. They are: *exaggeration, incongruity, automatism, character inconsistency, surprise,* and *derision.*

Exaggeration is intensification or enlargement through overstatement. Most people are not as miserly as Harpagon in Molière's play, nor as finicky as Felix in Simon's *The Odd Couple.*

Incongruity refers to conflicting elements that in some way deviate from the norm, such as a man's tuxedo worn with a tie-dye T-shirt.

Automatism is repetition, as in a person's acting without thought rather than rationally (like a mechanical person). It includes a visual or verbal gag repeated time after time, thus becoming funnier each time. Suppose for the first three entrances a character walks into a heavy floor lamp. On the fourth entrance she approaches the lamp carefully to see that she does not bump it. Someone calls her, and she turns her head to listen. She murmurs a reply and walks into the lamp.

Character inconsistency, similar to incongruity, exposes a trait that does not seem to fit in with the rest of a character's personality. In *Arsenic and Old Lace,* for example, the two elderly women seem to be almost a personification of goodness, except that they murder lonely old men.

Surprise includes many of the other comic devices. It is the unexpected. We know that each joke will have a punch line that we anticipate, but don't know ahead of time. The pun, the wisecrack, or the insult can surprise us. In *The Importance of Being Earnest,* the audience expects to hear a criticism when Jack admits to Lady Bracknell that he smokes. Instead, she responds that it is a good thing he does, because a man needs an occupation.

Derision is mocking people and institutions. Writers often deride hypocrisy, pomposity, or ineptitude. Yet if derision becomes too bitter, it defeats its purpose. Sarcasm can make the audience feel sorry for the intended victim.

Courtesy of Ferrum College, Virginia

Figure 10.4

British director John Hodgson rehearsing with actors for a Blue Ridge Dinner Theatre production of *Charley's Aunt,* a farce by British playwright Brandon Thomas written in 1935. In this play, an Oxford student is forced to impersonate his friend's wealthy aunt from Brazil so that the friend can propose to his sweetheart under the proper conditions.

Closely related to derision is **satire,** sometimes classified as a subgenre of comedy. Satire also ridicules, but for the purpose of reform. It is gentler than sarcasm. Gilbert and Sullivan's *H.M.S. Pinafore* satirizes the British Navy.

Types of Comedy

Because there often is such a mingling of types, comedy frequently seems to defy any sort of categorizing. However, the two extremes are *high comedy* and *low comedy.* This doesn't mean that one is better than the other, but only that the appeal differs. **High comedy** uses verbal wit and so appeals more to intellect. **Low comedy** is largely physical or slapstick.

According to playwright S. N. Behrman: "The immediate concerns of the characters in a high comedy may sometimes be trivial; their point of view must never be. Indeed, one of the endless sources of high comedy is seriousness of temperament and intensity of purpose in contrast with the triviality of the occasion."[7]

High comedy includes **comedy of manners,** which pokes fun at the excesses and foibles of the upper class. At the other end of the spectrum is **burlesque,** which relies on beatings, accidents, and, often, vulgarity for humor.

Romantic comedy usually is gentle in showing the complications the hero and heroine face in their quest for living "happily ever after." **Situation comedy** places the characters in unusual circumstances, whereas **character comedy** deals with the eccentricities of the individual.

All types of comedy have common ground. First, they establish a comic framework. Second, the humorous aspects are exaggerated, both in writing and performance. Third, comedy relies on timing. Fourth, the characters tend to be more stereotyped than in tragedy. Often, the writer is concerned with plot involvement rather than with characterization.

Melodrama

Like comedy, melodrama ends happily, at least much of the time. Like tragedy, it treats a serious subject, and the audience identifies with the protagonist. Rather than exploring a character's inner being, however, pure melodrama presents one-dimensional characters—either all good or all bad. When it deals with the painful and the serious, the subject matter is exploited only for its theatrical value. Melodrama often appears to show three-dimensional characters in conflict, but the struggle usually is only surface, and the audience knows that good will triumph. Action generally is much more important than characterization.

Melodrama offers entertainment and escapism, but it can bring the plight of individuals and groups to the attention of the audience. Within recent years, melodrama has become more realistic. The characters are less stereotyped, and sometimes the play does not end happily. There are still exaggeration and scenes of suspense and high excitement. Modern melodramas range from Shaffer's *Sleuth* to Maxwell Anderson's *The Bad Seed,* which is about a little girl who is evil. Though melodrama has changed outwardly, it has the same basic appeals: a virtuous hero or heroine, a despicable villain, and sensation.

Farce

A fourth genre is farce, somewhat similar to melodrama in that coincidence or fate can play a large part in the outcome. Farce is more similar to comedy than to tragedy. The primary purpose is entertainment. The appeal is broad,

[7] S. N. Behrman, "Query: What Makes Comedy High?" *The New York Times,* March 30, 1952.

and it takes little imagination or intellectual effort to follow the plot. Like melodrama, farce has stock characters who are one-dimensional. The plots are highly contrived and rely on physical actions and devious twists to hold the audience's attention. The play contains no message of significance, and the progression shows only how the major characters manage to release themselves from entanglements. Throughout the years the form has changed little.

William Butler Yeats describes farce this way:

> A farce and a tragedy are alike in this, that they are a moment of intense life. An action is taken out of all other actions; it is reduced to its simplest form, or at any rate to as simple a form as it can be brought to without our losing the sense of its place in the world. The characters that are involved in it are free from everything that is not a part of that action; and whether it is, as in the less important kinds of drama, a mere bodily activity, a hair-breadth escape or the like, or as it is in the more important kinds, an activity of the souls of the characters, it is an energy, an eddy of life purified from everything but itself. The dramatist must picture life in action, with an unpreoccupied mind, as the musician pictures her in sound and the sculptor in form.[8]

Because many farces are concerned with illicit sexual relationships and infidelity, they have been criticized for their immorality. But they neither condemn nor condone illicit sex. They are amoral in their outlook. The aim is to provide laughs for the audience by presenting a pattern of humorous actions.

The success of a farce relies heavily on the actor and director. They must present ludicrous actions and deliver gags and absurdities of speech. A farce that is delivered well in one language probably could succeed before an audience that speaks only another, because much of the humor is visual. Farce uses many of the devices of comedy: automatism, incongruity, derision, and physical violence.

The plot often relies on misunderstanding, mistaken identity, deception, and unfamiliar surroundings. The characters are the victims of their vices, and when caught, they appear ridiculous. An example is Georges Feydeau's *The Happy Hunter.* The title has a double meaning: The protagonist wants his

---

[8] William Butler Yeats, "Language, Character and Construction," in Toby Cole, ed., *Playwrights on Playwriting* (New York: Hill and Wang, 1960), p. 37. Reprinted from *Plays and Controversies* (London: Macmillan & Co., Ltd., 1923).

wife to think he is hunting game, when actually he is "hunting" illicit female companionship. The action is highly improbable and the entanglements along the way are completely divorced from reality.

Tragicomedy

Throughout the history of Western theatre there has been a mingling of the comic and the tragic. There is some humor in Sophocles' *Antigone* and in several of Euripides' tragedies, all written during the fifth century B.C. in Greece. Many of Shakespeare's tragedies include scenes of comic relief. Probably one of the most familiar is the gravediggers' scene in *Hamlet.* There is even more mixing of comic and tragic elements in Shakespeare's *Troilus and Cressida* and in his romances.

Within the past few decades the term *tragicomedy* has been applied to various types of drama. The term is a paradox. A protagonist who is a truly noble figure cannot appear comic. Neither can a humorous character possess the scope of a tragic hero. Nevertheless, some plays do mix elements of tragedy and comedy. Often the term is applied to absurdist plays. There is a great deal of controversy over what the form really is and when it began to exist as a new form. Some theatre scholars suggest that we discard the term altogether and call such plays tragic comedies or comic tragedies.

It takes a skillful playwright to mingle the serious and the comic effectively. Tragicomedy is one of the most difficult genres. The playwright must advance the plot without totally confusing the audience. The play must reflect the way life itself intermingles the tragic and the comic. Often, the writer of tragicomedy will present a situation that appears to be comic, and later let the audience realize that it is serious.

Harold Pinter's *The Birthday Party* is a total mingling of the comic and the serious, and some scenes even can be taken either way. The action occurs in a cheerless rooming house run by Meg and Petey. Stanley, a pianist who has sought refuge from the world, is the only boarder. Two men who seek lodging in the house suggest that a birthday party be held in Stanley's honor. During the party the two men destroy Stanley's personality and leave him speechless before they take him to their big black car waiting outside. It is never made clear why the two men are after him. Pinter called the play a "comedy of menace." The purpose is to point up the lack of contact among people. The situation appears funny, but its point is melancholy.

Playwright Eugène Ionesco said he wants his audience at times to view the tragic as comic and the comic as tragic. Although such plays as *The Lesson, The Killers,* and *Rhinoceros* present an unhappy outlook on life, they are written in such a way as to be amusing. One reason is that Ionesco often employs automatism. Examples are the repetition of nonsensical lines in *The Lesson* and the discussion about Bobby Watson in *The Bald Soprano.* To point up the comedy Ionesco wants ludicrous situations to be played with deadly seriousness.

Often in tragicomedy the audience is jolted from comedy to horror, as happens in *Who's Afraid of Virginia Woolf?* Whatever method the writer chooses to mingle the elements, the genre is well established.

Other Drama Forms

Many modern plays defy classification in any genre. Some are serious plays that have more depth than melodrama but lack the scope of tragedy. An example is Lorraine Hansberry's *A Raisin in the Sun.* The protagonist, Walter Lee Younger, changes his outlook on life and thus succeeds in keeping his dignity.

In modern plays the characters frequently are three-dimensional and we can empathize with them, but their actions are neither serious nor tragic. Often, too, modern characters are people with ordinary problems. In Tennessee Williams' *Cat on a Hot Tin Roof,* the character Big Daddy is stereotyped, but he is neither all bad nor, certainly, all good. Such, too, is the case with Maggie and Brick. Big Daddy will die, but the younger people are reconciled. The play is by no means humorous, yet neither does it end in defeat. In a sense Maggie and Brick are triumphant, but the play is not totally melodramatic in that the action is plausible.

Chapter Eleven

Architecture and Space

Theatres can spring up almost anywhere—in barns, warehouses, banquet rooms, and churches. In big cities and in small communities, plays are presented in parks, vacant lots, cultural centers, and school auditoriums. In fact, theatre can exist in any space large enough for the performers and the spectators.

We tend to think that going to the theatre means entering a specific structure designed solely for the purpose of presenting live productions. Yet theatre began in much simpler environments. In the 1960s, there was a move to bring theatre to those who wouldn't otherwise have the means or inclination to attend a performance. In fact, this concept of bringing theatre to the people is nearly as old as theatre itself. Throughout history, performers have gone from community to community or house to house to present short plays. Actually, the only requirements for a theatre are that the audience be able to see and hear and that the performers have enough space in which to present the play.

To a great degree, the type of theatre structure affects audience expectations and even helps determine the type of audience. Many people who stop to watch a performance in a community park might not don formal clothing to attend a professional production at a nearby cultural center. Theatres draw different audiences because of their architectural features. As a general rule, the more ornate the theatre, the more exclusive the audience. In the past few decades, new theatres have leaned toward simplicity of design to attract more varied audiences and to focus on the performance itself instead of on the gold-leaf designs bordering the walls. The architecture of the theatre has a bearing on what play is successful. Mountain Playhouse in Jennerstown, Pennsylvania, is a stock theatre in a converted barn. The setting is quite different from the Vivian Beaumont Theatre at Lincoln Center for the Performing Arts in New York City, and from the old opera houses of the nineteenth century with their intricate carvings and statues in recessed niches.

Areas of the Theatre Structure

The theatre can be divided into two distinct parts, the "player area" and the "audience area," or the private and the public areas.

> This particular spatial relationship thus characterizes theatre even when it is not enclosed in a physical structure, and it sets theatre apart from spatial organizations employed in other cultural systems. . . . The church or temple has perhaps the closest systematic architectural relationship to the theatre, since it involves the meeting of a secular celebrant with a sacred celebrated, but the sacred may be only spiritually or symbolically present, not spatially, as a player must be. Certain religious structures, such as the traditional Quaker meeting house, are thus able

Superstock

Figure 11.1

The upper foyer of the Theatre Amazonas in Manaus, Brazil.

to avoid the setting aside of a "sacred" space within their confines. Without a player's space, however, there would be no theatre.[1]

[1] Marvin Carlson. *Places of Performance: The Semiotics of Theatre Architecture* (Ithica, N.Y.: Cornell University Press, 1989), pp. 128–129.

Even in experimental theatre, where the actors attempt to make the audience a part of the production, the areas, though they overlap briefly, still are separate "where each performer may have only a private 'pocket' of performance space." But "even when no *specific* space is set aside for players . . . , the actor . . . [inhabits] a world with its own rules, like a space traveler within a personal capsule, which the audience, however physically close, can never truly penetrate."[2]

Overall, the private area includes the acting space and other spaces that support it—dressing rooms, scene shops, and storage areas. The public area comprises the seats, the lobby, the cloakroom, and so on.

Another way to classify the areas is to separate them into four categories: (1) the performance area, whatever its shape and/or dimensions; (2) the performance support areas, such as the costume room; (3) the audience areas (seating, concession stand, restrooms, lobby, etc.); and (4) the administrative areas (offices and, perhaps, the ticket booth, though the ticket booth could be classified either as part of the audience or the administrative areas).

Each section is dependent to some extent on each of the others. For instance, a theatre would not be likely to have a large stage area and a small seating area, nor vice versa.

Much of the building's design depends on the theatre's purpose and on the budget for erecting or adapting the building. Another factor is the relationship between actor and audience—separation, as in picture-frame staging, or intimacy, as in arena theatre, where the audience is close to the performer.

Although a theatrical production requires nothing more than an open space large enough to accommodate performers and spectators, there are four basic forms theatre takes structurally: proscenium- or picture-frame; arena stage; thrust stage; and found space, or environmental theatre.

The Proscenium Theatre

The traditional type of theatre is the **proscenium theatre.** The proscenium or proscenium arch frames the stage in much the same way a painter frames a landscape. The audience members, seated facing the opening, are asked to believe that they are viewing the action of a play through an imaginary fourth wall.

[2] Carlson, p. 130.

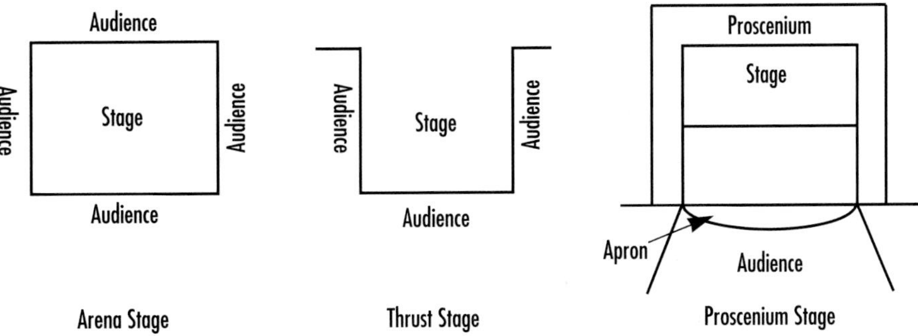

Figure 11.2

Three different theatre structures.

Scenery

Because there is a psychological as well as a physical separation of audience and actors, a setting can be portrayed more realistically in a proscenium theatre than in any other type of structure. With this type of stage the scenery that is used most often is a **box set,** or **flats** fastened together to look like the interior walls of a room or several rooms. The flats are frames made of one-by-three boards, usually covered with canvas and painted. Flats can be constructed to incorporate doors, windows, or fireplaces. Often, the scenery for a proscenium stage looks as much as possible like an actual, specific location. The box set offers further realism by providing an environment in which the actors can perform, with the setting surrounding them.

Sometimes other types of settings are used. The **backdrop** or, simply, **drop** is usually theatrical muslin, canvas, or occasionally luan, a very thin wood, that stretches across the stage. The drop is weighted at the bottom and painted to represent scenes. With drops, top curtains called **teasers** and side curtains called **tormentors** mask the backstage areas and the **fly space**—the performance support area behind the top of the arch, above the floor of the stage. At other times, **wings,** or flats that stand independently, are placed at intervals from the front of the stage to the back. Sometimes the latter type of scenery, called the *wing and drop* because the flats extend into the wing or side areas of the stage, is used for unspecified locations. It is painted in neutral shades for various changes of location indoors or outdoors, which the audience is asked to imagine.

Drops are useful because they can be flown, that is, raised into the fly space. Musicals, for instance, often require quick changes of scenery. It is simple to raise one drop and lower another. The drops attach to rods called **battens,**

W. B. Nickerson

Figure 11.3
A set for a production of Robert Bolt's historical drama, *A Man for All Seasons.*

which can be raised and lowered in a matter of seconds using a system of ropes and pulleys called the **counterweight system.**

The disadvantage of using backdrops with side curtains is that the actors now must play in front of the scenery. They cannot be part of the scenic environment. Thus, this sort of scenery lends itself better to presentational productions. Wing and drop settings can be used as interiors, but they aren't as realistic as box sets. Sometimes they are used to represent interior scenes for period plays written before the box set was developed.

Scrims, or semitransparent cloths, sometimes are used for drops. When lighted from the front, they appear opaque and the audience sees a painted surface. Backlighting allows the audience to see through them, creating a dreamlike effect.

Not only drops, but two-dimensional set pieces such as walls or cutouts of trees or rocks (and even some three-dimensional pieces) can be flown. For example, in the musical *Once Upon a Mattress,* based on the fairy tale "The Princess and the Pea," a large bird cage is used, and the "bird" is a person. The cage can be stored in the fly space until it is needed, then lowered into place.

Another type of setting used in the proscenium theatre is the **wagon stage,** a set constructed atop a platform that can be rolled on and off stage. It sometimes fits into grooves in the stage floor. Wagons can be effective for quick scenery changes when the theatre has a large enough wing space for storing them when not in use. Wagons aren't practical when space is limited or when many scene changes are required. They can be large enough to cover the width of the stage, or smaller for intimate scenes.

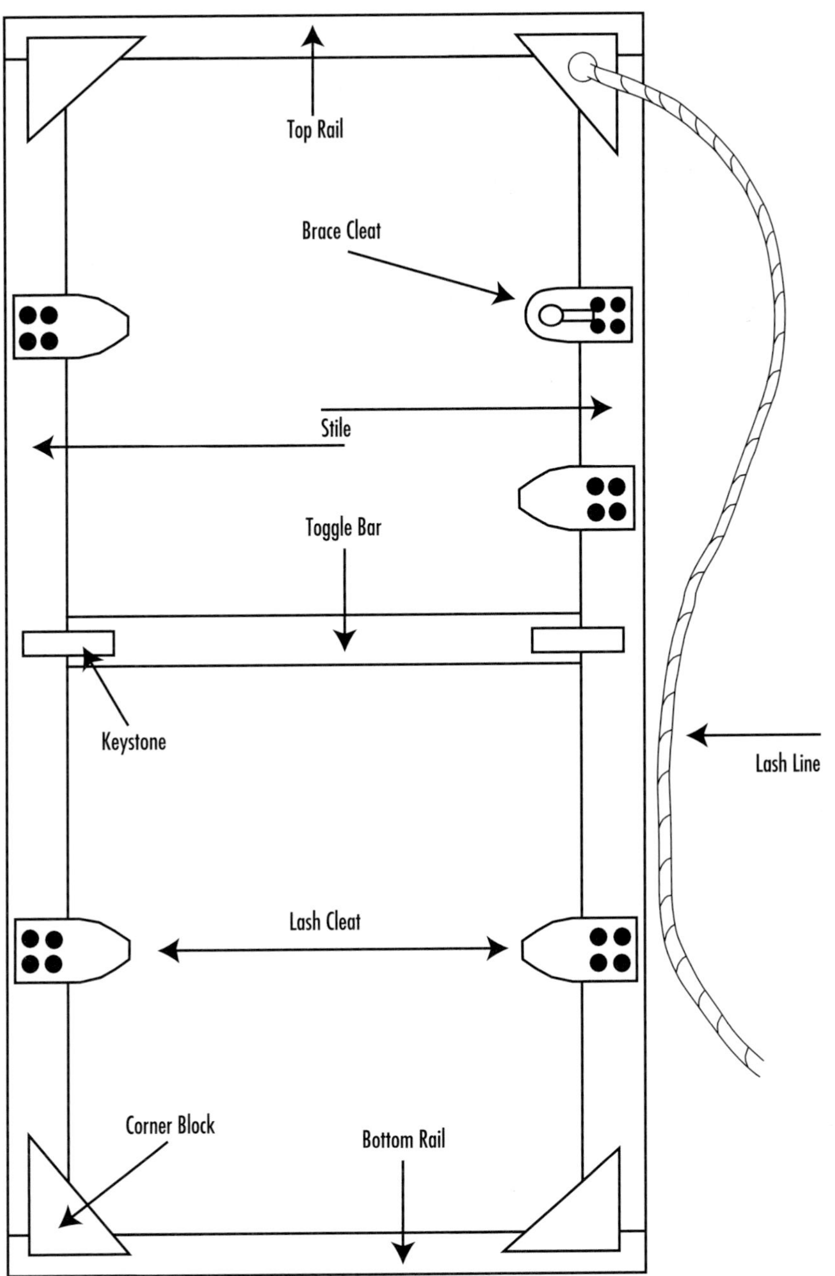

Figure 11.4

Parts of a flat, which are frames that may be fastened together to create a box set.

Other elements sometimes have been added to proscenium stages to provide further spectacle. Most, however, have not remained in use long. One is the **elevator stage.** The stage itself is an elevator that can raise and lower entire sets. Another type, still in use in some theatres, is the **revolving stage.** A circular portion of the stage floor is constructed on top of a shaft that is run by a motor and rotates the cutout portion of the stage floor. This allows two sets to be constructed back-to-back and changed quickly.

The revolving stage can also be used in other ways. For instance, when Ray Bradbury's play *Fahrenheit 451* had its world premiere at San Diego State University in the 1980s, William R. Reid designed a set that could be adapted, largely through rear-screen projection, to many locales. At several points in the play two of the characters strolled from one locale to another. To provide the illusion of covering distance, the stage revolved as the two actors "walked."

The designer in a proscenium theatre plans the setting and placement of furnishings so that the audience can have a clear view of the set from any seat in the house. Because of this, box sets are wider at the front of the stage than they are toward the back.

Stage Areas

During the Italian Renaissance, stages were *raked,* or sloped gradually upward toward the rear wall of the theatre. That's why we use *upstage* to refer to the area furthest from the audience. The area closest to the audience is *downstage. Stage Right* is the portion of the stage to the right of an actor facing the audience, and *Stage Left* is to the actor's left. The other portions of the stage draw on these terms. *Down Right* is closest to the audience and nearest the right side of the stage. *Up Center* is closest to the back wall and in the center of the stage.

In most proscenium stages there is an **apron,** or **forestage,** that projects out in front of the proscenium arch. It can be almost any size. The more it projects, the more playing space there is near the audience. Forestages are used particularly for presentational plays, and sometimes are constructed and added as part of the setting.

Advantages and Disadvantages

One of the greatest advantages of a proscenium stage is the variety of special effects that are possible. Since the stage and auditorium are separate, the front curtain, or **grand drape,** can be closed to mask changes and to indicate the end of an act. Any number of settings or set pieces can be flown in, wheeled in, or changed by hand. Properties can be stored backstage and

Culver Pictures

Figure 11.5

A view from the proscenium of the Moscow Art Theater (The Alexander Theater).

carried on when needed. Because the backstage area is masked, the actors can wait immediately offstage to make their entrances.

A disadvantage is the psychological and physical separation of the audience and actor. According to Richard Southern: "The cardinal problem about the proscenium-arch convention is that it creates a line. It is no more than ordinarily difficult to play *behind* that line; but it is very difficult indeed to discover in what tone to handle a passage where you propose to *cross* that line."[3]

The Arena Theatre

In **arena staging,** the audience surrounds the action. Although often referred to as theatre-in-the-round, the playing area usually is a square or an oval. It has historical precedent in the arena-style theatres of ancient Greece.

> Theatre in the round means three things; the first is obvious—it is a theatre where the audience completely surrounds the action on all sides. The second follows from this but is not so immediately obvious—it is a theatre where it is quite impossible to give the effect of a painted picture come to life. The third is that, speaking in general, it is a theatre which has no stage. Thus it can be properly called an *arena theatre.*[4]

As opposed to a picture-frame stage where the action is on a raised platform, the playing area for an arena theatre generally is lower than the seating area, which slopes downward. The seats closest to the playing area are at the lowest point.

Scenery

Because the audience surrounds the action, arena theatre has many requirements of setting not found in proscenium staging. There can be no realistic box sets, although scrims sometimes are used with backlights. Although the setting cannot be as realistic as that of the proscenium stage, the properties for representational shows have to be more realistic. The audience sits closer to the action and can spot substitutes.

---

[3] Richard Southern. *The Seven Ages of the Theatre* (New York: Hill and Wang, 1961), p. 275.
[4] Southern, p. 284.

Makeup in arena theatre must be more subtle and costumes more realistic. Properly dyed and lighted costumes on a proscenium stage can look rich and costly from the audience, even when constructed from a relatively inexpensive fabric. For example, monk's cloth can look like brocade. However, audiences in an arena theatre would immediately detect such fakes.

The designer in an arena setting has to be careful to include set pieces and furniture that are low enough that the audience member seated closest to the action can see over them.

Advantages and Disadvantages

In arena theatre there is a grid above the stage, and the lighting instruments always are in view of the audience, whereas in proscenium theatre the lighting instruments can be masked behind the teasers (short curtains) or focused on the stage from points in the ceiling of the auditorium.

There are other problems of concealment. The actors are in view of the audience at all times or have to make long entrances and exits down the aisles. Changes in setting are limited and must occur in full view of the spectators.

Another disadvantage of arena staging is that the director cannot be so concerned with presenting an aesthetically pleasing picture. A bigger concern is to make sure that all of the audience will be able to see at least most of the action. Difficulties arise when bodies must fall from closets, when someone must appear to be dead for a long period in view of the audience, and when someone has to exit quickly. (Chapter 14 discusses the special demands arena staging makes on a director.)

Still, arena theatre has many advantages. Most important, the audience is close to the action; there is not the physical barrier of the proscenium theatre. There can be more intimacy between spectator and performer, and there can be more subtleties of facial expression and movement than in a theatre where the audience is seated a great distance from the playing area. Indeed, with arena staging performers and audience members feel shared involvement.

A major advantage is that almost any room or space can be adapted for arena staging. The playing area itself can be much smaller because it is three-dimensional—unlike the two-dimensional effect of the picture-frame stage. Also, because the audience closely surrounds the action, the seating area covers a smaller space than in proscenium theatre, where the spectators view the action from only one side and generally sit farther from the stage.

The Thrust Stage

The third major type of theatre structure is the **thrust stage.** Sometimes the playing area is raised above the level of the audience, but most often the audience looks down on the action, as in arena theatre.

Basically, a thrust stage consists of an open playing area similar to that of an arena theatre, with a stagehouse or wall in the background through which the performers enter and exit. The audience area is three-sided. The arrangement probably resembles ancient Greek staging—after the appearance of the *skene* building in Greece's Golden Age—more closely than either of the other theatre structures do. (See page 4 in Chapter 1 for an illustration.)

Because there is a stagehouse at the rear, more scenery can be used than is possible in arena theatre. At the least, there can be a background for the action if the director and designer want one. There also is a place for storing properties and set pieces, which can be changed more quickly than in arena theatre, although the changes still occur in full view of the audience. As in arena theatre, lighting instruments hang in view of the spectators, and there can be no curtains.

The audience can become more involved than is generally possible in a proscenium theatre, because they are closer to the action, but again realistic properties must be used for a representational production.

Variations of Stages

There are several other types of stages, but they are variations of the proscenium, arena, and thrust stages. *Modified thrust stages* are theatres with a proscenium opening and a large apron that projects into the audience. *Platform stages* are similar to proscenium stages, but without a framing device. Theatres occasionally have ramps reminiscent of beauty pageants, but most often the ramps are part of a setting for one play rather than a permanent part of the theatre structure. There have been experiments with *wraparound stages,* which form an arc around part of the audience, similar to the film industry's experiment several decades ago with Cinerama. Many theatres also have both a proscenium opening and *side stages,* or small playing areas, in front of and to the sides of the proscenium opening. Here, intimate scenes with simple settings or a few characters can be played.

There is a great deal of difference among structures of a single type. Some proscenium theatres seat only a hundred spectators and have a small stage, whereas others seat several thousand, before a giant stage. The difference in size does have an effect. In a large theatre there is not the intimacy of a small one. The actors have to project their voices more and use broader gestures and movements to convey physical action. They forgo the subtleties of facial expression and the nuances of vocal tone that work in small theatres. On the other hand, a small theatre would not be able to handle elaborate productions such as *Cats.*

Many theatres—particularly those with several performance areas—contain a flexible staging area, or what sometimes is referred to as a **black box.** It allows for various staging and seating areas with temporary seats that can be moved according to the way a production is staged. The staging area can be anything from a thrust stage to an arena stage to a modified proscenium stage. San Diego Repertory Theatre, for instance, which occupies the bottom level of Horton Plaza shopping center, usually runs two productions concurrently. One is performed in what is called simply The Space, which can be arranged to suit any number of seating and staging arrangements. Although it can seat several hundred spectators, the typical black box is smaller, often seating only fifty to a hundred spectators. Many colleges and universities have such experimental theatres, largely for productions that are directed, designed, or written by students.

Environmental Theatre

Environmental theatre, or **found space,** means adapting whatever space is available to a theatrical production. Antonin Artaud of France was an advocate of this type of theatre. He believed theatre should affect more people more directly than has been the case throughout much of theatre history.

The term *environmental theatre* was introduced by Richard Schechner. Jerry N. Rojo, who designed for Schechner's Performance Group, says: "The term *environmental theatre* defines an aesthetic approach to production. It provides highly controlled conditions so that transactions involving performer, space and text may be developed organically."[5]

Schechner also was an advocate of drastic change in the audience-actor relationship. With his group, he presented plays in an abandoned garage in New York City. He experimented with seating audience members at various places, in various groupings, and even amidst the action. Sometimes the spectators sat on scaffolding and ledges.

The purpose of using found space is to break down all barriers between stage and auditorium so there can be more direct communication between actor and audience.

Rojo explains the experience this way:

> The environmentalist begins with the notion that the production will both develop from and totally inhabit a given space; and that, for the performer and audience, time, space and materials exist as what they are and only for their intrinsic value. All aesthetic problems are solved in terms of actual time, space and materials, with little consideration given to solutions that suggest illusion, pretense, or imitation. An environment, for example, never creates an illusion of, say, a forest, although actors and

[5] Jerry Rojo, "Environmental Design," in *Contemporary Design U.S.A.*, Elizabeth B. Burdick et al., eds. (New York: International Theatre Institute of the United States, Inc., 1974), p. 20.

audience may discover danger literally in a precarious arrangement of platforms, or a sense of safety may be achieved where a high place is conquered. In the more traditional theatre experience, the production is appreciated from *outside,* in a world especially created for the relatively passive observer. In the environmental experience, on the other hand, appreciation generates from *within* by virtue of shared activity. Each environmental production creates a sense of total involvement.[6]

Found space includes street theatres. Actors may perform in the street to provide cultural experience, to entertain, or to express the concerns of the audience.

Offstage Areas

Whatever the type of theatre, many behind-the-scenes areas directly affect the production. The "player" area alone is many times the size of the stage. The area from the proscenium opening to the back wall should be about one-and-one-half times as deep as the proscenium opening is wide, both for actors to have adequate crossing space from one side of the stage to the other, and for storage of props or set pieces. The wings and fly space should allow for scenery to be shifted quickly and easily, and so must be large enough to give stagehands and technicians room to store and move scenery and set pieces.

In a proscenium theatre, generally a teaser keeps the audience from seeing the battens from which lights and scenery are flown. Ideally, the fly space should be at least two-and-one-half times the height of the proscenium arch, so that full-length drops or other set pieces cannot be seen by the audience.

The wings on both sides of the proscenium opening (masked or hidden from the audience's view by tormentors) should at least equal the width of the proscenium opening. The wings are used for storing scenery and properties and for providing space for actors to wait prior to making entrances.

In nonproscenium theatres, the storage space, of necessity, is farther from the playing area. There should be storage space underneath the stage, as well, accessible by trapdoors that accommodate both equipment and human beings. The stage floor itself should be of a soft wood, generally pine, so there is no problem either in using nails and screws to anchor scenery, or in ruining expensive wooden floors.

[6] Rojo, p. 20.

Michael Whittaker

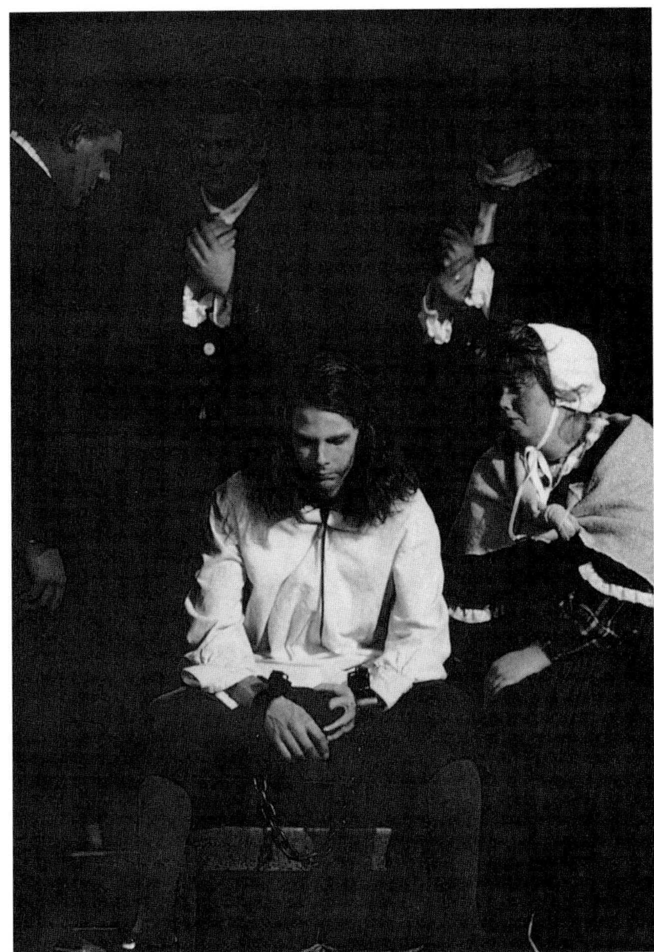

Figure 11.6

Lighting played a crucial role in the staging of Arthur Miller's *The Crucible* at Buena Vista College, Iowa.

Lighting and Sound

A theatre uses three different sorts of lighting systems: house lights, work lights, and stage lights, all of which are operated by separate controls. The house lights are in the auditorium and provide illumination for audience members to enter and exit. The work lights are used for rehearsals, for erecting sets, and for hanging the stage lights. Since the stage lights are hung differently for each show, it would be impractical to use them for general illumination, and they also are expensive to operate.

The main criterion for stage lighting is to provide good visibility. Like the two other systems of lights, they are separately controlled. During the course of a production, a lighting operator runs the lights from a control room at the rear of the theatre. Often it's a glass-enclosed room that affords a good view of the stage. (Stage lighting is discussed in detail in Chapter 15.)

A theatre also needs three types of sound systems: one that provides sound effects for a play, as well as any recorded music; an intercom system that allows technicians and/or theatre artists to talk to one another, and from which the stage manager can run the show during performance; and a public address system for communicating with the audience.

Figure 11.7

A stagehand in the scene shop at Midwestern State University (Texas) Theatre Department, working on a set piece for a production of Michael Frayn's *Noises Off*.

Scene, Costume, and Property Shops

Scenery and set pieces are constructed and often painted in the scene shop, although some theatres have a separate paint shop. Ideally, the scene shop should be the same size as the combined wings and stage space.

It should be near the stage and, if possible, on the same level and close to both a loading dock and the playing area, so scenery or supplies can easily be transported from one area to the other. The doors to the shop should be large enough to accommodate wagons, flats, and other large set pieces.

Costumes are built, dyed, repaired, and generally maintained in the costume shop, so it must be equipped with sewing machines, ironing boards, dress forms, fabrics, storage space for finished work, and full-length mirrors. It should have fitting areas, counter space, sinks, and washing machines, and there should be an area for long-term costume storage.

Some theatres have property shops, but large props usually are built in scene shops. There also should be an area near the stage to store props for

Figure 11.8

In the costume shop at the Department of Theatre in the University of Illinois at Urbana-Champaign, a designer fits a performer for a costume originally designed for a production of *O Pioneers!*

Bill Wiegand/University of Illinois at Urbana-Champaign

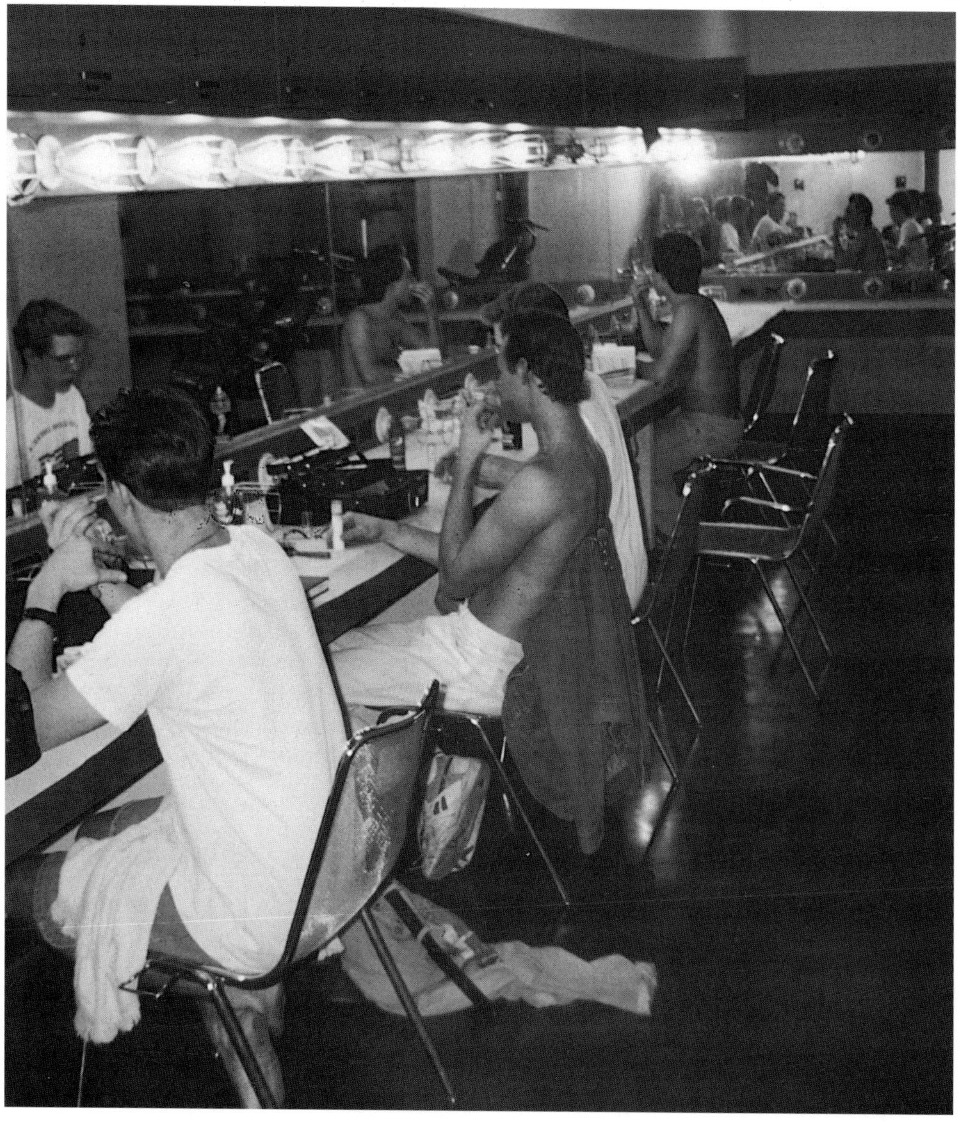

Figure 11.9

The makeup and dressing room area at Midwestern State University Department of Theatre, where actors are preparing for a performance of *Noises Off*.

current productions. Another work and storage area is the electrical shop where lighting instruments are maintained and repaired.

Dressing Rooms, Makeup Rooms, and Other Areas

Dressing and makeup rooms ideally are located close to the playing area for easy access. There are two areas—one for men, and one for women. Each contains makeup tables and mirrors that are adequately lighted. Professional theatres in particular also have "star" dressing rooms that are smaller and isolated from the larger areas. Each area should have space for storing hats, wigs, makeup kits, and, of course, space for hanging costumes that will be used in the various scenes or acts.

Many theatres have large rehearsal rooms that approximate the size of the stage. Many also have a **greenroom** where actors not only can relax before and between acts of a performance, but where press conferences can be held. Sometimes, food and beverages are kept here for those working on a production. Educational theatres also need space for classes.

The audience areas include a box office, cloakrooms or coat check areas, rest rooms, public telephones, drinking fountains, and refreshment stands, as well as the auditorium itself. The auditorium should have easily accessible seating and a pleasant decor that does not distract the audience. The area should be free from outside noise.

Professional theatres in particular have a variety of offices for directors and designers, as well as publicity, financial, and operations personnel, each with the appropriate office equipment.

Just as the types of writing and performance in theatre are changing, so are the concepts and manners of production, which makes theatre much more exciting than ever before.

Chapter Twelve

The Playwright

Playwrights, unlike other theatre artists, do much of their work alone.

> With the exception of a self-indulgent misanthrope, no one is quite so much alone as a writer, unless, of course, he owns a collaborator, in which case no two people are quite so much alone together.[1]

The playwright, working in solitude, begins the creative process that results in a production before an audience. Due to background and experience, each playwright has a different perspective, a different starting point. Even documentary plays are both more and less than the history they portray, since the dramatist, by the very fact of choosing and eliminating, is editing.

Because a play begins as one person's work, playwrights have more freedom than other theatre artists—their observations, experience, background, sensitivity, and skill are the only limiting factors of their work.

It has been said that the actor and audience are the only essentials of theatre. Yet an actor cannot exist as a separate entity. A performer needs a script, either created by the actor or by another. This script is the spring from which the production flows.

If playwrights are honest in their work, they try to present the truth of life as they see it. At the same time they give their writing a greater sense of direction than day-to-day life usually has and they try to make a play relevant to an audience by presenting conflict or problems that symbolize a universal concern. For instance, we can identify with Willy Loman's sense of failure in *Death of a Salesman,* with Tyrone's feelings of insecurity in *Long Day's Journey into Night,* with Oscar Madison's feelings of frustration at Felix's compulsive neatness in *The Odd Couple,* and with Hamlet's lust for revenge. We've all felt insecure and frustrated and vengeful. We have all experienced failures of one sort or another.

Plays almost always deal with characters' passions, those things that they care about, maybe even too much. Plays are about strong feelings and beliefs, about standing up for beliefs, about achieving, as Don Quixote called it in *Man of La Mancha,* "The Impossible Dream." For a play to successfully portray these passions, the characters need to chase their dreams or their solutions to the ultimate.

Jeffrey Sweet, author of such plays as *Porch* and *The Value of Names,* feels that "the best theater has not been separate from the society of which it is a part."

---

[1] George Oppenheimer, ed. *The Passionate Playgoer: A Personal Scrapbook* (New York: The Viking Press, 1958), p. 221.

He says that "most of the glorious moments of the American stage can be traced to some degree of social awareness. . . . Most of the greatest achievements have been the product of artists who were deeply involved in the passions of their times."[2]

In any important scenes a playwright needs to make sure that the content touches on incidents that shape the character.

What I need to do is think about something often for a year or so and then set aside time to write the play. I don't tend to have ideas, try them out, and then get rid of them. I wrote the first scene of *The Heidi Chronicles* when *Isn't It Romantic?* was in rehearsal, and then it just sat there for two years. I don't get that many ideas for plays and I don't write that many plays that often. My plays tend to come once every three years or so. Sometimes I'll think of something and say, gosh, that's a really good idea—not for me, for somebody else. And then I won't write it.[3]

—Wendy Wasserstein

I try to tell an interesting story, and then, usually, as I'm telling it I try to figure out things going on inside of me. That becomes what they call the theme of a play.[4]

—Michael Weller

What's this idea going to do that others I've seen don't do? How is this going to affect the way an audience thinks, feels, dreams about a particular subject, a particular feature of the perceptual world around us? What can this play do to make them deal with it in a way they haven't seen before? How can it make them see the values they have and make them question these values? Because affecting the audience is why one writes a play to begin with. You don't write it for yourself, the actors, or the director. You're there to do something to the audience.[5]

—Lee Blessing

---

2 Jeffrey Sweet. *The Dramatist's Toolkit: The Craft of the Working Playwright* (Portsmouth, N.H.: Heinemann, 1993), pp. 161–162.

3 Buzz McLaughlin. "Conversation with Wendy Wasserstein," *The Dramatists Guild Quarterly* (Winter 1994), p. 6.

4 Dale Ramsey. "Albee, Weller, Blessing on the Playwright's Craft," *The Dramatists Guild Quarterly* (Autumn 1993), p. 9.

5 Ramsey, p. 11.

> I found the use of notebooks very helpful, because often I would get an idea that I would be very excited about (and I do a lot of thinking before I write), but then I'd get distracted and one day I'd wake up and the idea would have just evaporated, vanished. No matter how rudimentary or primitive or unlikely, if an idea comes to me I keep it in a notebook. Then I found that something mysterious happens, and I get more interested in one idea than another idea.[6]
>
> —Horton Foote

Getting and Developing Ideas

To write work that is practical to produce, a playwright has to know the theatre—the technical aspects, what sort of scenery is practical, and how actors approach their roles.

The dramatist's job compares with the actor's in that both assimilate a diversity of material into a production. Both select, heighten, and expand.

Even in improvisational theatre—that which is created on the spur of the moment—an idea has to come from somewhere. An audience may suggest a line or a situation that the actors must immediately build into a brief play. In these circumstances the performers and the audience collaborate in developing ideas. Sometimes a theatre company or a group of actors improvises a play. Examples are *Hatful of Rain* and *Godspell.* Jeffrey Sweet describes getting together with two friends to improvise from an outline he had written. "Stephen, Sandra, and I sat around a cassette recorder and improvised our way through this scene three times. I then transcribed the three versions. I edited what I thought were the most effective passages and wrote some new material until I had the final piece, a short play called *Cover.*"[7]

Yet most theatrical productions involve a script completed by one person but to which others add their interpretations. Where do these scripts come from? How do the ideas occur and germinate?

Ideas can come from anywhere, from reading a news item or feature story to overhearing a random snippet of conversation. Dramatists then add on to what they have read or heard. Often, in seeking ideas to develop, playwrights follow and advise the following strategies:

1. Take something important or relevant in their lives and examine it. White South African Athol Fugard's 1990 drama *My Children! My Africa,* for

---

[6] Buzz McLaughlin, "Conversation with Horton Foote," *The Dramatists Guild Quarterly,* (Winter 1993), p. 17.

[7] Sweet, p. 84.

Figure 12.1

Horton Foote.

instance, concerns the politics of his country in relation to apartheid. Many playwrights, such as Eugene O'Neill in *Long Day's Journey into Night* and Edward Albee in *Three Tall Women,* base some of their work on themselves or their families.

2. Begin by examining their feelings. In *FOB,* David Henry Hwang looks at the clash between Chinese and American cultures, examining what can happen to first- or second-generation Americans who live in one culture at home and are thrust into another at school or in the outside world.

This isn't to say that every play has to have an intense message. Neil Simon's earlier plays exist largely to entertain. Yet they do have something to say.

Barefoot in the Park (1964), for instance, is about the need to compromise in order to get along in life. A later play, *Broadway Bound* (1986), is entertaining, yet it is more serious in its examination of a family's problems.

BROADWAY BOUND

Neil Simon
From Act I

JACK: There is no other woman.

KATE: I don't care. Stop it anyway.

JACK: Look, I know I've changed. I know I'm different.

KATE: Yes, you are.

JACK: I've stopped feeling for everything. Getting up in the morning, going to bed at night . . . . Why do I do it? Maybe it was the war. The war came along and after that, nothing was the same. I hated poverty, but I knew how to deal with it. I don't know my place anymore. When I was a boy in temple, I looked at the old men and thought, "They're so wise. They must know all the secrets of the world" . . . . I'm a middle-aged man and I don't know a damn thing. Wisdom doesn't come with age. It comes with wisdom . . . . I'm not wise, and I never will be . . . . I don't even lie very well . . . . There was a woman. (KATE *stares at him)* About a year ago, I met her in a restaurant on Seventh Avenue. She worked in a bank, a widow. Not all that attractive, but a refined woman, spoke very well, better educated than I was . . . . It was a year ago, Kate. It didn't last long. I never thought it would . . . and it's over now. If I've hurt you, and God knows you have every right to be, then I apologize. I'm sorry. But I'll be truthful with you. I didn't tell it to you just now out of a great sense of honesty. I told you because I couldn't carry the weight of all that guilt on my back anymore.

(JACK *waits quietly for her reaction.)*

Antonio Skármeta chose to write his play *Burning Patience* about the Chilean poet Pablo Neruda, set against a background of the evils of a fascist government.

3. Choose to write about something that arouses their curiosity. *Rupert's Birthday* by Ken Jenkins examines how one incident in a woman's childhood, helping to birth a calf, affected her entire life.

A play such as this sets up a situation and then says "what if . . . ." What if a few high-school girls stop in at a restaurant and see an older man staring at them? What if they become uncomfortable, and one of them decides she has to know why he's staring? And what if she's wearing an old high-school letter jacket that she picked up at a thrift store? And what if this jacket had belonged to the man's son? And what if the son is dead?

This is what happens in Mark O'Donnell's *Fables for Friends.*

4. Choose a subject or a situation that is haunting. Tennessee Williams based much of his writing on his sister, who had had a lobotomy. Arthur Miller was haunted by the McCarthy hearings, and so used the analogy of a witch hunt in his play *The Crucible.*

5. Begin with a real person, current or historical. Molière is said to have used himself as a model for the hypochondriac in *The Imaginary Invalid.* Examples of other plays based on real people are *The Miracle Worker* (Helen Keller and Annie Sullivan), and *Amadeus* (admittedly loosely based on Mozart's life). To a degree, events will influence the content, but the playwright is free to interpret events and express feeling about them.

6. Begin with a set of circumstances. Charles Kray did this with *A Thing of Beauty,* which is set in Nazi Germany and tells the story—based on fact—of Edith Stein, a Jewish woman who has become a Carmelite nun, Sister Benedicta. Tina Howe used both the circumstances and her memories ("hauntings") in *Painting Churches,* which takes place as the mother and father are leaving a house in which they've lived for years.

7. Begin with a setting. Louis Phillips must have done this with his comedy *Carwash,* in which vehicles driven through the Charm School Car Wash fail to come out the other side.

8. Adapt a play from another medium. Playwrights have adapted plays from novels, biographies, nonfiction books, or collections of stories. Some stay faithful to the original, while others interpret broadly. Examples are Stephen Sondheim and James Lapine's *Into the Woods* (fairy tales), Wendy Kesselman's *My Sister in This House* (an article about a crime), and Martin B. Duberman's *In White America* (historical documents, newspapers, diaries, and other records).

Choosing the Audience

Near the beginning of the writing process, playwrights must decide why they want to write a play and whom they want to reach. Often, this is a subconscious decision. Yet, as William Archer says, "The drama has no meaning except in relation to an audience. It is a portrait of life by means of a mechanism so devised as to bring it home to a considerable number of people assembled in a given place."[8]

[8] William Archer, *Play-Making: A Manual of Craftsmanship* (New York: Dover Publications, Inc., 1960), p. 9. Reprinted with permission.)

How can playwrights then go about interesting an audience in what they have to say? Almost any idea, if it's universal, can be the basis for a play. The manner in which it is presented—the characters, the setting, the dialogue, and the situations—determines whether it will hold an audience's attention, and also determines the sort of audience. The musical *Godspell* obviously appealed to a younger audience than did *Evita,* even though both had successful runs in New York a number of years ago. *Godspell* takes place on a playground where a group of young people enact Christ's parables and episodes from His life, according to the book of Matthew. *Evita* is a biographical opera about the life of Eva Peron, who rose to power in the 1940s in Argentina.

Theme is what a playwright wants to say to an audience. It's the play's central message and so is tied closely to audience response. How does the playwright want the audience to feel after the final curtain? Why? Is it simply to call attention to a serious problem the dramatist feels is important, or to look more closely at their own values?

Playwrights sometimes attempt to reinforce a common belief, as Thornton Wilder did in *Our Town,* which says we should learn to pay attention to each other and to make the most of our lives and our relationships. A writer may deal with something that is relatively alien to the experience of the audience. The goal then is to enlighten the audience. Historical plays often fall into this category, though many have other themes as well. Paula Cizmar's *The Death of a Miner* is alien to most people in its story about coal miners in West Virginia, but, of course, its concern with human rights is not alien, nor is Elizabeth Wong's *Letters to a Student Revolutionary*—even though it takes place in China and deals with the massacre of students by a government that allows no freedom of choice or expression.

Even when situations and characters are strange or different, they have to have elements with which the audience can identify. To have meaning for an audience, a play must deal with human emotions and problems. Most often audience members want to identify with and care about the central character.

On the other hand, Bertolt Brecht is highly regarded for his theatre of alienation, in which ideas and situations are more important than characters. Brecht sometimes had the actors add "he said" or "she said" after each line so they would remain emotionally detached from their roles. In *Mother Courage and Her Children,* for instance, Brecht emphasized social or political problems more than characterization, yet managed to express strong sympathy for the human condition.

In absurdist drama, which purports to point out the absurdity of life without making any judgments about it, the human condition rather than the individual characters is important, since the characters often exhibit traits of automatism and speak with illogical or disjointed dialogue.

To George Bernard Shaw, ideas were more important than characters, who sometimes carried on long conversations on philosophy and religion, as in the "Don Juan in Hell" scene from *Man and Superman.* Occasionally a writer will simply lead the audience in a particular direction, allowing them to interpret and draw conclusions, such as that racial and sexual stereotyping is wrong, as in David Henry Hwang's *M. Butterfly,* in which a man is duped over a long period of time into believing an Asian man is really a woman.

An audience is more willing to accept the theme if they are in at least partial agreement with it, for example, that war is morally reprehensible. This accounts for the success of many plays, from George Bernard Shaw's *Arms and the Man,* in which Captain Bluntschli carries chocolates in his cartridge belt, to Lavonne Mueller's *Five in the Killing Zone,* in which five soldiers in Vietnam have to identify body parts. .

There has to be common ground where the playwright and the audience meet. Audiences relate the action onstage to their own backgrounds and personalities. Here is what David Ives, writer of *All in the Timing* and *Lives and Deaths of the Great Harry Houdini,* says about the subject:

> I think of theatre as an arena for communal empathy. To write for the theatre, you have to have a kind of imaginative empathy for people in order to understand how and what they feel. You then bring that to an audience. The audience has to empathize with what you're saying, and the actors have to empathize with what you've written, and all the people who put a production together have to empathize with each other for the space of four or eight weeks. I think of theatre as this great civilizing arena where people find a common ground. It's where, in one way or another, we realize that we're in the same leaky boat, and we realize it in person.[9]

Beginning the Play

There is no particular way to begin writing a play. Some writers start with a theme, others with a section of dialogue, others with a situation or a setting. Many playwrights feel as Edward Albee does:

> I'm not a didactic writer. I don't start with thesis, and then create characters, and then create a situation to illuminate the predicament. . . . Writing, for me, is something of an act of discovery, of discovering what I'm thinking about.

[9] Stephanie Coen, "No Comparisons," *American Theatre* (Vol. II, Number 6, July/August 1994), p. 26.

Figure 12.2

A scene from the original 1956 Broadway production of the play *The Diary of Anne Frank,* featuring Joseph Schildkraut as Mr. Frank and Doronne as Anne Frank. Playwrights Goodrich and Hackett utilized Anne's diary for the stage play as well as for the 1959 film adaptation.

I really don't know the origins. They're difficult to trace. With the exception of *The Death of Bessie Smith*—which I wrote for specific reasons after reading, on the back of a record album, how Bessie Smith died—I can never remember the specific origin of the plays I write. When I discover that I am thinking about a play I've already gotten the idea for the play. As for the exact moment it came to me—it's awfully hard to answer.[10]

[10] Roy Newquist, *Showcase* (New York: William Morrow & Co., Inc., 1966), p. 19.

A writer needs a balance between what is common to all of us and what is unique to the individual. Many plays have dealt with children or young adults, each with a different perspective. The musical *Grease,* presented on Broadway in the 1970s and revived in the 1990s, did little more than present a facet of teenage life in the fifties. Compare this with William Gibson's *The Miracle Worker,* which is much more specific in its focus on the relationship between Helen Keller and her teacher, Annie Sullivan, or Frances Goodrich and Albert Hackett's *The Diary of Anne Frank.* What makes the dramatization of the real-life story of Anne Frank so successful is that the title character has feelings universal to teenage girls, even while holed up in an attic in Amsterdam for two years, where she and her family are hiding from the Nazis.

Many writers have examined the social climate with the idea of changing it for the better in some way, for instance, as Alice Childress did with racial stereotyping in *Florence* and *Wine in the Wilderness.*

It's advantageous for playwrights to be aware of the world around them, to be attuned to what they see and hear, and to recognize prevailing attitudes and concerns so they have more specific information to draw upon in creating a set of circumstances or a character. Not only does this provide the source and substance for a play, it lends veracity to the writing.

Characterization

The most memorable element of most plays is the characters. Chances are that if you are asked about a play you saw, you will begin, "Well, it was about this woman who . . . ." Most often, we identify with people first and ideas or subject matter second.

Tennessee Williams says:

> My characters make my play. I always start with them, they take spirit and body in my mind. Nothing that they say or do is arbitrary or invented. They build the play about them like spiders weaving their webs, sea creatures making their shells. I live with them for a year and a half or two years and I know them far better than I know myself. . . .[11]

11 Tennessee Williams, "Critic Says 'Evasion,' Writer Says 'Mystery,'" *New York Herald Tribune,* April 17, 1975. Reprinted in *Tennessee Williams,* ed., *Where I Live: Selected Essays* (New York: New Directions Books, 1978), p. 72.

Knowing the Characters

Just as in life it is impossible to learn everything about another person at first meeting, a playwright's relationship with the characters is a changing and growing process. Yet Williams says that although he knows his characters better than himself, "they must have that quality of life that is shadowy."[12]

After developing the characters, a playwright needs to decide what parts of them, which of their traits, an audience should see. Novelists can write pages about personality, background, motives, or actions. Playwrights describe character only through appearance or dialogue. A playwright has to be more selective than a novelist, since a play takes only a limited amount of time on the stage. Joyce Carol Oates, a novelist who later began writing plays, compares the two forms to swimming and jogging:

> Both are exercises and can be very rewarding, but they use completely different muscles. The challenge of the theatre is to make the characters vivid enough to be alive on stage and carry the weight of the action. The prose narrative voice doesn't require this; you're telling a story. . . .

Oates explains that writing a play is unlike writing fiction because "I can't tell the story—they [the characters] have to tell their own stories."[13]

A character has to want something, which he or she then tries to obtain. Often the reaction, rather than the problem, is more important because it shows a different side to the person, giving the play life and making it more enjoyable. Most plays deal with something that touches directly on the central character's past, that brings about reactions based on important personality traits.

Characters are both pushed by the past and pulled by the future. Thus, characters are set on a course that has to continue throughout the play. Like human beings, they are individuals with different perceptions and experiences. Thus, each character reacts differently in similar situations.

In *Death of a Salesman,* Willy Loman's wife Linda cannot understand why he found suicide necessary. All the bills are paid, and she and Willy wouldn't have needed much to live on. She says that he had the wrong dreams. Because of the kind of person he is, Willy reacts differently from anyone

---

12 Williams, p. 72.

13 Laurence Shyer, "The Sunny Side of Joyce Carol Oates," *American Theatre* (Vol. 11, Number 2, February 1994), pp. 25–26.

else in similar circumstances. It would not be logical, for instance, for Regina in *The Little Foxes* to commit suicide because she has failed financially. Nor would Willy ruthlessly trample anyone in his path to achieve success, as Regina does.

In addition to their uniqueness, characters should possess universal qualities—traits and feelings with which we all can identify. These draw us to the characters, help us to sympathize with their plight, and generally make us care about their lot.

Although major characters are fully developed by the playwright, minor characters are not. If they were, the audience might identify with them too strongly and be disappointed when they disappear from the play. Often, minor characters are included only to advance the plot. Consider Ben, Willy Loman's successful brother, who is a symbol of Willy's own lack of achievement. In Neil Simon's *Barefoot in the Park,* the delivery man is included only as a means for Corie's mother to keep reminding her of all she's left behind by marrying Paul, a struggling young attorney.

Revealing a Character

One way of revealing a character is by having other characters talk about him or her. But we don't learn much this way. People's views of others are colored by their own personalities. We have to meet someone to discover what that person is really like.

In Tina Howe's *Painting Churches,* it's much more effective to see firsthand that the three characters, though tied by blood and feelings, nevertheless exist in their own worlds than it would be to have a narrator tell us these things. We learn firsthand that Gardner, the father, a well-known and highly respected poet, seems to be experiencing the beginning stages of senility. His wife Fanny creates her own world in which she amuses herself by buying hats in thrift shops and ignoring or pushing away the seriousness of her husband's mental state. The daughter, Mags, appears to be concerned with her parents, yet is more interested in painting their portrait and having them accept it as good.

Dialogue

Dialogue has three main functions: to reveal character, to create atmosphere, and to advance the plot. To accomplish these purposes, the dialogue:

- has to have clarity;
- has to be appropriate to the character, the situation, and the setting;
- has to be natural.

Clarity

No matter how uneducated the characters, no matter how strong an accent or dialect, the audience should not have to strain to understand what they say.

Appropriateness

The dialogue not only has to fit personality, but it has to depict character. Some people are more hesitant than others. Some are shy, others outgoing.

The dialogue has to be appropriate to the mood. It needs a rhythm and flow that fits the emotions of the scene and the characters. Usually, the more passive the emotion, the longer and smoother the sentences and speeches. Abrupt, staccato speeches indicate just the opposite.

Naturalness

Since most plays present the actors as real people in real situations, the dialogue has to sound like everyday speech. Yet nobody speaks the same as anyone else. People in one part of the country have different vocal patterns and inflections than people in other parts. Even those who grew up in the same area speak differently due to different interests or personalities.

Environment helps to determine speech patterns. It's common for a Northerner to live in the South for a few months and to acquire the beginnings of a Southern accent. Schooling contributes to speech patterns and habits. Someone with little formal schooling may use poor grammar, or depending on personality, may compensate by speaking carefully or precisely.

Dialogue Versus Conversation

Dialogue and conversation are similar, it wouldn't work to use real conversation on the stage. Most conversations tend to ramble. They're often social in nature and thus inconsequential in content. On the other hand, dialogue has to have more of a purpose. Even when the main point of a particular play is lack of communication, the dialogue has to be selective. *The Bald Soprano* takes the everyday lack of awareness and exaggerates its absurdity. People usually are able to recognize their husbands or wives; they don't become shocked over someone's tying a shoelace.

Dialogue makes a point. It's not as repetitive as normal conversations. In order to establish a character and quickly advance the plot, it's less redundant. Of course, all these rules can be relaxed in pointing up an important character trait.

Using Physical Activity

Sometimes pantomime can be more effective than dialogue in revealing character or advancing the plot. The following occurs near the end of *Long Day's Journey into Night.* Mary, addicted to morphine given to her by a "quack" doctor, has lost touch with reality.

LONG DAY'S JOURNEY INTO NIGHT

Eugene O'Neill
From Act IV

TYRONE: *(Heavily.)* I wish to God she'd go to bed so that I could too. *(Drowsily.)* I'm dog tired. I can't stay up all night like I used to. Getting old—old and finished. *(With a bone-cracking yawn.)* Can't keep my eyes open. I think I'll catch a few winks. Why don't you do the same, Edmund? It'll pass the time until she—

(His voice trails off. His eyes close, his chin sags, and he begins to breathe heavily through his mouth. Edmund sits tensely. He hears something and jerks nervously forward in his chair, staring through the front parlor into the hall. He jumps up with a hunted, distracted expression. It seems for a second he is going to hide in the back parlor. Then he sits down again and waits, his eyes averted, his hands gripping the arms of his chair. Suddenly all five bulbs of the chandelier in the front parlor are turned on from a wall switch, and a moment later someone starts playing the piano in there—the opening of one of Chopin's simpler waltzes, done with a forgetful, stiff-fingered groping, as if an awkward school-girl were practicing it for the first time. Tyrone starts to wide-awakeness and sober dread, and Jamie's head jerks back and his eyes open. For a moment they listen frozenly. The playing stops as abruptly as it began, and Mary appears in the doorway. She wears a sky-blue dressing gown over her nightdress, dainty slippers with pompons on her bare feet. Her face is paler than ever. Her eyes look enormous. They glisten like polished black jewels. The uncanny thing is that her face now appears so youthful. Experience seems ironed out of it. It is a marble mask of girlish innocence, the mouth caught in a shy smile. Her white hair is braided in two pigtails which hang over her breast. Over one arm, carried neglectfully, trailing on the floor, as if she had forgotten she held it, is an old-fashioned white satin wedding gown, trimmed with duchesse lace. She hesitates in the doorway, glancing round the room,

her forehead puckered puzzledly, like someone who has come to a room to get something but has become absent-minded on the way and forgotten what it was. They stare at her. She seems aware of them merely as she is aware of other objects in the room, the furniture, the windows, familiar things she accepts automatically as naturally belonging there but which she is too preoccupied to notice.)

JAMIE: *(Breaks the cracking silence—bitterly, self-defensively sardonic.)* The Mad Scene. Enter Ophelia!

(His father and brother both turn on him fiercely. Edmund is quicker. He slaps Jamie across the mouth with the back of his hand.)

TYRONE: *(His voice trembling with suppressed fury.)* Good boy, Edmund. The dirty blackguard! His own mother!

JAMIE: *(Mumbles guiltily, without resentment.)* All right, Kid. Had it coming. *(He puts his hands over his face and begins to sob.)*

Writing and Rewriting

Some writers say that they record whatever comes to mind. Yet most writers have some sort of an idea about the progression of events, the theme, or even the resolution before they put words on paper. Some work out an intricate synopsis before starting to write. Others use only a minimal outline. According to Edward Albee,

> When I'm writing I work, more or less, in two parts. I think about a play at least a year before I start writing it down. The actual writing is rather brief—three months for a long play, four hours of work each morning, six days a week. I do revision in the afternoon. But other playwrights work very differently . . . . The only awful thing about being any kind of writer is that one is not engaged in a nine-to-five job working for somebody else. One is one's own boss, and one is quite alone, and one's self-discipline must be enormous.[14]

A writer often begins planning a play by choosing and analyzing the characters and their relationships and then goes on to determine the type of setting.

[14] Newquist, pp. 26–29.

Marc Connelly describes his collaboration with George S. Kaufman on the play *Dulcy* like this:

> All our free hours were spent on building the outline of the play. George and I established working methods then that we have followed through all the years we worked together. Having decided that our play should be in the mood of a warm but satiric comedy, we first fumbled about trying to visualize characters and plot progression. As Dulcinea—immediately shortened to Dulcy—was to be a girl of eccentric impulses, we saw possibilities in her engaging as a butler a convict thief, out of jail on probation. She also was the kind of girl who would invite, among ill-assorted weekend guests, an egomaniac movie producer, so we invented one she had met at a dinner party. Quickly, the characters, their development, and the narrative progression were sketched in great detail. Within a few days we had a completely articulated synopsis of about twenty-five pages. We then individually chose scenes for which we had predilections, wrote drafts, and then went over them together for improvement.[15]

The Opening Scene

Each play should start with a "hook" that captures the audience's attention immediately. A playwright therefore usually begins with a high point, as in the following scene, which opens Terrence McNally's *Frankie and Johnny in the Clair de Lune.*

AT RISE: Darkness. We hear the sounds of a man and woman making love. They are getting ready to climax. The sounds they are making are noisy, ecstatic and familiar. Above all, they must be graphic. The intention is a portrait in sound of a passionate man and woman making love and reaching climax together.

The real thing.

They came.

Silence. Heavy breathing. We become aware that the radio has been playing Bach's Goldberg Variations in the piano version.

By this point, the curtain has been up for at least ten minutes. No light, no dialogue, just the sounds of lovemaking and now the Bach.

15 Marc Connelly, *Voices Offstage: A Book of Memoirs* (New York: Holt, Rinehart and Winston, 1968), pp. 59–60.

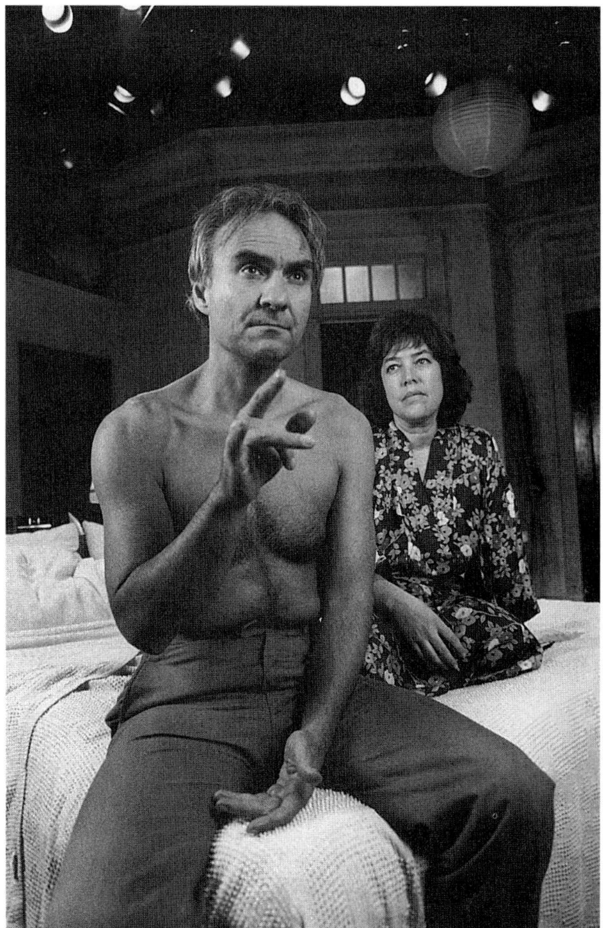

Figure 12.3

A scene from *Frankie and Johnny in the Claire de Lune,* the 1987 Broadway production starring Kathy Bates and Kenneth Welsh.

FRANKIE: God, I wish I still smoked. Life used to be so much more fun. *(JOHNNY laughs softly.)* What?

JOHNNY: Nothing. *(He laughs again, a little louder.)* Oh, God!

FRANKIE: Well it must be something.

JOHNNY: It's dumb, it's gross, it's stupid, it's . . . *(He howls with laughter.)* I'm sorry. Jesus, this is terrible. I don't know what's gotten into me. I'll be all right. *(He catches his breath. FRANKIE turns on a bedside lamp.)* Really, I'm sorry. It has nothing to do with you.

FRANKIE: Are you okay now?

JOHNNY: Yes. No! *(He bursts into laughter again. And now FRANKIE bursts into laughter: a wild, uncontrollable, infectious sound.)* What are you laughing at?

FRANKIE: *Barefoot in the Park:* I don't know! *(Now they are both laughing hilariously. It is the kind of laughter that gets out of control and people have trouble breathing. FRANKIE rolls off the bed and lands on the floor with a slight thud.)*

JOHNNY: Are you okay?

FRANKIE: No! *(Now it is FRANKIE who is laughing solo. It is a wonderful joyful sound: a lot of stored-up feeling is being released.)*

JOHNNY: Should I get you something?

FRANKIE: Yes! My mother!

JOHNNY: A beer, a Coke, anything?

FRANKIE: A bag to put over my head!

JOHNNY: You really want your mother?

FRANKIE: Are you crazy?

JOHNNY: You have the most . . . the most wonderful breasts.

Planning the Exposition

A writer also can plan the exposition ahead of time. *Background exposition* deals with the opening situation of the play, the *progressive exposition* continues throughout and is related to the unraveling of the plot and the revelation of character.

There are many techniques for presenting exposition, such as:

1. Using a narrator, such as the Stage Manager in Thornton Wilder's *Our Town,* who becomes the "bridge" between scenes. This works well because of the way the play is written. Generally, however, the narrator tends to distance the audience from the characters.

2. Using flashbacks, a means of "showing" past events that have a direct bearing on the play. This can be effective since the action of a play, unlike a novel, occurs in a continuing present time. This means that even when we travel backward in time to pick up a scene of this sort, we restart the clock, so to speak, so that the audience "sees" the scene as it is occurring.

3. Through characters talking about another person. An example would be the scene in *The Fantasticks* where the fathers of Matt and Luisa sing about knowing how vegetables will turn out once you plant them, but the difficulty in knowing how children will turn out.

4. Through such devices as meetings, partings, reunions, or other special occasions where people are likely to reminisce.

5. Through situations in which people are introduced to each other and try to find common ground for conversation.

6. Through touches of anger or irritation in dialogue. "Damnit, Charlie, this is the second time today I've had to clean up your dishes. Half the time you don't put your clothes in the hamper or hang up your jacket."

7. Through scenery, lighting, costuming, props, and makeup. The setting, unless it's abstract, shows the location and often the circumstances of the characters. The lighting and costuming can give clues to the season and the time of day, for instance.

8. Through conflict, which not only is more interesting but also moves the plot forward, since the conflict usually has its basis in the central problem.

It may take many drafts before a dramatist is satisfied with the result. The revisions may include rearranging the scenes, cutting sections or speeches, adding new scenes and dialogue for clarity, or trimming and sharpening the dialogue.

Even when the playwright is satisfied, the producer, the director, the actors, and the technical people may suggest or insist upon additional alterations.

Presenting the Play

> You know you're a writer when your ultimate reward is not the money that comes with it, but the precious opportunity to write again. And again. To let the hearts and minds and souls of your characters live inside you again and again as you head to work or do chores around the house. What greater feeling is there than that? Playwrights know what I mean.[16]

It isn't an easy task to have a play produced. Often writers have a better chance of having their work presented in theatres with which they are affiliated, or at least where they know someone on the staff.

Many theatres have play development programs, offering staged readings to plays they feel have the potential to be successful. That is, actors rehearse the play a few times but read from the books. They perform physical actions and use props, which (despite there being no specific set) gives a better idea of how the play will move.

Even after a first production, a play may need extensive rewriting. Things come across differently from the way they do in a reading when the play is performed before a theatre audience.

---

16 Philip Vassallo, "The Reasons to Write," *The Dramatists Guild Quarterly* (Autumn 1994), p. 35.

Playwrights have the choice of submitting their work to producers, contests, professional theatre companies, educational theatres, community theatres, various summer theatres, and drama publishers.

Producers and publishers are listed in such books as *Dramatists Sourcebook,* published each August by the Theatre Communications Group in New York, and in *The Playwright's Companion,* published yearly by Feedback Theatrebooks of New York. Each has a fairly comprehensive list of producers, publishers, and agents as well as listing various playwriting prizes, festivals, conferences, and workshops for playwrights.

Many playwrights join the Dramatists Guild, which publishes both newsletters and quarterly journals giving many listings of theatres looking for scripts. There are a variety of organizations, including arts councils in many states, that provide grants or aid to playwrights. Some offer an opportunity for production.

Gallery

Plates 1–19: Photographer, Brent Nicastro, Madison, Wisconsin

PLATE 1

Elaborate costume design and makeup was chosen for the character of Ravana, the Demon King of Lanka (M. P. S. Namboodiri) in *Tales from South Asia: The Story of the World's First Play*, as scripted and directed by Sharon Grady and Phillip Zarrilli and produced in 1992 at the University Theatre (University of Wisconsin-Madison).

PLATE 2
For a 1986 production of *Godspell,* a musical based upon the gospel according to St. Matthew, with music and lyrics by Stephen Schwartz, CTM Productions of Madison, Wisconsin, chose a whimsical assortment of costumes for five of the characters, shown here during a rehearsal.

PLATE 3
Dramatic lighting was key in this breakfast scene in Nöel Coward's 1930 comedy *Private Lives,* produced in 1995 by the Madison Repertory Theatre at the Isthmus Playhouse (Madison Civic Center, Wisconsin) and directed by D. Scott Glasser, with lighting designed by Thomas C. Hase.

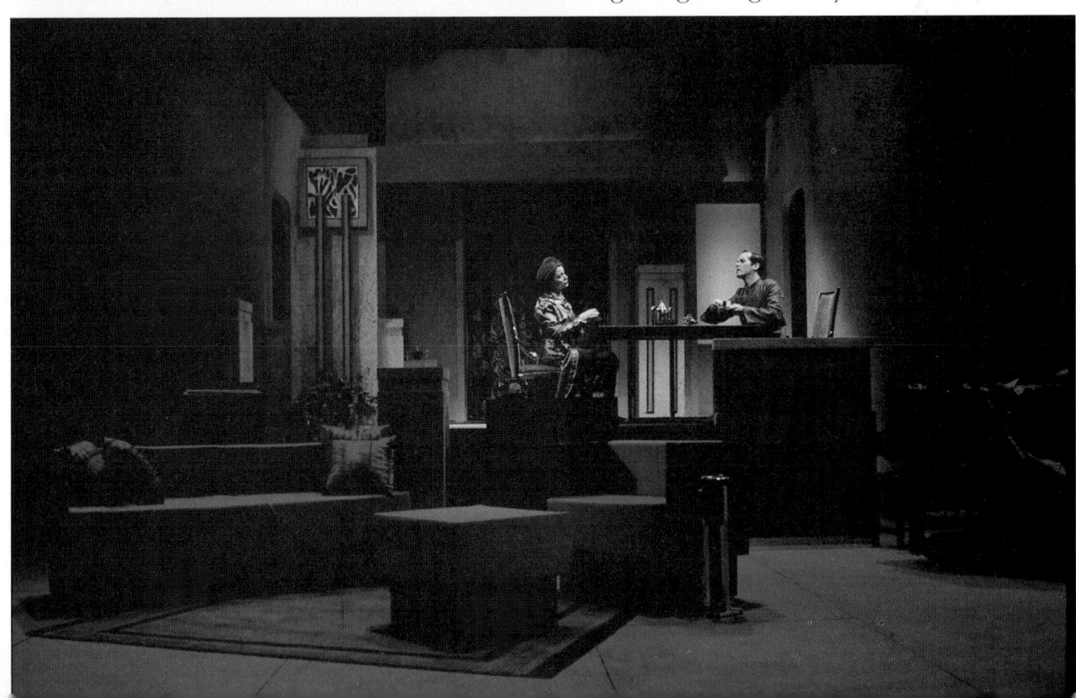

PLATE 4

A scene at Herr Schultz's Fruit Shop from the musical *Cabaret,* based on the book by Joe Masteroff and featuring music by John Kander with lyrics by Fred Ebb, from a 1993 University Theatre (University of Wisconsin-Madison) production directed by John Staniunas, with scenery and costume design by Dana Lauren Kenn. The lighting design was by Erik Appleton.

PLATE 5

In this scene from Daniel Sullivan's *Inspecting Carol,* a comedy-farce, Jason W. Bohan plays Wayne, a would-be actor whom Kevin (Stacy Loomis, right) mistakes for a representative of the National Endowment for the Arts. A 1995 University Theatre (University of Wisconsin-Madison) production, *Inspecting Carol* was directed by Ed Amor, with scenery design by Joseph Varga.

PLATE 6
Another scene from *Inspecting Carol* shows a play within a play, an NEA-funded production of *The Christmas Carol,* which The McClosky Street Theatre, a small community theatre in a fictional midwestern city, is working on as the time for inspection arrives.

PLATE 7
In Act Two from *Inspecting Carol,* the director of *The Christmas Carol,* Zorah (Karole Spangler) makes a dramatic entrance just prior to her attempt to seduce Wayne.

PLATE 8
In the final scene of *Inspecting Carol,* the real NEA representative, Betty (Natalie Buster), in costume as Elizabeth I, appears on the stage of the McClosky Street Theatre.

PLATE 9
The masked ball scene from Act One of the 1995 University Theatre (University of Wisconsin-Madison) production of Shakespeare's *The Tragedy of Romeo and Juliet,* directed by Karen Ryker.

PLATE 10

In a scene in Act II of the same production of *Romeo and Juliet,* Mercutio (Jim Nolan Lobley, in red) jests with the Nurse to Juliet (Karen Prager), as Benvolio (Daniel Dennis) and Romeo (Sean Bradley) look on.

PLATE 11

Friar Laurence (Tom Haig), who secretly married Romeo and Juliet, has just told Romeo (Sean Bradley) that he has been banished from Verona for killing Tybalt, Juliet's kinsman, during a duel. The Nurse (Karen Prager) looks on as the Friar tries to console Romeo in this scene from Act III of *Romeo and Juliet.*

PLATE 12

In Act IV of *Romeo and Juliet,* Juliet (Jeany Park), having taken the potion Friar Laurence secretly gave her, appears to be dead the morning she is supposed to marry Paris (Stacy Loomis, center standing). Note the strategic use of lighting for this scene in Juliet's chamber to indicate the morning and to focus on Juliet.

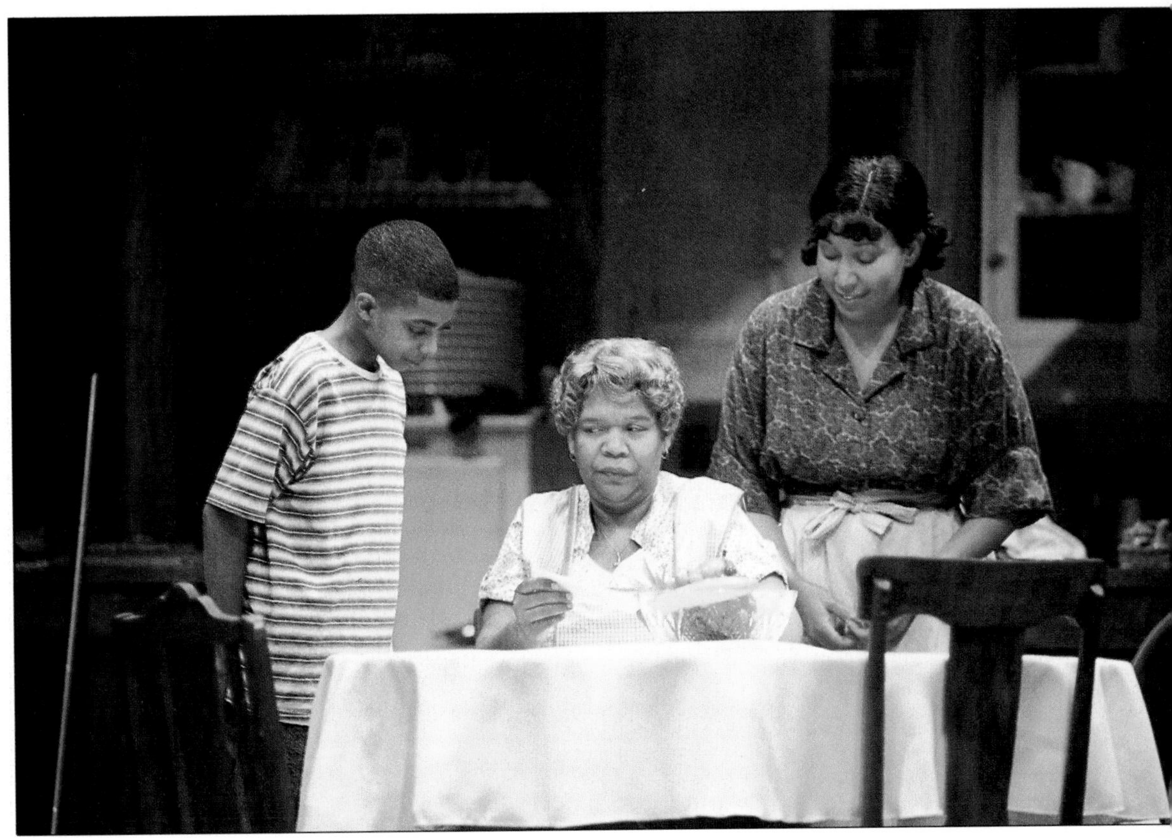

PLATE 13

In a scene from a 1996 New American Theater Center/Madison Repertory Theatre production of Lorraine Hansberry's *A Raisin in the Sun,* Lena/Mama Younger (Audrey Morgan) examines a check for $10,000, an inheritance she has just received. Edward G. Smith directed this production at the Isthmus Playhouse (Madison, Wisconsin, Civic Center).

PLATE 14
In a later scene from a rehearsal of the same production of *A Raisin in the Sun,* Walter Lee Younger (Cedric Young) laments losing the $10,000, as Mama/Lena Younger, his wife Ruth (Vikki J. Meyers), and Beneatha Younger (Jenna Ford) listen.

PLATE 15
In another scene from the same production of *A Raisin in the Sun,* Walter explains how love has gone out of his marriage because of Ruth's constant nagging, as Ruth stands behind the sofa and Mama stands in the kitchen.

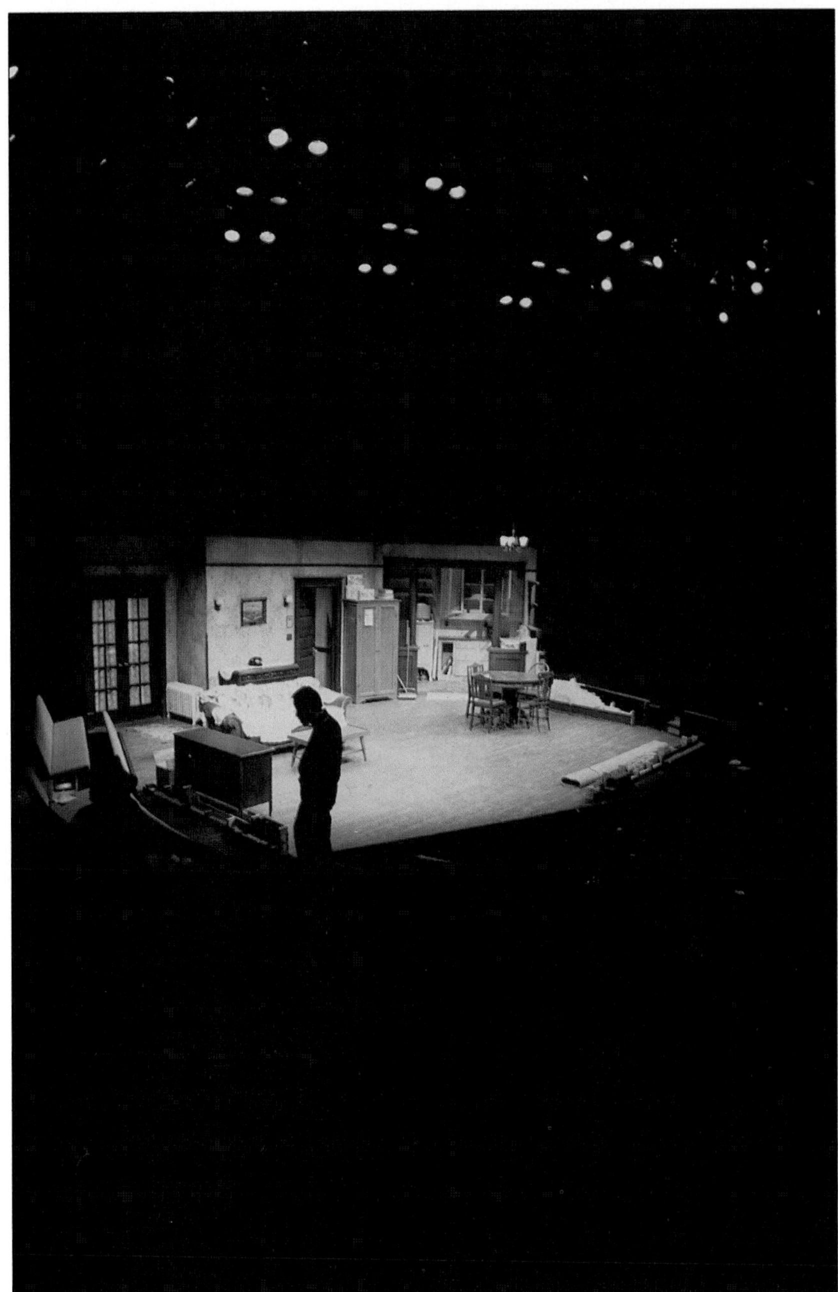

PLATE 16

Following the final dress rehearsal for *A Raisin in the Sun,* Madison Repertory Theatre Artistic Director D. Scott Glasser (standing, in silhouette) consults with guest director Edward G. Smith as lighting designer John Fraustchy runs through lighting cues.

PLATE 17
Director Robert Skloot consults with actors Quint Strack, who plays Cole, and Maria dePalma, who plays Keely, during a rehearsal for a 1996 University Theatre (University of Wisconsin-Madison) production of Jane Martin's gripping drama about issues in today's abortion rights debate, *Keely and Du.*

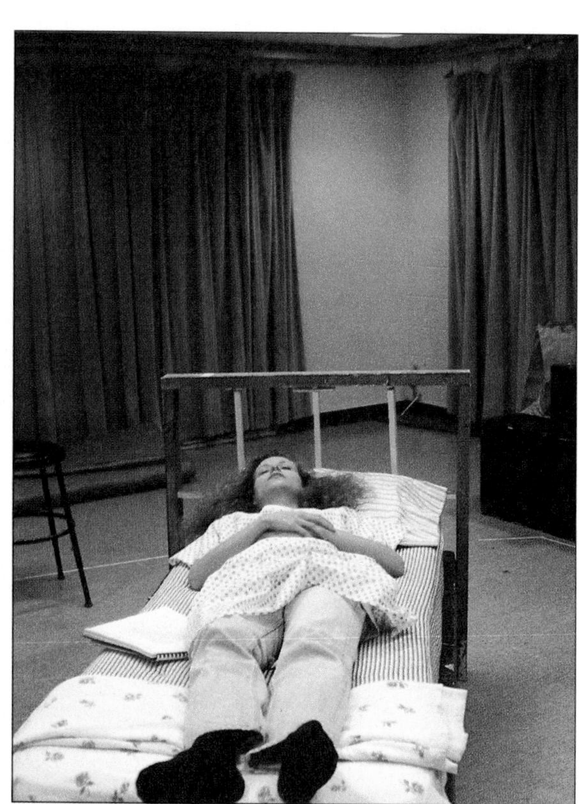

PLATE 18
Maria dePalma, playing Keely, a pregnant rape victim, rehearses a scene from *Keely and Du* in which she prepares for a confrontation with Du, a woman who is charged with her care.

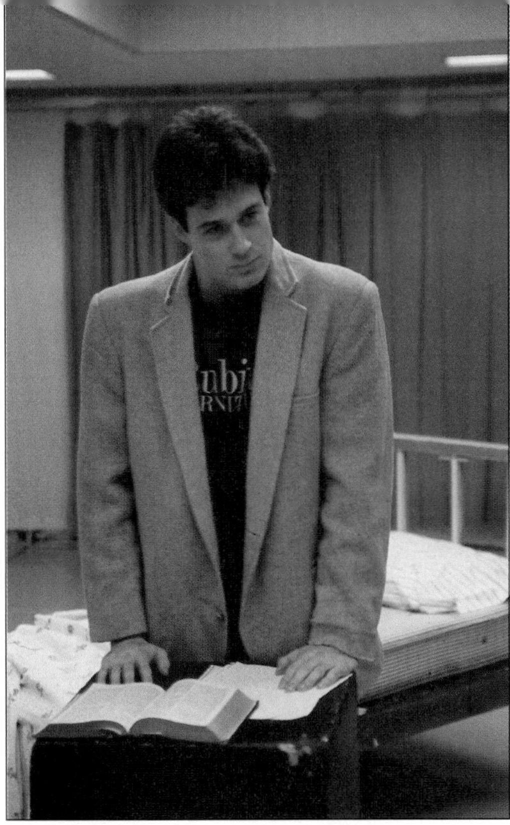

PLATE 19
Jeff Morrison, who plays Walter, an ardent pro-life minister in the same production of *Keely and Du,* studies the script during rehearsal.

PLATE 20
In this scene from Tony Kushner's *Angels in America, Part One: The Millennium Approaches,* Roy Cohn (Ron Leibman) has a playful encounter with Joe Pitt (Jeffrey King) at a cocktail party. This 1992 Mark Taper Forum (Los Angeles) production of *Angels in America,* which explores the gay community, discrimination, AIDS, and public policy, was directed by Oskar Eustis with Tony Taccone.

Plates 20–23: Photographer, Craig Schwartz

PLATE 21

In a scene of a shared drug-induced dream from *Angels in America,* Prior Walter (Stephen Spinella, left), who speaks about gay life and discrimination, confides in Harper Pitt (Cynthia Mace), Joe's wife.

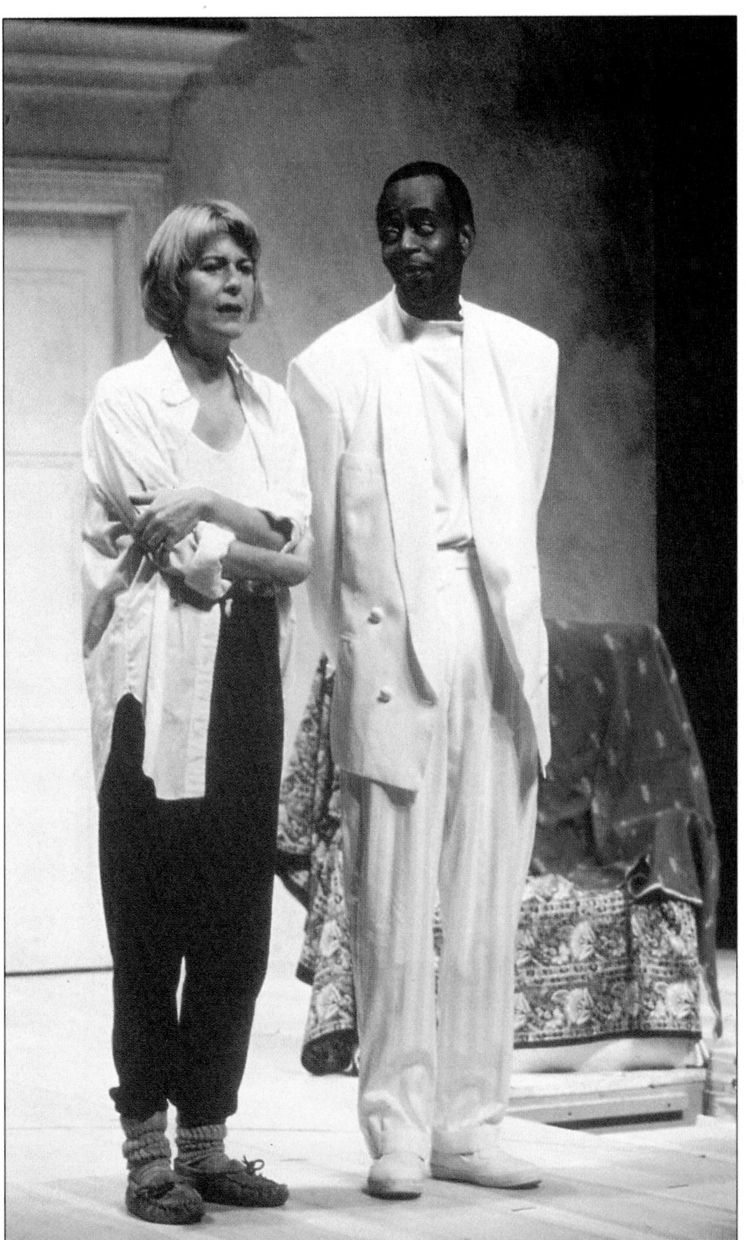

PLATE 22
In another dream scene from *Angels in America,* set in 1986, Harper (Cynthia Mace) talks with Belize (M. Todd Freeman), who is the nurse to dying AIDS victim Roy Cohn.

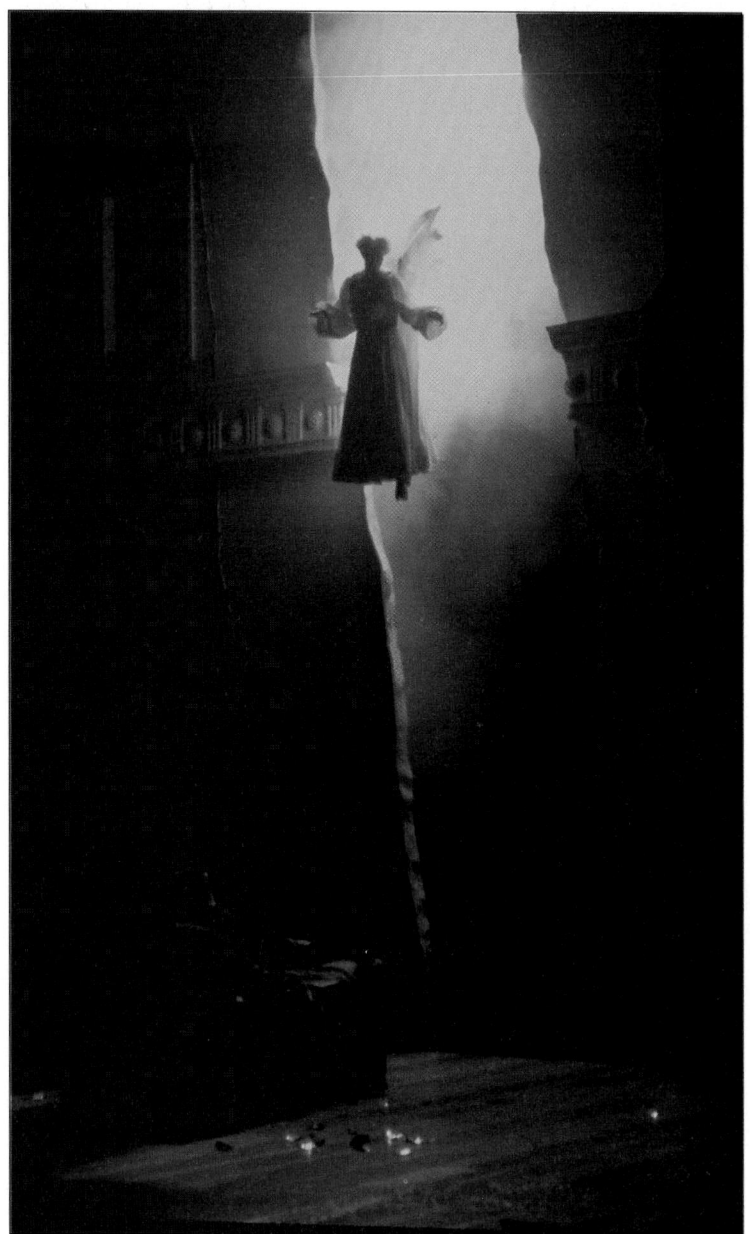

PLATE 23
The Angel (Ellen McLaughlin) descends to Earth in this final scene of *Angels in America, Part One: The Millennium Approaches.* Set Designer for this Mark Taper Forum production, presented in association with the New York Shakespeare Festival, was John Conklin; Lighting Designer, Pat Collins.

Chapter Thirteen

The Actor

Theatre cannot exist without an actor, the person with whom the audience most closely identifies, the one who provides the glamour, who personifies theatre in the eyes of the spectator. Yet, according to British psychologist Brian Bates, the general attitude toward actors is confused.

> We admire them and detest them. We deify them and sneer at them. We watch in our millions when they appear on television interview shows, but then we require them to talk about the most trivial aspects of their lives. And while a few actors are rewarded with knighthoods, others are served up for breakfast as titbits *[sic]* of notoriety beneath the cheap headlines of the popular press.[1]

Despite the admiration, the sneering, the constancy of performers in the public eye, actor John Gielgud says, "Of all the arts, I think acting must be the least concrete, the most solitary."[2]

Why, in light of the prominence of the actor among theatre artists, is he or she the most solitary? Perhaps because in some ways an actor's work is similar to a playwright's examination of self, of delving inside for answers to questions, of focusing inwardly.

Later, of course, the actor takes what comes from inside and makes it real for an audience in an attempt to persuade them that what they are seeing is much like life itself. "If somebody asked me to put in one sentence what acting was, I should say that acting was the art of persuasion."

> The actor persuades himself, first and through himself, the audience . . . . At the most high-faluting, the actor is as important as the illuminator of the human heart, he is as important as the psychiatrist or the doctor, the minister if you like.[3]

Where other artists use canvas and paint, or fabric and light to birth their work, actors rely on little else but themselves. They have setting, lights, makeup, and costumes, but these are accessories, accouterments. The actor alone is on display.

---

[1] Brian Bates, *The Way of the Actor: A New Path to Personal Knowledge and Power* (London: Century, 1986), 15–16.

[2] John Gielgud, *Early Stages* (New York: Macmillan, 1939), p. 311.

[3] Hal Burton, ed., *Great Acting* (New York: Bonanza Books, 1967), p. 23.

Painters frame and hang their work at exhibits; authors publish novels. But actors exhibit themselves; their art is themselves, not divorced and apart. The art they exhibit is the most direct and intimate of all, and because of this one of the most demanding.

According to Tony Award winner Mary Alice:

> What an actor has is himself or herself: the body, the mind, the imagination, the psyche, the voice—whatever makes up me. This is the instrument and learning how to use this is very important. It's related to knowing oneself—who I really am, how I really think, how I really feel, being very honest in my life so that I can be very honest in my work. How can I bring truth to a character that is written by someone else? How can I tell that person's story if I don't know my own?[4]

A ballerina dances; a vocalist sings; a reader interprets a poem or a piece of prose. Actors often use all these arts in a given performance.

Painters can change a landscape or even discard it if it fails to meet their standards. Actors have only one given moment to convey their message, and then the moment is past.

Noel Coward summed up the demands an actor faces onstage:

> You've got first of all to remember the character you've learned and studied and know about; you've got to remember your voice pitch, which has got to reach the back of the gallery, without shouting; you've got to remember your other actors—vitally important to get their eye, speak to them, not to the audience, to them. Then you've got to listen to the audience's reaction. . . . I believe that all acting is a question of control, the control of the actor of himself, and through himself of the audience.[5]

---

[4] Joan Jeffri, ed., "Mary Alice," *The Actor Speaks: Actors Discuss Their Experiences and Careers* (Westport, Conn.: Greenwood Press, 1994), p. 23.

[5] William C. Young, "Noel Coward," *Famous Actors and Acresses on the American Stage* (New York: R. R. Bowker Co., 1975), p. 226, from an interview on the BBC by Michael MacOwan, 1952.

Figure 13.1

Actors at Ferrum College (Virginia) rehearse a scene from a production of *Charity for All,* a local historical drama written and directed by R. Rex Stephenson.

Onstage and Offstage Acting

To convey their art, actors rely on mimetic instinct, developed more fully than that of the average person. As renowned British actor Michael Redgrave once said, "It is a truism that actors are born and not made; another truism that acting cannot be taught. The basis of acting is undoubtedly instinctive."[6]

Even if acting is instinctive, the person who successfully plays the role of history student in real life may have difficulty playing the role of a serious history student in a stage production. On the other hand, the stage actor who never studied history may successfully portray such a role, relying on other experiences to "feel" the part.

When we see actors in a performance, we can be fairly certain that they always are aware that they are acting, that they are playing to a particular audience. Everyday role playing often is an unconscious act. A student returning home after class does not consciously think, "Now I am going to assume the role of a roommate, friend, or relative." Actors on a stage are conscious of their surroundings. They remember to move in a certain manner, to use properties in a particular way at a certain time, and always to project their voices to fill a theatre. They are aware of body placement, of the arrangement of the other actors, and what is expected of each as a part of the total production. Role playing is more spontaneous. In trying to reach a goal, people in everyday life may have several alternatives. For the actor (unless the situation calls for improvisation), a playwright has written the script, the director has planned out action, and the scene occurs within a certain framework and setting, still, of course, with room for the actor's own creativity.

An actor is more aware of fitting into an overall scheme than is a ruthless business tycoon who tramples everyone to reach the top. The actor must consider (except in one-character plays or performance pieces) that constantly to dominate the scene means failure for both the performer and the production.

Helen Hayes once said of acting, "What you're doing . . . is projecting yourself into someone else entirely, into the mind of the author, into the being of the character. You are trying to settle down to be comfortable in that character and speak the author's words. You are merely an instrument for what he is saying."[7]

Because each person possesses the rudiments necessary to becoming a professional actor, it often is difficult to distinguish acting from role playing. In realistic productions the actor who most successfully conveys the impression of life or of being natural is the most successful. Therefore, it may seem that

---

[6] Michael Redgrave, *The Actor's Ways and Means* (New York: Theatre Arts Books, 1953), p. 30.

[7] Roy Newquist, *Showcase* (New York: William Morrow & Co., Inc., 1966), pp. 204–05.

there is little difference between "acting" in life and acting on the stage. However, live theatre is not and can never be life.

There is an old saying: "Everyone thinks he can be a writer." The same is true of acting. Because we each use the mimetic instinct and because stage acting appears to be like life, many people think there is nothing difficult about appearing in a play. All you have to learn is to project your voice a little more than normal, and you can do just as well on the stage as the next person can.

To become an actor requires a strong drive to succeed—a drive that most often is a prerequisite to endless training and years of hard work. Geraldine Page explains:

> I read everything I could about people in the theatre. The ones who stayed in the business for a long time and established themselves, strangely, took an average of about ten years to get a foothold. . . . So I said, "Oh well, it'll take about ten years and the broader a base I can build, the firmer I'll be." But then the tenth year began to go by. And I had always had this conviction that "I've got it and I'll get it. I'll get well-paid and I'll get recognition someday because I'm terrific." I'm still my best fan. So, the ten years were almost up, and I was talking to some of my acting friends and I heard this same firm tone of conviction from them. I thought, now wait a minute. Evidently this subjective feeling that you are it, that you are anointed and that you're going to live happily ever after is not a full guarantee.[8]

Even performers who have acted professionally for years often continue their studies. Just as a dancer spends years on elementary exercises and a singer repeats scales endlessly, the actor keeps practicing.

Tools of the Actor

Any art that belabors its medium or draws attention to technique is not good art. We appreciate a piece of sculpture for its beauty, for the freedom and flow of its line. In turn, we appreciate acting that involves us in a total production and that fails to call attention to itself. If we stop to think that an actor is performing well, he or she probably is not.

[8] Joan Kalter, ed., "Geraldine Page," *Actors on Acting* (New York: Sterling Publishing, 1979), pp. 14–15.

> It is wrong to suppose, as many actors do, that a true inner feeling will inevitably express itself in a true outward form. This will only happen when the voice, the speech, and the body have acquired by rigorous training and discipline a flexibility instinctively at the command of the inner truth, and no physical technique is of any use to an actor until it is so much an organic part of him that he is not really conscious of its employment.[9]

The Mind

As important as any of the other aspects of an actor's mind is the willingness to learn. Stage and film actor Paul Muni once said:

> If I were to use a principle at all in acting, . . . it would be that if the mind—the basic generator—functions alertly and sums up its impulse and conclusions to a correct result, it is possible for the actor to achieve something creative. Technique, which comes with practice, gives you a firm foundation on which to build your structure. But unless the mind sends out the sparks, the forces that stimulate the body to perform a series of actions that generate a spontaneous emotion, nothing creative can happen.[10]

Actors, of course, need to understand the techniques of acting—the various styles in which a production can be presented, and how to execute these styles. This is an intellectual process. Then they analyze; they try to discover the most effective way to project characters, emotions, and reactions. This is technique. "The best definition of technique I know," actor Hume Cronyn explains, "is that means by which the actor can get the best out of himself."[11]

The Body

Much more is involved, however, than mental processes alone. Actors' bodies must be in shape to sustain high levels of performance. Actress Sybil Thorndike puts it simply: "You've got to be like iron."[12]

---

9 Phillip Burton, *Early Doors: My Life and the Theatre* (New York: The Dial Press, Inc., 1969), p. 165.

10 Young, "Paul Muni," p. 841.

11 Newquist, pp. 66–67.

12 Newquist, p. 50.

Even after years of performing, Sir Laurence Olivier refused to rest on his accomplishments:

> I keep myself very fit now, I have to. I go to a gym twice or three times a week, not merely to look tremendously muscular, but I have to keep fit for my job. I'm determined to hold on to my job. I love it. But it is no use pretending it doesn't involve a certain amount of overwork, because it does. I've seen a lot of contemporaries get a bit under the weather with such work and I'm determined not to.[13]

Not only does the actor try to stay fit for good health, the demands of a role may require an athletic body. Actors often are called upon to perform exhausting feats, such as sword fighting or dancing.

The Voice

To be most effective, actors should develop their voices to its fullest potential. They should understand how the voice works and learn proper exercises to improve its use.

This means learning to portray emotions through various vocal qualities, to make pitch and volume fit the situation and character, to project, and to articulate clearly without calling undue attention to the words.

The voice has to have strength and endurance. It should be flexible to fit a variety of circumstances. The actor needs to have complete control over it. By doing proper exercises, much like a singer's, actors learn to use the voice without strain.

The Self

It has often been said that actors should never look upon any experience in life as wasted. Years later, a certain incident or feeling may suggest an approach to a character or a scene. Anything a person sees or hears can be useful in assuming a role.

In this regard, renowned actor Hume Cronyn says that an actor "must become so facile in the use of your physical equipment that it will respond instantly and do what you want it to do." Yet even so, a person could still be "a bloody awful actor."

---

13 Hal Burton, p. 16.

> Without the inner things—without being able to call on qualities of emotion or spirit—you're stuck with only a husk, a frame, a case. How do you go about developing what should be inside? How can you exercise that inner person, enrich it, make it immediately responsive? This is much more difficult because it's infinitely more subtle. . . .
>
> How one charges the batteries, how one learns and grows in the sense of total artistic appreciation and an understanding of the world we live in and our particular society, is a much more subtle and complex thing. One can't awake in the morning and say, "From now on I'm going to be aware, aware, aware. I'm going to be like a sponge and soak it up." You can't do it mechanically, yet without one's emotional antennae constantly aware of how people behave, respond, and react, without some degree of analysis of your own surging emotions—particularly in the moments when they're ungoverned—you're not growing. You have to find out these things because that's the grist of your mill. . . . All this must be, in turn, lent to the author by being brought to bear on the given emotional conflicts of a play.[14]

Much of an actor's training, in other words, should be self-training. Many people go through life paying little attention to the things or people around them, even to their own feelings. Yet the person who is able to *feel* both physically and emotionally, who has reservoirs to draw upon, has the better chance of success on the stage.

An actor has to be able to get outside self and see the world from different points of view. Only by using their imaginations and by being sensitive can actors project themselves into characters and situations.

Freeing the Imagination

Youngsters have no problem using the imagination. They play house or space travelers. They pretend/believe their stuffed animals are real, as Hobbes was real to Calvin in the comic strip *Calvin and Hobbes.* But Hobbes—a stuffed toy—came to life only when he and Calvin were alone. Unfortunately, this is how life is for many people, able only to pretend when they are alone. This is because most of our lives we've been told to pay attention and stop daydreaming.

---

[14] Newquist, pp. 66–67.

An actor or director or designer needs to let the imagination soar, to imagine what it is like to live in fear of being ousted as a ruler (Henry in Goldman's *Lion in Winter)* or to have been treated merely as a toy (Nora in Ibsen's *A Doll's House*).

Observation

Actors imagine how they would react in certain circumstances, so that they can play their roles effectively. They observe how other people stand, move, and sit, and how they react to pressure, happiness, anger, and all the other emotions. Performers get into the habit of observing and recording in their memories the way individuals talk and any idiosyncrasies of character that might be transferred to a role.

Mercedes Ruehl describes an exercise involving a character sketch assigned in a workshop she attended:

> You would study somebody on a subway, or a bus, or walking down the street; and the first thing you would do is, you would take them in. Like, I would notice that you're sitting with your leg crossed; and you're not looking at me straight on, but slightly at an angle. And that there is a smile, and that you wear lip gloss and that you have a very bright, keen, scrubbed healthy face and the long hair. And I would notice how your clothes make you sit. And then you have to get close enough to see what they smelled like. Every sense had to be involved in this character sketch. And if you didn't hear them talking, you would have to engage them in a conversation. Then you would have to watch how they gesture when they talk, and you would try to get just the timbre and the rhythm of their speech, and the accent. And as you were describing this person to the class, you would be incorporating every characteristic as you described it. What you were going for was a transformation—that thing that hooked you finally into the life of this other character.[15]

Becoming Creative

Creativity is often intuitive, based on prior knowledge. A good actor is not afraid to experiment—to see what works with a characterization and what doesn't. The actor maintains an openness of feelings and perceptions and is able to draw upon and mold them to fit a characterization.

15 Joan Jeffri, ed., "Mercedes Ruehl," *The Actor Speaks,* p. 165.

Through characterization, actors present an illusion of life. Just as a child pretends that a stick of wood is a polished sword, so the actor creates an illusion that suggests reality to an audience. Actors take what previously has been internalized and externalize it.

Formal Training

Actor training involves both the body and the voice. According to vocal consultant and dialect coach Elizabeth Smith:

> Body and voice are closely related. Posture has a great deal to do with the efficiency with which you can breathe. Ideally you're trying to rid the body of unnecessary tension, and you're trying to make it easier for someone to use their breathing mechanism. Breath is to voice what gas is to a car. It's the fundamental energy that makes it work.[16]

Actor training often begins with classes in oral interpretation, singing, dancing, and fencing—the last not only as an end in itself, but as a means of body control. There are some schools that have actors participate in team or individual sports to improve reflexes and to build stamina. Sometimes the games move into pantomime—playing ball games with imaginary equipment. Through these exercises actors learn to concentrate on how people actually respond in various situations.

As another exercise, an actor often is told **given circumstances** or basics and must proceed from there. Given circumstances are the background information (exposition) that sets a scene and establishes characters. After they receive the information, the actors create the action or carry the scene to its conclusion. The given circumstances could be as simple as being asked to take out the garbage when interested in watching a television show, or bursting into an adjoining apartment to complain about the noise of a wild party. Similarly, actors may participate in exercises in **sense memory,** that is, remembering and portraying anything sensory—walking in a light rain or eating an apple.

Less traditional forms of training include psychological and emotional exercises to stimulate the senses. In addition to developing sensitivity to self, others, and the environment, such training builds confidence and breaks down inhibitions. Often, the training is closer to role playing than to acting.

---

16 Candi Adams, "Elizabeth Smith: Articulating the Actor," *American Theatre* (January 1994), p. 29.

Figure 13.2

Actors go through a series of exercises as part of an acting class in the Department of Theatre at Northwestern University.

Sensitivity training has valid uses in many areas of the actor's development. One exercise, for instance, is to have actors work in pairs. One is blindfolded for a short period of time and must rely on the other for guidance. Not only can this exercise help an actor to develop trust in another person, it can sharpen the senses other than sight.

Newer forms of actor training look back to ritual and tradition. The new movements often are reactions against some parts of the old, at the same time embracing some of their aspects. For example, at the Polish Laboratory Theatre in Wroclaw, founded by Jerzy Grotowski in the late 1960s, rigorous training exercises are based in such diverse areas as gymnastic movements, Chinese classical ballet, and yoga.

Technical Requirements

Actors must know the stage areas and the implications of various types of movement. They know that curved movement under many circumstances can indicate indecision, whereas one of the strongest movements in projecting determination is from Upstage Center (the central area near the back wall) to Downstage Center (the area closest to the audience). They understand what body positions can suggest and know how to balance the stage picture.

Actors may be called upon to do almost anything on the stage. Often they must handle unusual properties or move naturally in cumbersome costumes. They may need to work with all of these elements, just to get their feel. They often may have to experiment with makeup to gain the right effects and to become used to moving about on a set built on different levels. An actor may have to sing or dance in addition to portraying a character.

Actors need to become acquainted with and be able to perform in a variety of styles—the unadorned movement of classicism, the gracefulness of romanticism, the earthy delivery of naturalism. They know that the audience and they themselves generally should be more involved in a tragedy or serious play, whereas both usually should stand somewhat apart from the roles in comedy. They should give the impression that they are sharing the joke with the audience in a comedy, and that they are playing for laugh lines while still maintaining balance between involvement and technique. Too much exaggeration, if it is inappropriate to a character, can destroy a role. So can too much naturalness, where the actor fails to project voice and actions.

Actors are responsible for communicating a variety of feelings with only a few words or gestures. They are oral interpreters who add their own interpretations to a written work while remaining true to the original purpose. Unlike writers or sculptors, they rely on many other artists, who in turn rely on them to present a successful play. They have a duty to the designers, the director, the other actors, the playwright, and most important, the audience. They must understand their roles and the whole play to fulfill this duty.

Approaches to Acting

Psychologist Bates says, "For most of us, the sensation of being taken over by an alien being, having our body possessed by an outside 'personality,' would be terrifying. We would fear we were going mad. But for some actors possession is not only what they experience, it is what they *seek* to experience."[17]

[17] Bates, p. 69.

For the actor there are many ways of achieving transformation; making the physical, emotional, even spiritual journey from one's being to that of a character, a role: another person. Quite often it is . . . a combination of disguise and performance. But to concentrate on the physical appearance only is to miss a fundamental aspect of the actor's art of transformation. An actor can *look* different from his usual self because he is different 'inside.' Entering into the psychological, mental, emotional world of a character can result in quite startling physical changes. Sometimes a physical transformation can be literally 'coloured' by inner concentration.[18]

This experience of "possession" accounts for many different actors being able to transform themselves physically, without unusual makeup or costumes, into the grotesquely deformed John Merrick in *The Elephant Man* by Bernard Pomerance, or to age fifty years over the course of a play and to do it convincingly. In effect, this involves, as least on one level, becoming the character.

The Internal Approach

In 1906 director Konstantin Stanislavsky of the Moscow Art Theatre first brought together all the elements that make up the internal approach, later referred to as the Stanislavsky System. The approach was a reaction against declamatory and extravagant acting styles, which relied on memorized gestures and posturing to portray emotion. Stanislavsky sought to present dramatic truth through an observation of life or nature. He taught that actors should seek truth of feeling and experience in the characters they play, finding the psychological depth of each role.

Stanislavsky wanted to find the true nature of creativity in the human being and subsequently discover the means for its development. He became increasingly interested in the operation of the subconscious and emotions. He formed the concept of **emotional memory**—remembering how one felt in a particular situation and relating that memory to similar circumstances of a character in a play. Most often, he felt, emotional memory isn't necessary, but it can be used if an actor is having difficulty feeling the emotion in a scene. He felt actors need to move, perceive, concentrate, and feel while on the stage—not merely pretend to do so.

[18] Bates, pp. 94–95.

The External Approach

Those who follow the external approach are largely concerned with technique. They think it is unnecessary to undertake the study of a role by trying to understand emotionally what a character does and says. It is necessary only to determine what the emotion is and then modify outward, observed signs of this emotion to fit the role. Sir Laurence Olivier felt that:

> Method actors are entirely preoccupied with feeling real to *themselves* instead of creating the illusion of reality. They want the absolute kernel of a character before starting to express anything. I decided, perhaps rather hurriedly, that this was wonderful training for film acting, where the camera and microphone can come right in and get your reality—the tiniest shade of your tone of voice, every little twitch of expression. But our problem on stage is to convey an illusion 50 or more yards away. That's where the big stretch comes—that's where imagination, where know-how above and beyond inner reality comes in. But I don't see that it matters where you start, inside or out, as long as the illusion ends up the same.[19]

Critics of the external approach say that the actors are using "tricks," because they are concerned with effect rather than feeling. They are, of course; but to some degree all portrayal of character involves "tricks" because the actors are aware of the audience and playing to them.

Often, the external can become internal. For instance, if we frown for a long enough time, we are going to be in a negative mood. If we smile, we begin to feel joy or happiness.

Those actors who play for effect are using the external method; those who seek the truth of the character are using the internal approach. Yet no matter which approach they use, actors have to be concerned with projection, the delivery of memorized lines, their spatial placement in relation to the other actors, and other technical aspects. Therefore, they perform on two levels—one concerned with analysis and technique, the other concerned with feelings and veracity and the appearance of life.

Acting is a combination of technique and "being" or feeling. It's been said that the best time for an actor to feel strong emotion is in the early stages of rehearsal. After that, he or she has to be in complete control, or else risk not being convincing.

---

[19] Young, "Laurence Olivier," p. 885, from Richard Merryman, "The Great Sir Laurence," *Life*, May 1, 1964, p. 81.

Other Approaches

Within the past few decades, methods of acting have begun to change. Part of the new experimentation in theatre can be credited to the Living Theatre of Julian Beck and Judith Malina, who sought to make drama fluid and poetic. They believed that new methods of acting should be discovered for new plays that were being written.

As Grotowski of the Polish Laboratory Theatre stated: "I believe there can be no true creative process within the actor if he lacks discipline or spontaneity."[20] Grotowski believed that the best approach to theatre and acting was to strip them of all nonessentials. That meant there should be no sets, make-up, lighting, or costuming. The actor, through discipline and control, creates these things in the minds of the audience. By controlled movement the actors create whatever they wish the audience to perceive. Impulse and reaction are simultaneous. The actor does not merely desire to perform a certain action but is incapable of not performing it. The skills become involuntary. The goal is to eliminate mental, physical, and psychological blocks. The result is the totally disciplined formation of a role in which all inhibitions are nonexistent and every phase of self is revealed.

Developing a Character

In reading a script, the actors see that the exposition or the development of the plot divulges certain character traits and uses these traits as a starting point, adding characteristics and features that are consistent with the character's personality.

Often, directors will have actors improvise a scene with the character. The scene is based either on the play itself or on an incident entirely divorced from the play. The actor learns how the character is likely to react in a variety of circumstances and becomes more comfortable with the role. The actors also project how the character reacts emotionally, psychologically, and physically to each situation and to the other characters within the play.

Analyzing a Role

Actors generally analyze a role in much the same way that the playwright (and the director) analyze the play as a whole. First, particularly if they rely on the inner approach, actors often seek the **spine** or **superobjective**—the goal the character wants to reach. The actor determines the overall goal first, and then

[20] Jerzy Grotowski, *Towards a Poor Theatre* (New York: Simon and Schuster, 1968), p. 209.

breaks the play into short scenes or units to determine the reason for the actions and reactions in each section. In this way, he or she understands how a character builds, how a personality unfolds or gradually is revealed, and where the focus should be in each section.

Defining the spine works best with realistic or naturalistic plays in which the characters approximate real people. One actor conceivably could discover a different spine for a role than does another actor. Often the director helps the actor interpret, but, except sometimes in premiere productions, the actor has no chance to ask the playwright what the goal of that character should be.

After determining the superobjective, the actor analyzes each individual scene to figure out its specific objective and how it contributes to the overall goal.

Determining the Character's Makeup

Actors go on to determine as much as they can about their characters by asking themselves certain questions. For instance, what is the character's physical makeup? Actors, of course, cannot drastically alter their basic physique, but they can change things such as apparent age, hair color, and posture.

Although playwrights indicate what a character is like or even describe him or her, rarely can the actor find complete information within the given circumstances, which really serve only as a starting point.

Next the actors determine as much as possible the characters' backgrounds, much as a playwright does. Where were they born? Where did they grow up? What are their educational, sociological, ethnic, and financial backgrounds? What are their present circumstances? The more an actor "knows" about a character the easier it is to make him or her believable on the stage.

The actors also determine how their characters view the world. What are their basic beliefs about life in general and the circumstances in the play in particular? How are they most likely to react in certain situations? What are their most important personality traits?

Because of time limitations the actors can present only a few of a character's traits. They decide which are most important to the audience and why. They determine which facets of the character's personality should be emphasized and which deemphasized.

As you learned, characters often are a combination of a type and an individual. For example, a universal trait is Oedipus's pride, whereas an individual trait is his limp. To individualize a character the actor often emphasizes a distinctive trait that may not be suggested in the script, but that immediately identifies the character in the minds of the audience. For instance, an actor portraying Tyrone in *Long Day's Journey into Night* could play with a silver dollar as a symbol that he has money, or pick up pieces of string and put them into drawers to indicate miserliness.

© T. Charles Erickson

Figure 13.3

Actors rehearse for a production of Shakespeare's *The Tempest* at the Yale School of Drama.

Determining Relationships

Another consideration is how a character feels about the other characters. Why? What is the character's self-image? How do these feelings relate to the theme or action of the play? As Katharine Cornell says, "To understand one's own character thoroughly one must see it in relation not only to itself but to the other characters in the play."[21]

Although the character analysis occurs before, or at least near the start of, the rehearsal period, the actor enters the role with the understanding that the character will continue to build until the play is presented. If this

[21] Young, "Katharine Cornell," p. 222, reprinted from an interview in *Theatre Arts Monthly,* January 1977.

were not so, much of the rehearsal period could be eliminated. Rehearsal involves exploring relationships and projecting the actors more completely into their characters. Building and growth often develop naturally once actors appear onstage together. It is much easier to act well when fellow actors are doing a good job; it is easier to establish the mood and to determine rhythm and pace.

Figure 13.4

Onstage positions for the actor include the full-front body position, strongest for an actor onstage. The quarter profile often is used when actors talk with each other. The further upstage an actor turns, the weaker the positioning usually becomes. The back position is rarely used.

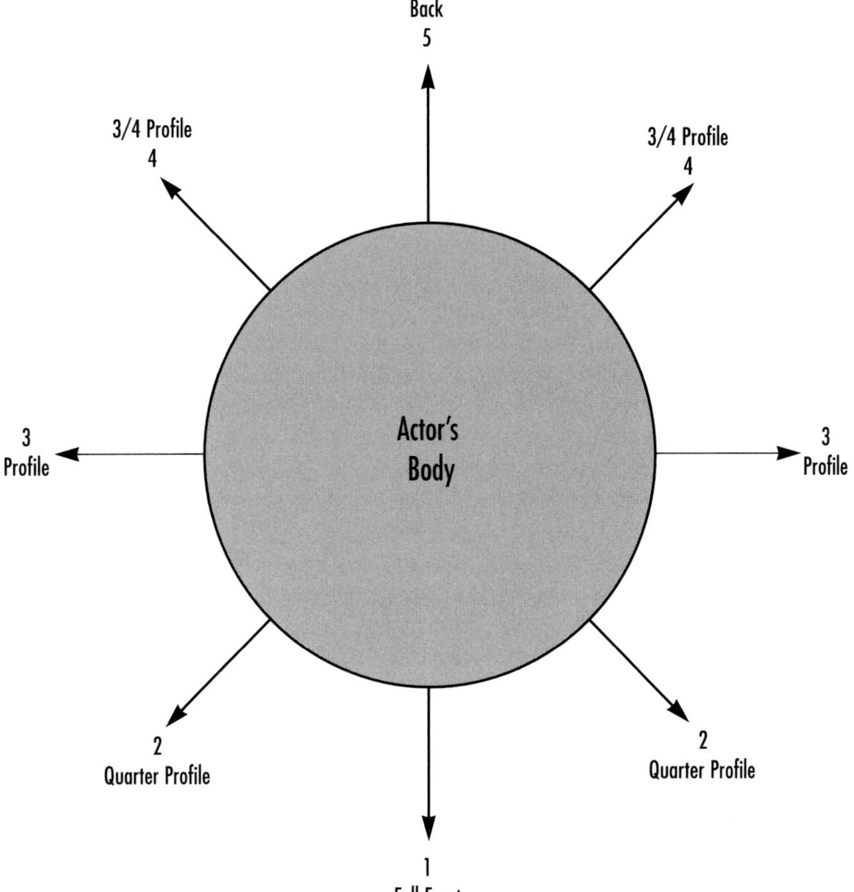

Memorizing Lines and Business

The rehearsal period begins with the memorization of lines and **business** (physical actions necessary to the advancement of the story or to delineating character). Once the actors have learned the sense of the scene, the lines become easier to learn and to remember. Directors sometimes have actors who have not yet learned their lines ad-lib a scene, using the ideas but not the exact dialogue. This exercise can help both in characterization and in giving the actors confidence that they do know the direction the action is taking.

Along with their own lines, the actors memorize their **cues,** the lines or actions preceding their own. They learn the sequence of ideas in order to convey the playwright's message or theme.

Most acting involves the ensemble concept, the willingness to yield to other actors when the script indicates they are the center of focus. Actors must understand each other's actions and speeches as well. Even when actors are not speaking, they listen to what the other characters are saying and react to what they hear. If not, the audience members will sense a false note in the performance.

Interpreting Ideas

Success in interpreting a role depends on the appearance of spontaneity. Unfortunately, it is common to see actors who have played their roles for a long time become automatic in their acting and responses.

Laurence Olivier once remarked, "I have a horror of a performance becoming mechanical, automatic, and I watch like a hawk for signs of it. Then we try to find fresh lines, fresh ideas and emotions—new deliveries to make them spontaneous again."[22]

While immersing themselves in their roles, actors also remain aware of technique. They are ready to meet unexpected audience response, and they watch for the occasional fluffs of lines or mistakes of technicians. Also, despite the fact that in real-life situations people sometimes become so angry that they scream and lose their voices, actors cannot afford to do so. They have to be aware of vocal technique and the technique of building a scene. If they wholly immerse themselves in the role, oblivious to outside changes or interference, they are letting themselves in for disaster.

There has to be a balance between the purely artistic and the purely technical; between credibility and projection. Actors, through training and experience, learn to trust their own intuition. If they begin to doubt themselves,

---

[22] Young, "Laurence Olivier," p. 886.

they will fail in their roles. They have to be confident that what they are doing is the right thing. They must be able to free themselves of doubts and inhibitions.

The actor's job, then, is to create, to interpret, to illustrate, to heighten, and to expand. The work bears the mark of the actor's own personality, because like all artists, actors give of themselves. Yet actors usually are interpreting the work of others, including the playwright, who provides clues to the building of a character, and the director, who provides only the basic blocking and interpretation.

The Business of Acting

Making a living as an actor, unfortunately, is almost next to impossible. Little more than 10 percent of those in **Actors' Equity Association** (the union for actors in legitimate theatre) are employed at any given time. And in all the actor's unions combined, only three thousand or so are working steadily. A much smaller percentage make a living as actors over their working lifetimes. Even those fortunate enough to land jobs in original New York productions may work only a few nights before the show closes due to poor reviews and lack of attendance.

Yet thousands try; thousands believe that they can make it. Some of them can, at least for a time. There are opportunities in nearly every medium-sized to large city to act for pay, and there are theatres off in small towns or even out in the country. There are non-Equity (nonunion) jobs, but most of them will barely support a performer—if they support him or her at all. The picture is bleak. Of course, there are many other jobs connected with theatre and many opportunities for acting in community theatres on a non-professional basis.

Those who do make it as stars, or at least who work much of the time, nearly always wait for years for their break.

> [S]ometimes I just want to get up in front of some bunch of kids and just say, "You know, you have to stay with something past despair." Because that point where all of my anger and pain and hurt and tired of wearing coats that were too cheap and not warm enough for these New York City winters and blah-blah-blah. That was a point of a certain kind of despair. And I just finally thought, "It's not going to happen. I could have sworn it was going to happen, but it's not going to happen." And in my life, at least, that was the point that I had to bust through and get on the other side. I had to stay with it past despair. And I think sometimes, you know, in relationships, just when you want to despair of the person ever

coming through, you stick with them. You don't close them out of your life. You don't close this theatre out of your life entirely. Don't close this dream out entirely. And sometimes that's when it happens. I guess you have to *want* to do it. As Tad, my great teacher, said, you have to be able to look somebody in the eye and unflinchingly say, "I would die if I couldn't do it. . . ."[23]

A Voice from the Past (Not Much Has Changed)

The following is part of a speech delivered in 1928:

> Until a few years ago the actors in America, owing largely, I presume, to the . . . fact that the theatre was not considered a fine art, pursued their calling under conditions which were little short of intolerable. They were overworked, often underpaid, subject to unfair and illegal treatment with no easy redress, and, off the stage, regarded, save for a few bright exceptions, with a more or less contemptuous eye. In a young country, such as this was not so long ago, it was natural that its inhabitants should turn more readily to the plow and the sword than to the buskin and the grease-paint. . . . Native play-acting was regarded askance as a career; and parents whose offspring took to it shuddered and curst and wept. The better class of young people did not then choose acting as a profession. The prejudice against that profession still in a measure continues. . . .[24]

Actors don't get second chances. That is, they must ignore outside distractions and proceed with their art. They cannot deliver a few lines, analyze what they have done, leave, come out on stage later, and then modify their behavior. All the planning has to be accomplished before the performing.

Further, actors must expect long hours of rehearsal and work at home, memorizing lines and analyzing and developing characters. Yet when actors do succeed, they know beyond a doubt that their job is one of the most fulfilling undertakings in any form of art.

---

[23] Joan Jeffri, ed., "Mercedes Ruehl," *The Actor Speaks,* p. 171.

[24] Gilbert Emery, "A Play Is Presented," *The Art of Playwriting: Lectures Delivered at the University of Pennsylvania on the Mask and Wig Foundation* (Philadelphia: University of Pennsylvania Press, 1928), pp. 97–98.

Chapter Fourteen

The Director

The director usually is the first theatre artist involved in bringing a script to life before an audience. Myriad responsibilities make the job one of the most exciting and satisfying. According to Harold Clurman:

> Direction is a job, a craft, a profession, and at best, an art. The director must be an organizer, a teacher, a politician, a psychic detective, a lay analyst, a technician, a creative being. Ideally, he would know literature (drama), acting, the psychology of the actor, the visual arts, music, history, and above all, he must understand people. He must inspire confidence.[1]

To be a director requires training and/or experience in various phases of theatre. Directors need a working knowledge of the principles of acting, scene and lighting design, costuming and makeup, as well as an understanding of how to prepare and balance a budget.

According to Jacques Copeau, "Directing is the sum-total of artistic and technical operations which enables the play as conceived by the author to pass from the abstract, latent state, that of the written script, to concrete and actual life on the stage."[2]

Selecting the Script

A theatre's success depends, in large part, on the scripts it produces. In many types of theatre, directors have at least some say in choosing a script, so they need to be able to judge what will be acceptable to potential audiences and what sort of people are likely to attend their productions. Of course, they also need to consider their own likes and dislikes.

If they are working with an established organization, directors choose plays that fit into the total season. If a college presents four productions a year, a director wouldn't want to do a melodrama when another is planned for the same season. Directors also have to consider plays done in recent seasons. If Alfred Uhry's *Driving Miss Daisy* was produced at a particular community theatre two or three years ago, it probably won't draw well in the current season, at least from the local citizenry. Directors also need to consider what has been done or is planned at nearby theatres.

---

1 Harold Clurman, *On Directing* (New York: The MacMillan Company, 1972), p. 14.

2 Jacques Copeau, "La Mise en Scéne," *Encyclopédie Francaise,* December 1955, from *Directors on Directing,* p. 214.

How do directors know what will be successful? They don't; they can only make educated guesses. Even the type of play that was a success in one season is not a guaranteed success in another. The socioeconomic and political climates change; tastes and styles differ from one year to the next. However, by studying trends and box office receipts, directors can make fairly accurate choices. This requires familiarity with a broad range of plays.

Directors also need to consider the type of theatre structure and the available talent. A small theatre group, or a theatre that has few seats and a small stage, would have a difficult time presenting a large-cast show.

Analyzing the Script

Scheduling a play is just the beginning of a director's work. The next task is to analyze the script to determine what the writer means to say and how he or she wants to say it. This, in part, determines the style of the production—both in the acting and design.

When the play is to be given its initial production, the director may have a chance to work directly with the playwright in asking questions of clarification or requesting rewrites. Yet according to Tyrone Guthrie, working with the writer may not help the director to understand the play:

> With regard to what the script is about, the last person, who, in my opinion should be consulted, even if he is alive or around, is the author. If the author is a wise man, he will admit straight away that he does not know what it is about. . . . The more important the work of art, the less the author will know what he has written.[3]

There are many playwrights, of course, who would disagree with this, though the statement does have at least a grain of truth in that plays sometimes are written on gut instinct. In other cases, however, the playwright knows exactly what he or she is doing. For instance, Joan M. Schenkar says that in *The Universal Wolf* the Grandmother is "the real Wolf of the tale, while Mr. Wolf is nothing but a patsy."[4]

---

3 Tyrone Guthrie, Transcript of a talk delivered before the Royal Society of Arts, London, March 10, 1952. From *Directors on Directing,* p. 214.

4 Rosette C. Lamont, ed., "Introduction," *Women on the Verge: Seven Avant Garde Plays* (New York: Applause Theatre Books, Inc., 1993), p. XXXIV–XXXV.

Figure 14.1

Guest director Nellie McCaslin discusses the script with cast members before a performance at the Blue Ridge Dinner Theatre, which produces plays in association with Ferrum College (Virginia).

Finding an Overall Concept

As they work with the script and later with the actors and designers, directors may change some of their concepts. Most, however, do work out the largest portion of their analysis ahead of time, first reading the script through a few times simply to get a feel for it. Then they may do research into the social, economic, and political climate of the period in which the play either was written or is set, and they may investigate the playwright's life to learn what influenced the writer and what was important in his or her life.

Director José Quintero feels "that the main function of the director is to translate something from the literary form into an active dramatic life" and that "it is mainly a question of translation."[5] Directors who believe, as does Quintero, that directors are translators, often look for a theme or a metaphor that is carried out in the design and acting. The purpose is to say that a particular play is "like" this facet of life or this particular set of circumstances. For instance, Archibald Macleish's *J.B.,* which uses the book of Job from the Bible as its starting point, often has been done with a circus metaphor. The highest platform in the circus tent represents heaven and the lower levels earth and hell. The idea is to provide a focus for the entire design and, subsequently, for the audience.

Interpreting More Closely

After deciding upon the overall concept, directors become more specific in their analysis, which is somewhat similar to that of the actor. Yet it is much more inclusive in that the director deals with the overall play, while actors are more concerned with how their characters fit into the drama overall.

Directors determine which elements are the most important for the audience's understanding of the play and which are less so. Often, directors will add elements that are not in the script. An example is adding further "hokey" business to a farce to accentuate the silliness of the character or situation.

The director next determines the basic action or the areas of conflict in the play as a whole and in each scene. Where does the major climax occur, and how can it be pointed up? Where are the minor climaxes in each scene, and how should they be presented? What is the prevailing mood or atmosphere? Is it nostalgic, comic, tragic, or sentimental? There often are subtle or abrupt

[5] José Quintero, interviewed by Jean-Claude Van Itallie, in Joseph F. McCrindle, ed., *Behind the Scenes: Theatre and Film Reviews from the Transatlantic Review* (New York: Holt, Rinehart and Winston, 1971), p. 256.

changes in mood throughout a play; however, there is a prevailing atmosphere or feeling that is most important to the script's message. John Millington Synge's *Riders to the Sea* has a heavy and somber mood throughout.

Directors determine how each character relates to the play as a whole and how the characters relate to each other, much as an actor does. Alan Schneider states: "To me a play is a series of relationships. A dramatic action . . . means a change in relationship."[6] Directors determine why each character is included and how each advances the theme. What struggle is the most important in providing the play's dramatic movement? What needs or desires do the characters symbolize? How is each unique?

The following are reconstructed "director's notes," showing part of the analytic process director Harold Clurman used in preparing for a production of O'Neill's *Long Day's Journey into Night.*

Director's Notes for LONG DAY'S JOURNEY INTO NIGHT by Eugene O'Neill[7]

(Directed with an American company for the Kumo Theatre, Tokyo, 1965.)

FIRST IMPRESSIONS

Guilt—a keynote

Apprehension-suspense

More guilt

Self-accusation

The characters are sustained by no faith.

The eyes of each character are on the other.

Foghorn—a desolate sound of aloneness.

Loneliness—everyone is alone with his or her own secret and guilt.

---

6 Alan Schneider, interviewed by Van Itallie, in McCrindle, p. 279.

7 Harold Clurman, *On Directing* (New York: The MacMillan Company, 1972), pp. 254–259. (His own notes on directing the play.)

The play is a self-examination, a search into oneself and into others. Through understanding to find forgiveness, relief, the connection of love which may overcome loneliness.

Long Day's Journey (self-examination) into Night (the darkness of the self). The journey to self-discovery. The search for the true self which has somehow been lost.

MARY: "If I could only find the faith I lost so I could pray again!"

Later, "What is it I'm looking for? I know it's something I've lost."

The spine of the play: to probe within oneself for the lost "something."

TYRONE

SPINE: to maintain his "fatherhood"—the tradition (the crumbling grandeur).

He is a *positive* character: he wants to sustain the structure of his home and family, above all, his wife whom he still loves. If she were well, he thinks, all would be normal. There would be no suffering, no crises. He hopes and hopes—so that he may not see the failure of his whole life, his part in that failure, his guilt.

He still clings to his religion: his faith in the theatre, his world. (He takes pride at never having missed a performance.) His gods are Shakespeare and Edwin Booth. . . .

But the tradition has been shattered in the struggle for existence in the dark days of America's Gilded Age. . . . Tyrone is "redeemed" by the discovery of the past in his son.

Tyrone's heartiness is something more than a sign of physical health. It is part of the fortitude in his *struggle* with poverty, his *struggle* to educate himself, to lose his brogue, to learn Shakespeare, to become a stage star. (The theatre is his religion.) But he has betrayed his religion through his fear of poverty. He wants land, which means security to him ("the farm"). He seeks roots, lost in the departure from Ireland and in the effort to grow new roots in the new and different American "soil."

It is hard for him to admit the least fault or guilt in himself. He can't even admit that he snores, that he drinks too much, that he is greedy. He does not, at first, understand his faults as a consequence of his background and situation. He must maintain his self-respect to be a father, a god, a leader, a man.

(American children of immigrants rarely understand their fathers. They are always disappointed in them. They do not appreciate the hardships of their fathers' struggle as immigrants or as "pioneers": *Desire Under the Elms, A Touch of the Poet.*)

"Socialism," for Tyrone, means destruction of the tradition. His sons blaspheme against the theatre, Shakespeare, etc.

He shuns "Wall Street"—the forces, which without his realizing it, have conspired to ruin him. He doesn't understand his life—or his country. Hence, his constant self-contradiction, his absurdity.

He's a good man, a soft man. He always yields to his better nature, to sentiment and affection. Like most actors, he is susceptible to compliments. He's an "old-time" actor: life was composed of work on the stage, stage lore, companionable drinking, dreams of glory, celebration of success.

Clurman goes on to analyze each character in depth and to find the spine for each.

Anticipating Design and Blocking

During the analysis a director also thinks in terms of setting and technical elements. What type of environment would best portray the atmosphere, mood, actions, and circumstances? What should the lighting suggest? What sorts of costumes should the characters wear? Should the makeup be realistic or exaggerated? At some point in the planning the director meets with the designer to present or discuss ideas. Some directors prefer to work out the overall design concept themselves, whereas others are open to suggestion.

After approving the set design, the director considers how much blocking to plan before the show is cast and rehearsals begin. As a general rule, directors plan the broad movements and leave the subtleties of gesture and characterization to the actor. Experienced actors are likely to have a sense of what is right for any situation, and directors may prefer to give them more freedom than they give beginning actors.

If the blocking has been planned in detail, rehearsals probably will proceed more smoothly, but there is a chance the physical action will appear too rigid and controlled. If there is too little planning, the director risks wasting time.

Casting the Play

The director has to be a good judge of human behavior, particularly in educational and community theatre. Because actors in these situations receive no

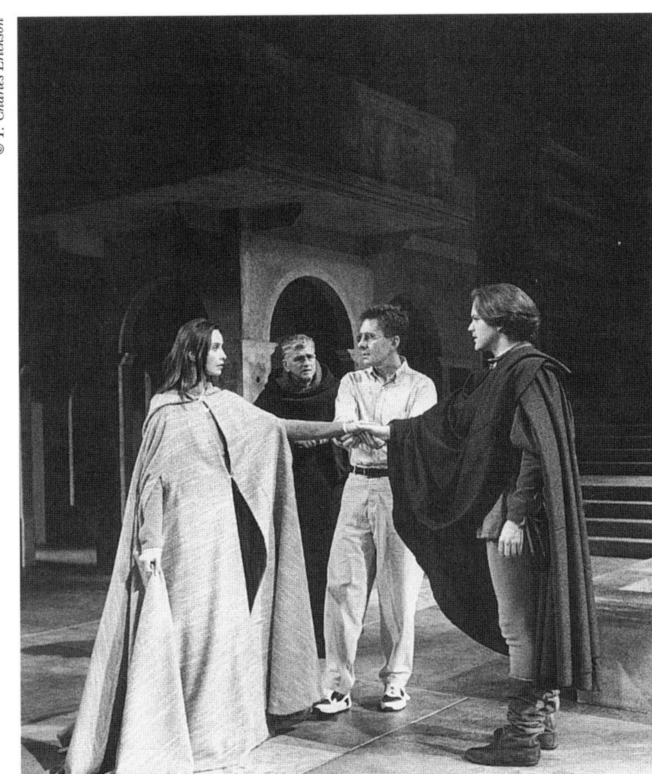

Figure 14.2

Director Mark Lamos works on blocking with actors, rehearsing for a Hartford Stage Theatre production of *Romeo and Juliet*.

financial compensation for their work, they must have other incentives for auditioning. The director tries to judge the actors' sincerity and reliability, as well as their talent. Another consideration is how well the actors and the director can work together, and whether a good rapport can be established among the cast members.

Although they have in mind the physical type they want for each role, directors usually do not precast shows, except perhaps for central characters in some professional theatres. Broadway shows, for example, often have been written with particular actors in mind.

Auditions

"Choose a good script," I sometimes advise students, "cast good actors—and you'll all be good directors!" There is more than a little truth in the jest. Casting constitutes the first step in the practical interpretation of a play.[8]

Most common is **open audition.** The actors all appear at a certain time and audition in front of everyone there. Often the director makes scripts available a day or more ahead of time and takes a few minutes at the beginning to summarize the plot of the play and to explain the circumstances. Sometimes directors allow the actors to audition for specific parts; at other times directors ask them to read certain sections or roles. Some directors prefer that the actors present a pantomime or an impromptu or improvised scene.

The open audition has several advantages. The director is able to judge how the actors will appear with each other, so there is little danger, for instance, of casting a father who is shorter than his thirteen-year-old son. The director also can see how well the actors relate to each other and how well their voices blend. An advantage for the actors is that they are able to judge the competition.

There are several disadvantages. One is that certain actors may have adverse reactions to the auditions of other actors, which can affect the way they read. Auditioning first, last, or in the middle may also affect how well an actor does. Further, if the auditions last a long time, the director may tire and lose concentration.

A second type of audition is the *interview.* The actor and the director meet without having anyone else present. Sometimes directors simply talk with the actors. Sometimes they have the actors read from the script or perform an impromptu scene. Advantages of this audition format are that the director can concentrate on one actor at a time and that the actors needn't experience the pressure of having to compete openly with others.

A disadvantage is that the director cannot see the way the actors look together nor how well they work with each other. Sometimes, too, the director has to read a part to cue the actor and loses concentration. In addition, because this type of audition often is held in an office or small room, the director is unable to consider vocal projection.

There are various other methods of auditioning. At times, for example, actors are asked to prepare a short scene of their choice to present either at open auditions or at interviews. Sometimes a director will interview actors and

[8] Clurman, p. 64.

then have them come to open auditions. In professional theatre, directors often interview experienced actors, while most of the other actors go to open auditions, referred to as "cattle calls," where they may be eliminated on the basis of physical appearance even before seeing the director.

At any type of audition, the director has many aspects to consider: how easily the actors move; their emotional depth and range; the quality, range, and projection of their voices; and their overall potential for a role. Some actors do not read well, but have the potential for growth and development in a role. Others read well at first, but fail to develop their characters much during rehearsals.

Often actors will need special abilities. For a musical, they may be asked to come to auditions with a prepared song to sing. They may perform their own dance steps, or be shown several steps to learn and execute.

Rehearsing the Play

After the cast is chosen and the technical elements are planned, directors devote most of their time to the actors. The rehearsal period can vary from a usual four weeks in professional theatre to six weeks in educational and community theatre. A shorter period is needed in professional theatre because the actors can spend an entire work day rehearsing, whereas in other theatres they have school and/or a job.

There are six stages of preparation: *reading rehearsals,* with the purpose of coming to a clear understanding and interpretation of the play; *blocking rehearsals,* where the action, movement, and business are worked out; *character and line rehearsals,* where the performers develop and build their characters and try to discover the most effective method of delivering their speeches; *finishing rehearsals,* in which all the elements of acting are developed and unified; *technical rehearsals,* devoted to coordinating the visual and sound elements with the total production; and *dress rehearsals,* in which the play ideally is given just as it will be in performance.

The length of the rehearsal period depends upon several factors. One is the background and experience of the actors. In educational theatre, the director often has to serve as a teacher. Also, some plays are easier to perform than others. It probably will take less time to ready a simple comedy for production than a musical in which the actors must memorize songs and dances as well as learn lines and build characters. The theatre schedule affects the rehearsal period. Often, summer stock theatres change the bill each week. In college or university theatres, plays sometimes are presented every two or three weeks during the summer.

The period of time needed for each type of rehearsal varies. When the business and blocking are intricate, blocking rehearsals have to be longer. This happens in stylized productions, for instance, where every movement is

Figure 14.3

Yale School of Drama actors listen as the director (at left) explains his interpretation of a scene from Chekhov's *The Cherry Orchard*.

planned. Character and line rehearsals take longer if the speeches are difficult and the characterizations unusually involved. Often, if there are many special effects, additional technical rehearsals will be needed.

In nonprofessional theatre, the director usually schedules rehearsals of no longer than two or three hours. There is little advantage in holding rehearsals of less than an hour, except, perhaps, to work with individuals.

Reading Rehearsals

For the first few rehearsals, it isn't necessary to have a stage or rehearsal hall. In fact, directors often prefer to have a relaxed atmosphere in which the actors feel free to discuss the script. Reading rehearsals are somewhat misnamed, in that the major purpose is to agree on a script's interpretation. During reading rehearsals, directors explain what they see as the play's theme and the effects they hope to achieve.

The idea for both the actors and the director is to come to an understanding of the basic action and motivation. At the first rehearsal, a director may have the actors read through the play to grasp the overall concept, without attempting to develop character.

The director may listen to the actors' ideas, often telling them to go ahead and experiment. If the director feels that the suggestions are appropriate or consistent with the overall concept or interpretation and add something of value, he or she usually tells the actor to go ahead with them. On the other hand, if the director feels the actions are inappropriate, he or she may suggest changes or encourage the actors to find ideas that are in keeping with the overall concept.

At some point the director may show sketches and floor plans to the actors so they can better visualize the action. After this, the cast is ready to move to a rehearsal hall or stage.

Blocking Rehearsals

One purpose of movement and business is to keep the play from appearing static and to give it life and activity. Another purpose, however, is to present an aesthetically pleasing picture in both the placement and movement of the actors. The director has to keep in mind that the stage picture is constantly changing and is perceived differently from each section of the audience. He or she needs to consider sightlines and which stage areas are the strongest for emphasis. Body position, focus, and levels all are used to emphasize specific characters, speeches, and scenes.

Movement has to be motivated by the script, or at least appear to be. The director cannot simply move actors to balance the stage without a seemingly logical reason for them to move; the blocking has to fit the situation and the type of play. In a funeral scene, for instance, the movement would be slower and more stately than in a party scene. Different types of characters move differently, and their movements provide variety and contrast.

There are two categories of movement and business: inherent and supplementary. The first is any action that advances the story or is an integral part of the plot. It includes exits, entrances, and phone calls. Supplementary business is added for effect, either to enhance the message of the play or to establish character. It includes how the actor stands, sits, or walks and is important in establishing personality traits and attitudes. It helps to establish the mood of each scene and the emotions of the characters.

Both inherent and supplementary business are used for focus. A moving actor, whether walking from one spot to another or fiddling with a prop, attracts more attention than one who is stationary. Focus also applies to the characters' use and placement of furniture, and it can provide psychological groupings, as when a family is united around a table.

Figure 14.4, which follows, explains varying strengths of stage areas and some of the circumstances a director has to consider when planning movement and blocking.

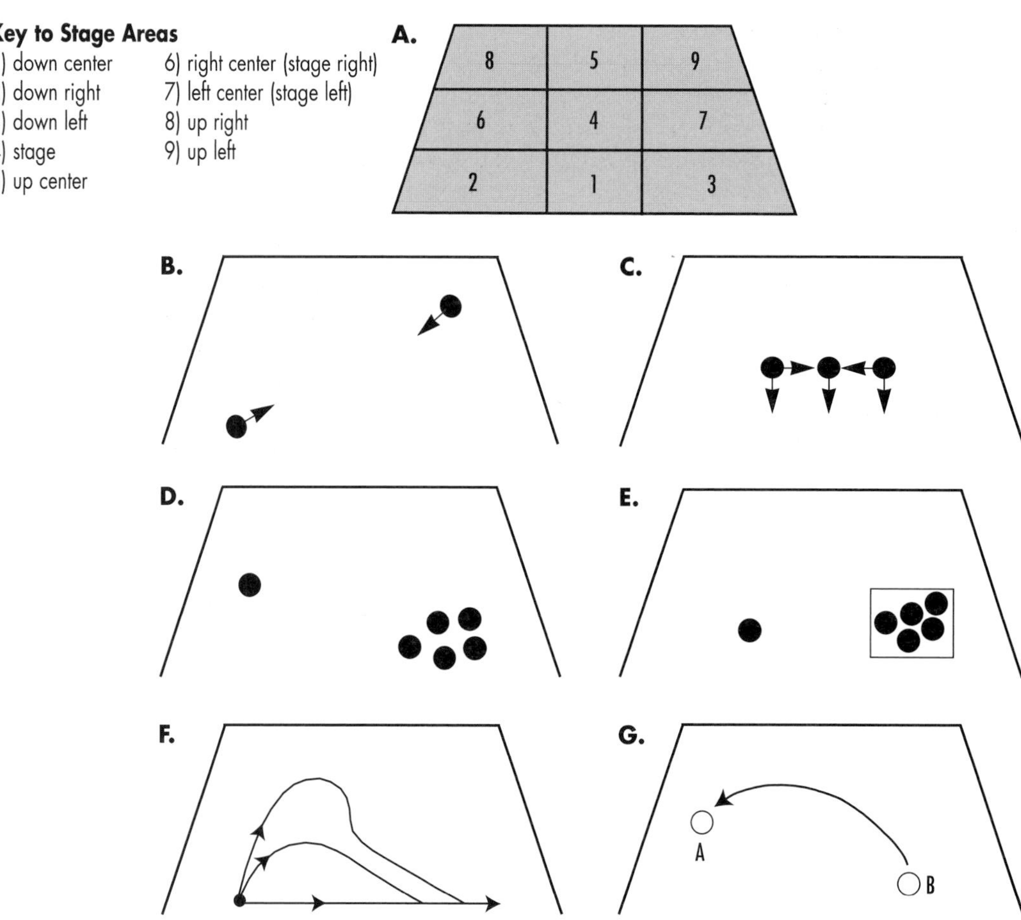

Figure 14.4

Stage areas, various movements of actors, and blocking.

In the top drawing (A) showing the numbered sections of the stage, the #1 area is the strongest. The areas decrease in strength the higher the number—if all else is equal. Of course, other factors affect relative strengths or weaknesses of any area. In the second drawing (B), the person in the #2 stage area actually is weaker than the one in #9 because of facing upstage or away from the audience. In the drawing to the right of this (C), all three actors can be of equal strength when facing front. However, if the two on the ends face inward, the middle actor then becomes a strong focal point. (Yet, if one of these wears a more colorful or unusual costume, this person will be the center of attention.)

Drawing (D) shows that the isolated individual receives emphasis, while the drawing to the right (E) shows that the emphasis is equal when the group stands on a platform.

Drawings F and G have to do with movement. The strongest movement, shown in drawing F, is straight across the stage. The other moves show decreasing strength or uncertainty. Drawing G, however, shows that it often is stronger to move in a curved line than a straight one because of final positioning. If the actor were to walk straight upstage from the #3 stage position, he or she would be facing away from the audience, which is a weak position.

Physical closeness sometimes implies emotional closeness, whereas distance often implies disagreement. A tendency to stay in certain areas of the stage can reveal much about the psychological aspects of a character. One who stays upstage can appear timid, whereas another who is downstage may come across as extroverted or confident. A scene appears weak if the characters constantly move behind the furniture rather than in front of it. Unless it's done deliberately to provide humor, a dominant character usually wouldn't stand looking up at a platform while browbeating a weaker character.

A director needs to be aware of providing unity and variety in picturization, as well as showing conflict, focus, emphasis, and characterization. Movement can complement or even replace lines. Finally, although movement is planned just after the reading rehearsals, it continues to build and change throughout the rehearsal period.

Character and Line Rehearsals

Beginning with the reading rehearsals, the actors have been working on interpreting their characters and lines. However, it is only after the blocking is finished that this becomes the focus of rehearsal. During this period a director usually encourages the actors to experiment in building their roles. This is the stage of rehearsal in which a character really begins to come to life. Line and character interpretation usually go hand in hand in that, once established, a character has a certain way of speaking.

During this phase, the director makes certain that the actor understands the significance of each line, since the method of delivery is just as important as the content in conveying the mood and message. This also helps the audience to understand of the significance of a scene. Ultimately, it is the director's responsibility to see that the lines are delivered in character and in accordance with the play's mood and style. Occasionally, the director has to provide more guidance than usual for the actor who has failed to grasp the style of the play or the intricacies of the character.

The director also is concerned with how the actors are projecting lines and character. For instance, a good rendering of character for television would not be suitable for a proscenium stage. Many of the subtleties of movement and facial expression would be lost, and the lines probably would not be loud enough for the audience to distinguish the words.

W.B. Nickerson

Figure 14.5
A dress rehearsal for Robert Bolt's *A Man for All Seasons.* During such rehearsals, it is unusual for the director to stop action.

Finishing Rehearsals

Action, interaction, delivery, and interpretation are refined and polished during the last few weeks of rehearsal. Up to this point the director has stopped scenes when necessary and corrected blocking or line delivery. Now, unless something major needs correcting, the rehearsals proceed without stopping. Often it is not until the finishing rehearsals that an actor can fully appreciate the impact of a role. The director usually takes notes and discusses inconsistencies between the running of the acts.

Until the finishing rehearsals it has been difficult to concentrate on the show's overall movement because there have been so many stops and starts. Now the director concentrates on the three broad aspects of movement: *pace, timing,* and *rhythm.*

Pace refers to the fastness or slowness in handling business and speaking lines. The pace will be faster in scenes of excitement or tension and slower in a relaxed atmosphere. All plays—even tragedies—lose effectiveness if they drag. Plays also suffer if the scenes are presented too quickly.

Timing refers to the use of pauses within or between speeches. It is important both in pointing up specific lines and actions and in emphasizing reactions, both in comic and serious plays. In a comedy, an actor needs to pause just the right length of time before delivering a punch line or a humorous action. In a serious play, for instance, when a character hears of the death of a relative or friend, it takes time to absorb the shock before responding. Pauses also are effective in drawing attention to a character or in showing that something momentous is about to be said.

Rhythm refers both to the flow of the language and to the matter of picking up cues and changing scenes. Every piece of literature, largely through the author's style, has a certain rhythm. David Mamet's *Glengarry Glen Ross* (about lack of scruples in the business world) has a very different rhythm than does Lanford Wilson's *Burn This* (which takes place after the accidental death of a young gay man and the encounter between his two roommates and his brother), although both deal with serious subjects. A play's inherent rhythm can be ruined by actors who pick up cues either too slowly or too quickly, although the former is much more likely.

Pace, timing, and rhythm are all tied closely to mood and emotional pitch.

Technical Rehearsals

By the time the finishing rehearsals end, the production should look as it will during the show's run. Out of necessity, during the usual two or three technical rehearsals the director will devote attention to the technical aspects of the production to the neglect of the actors. If the director has planned well and worked closely with the designers, there shouldn't be much to do, except to help the designers, or, more likely, the various stage technicians, to correct minor details.

Dress Rehearsals

There's an old saying: A bad dress rehearsal means a good opening. This simply is not so. Sometimes there can be a successful opening night despite a

Michal Daniel

Figure 14.6

During a dress rehearsal, the director has an opportunity to check all the technical elements of a scene, particularly important in a complicated production such as this Guthrie Theatre (Minneapolis) performance of Girish Karnad's *Naga Mandala*.

poor dress rehearsal, but never because of it. The dress rehearsal is a tryout of the production, much as a Broadway-destined production tries out either at the theatre where it will be presented (in what is termed *previews*) or out of town.

Usually there are two rehearsals in full costume with all the technical elements. Directors sometimes invite guests so that the actors can become accustomed to playing to an audience. From now on, the director's job technically is finished, unless the play has a long run, as may be the case in professional theatre. Then the director may call rehearsals to correct inconsistencies that have crept into the performance. During long runs, additional rehearsals may be necessary when one actor replaces another. Sometimes the entire cast rehearses with the new actors. At other times, the director, an assistant, or a production stage manager may rehearse the replacements with only certain members of the cast.

Occasionally, directors like to watch and take notes at early performances, then give them to the actors some time before each succeeding night of the play's run. This is particularly true in community and educational theatre.

Directing in Arena Theatre

Many of the principles of directing are the same for arena theatre as for proscenium, but there are some differences. The director has to pay more attention to small details and subtleties of characterization, because the audience is closer to the action.

Although furniture can be placed in closer approximation of real life on an arena stage than on a proscenium stage, it is both ineffective and monotonous to line the edges of the stage as in a real living room. Some of the furniture, at least, can be centrally placed, and then the actor can play toward the audience rather than toward the center of the stage. Some directors place the furniture at the corners of the arena so that each section of the audience will have a good view of each actor at least part of the time.

Figure 14.7

An arena stage theatre director establishes stage areas using a clock method or compass directions.

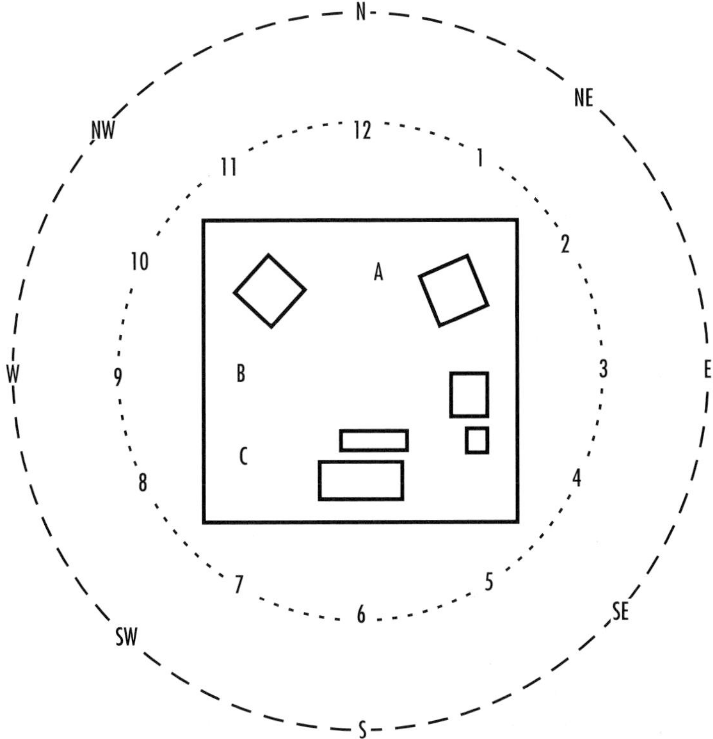

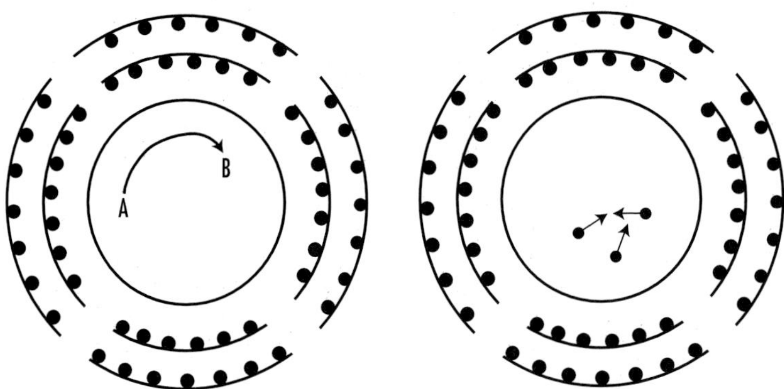

Figure 14.8

In arena theatre, movement is ideally directed in a curve for the benefit of the audience. For the same reason, a triangular arrangement is usually used for three or more actors, so no one segment of the audience is unable to see actors.

The arena stage director also does not have the same control over picturization as in proscenium theatre, since the groupings of characters will be viewed from all sides. Focus is similar in arena theatre to that in proscenium theatre. The actor who is standing is more dominant than the one who is sitting, and the audience pays more attention to the moving actor than to the one who is still. There is an advantage in that there are no weak areas—except, possibly, center stage—because only half the audience can see the face of an actor who stands there. The actor who plays off center but faces center is facing more than half the audience. An actor in an aisleway or corner can, just by a turn of the head, face all of the audience. There is more variety in playing area because the groupings are more moveable. Although there is a loss in emphasis through grouping, the director can make better use of depth in movement.

Body position is of little value in arena staging, since an actor who is open to one part of the audience is closed to another. Similarly, upstage for some viewers is downstage for others. Often, the director will designate areas of the stage to correspond to the face of a clock. One area is the twelve o'clock position, one the three o'clock, and so on. The positions remain constant and are referred to in terms of the clock rather than as Down Right or Down Left. Another method is to designate positions according to geographic directions, such as Northeast or South. Both are shown in Figure 14.7.

Spacing is unimportant; an actor separated from the group at one angle appears to be part of it at another. Body positions relate to the other actors and not to the audience, but the actor can move away from or come closer to the other actors and give a sense of psychological closeness or separation. Often the movement is curved, so that the actor making a cross is open to several areas of the audience. In proscenium theatres such curved movements can denote weakness or indecision, but in arena theatre they are not so likely to carry these connotations unless the actor moves slowly or hesitantly. Weakness or strength in arena theatre depends on how the actor executes a movement.

If the actors keep at least four feet of space between each other, the scenes will be opened for all parts of the audience. If two actors face each other directly at close range, each one's back is to part of the house, meanwhile blocking the other actor from the same part. It is better if each stands slightly sideways in relation to the other. Most positions are not bad if they are held only briefly. Even subtle changes in movement give the audience the impression of having a better view.

In two-character scenes the director can place one or both actors near an aisleway, providing better sightlines. Often, since the actor speaking cannot be the center of attention for the entire audience, reactions through facial expression and movement become more important in arena theatre.

It is easier to block three characters, because there can be a triangular arrangement. Now most of the viewers will be able to see one actor full front and another in profile. Large groups can be divided into several triangles.

Movement can be less restrained and more natural in an arena, but it should have meaning. Any placement of actors should be aesthetically pleasing to as much of the audience as possible. The overall tempo or pace usually is faster because the lines and characterization do not have to be projected so far. Still, a comedy would proceed more quickly than a tragedy, of course, and actors still would have the same considerations about pauses and timing as in any other type of theatre.

One aspect of tempo that requires more rehearsal in arena theatre is entrances. The actor has to walk down an aisleway and must not arrive too early or too late. The director makes sure that the audience knows early in the action just where each of the aisleways is supposed to lead.

In casting for the arena stage, the director takes more care in choosing the right physical type, because makeup and costuming, at least in realistic plays, are more subtle. The director also must take care in choosing the play. Although most plays can be adapted for arena staging, it may be difficult to present extravagant musicals. Plays with many changes of locale also will be difficult to stage with any appearance of realism.

A director would have to consider many of the same things in blocking and rehearsing a play for the thrust stage as is the case for arena staging. Although a third of the audience faces the wall behind the stage, the other two-thirds face the action from the two sides. Thus, picturization must be handled much as it is in arena theatre.

There can be more background scenery than in arena theatre, although the director and designers must consider that the portion of the audience on either side of the stage would not have a clear view of two-dimensional scenery, such as painted backdrops or flats. On the other hand, there is at least some storage space through the doors behind the stage, and there is not the problem of timing entrances down long aisleways.

Chapter Fifteen

The Designers and Supporting Artists

The designers of the theatre production are as responsible as the director for making a dramatic presentation appropriate and pleasing. Even when the director has definite ideas about how a setting or lights or audio should be handled, or how costumes or makeup or props should appear, the designers—in carrying out the director's wishes—add their own personalities, their way of viewing the world, to their work.

Scene designer Michael Olich says he believes "absolutely" in collaboration. "It's the drug, the hook that has made me an addict of the theatre. . . . As frustrating as communication can be at times, it's also ecstatically energizing when ideas that come from outside of you draw you outside of yourself as well."[1]

The Scene Designer

One of the collaborators is the scene designer, whose work must be as aesthetic as that of a painter and as practical as that of an architect. At the same time, the scene designer's work is different from either of these fine arts because it is not complete in itself. After the setting is constructed, it requires the actors, the costumes, the lights, the makeup, and the properties to complete the picture. Throughout the production, the picture changes continuously as the actors move and the lights come up or fade.

The Scene Designer's Background

To design a practical and aesthetically pleasing set to match a variety of styles and historical periods, a designer needs training, experience, and talent in many different areas. For instance, there is a big difference between constructing an apartment on stage and constructing an apartment building. Scene designers know how to adapt architectural design to a theatre production. They know enough about stage carpentry to design a set that can be built without major difficulty. They plan so that scenery can shift quickly and quietly. This means that they build both illusion and practicality into their designs so that the settings elicit certain emotional responses from the audience at the same time that they are easily functional.

Scene designers need to be acquainted with the principles of lighting and know how light will affect their sets. They should know the emotional impact of various colors, textures, and masses. They must be familiar with the materials used in set construction and recognize which of these are best for particular effects.

[1] Michael Olich, "A Strong Conceptual Hit," from "And Another Thing: Interviews with Four Designers Who Also . . .", *American Theatre,* October 1993, p. 40.

Figure 15.1

Theatre is a collaborative art, as the director and set designer work with lighting, sound, and costume designers to create an aesthetically pleasing production. From a performance of *The Bakkhai* at the North Carolina School of the Arts.

Of course, they also should be acquainted with interior decorating in order to adapt various decors to the requirements of the stage. Then they must be able to visualize suitable furniture, and how this furniture will modify the stage picture. Designers must be familiar with current styles and know where to research period furniture and architecture.

Designers should be familiar with various theatrical styles from expressionism to realism and know how each of these can reinforce the director's concept or vision. According to Francis Reed, "The search for an appropriate style is the key decision facing any production team. As noted, the extent of the departure from reality can vary in acting, costume, setting and lighting—although each must be internally consistent and complementary to the others."[2]

[2] Francis Reid, *Designing for the Theatre* (London: A & C Black [Publishers] Limited, 1989), p. 29.

Designer Donald Oenslager says: "Wherever he works, the designer is an artist and craftsman who translates the world around him into the theatrical terms of the stage."[3]

"CAMPING OUT"

Nancy Franklin
from The New Yorker

[John Arnone's set for the Broadway revival of the musical *Grease*] . . . is a replica of a school-auditorium stage, complete with steps at the sides, and gives the show, slick as it is, the spirit of a high-school production. . . . On the first day of school, the students of Rydell High, Class of '59, come onstage carrying big pieces of cardboard painted yellow to look like a school bus, and there are other moments when you have the illusion that the students are just using what's at hand to put on a show when the greasers, out at night, use their flashlights as microphones, or when one of the girls, in a scene in a bathroom, sings to a bar of soap. . . . One part of the set—and it's a big part—seems all wrong, though: a huge collage of images meant to evoke the fifties frames the stage, and it's done up in Day-Glo pinks and greens and oranges, which are the colors of another decade and, in any case, tire your eyes out before the show is half over. The excess of color works better in Howell Binkley's lighting and in Willa Kim's witty sendups of fifties fashion clichés—skirts with telephones, champagne glasses, flamingos, Scottie dogs, and Hawaiian palmscapes, and, for the boys, an endless variety of black-and-white plaid pants and shirts. . . .

Functions of Scene Design

Beyond providing a channel for the playwright's message, the setting helps convey the theme and provides information essential to the understanding of the play. It fulfills the director's interpretation; provides an environment, mood, and playable area for the actor; remains faithful to the playwright's style; and complements the work of all the other designers.

[3] Donald Oenslager, *Scenery Then and Now* (New York: W. W. Norton & Company, 1936), p. 11.

W. B. Nickerson

Figure 15.2

A scene designer at work on a set for a production of *Tartuffe*.

The design provides a framework for the action and a *focal point,* where the audience's attention is directed. Even though the focal point may change from scene to scene, every member of the audience must have an undistorted view of each. For example, one scene may take place in a bedroom and another in the kitchen. The focus may be provided in part by lighting, but the designer makes each location, bedroom or kitchen, interesting and easily seen from any part of the audience.

A setting must be designed for easy use by the actors. For instance, treads on steps in a set usually are wider than those in a house so the actor can concentrate on action and character rather than on where to step.

The setting presents an aesthetically pleasing image, which, however, should not be so elaborate that it calls undue attention to itself. It should provide exposition for the audience. The set also can locate time and place. The style of architecture and the furnishings can indicate the historical period and whether the play takes place in an upper-class home or in an office. For instance, Tony Cucuzzella's design for Victor Herbert's *The Red Mill,* produced in the mid-1990s by the San Diego Comic Opera Company, immediately showed the audience that both the hotel and the mill were in advanced disrepair. The arms of the windmill were tattered; pieces of the hotel kept falling off throughout the performance. The architecture told the audience that they were in another country, probably Holland, and that the time was the past—as seen in the styles of the buildings. At the same time, in the background, a white cloud was projected onto a blue cyclorama, suggesting that although the buildings were falling apart, the mood was still lighthearted.

Of course, providing exposition does not mean that the setting has to appear as if it is an actual environment. Depending on the type and style of the play, it can be more a suggestion of environment than a representation.

Balance and Harmony

The set should be balanced, either symmetrically or asymmetrically. **Symmetrical balance** means that the left half contains exactly the same elements as the right half. Scene designers often use symmetry for staging Greek plays.

Asymmetrical balance is achieved through mass, color, and shape that differ from one side of the stage to the other. If, for instance, a huge grey brick wall were facing front at Stage Left, another object or combination of objects should go at Stage Right to counterbalance the feeling of heaviness. The designer might use dark colors, a grouping of heavy furniture, or platforms to achieve the counterbalance.

A well-designed setting should have harmony and balance. Each element should appear to belong, to be consistent. In Kaufman and Hart's *You Can't Take It with You,* each member of the household has a separate interest, such as writing, dancing, or making firecrackers, and these interests show up in a diversity of elements in the set. Although diverse, the mixture contributes to the theme of nonconformity, which provides harmony to the production as a whole. On the other hand, if a person were to design a setting for Wilder's *Our Town* using the bare stage with only a ladder to represent the second story of the Gibbses' house and sawhorses and a plank to represent a soda fountain, but then constructed a box set and placed actual furniture in the Webb household, the set would not have harmony.

Figure 15.3

A stagehand works on the scenery ("dutching," applying a strip of muslin with glue to cover the cracks), for a production of *Noises Off* at Midwestern State University Theatre (Texas). Pastels were used for the design of this particular set.

Colors and shapes help convey the style and genre. Curved lines and shapes, for instance, can convey lightness or gracefulness, whereas straight, angular shapes can convey austerity or somberness.

A designer often may exaggerate an element of the setting to point up an aspect of the play. For instance, set pieces for a farce may be two-dimensional like the characters. In showing the characters' tastes, interests, hobbies, and financial status, the set becomes almost a character in itself.

Planning a Setting

The scene designer's work begins with a study and analysis of the script, first to determine the mood and theme. Then come practical questions: How many doorways are needed? Where do they lead? Are windows, fireplaces, or levels needed? How can the set add to the effectiveness of the action?

Designer David Jenkins likes to read a script "as early as possible—and then let the ideas wash over [him]":

> You can read the script and then, say, a week later you really start to work on it. That week that you waited, somewhere you're walking down the street, or you're lying in bed, trying to go to bed at night, your thoughts start, and you are actively beginning to work then.[4]

Next, the designer often researches building architecture, both historically and geographically, since a type of structure seen in one country or even one part of a country may never have been erected in another.

Once they have ideas in mind, designers prepare sketches for the director. Sometimes directors have definite ideas about the setting; at other times they give the designer a free hand. In either case the director sees to it that the proposed design meshes with the work of the other theatre artists.

Figure 15.4

This floor plan shows a scale drawing of the exterior setting for a production of Jack Kirkland's *Tobacco Road.* (1/4 inch equals 1 foot)

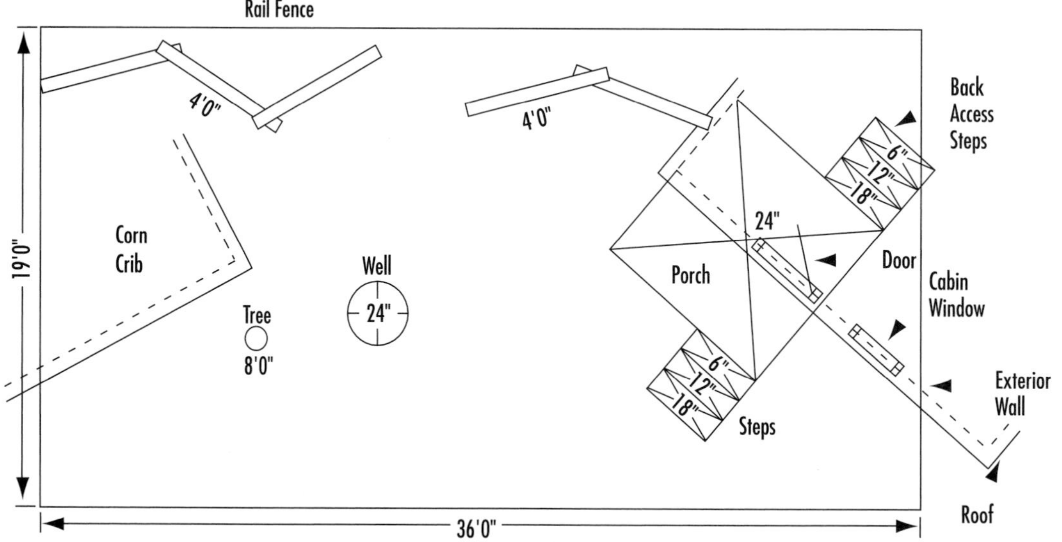

[4] Arvid F. Sponberg, "David Jenkins, Scene Designer," *Broadway Talks: What Professionals Think About Commercial Theater in America* (New York: Greenwood Press, 1991), p. 119.

After the director approves the preliminary sketches, the designer prepares more exact plans for the construction of the set. A **floor plan** (also called a *ground plan*) of the setting as viewed from above shows how the set fits the stage. Sometimes the designer draws several floor plans, showing a shifting of furniture, so that the director can visualize where to place the actors. Some designers use storyboards that show the set lighted from different angles, for instance, or with furniture arranged differently for different scenes.

Often, the designer constructs a model of the set so the director can see what it will be like. The plans and model are on a scale of one-fourth inch (or occasionally one-half inch) to the foot. Then the designer may draft elevations, showing the height of platforms, steps, other three-dimensional shapes, and flats. Often the designer prepares a sectional view of objects to show the method of construction, or isometric views that show an object from the corner and slightly above to give the builders a clear understanding of the platform or figure. Copies of the drawings and plans go to the director, the technical director, the stage manager, and the head of the construction crew.

Lately, more and more designers are using computers with a variety of software programs developed to make their work less tedious and the drawings and computer-generated models more easily understood by the technician. Perspective drawings are much easier to do, and the computer design has the advantage of being able to show the entire setting or any portion of it from various angles, drawn in three dimensions.

Computer programs, singly or in combination, are able to insert or take away portions of a design and show multilayered examples.

Another advantage is the use of templates for various types of stages or for furniture and costuming.

After the planning, the scene designer's duties differ in various types of theatres. Particularly in educational and community theatres, the designer chooses the furniture and set dressings and supervises the set construction and scene painting.

FROM "THE ESSENTIAL MING CHO LEE

What Would American Scenic Design Be Without Him?"

Mel Gussow

The dean of American scenic designers, [Ming Cho] Lee is a master of his art in theatre, dance and opera. Through his work and through his teaching, he has become one of the most influential people in his field. During his 25 years at the Yale Drama School, 20 of them as co-chairman of the design department, he has trained scores of successful designers. . . . .In so doing, he is carrying on the tradition established by designers reaching back to Robert Edmond Jones. Theatre design is that rare art that continues to operate through the apprentice system, as established designers pass on their knowledge and techniques to younger designers. . . .

In his own designing, Lee is the enemy of decoration, of effects, of anything that detracts or distracts from the drama. The idea that theatregoers might actually applaud a set offends his scenic sensibility. . . . He does not like excessive or useless scenery, scenery that makes its own architectural statement and does not complement the play. . . .

His steadiest employment was as a principal designer for the New York Shakespeare Festival. In 11 years, he did 22 Shakespearean productions as well as many contemporary plays, including *Hair* in 1967 and *for colored girls who have considered suicide/when the rainbow is enuf* in 1976. His adventurousness in new works is exemplified by the striking background he designed for Jack MacGowran's one-man evening from the works of Samuel Beckett. With its cloudlike swirls, the set looked like a closeup section of a Turner painting.

Because of his Shakespeare designs for the Delacorte Theater in Central Park, Lee became identified with vertical sets. Often he used stairs, metal piping and scaffolding, an approach that was particularly suited to the Delacorte sightlines, but one that he felt was not necessarily conductive to other stages.

Lee's work has also been affected by what was happening in the world outside the arts. Increasingly he has been able to demonstrate that stage design can express social relevance, as in his design for Berkeley Repertory Theatre's large-scale 1993 dramatization of Maxine Hong Kingston's *The Woman Warrior*. . . .

[H]e has won only one Tony award, in 1983, for the imposing mountain he designed for Patrick Meyers's *K2*. . . . [I]t is not one of Lee's favorites. It was explicit, overpowering and in the New York production of the play, it depended too much on surprising the audience. . . . Since then, partly in reaction to *K2*, Lee has often created low horizontal designs. . . .

For him, design is a process of distillation. Repeatedly he says to himself, as he does to his students, "you don't need it." The search is often for "an icon," a single object, perhaps a hanging, to represent the central theme. When the set is finally in place, "the people who are living the life on stage are paramount. The design is to create a world in which that event can take place. But when the image becomes so overwhelming that the action is not needed, then I have a problem doing it. I don't know how to design for an audience. I have to design for the work."

The Lighting Designer

When electric lights first came into use in the theatre, they simply illuminated the stage to enable the spectators to see the action. Modern lighting, like scenery, enhances the total production.

There are two categories of stage lighting: *general* and *specific.* **General lighting** provides a well-lighted performance area. **Specific lighting** provides special effects, enhancing the playwright's message through intensity and color.

Dim lights can suggest a foreboding, mysterious atmosphere, whereas bright lights often mean "lightness" in treatment of subject matter. There are exceptions, however. Sledgehammer Theatre's production of Bertolt Brecht's *Drums in the Night,* presented in San Diego in 1991, focused "painfully bright" lights on the audience deliberately to make the spectators uncomfortable.

Functions of Lighting

Lighting complements the other areas of design and helps to convey the mood and message of the play. It provides **selective visibility.** Often only certain areas of the set are important to the action. In such cases, the lights can provide a point of focus by fading to black on the areas to be deemphasized and coming up on the important areas. Large follow spots sometimes are used (particularly in musicals) to focus on the star performer.

Lighting can provide exposition by showing time and place. A bright light can indicate midday in a warm climate. Blazing chandeliers can indicate nighttime in a wealthy household.

Of course, lighting, like scenery, is a symbol. It suggests; then it is up to the audience to use imagination. For example, a common table lamp onstage would not provide enough illumination. Its light must be intensified, usually by focusing additional overhead lighting on the lamp.

Another function of lighting is to reveal or define mass and form. Properly lighted, a papier-mâché rock can become real for the audience. Lighting also contributes to and complements the style of the production.

Lighting Components

Lighting consists of two components: a *source* and a *system of control. Source* means the lighting instruments. The two major kinds are **floodlights,** which are nonfocusable and have no lens, and **spotlights** (spots), which can be focused and usually do have a lens. Floodlights usually are for general illumination, such as for lighting backdrops, whereas the various types of spots are for specific illumination.

Spots come in various sizes and can focus from a very small area to a large one. Most have a metal frame into which gelatins can be fitted for emotional

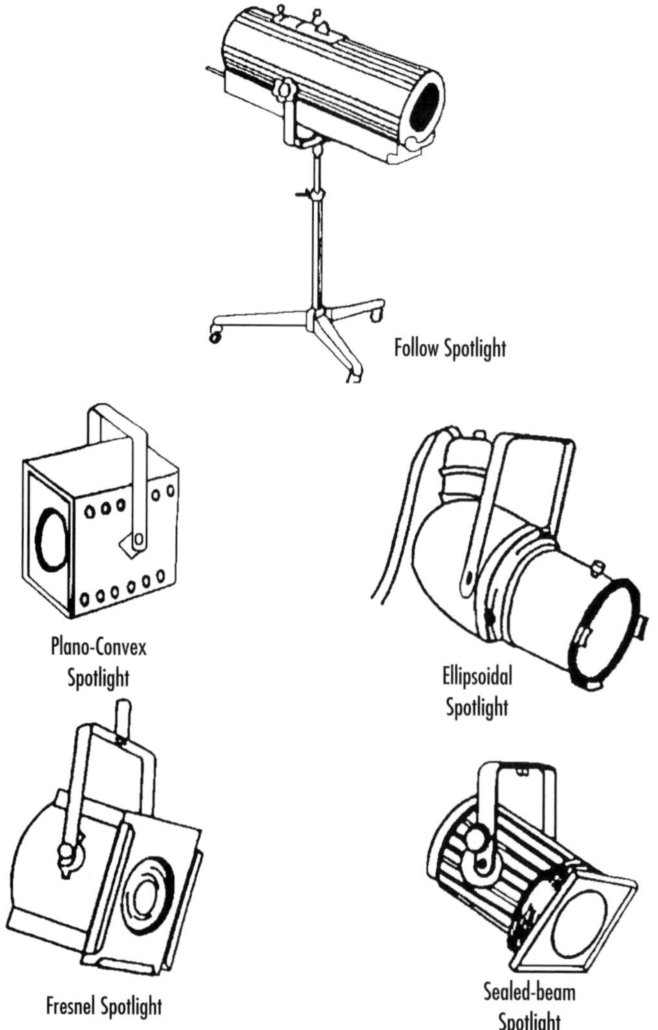

Figure 15.5

Types of spotlights.

effects. A gelatin is a color transparency—translucent plastic placed in front of a lighting instrument to add color to the lighted area.

One of the most common spots is a **Fresnel** (frā-nel'), named for the French physicist Augustin Fresnel (1788–1827), who developed it for use in lighthouses, and which provides a circular or oval area of light. The lens that covers the lamp (bulb) softens the edge of light so that it's difficult to define exactly where the lighted area ends. An advantage is that this same softness blends in with light from other instruments to provide a sense of continuity or evenness. Fresnels range in size from a three-inch diameter to twelve inches (or even larger in television studios).

The other most common spotlight is the **ellipsoidal reflector,** which is brighter than a Fresnel and more controllable. It has a framing device that allows the area the light strikes to be specific. The edge, unlike that of the Fresnel, is exact. It can provide a contrast from intense brightness to total darkness with no "spill" into the unlighted area. An ellipsoidal reflector can be used at almost any distance from the stage (whereas Fresnels generally are placed within forty feet).

Another common source of illumination is the **striplight,** a long, troughlike instrument with lights a few inches apart along the length of the trough. Often, strips light the cyclorama, or circular curtain surrounding the sides and rear of the acting area in exterior scenes, providing the illusion of distance. There are a variety of other instruments, which are used less frequently. One is the **beam projector,** which casts a narrow, intense light used, for instance, to simulate sunbeams. In effect, it is a tiny version of searchlights—those associated with shopping mall openings or film premieres in earlier eras, and which cast their rotating beams up into a night sky.

The Dimmer Board

The control system is the **dimmer board** (or switchboard), the panel from which the lights are operated. It allows the lighting technician to dim from one area to another and to control both the intensity of the light and the direction from which it originates. It also can provide control over color. For example, if a play were to progress from noon to evening, the lighting technician could change the direction of the light by switching from one set of instruments to another. Various colors of gelatins could indicate increasing darkness. For most ordinary lighting, a warm color is used.

Bill Wiegand

Figure 15.6

A lighting technician and the stage manager go over light cues on the control board at the Department of Theatre of the University of Illinois at Urbana-Champaign.

Many newer boards are computer controlled, that is, they keep a record of each change, and so can come up with any combination or "cue" whenever necessary and can maintain the combination for as long or as short a time as needed. Lighting designer David Hays defines a cue as "the pace and orchestration of the shifting light."

> Do we want the audience to ponder a certain line? Should we therefore leave a glow on that actor's face as we fade? But is it the actor pondering the line, or the audience? Perhaps a simple pause before the next scene, without featuring the actor, is best. Or does energy and content demand a quick pickup on new entrants even as the old scene fades?[5]

The lighting instruments generally are not plugged directly into the dimmer board, since this could cause a mass of cable twistings, making each hard to trace to its receptacle, as well as causing a lot of other problems. Instead, the instruments are plugged into receptacles connected to cables that lead through the walls to the dimmer board. A number of instruments are controlled from each switch or all from a master switch.

Planning the Lighting

People often think of the lighting designer as an expert electrician rather than as an artist. Certainly, designers know a great deal about electricity, and many of them do have an electrician's license. In addition, however, they are as creative and imaginative as the other theatre artists, and they possess a general knowledge of all areas of theatre production.

Lighting designers work closely with the director and the other designers to provide a cohesive image for the audience and to convey the mood of the play. They analyze the script to determine the source of light for each scene and plan how to indicate time, place, and even season. At the same time they make certain that the lighting does not call attention to itself.

> A lighting concept may seem obvious when a huge transformation is heaped on to a play. "Let's do it as if we've just been swallowed by a

[5] David Hays, *Light on the Subject: Stage Lighting for Directors and Actors and the Rest of Us* (New York: Limelight Editions, 1989), p. 61.

whale!" Hold it—is that a concept or just a locale? If the play is *Hay Fever* you've only switched it to a quirky set. Does it really change what happens between the actors? That's what the lighting designer must question. In this whale—are the characters trapped forever? Is there hope—light at the end of the gullet? Is there light only when the whale yawns, and it comes in striped by baleen strips like vertical Venetian blinds? Do we have flashlights with expiring batteries? Does an inrush of phosphorescent organisms supply us with a useful glow?

Silly, but not necessarily so if the play is *Pinocchio,* where Father Gepetto has come to the end of the world, the pit of despair, the belly of the beast. The symbol of the whale is right and profound. Perhaps his son comes to him as his candle, the shred of his remaining light, is used up and about to flicker out. Now you can get your teeth into it.[6]

Lighting designers understand where to hang lights for the best effect. They know that an actor or a set piece is lighted from various angles to appear three-dimensional. They know the psychological effects of lighting. For instance, people are more alert in high intensity lighting, which the designer could use for a fast-moving comedy. At the same time the designers recognize that many quick changes in lighting tire an audience.

The designer plans to control three aspects of lighting: *color, intensity,* and *distribution.* Warmer colors (in the form of gelatins), such as yellow to amber shades, generally are used in comedies, cooler colors in serious plays. For maximum visibility yellow is best, whereas orange and red tend to inhibit visibility, as do blue and green. Colored light most often is used because white light glares and hurts the eyes.

The designer can plan color in lighting symbolically, but always in conjunction with the other elements of design. For example, focusing a red hue on an actor could indicate a state of health, or it could be associated with shame, embarrassment, or passion. The color in lighting is directly related to the color of the other scenic elements. Most often a designer avoids green light, except for an eerie effect, because it suggests an unearthly or ghostlike quality. Mixtures of color in makeup, costuming, and lighting also can produce undesirable effects. When you color a surface with a yellow crayon and then cover the yellow with blue, you end up with green. The same kind of overlap can happen if the lighting designer does not take the other visual elements into consideration.

---

6 Hays, pp. 87 and 89.

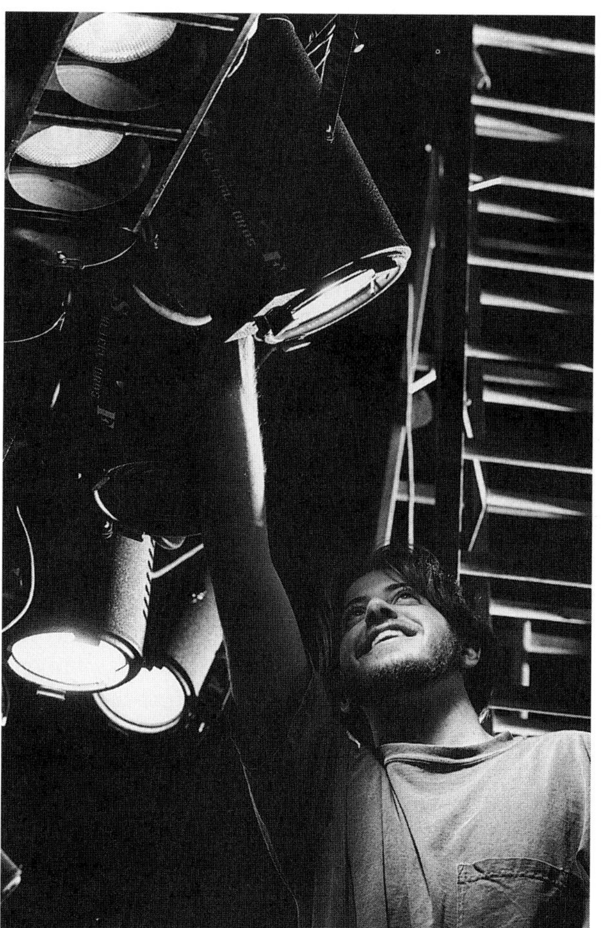

Bill Wiegand

Figure 15.7

A stagehand at the Department of Theatre of the University of Illinois at Urbana-Champaign adjusts a Fresnel light to a broad "wash" of light on the playing area of the stage below.

The Lighting Plot

Lighting does not remain static, but becomes a new design with each movement of an actor or each change in intensity or focus.

Once designers determine what is needed to light a set, they make a lighting plot, a mixture of general and specific lighting for illumination and shadow, and an instrument schedule, which includes such information as the instruments to use, where to hang them, and where to focus them. They take a floor plan of the set and draw in the location of each instrument and the area the light will hit. In a proscenium theatre the acting area most often is lighted from overhead, from the back, and from instruments placed somewhere in the auditorium.

The designer divides the stage into areas, using a minimum of two instruments for specific illumination in each area. Two or more are needed to eliminate long shadows and to light each side of the actor or set piece. The designer also prepares a list of the lighting cues, so the technician knows exactly what

Bill Wiegand

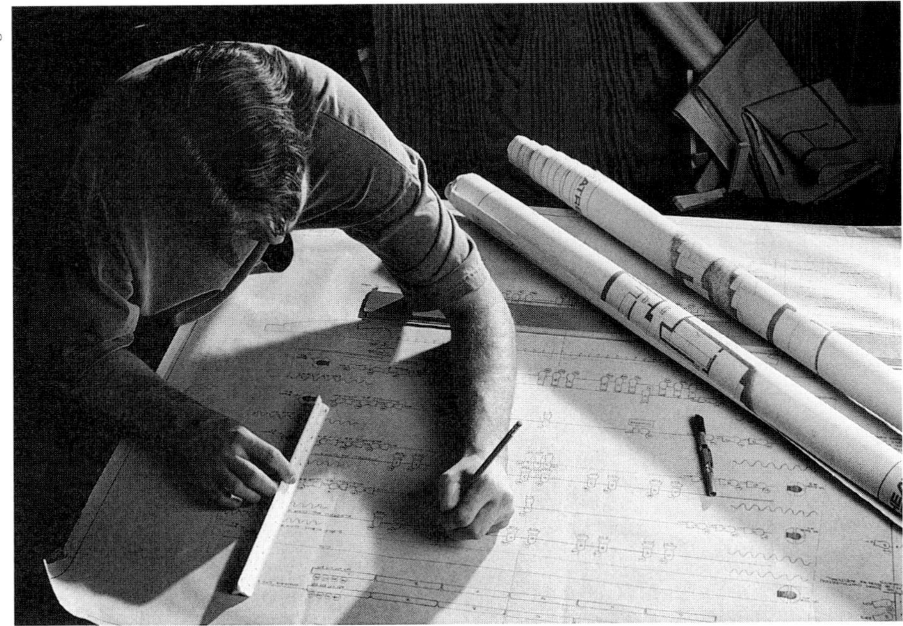

Figure 15.8

A designer in the Department of Theatre of the University of Illinois at Urbana-Champaign is shown here working on a lighting plot for an upcoming production.

to change and when. Once the lighting is set the way it will remain throughout the production, the designer's job in effect is finished, except that in many community theaters, for instance, he or she may be in charge of the lighting crew.

The Costume Designer

Costuming in a play, like clothing in real life, conveys a lot of information, such as the character's occupation. An actor playing a businessman wears a different outfit than does an actor playing a Roman Catholic priest. Clothing also reveals personality. A formal person wears different clothing than an easygoing person. Costuming also can indicate how a character feels. In everyday life people often wear colorful clothing when they are in a positive mood. Conversely, a person who feels depressed is likely to dress in drab colors. Each person develops an individual style. One person may prefer to wear jeans and a T-shirt for relaxed occasions, while another feels comfortable only in dress slacks and a shirt or blouse that buttons. We associate each of these styles with different personalities.

A woman with dangling bracelets probably would be more outgoing than one with little or no jewelry. There is the old cliché of wearing a red carnation to be recognized. Most people don't wear red carnations, but many people do choose a distinctive touch—bow ties, big earrings, or a cowboy hat, for example. Such features in a costume tell us about the character's self-image.

Costumes can also tell the audience many things about a character's situation. If an actor entered wearing a tennis outfit, a playgoer might assume several things: the character plans to play tennis or has just finished playing tennis; he is athletic and competitive; he has free time; and he wants exercise.

Costuming for the stage conveys the same sorts of messages as everyday clothing, but the effect is heightened. Of all the scenic elements, costuming and makeup provide the strongest clues to character. They are the most personal elements of design, and the audience perceives the character, costume, and makeup as a unity.

The designer takes into consideration the character and the way the actor is playing the character. In turn, the actor may be influenced by the costume to play a certain way. For instance, an 1880s dress suit may help an actor feel more completely the formality of the role.

The costume is that facet of the design that most identifies and supports the character, and thus, like the actor's gestures and movement on a vast stage, and like the oversized living room that is part of the set, the costumes often must be bigger than life to project personality and character to the audience. Generally, the more exaggerated the style of the production, the more exaggerated the costumes.

At the same time, a costume should give the actor freedom of movement . . . unlike actual clothing worn in various historical periods.

Designing the Costumes

> I have two approaches and it depends which one has kicked off. I either will start drawing it and never think about color, think about character, think about design, think about you know, blocking all the scenes . . . seeing what the look is, and then going in and carving it out. I may start with the leading lady. I may leave her till the very last. Just depends how the show hooks into me. . . . Then I will go back and I will palette the whole show. And I have thousands of five by three cards with fabrics stapled onto them that I make my palette out of. I go right into the fabric. . . .
>
> If I start with, let's say, the overall color scheme, I will do that entire show, and if I'm working with a director who can abstract himself enough to understand—to look at the colors and see, I will share

it with him. Try to. It's very hard to do, because it's like abstract painting. I'm painting with fabric. And then I will draw the show.[7]

The costume designer has to have a specialized background and a flair for style—not only the style of the character, but the style of the actor playing the part. What one actor feels comfortable wearing could inhibit another. The actor should feel at ease with the costume, both in characterization and in appearance. The designer keeps in mind what actions the actor will be performing, and whether a particular design will aid or hinder these movements. A gown that is appropriate for the straight play *The Importance of Being Earnest* might not work for the musical version *Earnest in Love;* yet both costumes must suit the historical period and the status of the character.

The costumer keeps in mind the character's motives and personality. When we watch old Hollywood westerns, we can tell immediately who is the "good guy" and the "bad guy" by the color of their hats and horses. Stage costuming usually is not so blatant in its symbolism, but tries subtly to convey mood and personality. Often the audience is not even conscious of the design.

Like the other elements, costuming must be consistent with the overall concept of the play. There should be no incongruity of character—a conservatively dressed character, for instance, wearing gaudy jewelry (unless the playwright means for the character to be inconsistent).

The designer has to be aware of what a color usually signifies. Just as red light tells us any number of things, so can red in costuming.

Color also serves as a point of focus. Although all the dancers in a musical are performing the same step, the lead dancer is emphasized through costuming that differs in color or style from that of the chorus. Color and style help identify groups as well as individuals. Just as opposing basketball teams wear different-colored jerseys, so do opposing sides in a play: The Sharks, one of the street gangs in *West Side Story,* dress differently from the Jets.

In many ways the costume designer's analysis of the script is similar to a director's or an actor's. Among the questions the designer asks are:

1. When and where does the action occur? Let's say it's 1888. But is the location New York or Russia? And is it a rural or metropolitan area?
2. What is the economic status of the characters? Are they blue-collar workers or business people?
3. What is the season and the time of day? Does the action take place largely indoors or out? If outdoors, is it late fall or the middle of July? What are the characters doing?
4. What are the characters like, and how does this influence their dress?

---

[7] Sponberg, "Patricia Zipprodt, Costume Designer," *Broadway Talks,* pp. 110–111.

There are many ways to conduct research into period costumes—museums, newspapers and periodicals on microfilm, private collections of period clothing, and so forth. In addition, there are many books that treat fashion through the ages, such as Doreen Yarwood's *Fashion in the Western World, 1500–1990.* Some that focus on costuming tell how to adapt and then build period costumes for the stage.

A costumer may be required to design any type of clothing from any historical period, even though many times it often is impractical to duplicate period clothing exactly. In past periods, women's costumes often were cumbersome and difficult to change. In the theatre quick changes often are required, so tear-way seams, snaps, and zippers are used. Fake furs take the place of heavy and hot real furs.

The costumer meets with the director before designing a show. Together, they work out an overall concept to avoid a clash of colors and styles from one type of design to another. Although costuming complements the other areas of design, it also provides contrast. An actor wearing light blue clothing in front of a light blue wall would seem to fade into the background.

Also, the designer has a knowledge of texture and fabric. From a distance and under light, inexpensive fabric sometimes appears costly. The costumer also recognizes that different fabrics or textures drape or hang differently. Stiff fabric tends to be more angular and severe, and possibly would be better suited for a serious play or a formal character than would a clinging fabric.

The costumer knows how a fabric will flow or cling as the performer moves. Properly designed costumes can help an actor to move in character. In the musical *Sugar* (later made as the film *Some Like It Hot*), Joe and Jerry dress as women and join an all-girl band to escape pursuing gangsters. Because the play takes place in the thirties, the two "girls" wear spiked heels. The heels help them take shorter, mincing steps.

The Makeup Designer

Like costuming, makeup aids the actors in their portrayal of character and helps them "feel" the part. It also helps identify the characters for an audience.

There are two types or categories of makeup: *straight* and *character.*

Straight Makeup

Straight makeup enhances or projects an actor's natural features. Under theatrical lighting a person's face tends to "wash out," so straight makeup brings out the actors' features more clearly.

Straight makeup begins with the application of a *base* or foundation, often redder in hue than normal skin color to compensate for the bright lights. The only considerations are that the makeup should be consistent with the actor's

Four By Five Inc./Super Stock

Figure 15.9

An actor uses a schematic (on right of table) to do his makeup.

natural complexion and coloring and with the character. In earlier periods, grease paint was used for the foundation; now, however, the foundation is almost always water-based. Called pancake makeup, it is much the same as everyday street makeup.

After the base is applied, features of the actor's face may be highlighted. Eyebrows usually are darkened, as are the eyelashes and rims of the eyes. Straight makeup is completed with a touch of rouge to the cheeks and lips.

Character Makeup

Although in many theatres, actors usually choose and apply their own straight makeup, often they need a designer for **character makeup**—particularly when the makeup is to alter their entire appearance, such as it does for the characters in the musical *Cats.*

A more common example of using character makeup is in making a person age. Then there are additional steps, such as adding wrinkles, after a base

UPI/Bettmann

Figure 15.10

A scene from the Chicago 1981 production of *Cats,* Andrew Lloyd Webber's first "megamusical."

is applied. Character makeup also includes such things as fake scars or "beauty marks," or, as in *Cyrano de Bergerac,* a longer nose probably made of putty. Often, crepe hair is glued to the face to represent beards or moustaches.

Facial features can be made more prominent through the use of highlighting, adding a touch of white. This can make eyes appear less sunken or a nose appear larger. The use of brown or black makeup, on the other hand, makes features seem to recede. It can make cheeks or eyes hollow, expressing illness or fatigue.

The face also can be changed through the use of latex, a sort of rubber that the makeup artist can build up on an actor's chin or cheekbones, for instance.

Planning the Makeup

Makeup designers, like the other designers, are acquainted with the theory of color and its symbolism. They know how each type of makeup will look under lights of a certain color. For instance, blue light will make rouge or lipstick appear black.

For any special needs, designers may prepare **schematics**—outlines of the head with the face divided into areas and planes. They use the schematics to indicate the color and special features to apply to each area. Also, it may be necessary to change a character's makeup during the course of the play to correspond with different physical and emotional states.

Stylized makeup, similar to character makeup in that it alters a character's appearance, also is nearly always planned by a makeup designer so that it meshes with the overall production style.

The Property Master

Another theatrical artist is the property master, who analyzes the script to understand the style, type, and number of properties needed.

There are three overall categories of props: *set props, set dressing* or ornamentation, and *hand props.* **Set props** include anything that stands within the set, such as furniture, trees, rocks, or, depending on the technical director's interpretation, even small platforms. **Set dressing** includes wall fixtures, paintings, plaques, vases, and figurines. **Hand props** are those objects an actor either carries onstage or handles while there. Often, the scene designer will choose the set dressing and sometimes the set props to make sure they are consistent with the overall design. At other times, the designer and property master work together in coordinating this aspect of the production.

Some productions require little in the way of props, while others list hundreds. For many shows the property master has to research historical items and build substitutes that appear accurate. More often, however, it's simply a matter of deciding what is needed and buying or borrowing it.

Properties are important for a number of reasons:

1. They add to a production's authenticity and/or style. An example is period furniture.
2. They augment characterization. Such things as constantly working on a partially knit sweater or twirling a cigar can go a long way in delineating personality.
3. They provide visual effects. The walls of a living room filled with paintings by Brueghel say something different about the occupant than do paintings by Pollock.

Although acting editions of previously produced scripts contain lists of properties by act and scene, for previously unpublished or unproduced shows the property master has no recourse except to go through the script carefully to determine all the properties needed.

In much the same manner as the lighting or costume designer, the property master makes plots. One of these lists where props are initially placed. Hand props may be placed, as required by the script, either onstage or offstage for actors to pick up and use; another shows how they are to be shifted during blackouts or intermissions.

Similar to the costumer, the property master often needs to do historical research, using many of the same facilities—museums, libraries, published historical material, and so on.

The Audio Designer

The audio designer provides the music and sound effects for a play.

> We are beyond the era of sound "effects." Sound is no longer an effect, an extra, a *garni* supplied from time to time to mask a scene change or ease a transition. We are beyond the era of door buzzers and thunderclaps. Or rather, door buzzers and thunderclaps are no longer isolated effects, but part of a total program of sound that speaks to theatre as ontology. Sound is the holistic process and program that binds our multifarious experience of the world. Sound is our own inner continuity track. It is also our primary outward gesture to the world, our first and best chance to communicate with others, to become part of a larger rhythm.[8]

Determining the Sound Design

An audio designer needs to determine what sounds are necessary to represent the style or "reality" of the production. This is important because too little sound can leave an audience vaguely unsatisfied and too much intrudes on the presentation. Even the way a particular sound is used is important. Suppose the stage directions call for a doorbell to be heard. The designer first needs to decide on the type of doorbell—a buzzer, a chime, several notes of a tune. A buzzer can sound intrusive or jarring; notes of a song can come across as either individualistic or "cutesy."

---

[8] Peter Sellars, "Foreword," Deena Kaye and James Lebrecht, *Sound and Music for the Theatre* (New York: Back Stage Books), 1992, p. vii.

The designer further needs to take into consideration why the doorbell is sounding. Is it to signify the arrival of an anticipated guest or an apartment manager bringing a previously threatened eviction notice? Should the sound seem angry, welcoming, frightening? Does it create a sense of anxiety or one of relief? Of course, these things go together to influence the volume of the sound, the length, the number of times the doorbell rings. In other words, when analyzing a script, the audio designer needs to pay attention to such things as mood, reason, style, and characterization.

The designer also needs to be acquainted with where specific sound effects can be acquired. Many designers maintain their own "libraries" of effects, gathered from such places as theatrical houses that sell recordings of particular sound effects, to private individuals who have specialized recordings, to various city or nature sounds the designers have taped themselves. This means, of course, that many of the sounds are prerecorded, but not necessarily all of them. The doorbell, for instance, can be "live."

The designer knows that an overall effect may include a combination of sounds. Suppose the action takes place outdoors in a rural area. The designer needs to ask what sounds a person would be likely to hear in such a setting, and maybe even go to a similar setting to experience these sounds—katydids, an occasional bird call, the far-off echo of a train whistle. But again, the designer has to determine the emotional or psychological content of the scene, and, subsequently, how to present these sounds and for how long. They'll call attention to themselves if they begin or end abruptly, if they're too loud, or even if they go on so long as to become intrusive or overwhelming.

No matter what the sound to be used, the designer must determine how to present it appropriately and in accordance with the style of the production and the genre, so that it matches the other elements of design—the pastel colors of the costumes, for instance, or the oppressive feeling of the setting.

Many effects are listed in the stage directions. Others may be indicated in the dialogue. At any rate, the audio designer needs to go through the script carefully to see that everything essential to the story and the plot is noted.

Of course, the sounds have to be timed appropriately. If they don't mesh with the action—that is, if they occur too early or too late—most likely they will come across as humorous.

Purposes of Sound

With the continued development of audio systems and mixers, the use of sound is becoming a sophisticated process—much more a part of productions today than ever before in theatrical history. There are, in fact, a variety of reasons for using sound in a production. The most obvious uses are those things that are an integral part of the action, such as the ringing of a phone, the firing of a weapon, or a rainstorm. Sometimes a playwright will want a particular piece of music played at a certain time, maybe because a character is to turn on a song that has meaning to him or her, or so it catches a character unaware and brings up old memories when heard on the radio.

Sound also is used to introduce or frame the play (or even a scene in the play). Arthur Miller specifies that *Death of a Salesman* should open with the playing of a flute. Tina Howe is very specific with the music she wants used throughout her play *Painting Churches,* both as a frame and to establish mood and character:

MUSIC IN THE PLAY

During the scene changes the opening measures of the following Chopin waltzes are played:

- As the house lights dim, the Waltz in A minor, opus posthumous.
- Setting up Act I, Scene 2, the Waltz in E minor, opus posthumous.
- Setting up Act I, Scene 3, the Waltz in E major, opus posthumous.
- To close Act I, the final notes of the Waltz in B minor, opus 69, #2.
- As the house lights dim for Act II, the Waltz in A flat major, opus 64, #3.
- Setting up Act II, Scene 2, repeat the Waltz in A minor, opus posthumous.
- To accompany the final moments of GARDNER's and FANNY's dance, the Waltz in D flat major, opus 70, #3.

Other effects besides music can introduce the action. David Rabe's *Hurlyburly* opens with a TV "droning out the early morning news."

A director or designer may only infer certain effects from what the playwright has written. In *Joe Turner's Come and Gone,* August Wilson, in part, has this to say after the list of characters and the setting and before the action begins:

William Gullete

Figure 15.11

A scene from *Joe Turner's Come and Gone* as produced at the Old Globe Theatre, San Diego.

> It is August in Pittsburgh, 1911. The sun falls out of heaven like a stone. The fires of the steel mill rage with a combined sense of industry and progress. Barges loaded with coal and iron ore trudge up the river to the mill towns that dot the Monongahela and return with fresh, hard, gleaming steel. The city flexes its muscles. Men throw countless bridges across the rivers, lay roads and carve tunnels through the hills sprouting with houses.
>
> From the deep and the near South the sons and daughters of newly freed African slaves wander into the city. . . .

This information might suggest using the sound of steel mills, barges on the river, men and women calling to each other, or trains unloading passengers.

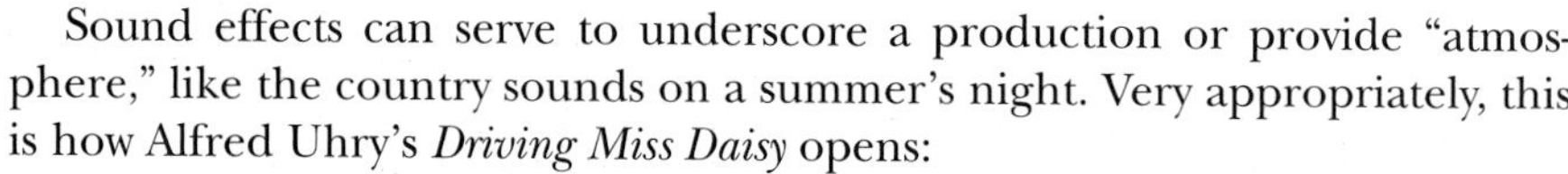

Sound effects can serve to underscore a production or provide "atmosphere," like the country sounds on a summer's night. Very appropriately, this is how Alfred Uhry's *Driving Miss Daisy* opens:

> In the dark we hear a car ignition turn on, and then a horrible crash. Bangs and booms and wood splintering. When the noise is very loud, it stops suddenly and the lights come up on DAISY WERTHAN's living room . . .

Sounds and music may suggest a particular period, as would the old *Inner Sanctum* radio show or "The Charleston."

A designer may decide to use *voice over.* An example of this is the voice from the sound booth in the musical *Chorus Line,* which tells the dancers onstage what to do. Or it can be voices unrelated to the characters, but used to provide effect or to present characters' thoughts, which then is a device similar to the soliloquy.

Music or other sounds (old newscasts, for instance) added to a production can show the passage of time, or the movement from one place and/or time to another. Similarly, music or other sounds can be identified with a particular character. Arthur Kopit opens *End of the World* with these directions: "MUSIC: *lazy, bluesy music for a hard-boiled detective. It is 'Trent's Theme.' Curtain up.*"

The sound has to be convincing within the framework of a play. In Arnold Ridley's *The Ghost Train,* where a wrecked train supposedly passes a railway terminal, it would be unconvincing if the sound did not begin at one side of the stage and progress to the other as the train passes by. The designer has to determine how to convince the audience of the train's movement. After determining the effects, the sound designer then prepares a sound plot, just as the lighting designer prepared a plot.

Chapter Sixteen

The Business Side of Theatre

Among those who work behind the scenes in theatre are the producers, the general and company managers, and the house and box office staffs. Others, whose work evolves directly out of that done by the director and the designers, are individuals and crews involved more closely with the production.

Before a play can be planned or presented, arrangements must be made for securing a theatre space, for promoting the show, for paying expenses, and, when required, for paying salaries. The producer can be an individual or a group. The manner of financing and the method of handling business arrangements depend on the type of theatre.

Producing in Educational and Community Theatres

In educational theatre, the school itself, or a department of the school, is the producer. In elementary and high schools one person often is in charge of all the arrangements. Money may be advanced by the school or by an organization in the school. In college, the expense of producing plays comes out of the departmental budget and/or other sources. While the community theatre also is the producer of its own shows, the setup is somewhat different from educational theatre. Most often, an elected board governs the practical aspects of planning a season and is responsible for approving expenditures.

The important consideration for educational theatre is to plan a balanced season, whereas community theatre's major concern is selecting plays that draw well.

Nonprofit Theatre

The commercial theatre in the United States, in the past and at the present, centers in New York City, with Chicago now considered by many to be the "second city." However, more and more professional theatres have been established throughout the country—repertory companies, various types of stock companies, dinner theatres, outdoor dramas, and children's theatre—in major cities as well as small communities.

Figure 16.1 (opposite page)

Educational theatre productions can be funded in a variety of ways. As shown on this program cover for the Franklin Pierce College production of *While Falling,* written by Robert Lawson, funding was in part from The Kennedy Center Corporate Fund, the U.S. Department of Education, and Ryder System.

KC/ACTF XXVII

Kennedy Center American College Theater Festival XXVII

Presented and produced by
The John F. Kennedy Center for the Performing Arts

Supported in Part by
The Kennedy Center Corporate Fund
The U.S. Department of Education
Ryder System

This production is entered in the Kennedy Center American College Theater Festival (KC/ACTF). The aims of this national theater education program are to identify and promote quality in college-level theater production. To this end, each production entered is eligible for adjudication by a regional KC/ACTF reprsentative, and certain students are selected to participate in KC/ACTF programs involving awards, scholarships, and special grants for actors, playwrights, designers, and critics at both the regional and national levels.

Productions entered on the Participating level are eligible for inclusion at the KC/ACTF regional festival and can also be considered for invitation to the non-competitive KC/ACTF national festival at the John F. Kennedy Center for the Performing Arts in Washington, DC, in the spring of 1995.

The KC/ACTF is a program of the Kennedy Center Education Department, which also includes youth and family programs, professional development opportunities for teachers, and performances for school groups, the Kennedy Center Alliance for Arts Education, the Performing Arts Centers and Schools Program, performance enhancement events, national and community outreach initiatives, the Kennedy Center Internship Program, and the National Symphony Orchestra education program. The Kennedy Center also works closely with Very Special Arts, an educational affiliate of the Kennedy Center.

Last year more than 800 productions and 17,000 students participated in the American College Theater Festival nationwide. By entering this production, our department is sharing in the KC/ACTF goals to help college theater grow and to focus attention on the exemplary work produced in college and university theaters across the nation.

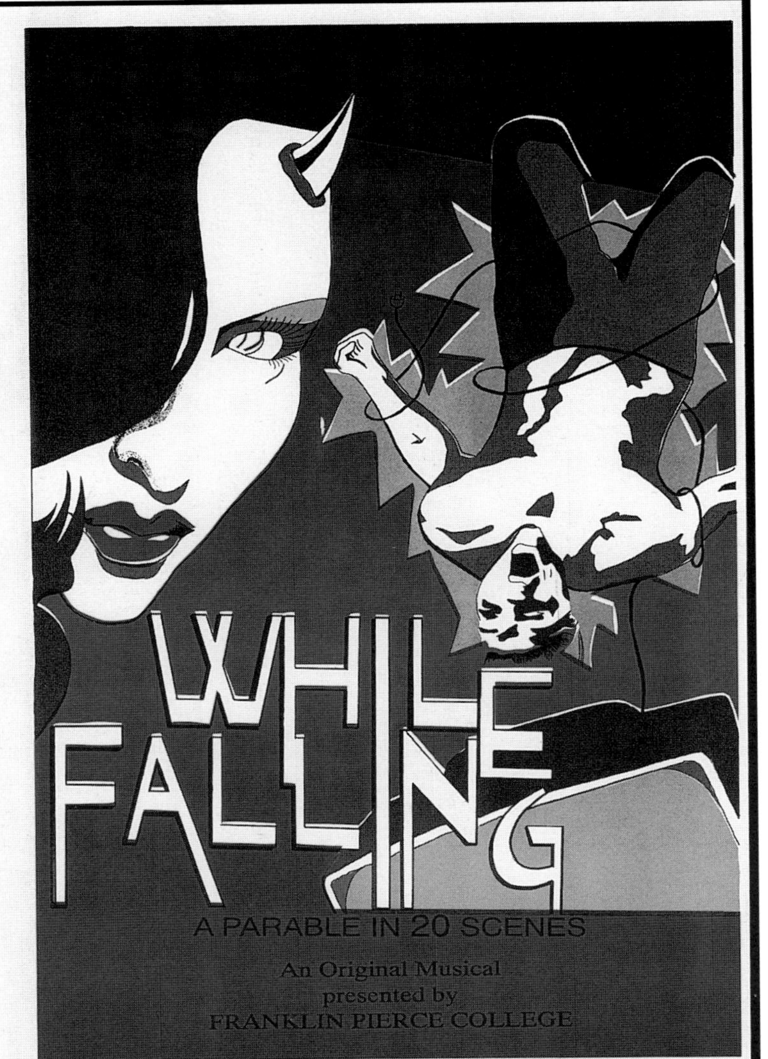

WHILE FALLING
A PARABLE IN 20 SCENES
An Original Musical
presented by
FRANKLIN PIERCE COLLEGE

Until the late 1960s or early 1970s, most professional theatre existed to make a profit. Then came a change that gained impetus in the 1980s, totally changing the face of professional theatre. It was the establishment of nonprofit regional theatres that do not rely totally on box office receipts to fund their operation. Rather, they are supported in large part by grants and donations, which is more in line with the way it has been done in Europe, with governments of various countries subsidizing the arts.

Theoretically, this allows theatres more freedom in what they choose to present. Often, the producer in this sort of theatre is the organization itself, and most often the grants and other monies received are for overall operation rather than a single production.

These theatres are subsidized by foundations, government agencies, individuals or corporations, or often a combination of these sources. This sort of theatre rarely existed in the first half of the twentieth century, and only lately has come to exist in nearly every major city in the United States. Included, for instance, are The American Repertory Theatre in Boston, The Goodman Theatre and the Steppenwolf Theatre Company in Chicago, The Mark Taper Forum in Los Angeles, and the Old Globe Theater and La Jolla Playhouse in San Diego. There are now more working artists in such theatres than in those that exist to make money for the producers. And the theatres, because they are culturally oriented and don't have to rely on box office receipts, are raising artistic standards. Yet, like their commercial counterparts, they are having problems:

> Nonprofit theatres across the country continued to struggle for economic health and survival in 1994, according to Theatre Communications Group's latest national survey of nonprofit professional theatres. Still unable to recover from the prolonged effects of the recession of the early 1990s, theatres once again failed to balance their budgets and experienced further audience attrition.
>
> Earnings did not keep pace with inflation as overall attendance figures reached a five-year low, mitigated at the box office only by price increases that countered the effects of fewer performances and lower attendance. . . .
>
> Federal funding and corporate contributions were virtually flat, falling below the inflation rate for the period. Fortunately for the overall picture of the field's health, however, the negative economic environment was tempered by several positive factors: Theatres reported impressive increases in individual giving and foundation grants, and funding from state agencies and from city and county coffers regained some lost ground by showing welcome increases.

Despite continued tight control of operating expenses, more than half the surveyed theatres ended the year with operating deficits, and some theatres were forced to suspend operations or close their doors permanently in fiscal 1994.[1]

Figure 16.2

Community organizations often sponsor their own amateur theatre productions. Here a group rehearses a scene from the musical *Dreamgirls* in a community center.

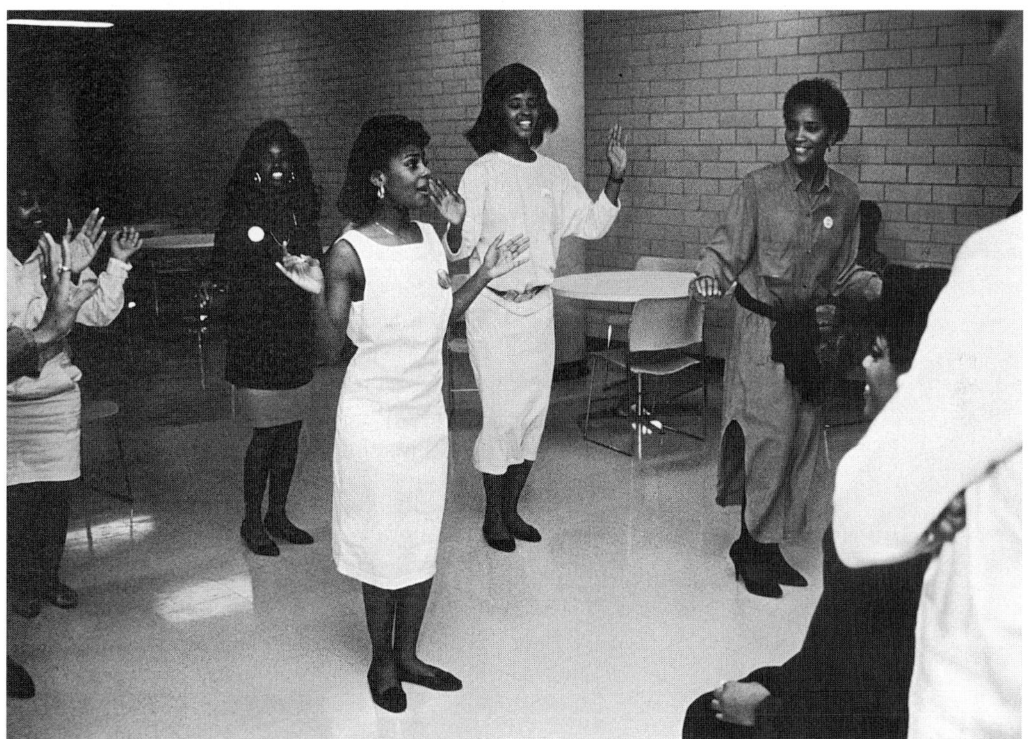

W. B. Nickerson/Evanston, Illinois

[1] Barbara Janowitz, *"Theatre Facts '94," Theatre Communication Group's Annual Survey of the Finances and Productivity of the American Nonprofit Theatre,* p. 2, insert in *American Theatre,* April 1995.

Broadway and Off-Broadway Theatre

When the booking of shows for a season and the casting for touring shows became centralized in the United States, the location was a small section of Manhattan on and around Broadway (a street) in New York City. Within the last few decades rising costs have made Broadway a risky venture, even for the most courageous producer. Most shows are presented to appeal to a mass audience, and untried playwrights have little hope of production. The Broadway producer is concerned, and rightly so, with staging a show that will be a hit. Even at that, the majority of shows never regain their initial investment.

Although location has something to do with calling a theatre Off-Broadway (many are located in the Greenwich Village area), the main factor is size. According to standards set by Actors' Equity Association, the union for stage actors, an Off-Broadway theatre can seat no more than 299 spectators. Whereas Broadway appeals to the mass audience to make money, Off-Broadway producers, if they choose, can present plays that have limited appeal. There is the occasional show that becomes so successful it moves to a larger theater. However, Off-Broadway, too, is becoming more commercialized than in the 1960s or 1970s, so that Off-Off Broadway has become in recent decades what Off-Broadway was in the 1950s and 1960s—a place for nearly any sort of theatre, and a wide range of experimentation.

The procedure for producing Broadway and most Off-Broadway shows is entirely different than for nonprofit theatre. Generally, a producer takes an option on a play. An option is a contract with the playwright, whereby the writer is paid a certain amount to give the producer exclusive rights for a limited time to produce the play. If the script is not produced within the time limit specified in the contract, the rights revert to the writer, who may seek another producer. Often, producers do take options on plays that they never present for one reason or another.

Once a producer takes an option—often after contact with literary agents who handle scripts—and definitely decides to produce the show, he or she makes the financial arrangements and rents rehearsal space and theatre. The producer may provide all the money for a production, but more likely will seek backers, known as "angels," who form a corporation just for the run of a show. The producer receives up to half the profits.

If a play is accepted for production and arrangements are made, the producer reserves the right to make suggestions and changes. The same right extends to the backers. Actually, the producer may take an option on a script only if the writer agrees to changes beforehand.

Here's how producer Cheryl Crawford describes her work:

Sometimes I think a producer is a person who is absolutely unable to do anything else, who has a strong interest in all the arts but the talent for none of them and enough business sense to know that

> sometimes you must dare to go to the edge of disaster to achieve what you desire. A producer is definitely a gambler. For the education of a theatre producer, the sky is the limit, which is what makes the profession so endlessly exciting. . . .[2]

Although producers have no direct working arrangements with the artistic end of a play in rehearsal, they approve any alterations that are made, because these changes will affect the show's audience-drawing potential. The producer's final responsibility is deciding when to end a show's run, whether it is after a day, a month, or several years.

If a production continues beyond opening night, it is up to the producer to meet all operating expenses and finally to begin splitting any profits among the investors. If the reviews are bad, the producer is the one who posts the closing notice, ending all arrangements.

It is becoming increasingly difficult to produce a play professionally in New York. Many people feel, as does Dramatist Guild president Peter Stone, that Broadway is in a "crisis period" for several reasons. Producers have "negotiated contracts somewhat carelessly," young people are more interested in television, videos, cable, and movies, and current audiences think a play is a failure if the seats at a performance are not all filled.

> So the sad fact is we have developed a paradox: We have a theater that is way out of line economically, and we have houses that are much too big for the available audience. And we have an audience that is so success-oriented that they won't consider a play that has three quarters of a house in it.

Stone states that perhaps the only possible solution is to concentrate on a unified New York theatre, instead of Broadway and Off-Broadway.[3]

Playwright Terrence McNally flatly proclaims: "'Where are the new American producers?' playwrights ask. We complain that there are no new American producers. We're right." He goes on to say that "if you're talking about serious American theater today you're no longer talking about on Broadway or off. You're speaking about the not-for-profit regional theater," whose "corporations have replaced the commercial producers who made off Broadway happen in the '60s."[4]

---

[2] Cheryl Crawford, *One Naked Individual: My Fifty Years in the Theatre* (Indianapolis: The Bobbs-Merrill Company, Inc., 1977), p. 1.

[3] Peter Stone, "Peter Stone on Broadway: Let's Call the Whole Thing Off," from "The State of the Theatre 1994," *The Dramatists Guild Quarterly,* Spring 1994, p. 8–9.

[4] Terrence McNally, "Terrence McNally on Off-Broadway: The New Establishment," from "The State of the Theater 1994," *Dramatists Guild Quarterly,* Spring 1994, p. 10–11.

Figure 16.3

A scene from the musical *42nd Street* as produced by the San Diego Junior Theatre, a nonprofit regional theatre.

It isn't only playwrights who feel this way. Producer Richard Horner states that costs are getting out of hand due to "featherbedding"—having, under union rules, to hire many more people than are necessary.

> I know that actors used to rehearse for no money, without being paid. Actors were commonly stranded in other cities when their shows closed on tour with no way to get home. There were great abuses. There's no question about it. . . . But, unfortunately, the pendulum has swung far in the other direction.[5]

[5] Arvid F. Sponberg, "Richard Horner, Producer," *Broadway Talks: What Professionals Think About Commercial Theater in America* (New York: Greenwood Press, 1991), p. 12.

One solution to the problem is a closer relationship among nonprofit and commercial theatres.

> On her installment last January as new chairman of the National Endowment for the Arts [1994], Jane Alexander called for wider collaboration by commercial producers and nonprofit resident theatres. The call . . . rekindled a debate launched formally at the First Annual Congress of Theatre (FACT) in June 1974, when Broadway producer Alexander Cohen invited 220 representatives from nonprofit and commercial theatres to convene in Princeton, N.J. His goal—which was not wholeheartedly embraced by the nonprofit emissaries who attended the meeting "on scholarship"—was to formulate cooperative solutions to the problems afflicting both theatrical sectors: growing financial needs in the burgeoning nonprofit community, and a moribund climate on Broadway. . . .
>
> Twenty years after FACT [First Annual Congress of Theatre] delegates mulled prospects of greater union between the commercial and noncommercial sides of the theatre, industry trends and strapped finances have forced both groups to live together under common law if not by holy matrimony. Forged out of necessity, the partnership shows signs of promise: Hope seems to lie in nurturing a cautious collaboration between commercial producers sympathetic to aims of nonprofit theatres, and managers of nonprofit theatres who can work these relationships to advance traditional goals—service to the community and fidelity to artistic purpose—without indulging foolish expectations of limitless cash flow. . . .
>
> Cooperation doesn't guarantee harmony, however, even after details of financial arrangements are hammered out. On Broadway and elsewhere, commercial producers are quick to yell foul when tax-advantaged, nonprofit theatres pose competition. Inside the nonprofit environment, the old debate persists: Do commercial aspirations constrain creativity and stifle voices that are not commercial enough?[6]

Members of the Business Staff

Besides the producer and the theatrical artists, there are many others involved in presenting a play. In New York theatre there are a general manager and a company manager. The former is the first person involved in the show after the producer decides to go ahead with it, negotiating agreements with the

[6] S. L. Mintz, "A Marriage of Convenience," *American Theatre*, November 1994, pp. 26–28.

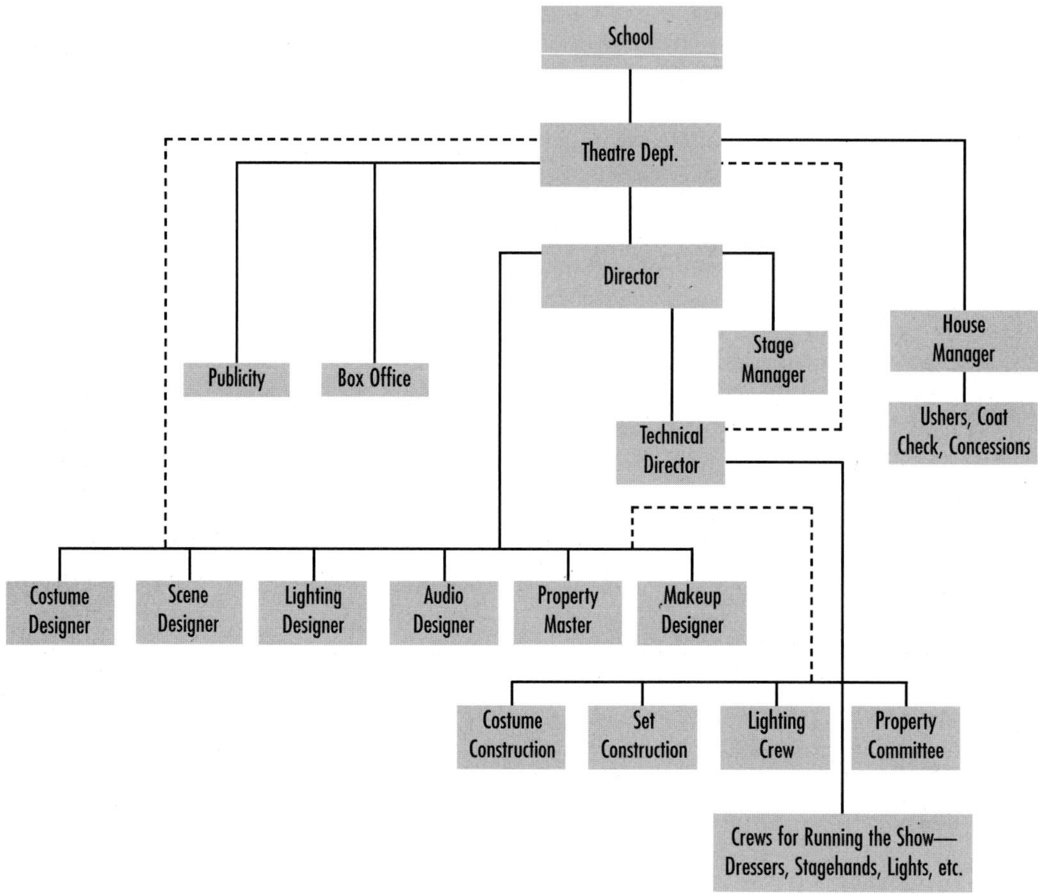

Figure 16.4

An organizational model for educational theatre.

director, the theater owners, the designers, and the stars. The general manager develops the production budget and sees that it's followed and that any profits are distributed among the investors.

The company manager is the producer's representative in the day-to-day business operations of a production, including seeing that everything associated with the project is on schedule and running smoothly. He or she oversees expenses, payroll, and ticket sales. Overall the job involves seeing that everything functions properly.

The house manager supervises a host of people, including ushers, doormen, and cleaners. The business staff also is extensive, with various secretaries, accountants, an attorney, and a press agent.

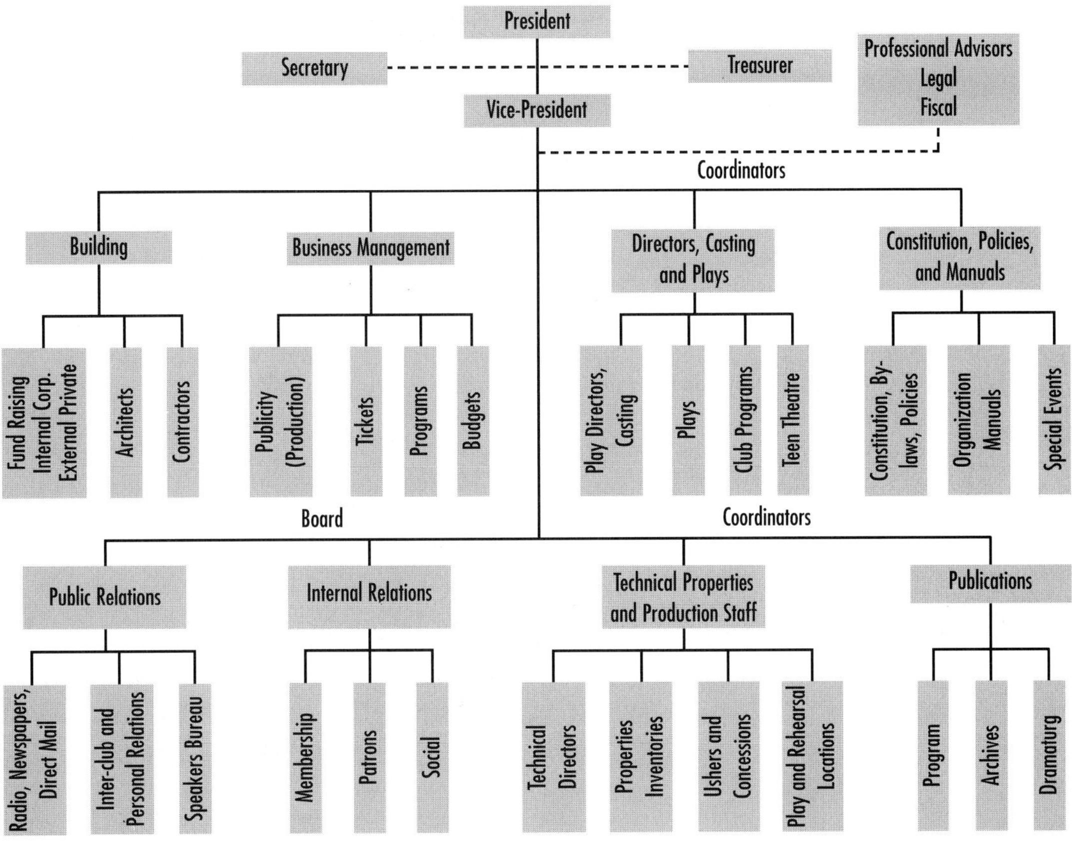

Figure 16.5

An organizational model for community theatre.

Although community and educational theatres generally do not have so extensive a staff as does professional theatre, there still are many members. The house manager usually is responsible for all front-of-the house matters. This work includes seeing that the theatre and the grounds are in proper order, arranging for ushers and ticket takers, sometimes arranging for the printing and delivery of programs, handling the checking of coats, and often being in charge of the concession stand.

Publicity managers or press agents also have many duties. The most important, of course, is to sell tickets. Second, they are responsible for projecting a good image of the theatre and for increasing public awareness of its existence and program. Last, they are responsible for publicizing each show. Although they have several others working with them, publicity managers have the final responsibility for all press releases for radio, television, and public appearances. The publicity manager works directly with the box office personnel, because both are responsible for ticket sales.

Backstage and Behind the Scenes

There are many other people who work backstage. Increasingly in the United States, theatres are hiring *dramaturgs,* whose duties vary, depending on the theatre. (Dramaturgs have been used in German theatre since the 1700s.) In some cases, they solicit, read, and even select scripts for production.

In effect, **dramaturgs** are literary managers of a sort, knowledgeable about the history, genres, and structure of drama. As such, they are available for answering directors' and actors' questions about the period in which a play was written or about its interpretation. Sometimes their duties include educating audiences through lectures, discussions, or articles in the play program.

A dramaturg usually works closely with the director in researching a play's background and in analyzing and interpreting the script.

Stage Manager

The stage manager usually is considered second in command after the director. The job actually begins two weeks before the rehearsal period begins. Although the stage manager serves as a liaison between the cast/crew and the management, he or she also acts as the director's representative in meetings with the actors and other theatre artists. If necessary, the stage manager takes over rehearsals and also helps solve any technical problems that come up. In effect, the job involves minor details that otherwise would confront the director.

Stage managing is a big responsibility, particularly after opening, when the stage manager "calls the show"—that is, announces cues for scenery shifts, lights, and sound. A stage manager is responsible for seeing that the entire production goes as rehearsed and according to schedule, and that the director's wishes are carried out from opening night until the production closes. In other words, stage managing involves seeing that everyone associated with the performance does the job according to plan and on time.

Production Stage Manager and Assistants

Some theatres differentiate between the stage manager and the production stage manager. Often the production stage manager arranges rehearsal times, recording sessions, and so on, at regional theatres where several shows are in rehearsal at the same time. For long-running productions, he or she sits in the audience to check that the show is going according to plan, both technically and artistically. Although qualified to do so, the production stage manager usually calls a show only in an emergency.

In various theatres there are other jobs such as *production assistant,* who works with the director, and *casting agent* (particularly in Broadway theatre), who chooses several of the most likely people for particular roles so that the producer or director can make a final selection.

Various theatres have technical directors who supervise building and erecting sets, and, of course, there are various crews who help build scenery and costumes, handle lights, prepare the sound effects, and run the show in production.

Critiquing a Theatrical Production

Throughout the text you have become acquainted with various aspects you should take into consideration when critiquing a theatrical production. To write a review or evaluate a performance, you simply need to look at the information in a new light.

Consider Who and What You Are

First, examine your background and beliefs.

Suppose you will attend a production of Kramer's *The Normal Heart.* What are your feelings about AIDS? About gay men? Why? How will this affect the way you view the show? Can you be objective in your critique?

What genres do you like or dislike? Why? Would you rather see a comedy, or do you prefer something you can "sink your teeth into?"

Take into consideration why you are attending a performance. Is it because you want to be there, because it's a class requirement, or because you have been given an assignment of writing a review?

You need to consider the audience the playwright intended to see the work. Does the play fit the audience? Another basis for judgment is whether the producer or director really paid attention to the type of audience the theatre usually draws.

You need to ask yourself:

How did the presentation affect me personally? Emotionally? Professionally? You should try to be honest in your judgment of the production. Yet your opinion is bound to differ from someone else's.

The following appeared after the opening of August Wilson's *Joe Turner's Come and Gone.*

"NEW CHAPTER IN WILSON SAGA OF BLACK LIFE"

by John Beaufort
The Christian Science Monitor
March 30, 1988

"Joe Turner's Come and Gone" is the most searching of the growing cycle of August Wilson dramas about the black American experience. It was preceded on Broadway by "Ma Rainey's Black Bottom" (the 1920s) and the current "Fences" (the 1950s), winner of the Pulitzer

Prize and other awards. The transcendent new work further explores the personal sufferings and struggles born of a diaspora that began with slavery and continued with the post-emancipation of blacks to the industrial North.

In the present work, the struggle is as much for self-identity and self-realization as for lost kinfolk. "Joe Turner" is set in Pittsburgh in 1911. Swinging in mood from the richly comic to the poignantly tragic, the play constitutes what Mr. Wilson has described as "a boardinghouse play." Its inspiration comes from a painting by the late Romare Bearden and its title from a W. C. Handy blues ballad about the actual Joe Turner. . . .

While Wilson's dialogue abounds in folk-flavored vernacular, his lyric flights . . . give "Joe Turner" its extra dimension of poetic drama. The author also proves once more that he has moved far beyond the conventional "race play." The crimes of Joe Turner are presented as merely part of the pattern of subjugation that black Americans have historically endured. . . .

It is obvious that Beaufort liked both the play and the production. Yet, in talking about Wilson's collection of work, *The Oxford Companion to American Theatre* says:

> This profusion of awards is baffling, for while the plays have powerful scenes or moments, they are basically an unhomogenized melange of styles and techniques. Wilson employs realism, mysticism, some extremely eccentric characters, musical segments and anything else that might work for immediate effect. As a result, the plays, except possibly for *Ma Rainey,* lack a sense of tone and a legitimate, sustained dramatic thrust.[1]

Set standards for yourself and for the production. Then, stay focused and involved. Of course, this is hard to do if the acting is poor, the designs inappropriate, or the blocking sloppy. Most likely you will then have to step back from what is going on and view it more from the "outside." At the same time, you have a right to be demanding of a good choice of play, a

1 Gerald Bordman, ed., *The Oxford Companion to American Theatre* (New York: Oxford University Press, 2nd ed., 1992), p. 718.

well-written script, and a well-executed production. To judge this, you need to be knowledgeable and sensitive—as to what can realistically be expected of a performance, given the company and the theatre, and in regard to your openness in evaluating what you are perceiving.

Two Halves of an Integrated Whole

A reviewer actually is critiquing two halves of the same integrated whole: the playwright/play and the physical production.

The Script

There are a number of things to consider about the writer and the script. For instance, when and where did the dramatist live? What were the economic and social conditions, and did they influence the subject matter and approach?

According to Hwang, *M. Butterfly* was influenced by stereotypes Westerners often have about Asians. Albee's *Three Tall Women* has a great deal that is autobiographical. The style and genres popular at the time the play was written also influenced the writer. How does this affect the play? What about the social influences? Is the viewpoint honest? Truthful? If not, why not? What in the play made you feel the phoniness? Was it the writing? The production itself?

What sort of structure does the play have? Is it easy to follow? Is there a dramatic problem? If so, what is it? What is the play's central message? What does the dramatist want the audience to think or feel after seeing a production of the play? How do you know this?

Did the play hold your attention? Were you interested in the ideas, the story, the plot, the characterization? What didn't interest you? Why? Were you able to suspend your disbelief and put yourself into the world of the play? Was the writing flawed?

Were the theme, the characters, the situation universal? Did the play deal with universal feelings, traits, and ideas? If not, was it at least timely? How do you think it will be viewed by audiences in ten, fifty, or a hundred years?

Many plays—particularly those that are political in nature—often do not hold up beyond a certain period. This is the case with much of the AIDS drama of today. In fact, much of it already seems dated. On the other hand, playwrights are still dealing with many of the same social issues Ibsen dealt with in his plays about women's rights or individual rights.

Is the treatment of material appropriate? AIDS drama, for instance, has evolved from agitprop to comedy. Why do you suppose this happened? Do you think it's logical? Desirable?

How well do you think the play stands up as a comedy, a tragedy, a farce? If it's a comedy, is it really funny? What comic devices are used?

Is the conflict logical? Does it have meaning for you—either in subject matter or treatment?

What symbolism, if any, does the writer use (in contrast to that imposed by the director and designers)? Is it workable and appropriate?

Is the background information clear? Is it presented unobtrusively? Is there adequate foreshadowing? Does the suspense build?

Does the setting fit the characters? The situation? The action?

Are the characters well drawn? Are they individuals? Is there enough contrast among them to make the situation and conflict interesting?

Are the characters three-dimensional? If the play is a farce, of course they shouldn't be.

Is it easy to pick out the central character or protagonist? Are the person's goals logical, worthwhile, fitting for the situation, the genre, the time period?

Can you easily determine the purpose each character has in the play? Are their actions realistic in light of what you know about them?

Is there a balance between the main characters' individuality and typification?

Is the dialogue appropriate to the situation? The mood? The characters? Does it give clues to personality and background?

Is the style appropriate to the genre, to the social class and background of the characters? To the region?

The Production

How well does the production stand up as a whole? How does it compare with other productions you've seen?

Is the production worthwhile? Did it effectively bring across the playwright's message?

Were the design elements integrated? Were they appropriate?

Did the director and performers understand what the playwright intended? Did their interpretations fit your idea of the play? Did they contribute to your appreciation of the play? Were the actors well cast? Were they competent in their skills and in their interpretation? Did they work together rather than trying to dominate the performance? Was the style of acting consistent?

What do you think were the goals of the production? If you are familiar with the play, do you think the director's interpretation is fair or accurate? What would you have done differently? Why?

Was the pace appropriate?

Finally, what is your recommendation? Should others see (or have seen) the production?

The Drama Critic's Responsibilities

If you are going to be writing a review for publication or presentation, here are some things to keep in mind.

1. Don't take cheap shots. Of course, you can be critical of something you think needs improvement. But just as a theatrical artist should not call

undue attention to self, a theatre critic should concentrate on reviewing the show, rather than on exhibiting his or her intelligence or trying to be sarcastic or funny.

2. If your review is to be presented to the public, be familiar with the playwright's work, if possible. Also, be familiar with the work of the designers, the director, and the actors.

3. Keep yourself out of the review; your audience wants to hear about the production, not about your background or beliefs or dramatic theories. Of course, give an opinion, but do it as honestly and simply as you can.

4. Be comprehensive. Don't spend half the review raving about how good or how bad the set design was. Give adequate space to all the important elements.

5. Do tell your audience about both the play and the production.

6. Do state what you think was most important about the production, what you think should be emphasized or downplayed and why.

7. Finally, discuss the play's relationship to the audience and to theatre as a whole.

Following are a few reviews to give you an idea of the sort of thing critics write and the diversity of their opinions. First is John Beaufort's entire review of August Wilson's *Joe Turner's Come and Gone,* from which the earlier excerpt was taken.

"NEW CHAPTER IN WILSON SAGA OF BLACK LIFE"

by John Beaufort

"Joe Turner's Come and Gone" is the most searching of the growing cycle of August Wilson dramas about the black American experience. It was preceded on Broadway by "Ma Rainey's Black Bottom" (the 1920s) and the current "Fences" (the 1950s), winner of the Pulitzer Prize and other awards. The transcendent new work further explores the personal sufferings and struggles born of a diaspora that began with slavery and continued with the post-emancipation of blacks to the industrial North.

In the present work, the struggle is as much for self-identity and self-realization as for lost kinfolk. "Joe Turner" is set in Pittsburgh in 1911. Swinging in mood from the richly comic to the poignantly tragic, the play constitutes what Mr. Wilson has described as "a boardinghouse play." Its inspiration comes from a painting by the late Romare Bearden and its title from a W. C. Handy blues ballad about the actual Joe Turner.

The action occurs in the simple but hospitable boarding house operated by Seth Holly (Mel Winkler), a hardworking factory hand and part-time tinsmith, and his good-hearted wife, Bertha (L. Scott

Caldwell). The $2-a-week rate covers room and two meals a day. The boarders include Bynum Walker (Ed Hall), an amateur "voodoo" man with claims to mystic healing and "binding" powers; Jeremy Furlow (Bo Rucker), a newcomer from the South with a guitar under his arm and an eye for the girls; Mattie Campbell (Kimberleigh Aarn), a pretty woman in search of the husband who deserted her after the death of their two children; and humorous, worldly-wise Molly Cunningham (Kimberly Scott).

The cheerful, occasionally explosive course of events takes a darker turn with the arrival of Herald Loomis (Delroy Lindo) and his 11-year-old daughter Zonia (Jamila Perry). Loomis, a one-time church deacon, has been a victim of the notorious Joe Turner, a bounty hunter who kidnaped blacks and sold them into plantation servitude. After completing his term, Loomis has taken to the road in search of the wife from whom circumstances separated him.

Seth's suspicions of the black-clad, seemingly sinister Loomis explode into hostility when a "juba" celebration leaves the stranger writhing and out of control. Although the benign Bynum proves his healing gift, it requires an even more violent eruption to bring the complex, multifaceted play to its affirmingly mystical resolution.

While Wilson's dialogue abounds in folk-flavored vernacular, his lyric flights (especially as spoken by Mr. Hall's Bynum) give "Joe Turner" its extra dimension of poetic drama. The author also proves once more that he has moved far beyond the conventional "race play." The crimes of Joe Turner are presented as merely part of the pattern of subjugation that black Americans have historically endured. No great stir is caused among the boarders when Rutherford Selig (Raynor Scheine), a white traveling tin salesman who earns a little on the side for tracking down lost loved ones, tells how his father used to apprehend runaway slaves for their masters.

The performance, staged by Lloyd Richards, Wilson's longtime collaborator, at the Ethyl Barrymore Theatre is sensitively attuned to the resonance of "Joe Turner's Come and Gone." Hall and Mr. Lindo create the central dynamic for a human drama of heroic proportions. Besides those already mentioned, the good cast includes Angela Bassett as Loomis's finally appearing wife and Richard Parnell Habersham as a little boy next door. A murky background of smokestacks and bridges looms above the cozy boardinghouse premises of Scott Bradley's setting. The Yale Repertory Theatre production, lighted by Michael Gionnitti and costumed by Pamela Peterson, expands the scope and range of what is becoming a magnificent project.

The Christian Science Monitor, March 30, 1988.

"'NO TIME' CONFUSING OVERLOAD OF IDEAS"

Michael Phillips

A year ago, Sledgehammer Theatre mounted Erik Ehn's "No Time Like the Present" as part of the Whitney Museum's spring performance series in New York. Now, a revised version of Ehn's mind-warp has opened at Sledge's home base, St. Cecilia's Playhouse.

It's tough stuff, even by Ehn's standards. It is, in fact, damn near impossible to access—and the way it has been staged, the access points have been plastered with signs saying DETOUR.

Previously, Sledgehammer has produced several of Ehn's "Saint Plays" and his disarming, lunatic one-act "New." The latter is one of his best in part because, like Mac Wellman's "Albanian Softshoe" (staged by the San Diego Repertory Theatre in 1989), it starts sane—with a conventional romantic triangle—and then goes nuts. Working from a tantalizingly cheesy science-fiction premise, "No Time Like the Present" starts nuts and keeps going.

The year is 2017. A series of nuclear accidents have altered the laws of physics, changing the speed of light and altering time. A first-year college student, Emily (Sarah Gunnel) takes the train home to Grand Central Station to spend Easter break with her divorced parents, Ray (Bruce McKenzie) and Bea (Dana Hooley). Because of time's free-ranging properties, she actually gets years younger as she approaches.

Events happen out of order. As the Last Living Physicist on Earth informs us on videotape: "You are listening to this interview before I'm actually giving it." Meantime: The Virgin Mary has set up a laboratory in a castle by the Hudson River, conducting Frankenstein-like experiments. In another subplot, five drunken sailors (represented by McKenzie's right-hand fingers) chug toward the North Pole in a stolen submarine, in hopes of adjusting the planet's axis and restoring Earth to "the good sense of linear time."

Ehn's dealing with some provocative, potentially hilarious concepts here. Emily's parents, Bea and Ray, reunite for a motel tryst, but it's strange; as Bea says, "Sex finishes before it starts since physics went kerflooey." On video the physicist speaks of various "home cures" being concocted to counteract the time problem, including a uranium cocktail called "Brightness"; other folks, he notes, "mix alcohol with bad poetry."

Ehn packs all his plays with allusions, Catholic iconography, odd mixtures of domestic realism and supernatural surrealism. This time he's packed too much into an elusively defined framework. The good ideas get mired; the density simply becomes overload.

Director Scott Feldsher loads it up further. It's his quietest, simplest images that work best. At one point McKenzie becomes a metronome, bobbing between Gunnell and Hooley, and it's a lovely literalized metaphor for the characters' confusion. The post-(or pre-?)coital motel room tableau prior to the offstage line, "Maid service!" likewise creates the right sort of simplicity amid the craziness. The production needs more moments like these. A *lot* more.

Set designer Jeff Crane's snakelike orange tubes and tendrils criss-cross all over the St. Cecilia stage, emanating from an upstage TV monitor. The environment works, and it's sharply, coldly lighted by Peter Smith. There's one especially good bit of Ethan Feerst video: The physicist (McKenzie) turns into a "Cabinet of Dr. Caligari"-style silent movie anti-hero, creeping along a hallway, smashing light bulbs as he goes. Elsewhere, though, the physicist's lectures are intentionally scrambled, so that we don't hear them clearly. It's frustrating.

Ehn's writing frustrates, too. He's written three plays, in effect, and the ones about the Virgin Mary and the drunken sailors never worm their way into the overall. "No Time Like the Present" is like Emily's train: Though the confusion is sometimes fun, you gotta run to catch up with it. And finally, Feldsher's staging isn't fun enough. It's heavy-ish; though it sounds oxymoronic, it could be described as lamely intense.

The San Diego Union-Tribune, April 17, 1995.

"SONS AND MOTHERS"

John Lahr

For one terrible moment at the beginning of "Three Tall Women," the pretension that has sunk so many of Edward Albee's theatrical vehicles in his middle years looms menacingly on the horizon. "It's downhill from sixteen on," says one of the women, a middle-aged character called B, who takes care of a rich, imperious, senile old bird called A and is herself a connoisseur of collapse. She goes on, "I'd like to see children learn it—have a six-year-old say 'I'm dying and know what it means.'" But then, as we and the old lady settle into the demented fog of her remembering and forgetting, it becomes apparent that Albee has found his way back to the sour and passionate straight talking of his early, best plays.

The last great gift a parent gives to a child is his or her own death, and the energy underneath "Three Tall Women" is the exhilaration of a writer calling it quits with the past—specifically, the rueful standoff between Albee and his mother, the late Frances Cotter Albee, who adopted him only to kick him out of the family home, at eighteen, for his homosexual shenanigans and later to cut him out of her sizable will. The play has earned Albee, who is sixty-six, his third (and most deserved) Pulitzer Prize, but the writer's real victory is a psychological one—honoring the ambiguity of "the long unpleasant life she led!" while keeping her memory vividly alive. Far from being an act of revenge or special pleading, the play is a wary act of reconciliation, whose pathos and poetry are a testament to the bond, however attenuated, between child and parent. "Three Tall Women" bears witness to the son's sad wish to be loved, but with this liberating difference: the child is now finally in control of the parent's destiny, instead of the parent's being in control of the child's. . . .

The New Yorker, May 16, 1994.

Glossary

Absurdism or theatre of the absurd: A movement of the 1950s and 1960s in which playwrights dramatized the absurdity and futility of human existence. Generally, absurdist drama is nonsensical and repetitive.

Acting area: The staging area used by the actors during a performance. Most often, it is divided to make the blocking and movement more easily explainable.

Actors' Equity Association: The professional stage actors and stage managers union.

Agitprop: Activist theatre; propaganda in the form of drama, which is designed and performed to agitate or stir viewers to political action.

Agon: In ancient Greek theatre refers to the major struggle of the protagonist.

Aesthetic distance: The detachment that allows us to appreciate the beauty of a work of art.

AIDS drama: Plays dealing with the AIDS crisis; begun shortly after the outbreak of AIDS, the plays have evolved from shock and despair to anger, political activism, and even comic relief.

Amphitheatre: Originally, the theatre of ancient Rome; now used to refer to any outdoor theatre.

Antagonist: Opposes the protagonist; the antagonist can be a person or persons, society, a force such as a flood or a storm, or a conflicting tendency within the protagonist.

Apron or Forestage: The area of a proscenium stage that extends in front of the grand drape.

Arena stage: The type of stage in which the audience surrounds the playing area.

Aristotle's elements: The six elements Aristotle felt were essential for tragedy are plot, character, thought, dialogue, melody, and spectacle.

Art theatres: A movement begun by Yiddish language companies to present theatre of high artistic quality.

Aside: A speech delivered directly to the audience by a character in a play; supposedly, the other characters on stage are unable to hear what is said.

Asymmetrical balance: Making mass, shape, and color differ from one side of the stage to the other, but keeping the total weight or mass the same so that there is a feeling of balance.

Audition: An actor appearing before a director or casting director to "try out" for a production. Auditions may consist of memorized pieces, cold readings of the script to be used, an interview, improvisation, or a combination of any of these.

Automatism: Visual or verbal gag that is repeated many times.

Auto Sacramentales: Spanish drama akin to medieval mystery and miracle plays in subject matter, yet similar to morality plays in the use of allegorical characters.

Backdrop or drop: Theatrical canvas or muslin that stretches across the stage, is weighted at the bottom, and is painted with scenes.

Backstage area: The area of the stage usually hidden from the audience's view. It includes the wings and the back wall. It is used for storage of scenery and props, for actors to await entrances, and so forth.

Ballad opera: Burlesqued Italian opera and satirized the current political situation. An example is John Gay's *The Beggar's Opera.*

Battens: Rods to which drops (or other scenery) are attached to be raised and lowered in a proscenium theatre.

Beam projector: A stage lighting instrument that throws a narrow shaft of light, used to represent sunlight and so on.

Black box: Flexible theatre space that allows for various staging and seating areas with temporary seats that can be moved according to the way a production is staged. The staging area can be anything from a thrust stage to an arena stage to a modified proscenium stage.

Blackout: Dimming or turning off the lighting to leave the stage in complete darkness.

Blocking: The planned movement or business in a play; the stage directions for the actor.

Bourgeois tragedy: Characterized by false emotion and sentimentality over the misfortunes of others, unlike sentimental comedies, the plays ended unhappily when the leading characters yielded to temptation.

Box set: A setting that generally represents an indoor location and is constructed of flats.

Broadway: The main commercial theatre district of New York City.

Burlesque: Derisive imitation; also a type of low comedy that relies on beatings, accidents, and vulgarity for its humor.

Burlesque farce: Popular during the 1700s, this form of drama poked fun at the sentimental drama of the time.

Business: Physical action taken by the actor.

Callbacks: The stage of the audition process when certain actors are asked to return for a second audition.

Catharsis: The purging of emotions; the release of emotional tension.

Character comedy: A play whose humor directly involves the actions and eccentricities of the central character.

Character inconsistency: Comedy that results from a trait that does not seem to fit with a character's personality.

Character makeup: Makeup that makes an actor appear different from normal.

Choregi: Wealthy citizens chosen by the *archon* or master of revels to pay for the training, costumes, and room and board for the chorus in ancient Greece. Each year one *choregus* was chosen per playwright.

Chorus: A group of actors or oral interpreters in ancient Greek theatre. They most often performed in unison. A chorus sometimes appears in plays of other historical periods and as singers and dancers in musicals.

Circular structure: A type of organization in which the action of a play shows no real progression from one point to another, but ends as it began.

City Dionysia: In Athens, the major festival honoring the god of wine and fertility, Dionysus, and at which plays were performed.

Classical drama: The plays from ancient Greece and Rome. Also used to denote any outstanding drama from any historical period.

Climax: The high point of the plot; the moment when an irrevocable action occurs that determines the outcome of the play.

Combination companies: In the nineteenth and early twentieth centuries, theatre companies that traveled (that is, visited a "combination" of theatres) for a season presenting a single play. At first, combination companies usually presented only road shows of current New York hits.

Comedy of manners: A play that deals with the foibles or amoral characteristics of the upper class.

Commedia dell'arte: Professional acting troupes who traveled throughout western Europe from the mid-fifteenth to the mid-sixteenth centuries. They improvised from outlines called *scenarios,* thus making their work adaptable to changing locations and situations. An actor continued to play the same stock character so long as he or she remained with the company.

Comic devices: Techniques that playwrights use in establishing a comic frame of reference. They include exaggeration (intensification and enlargement), incongruity (unlike elements appearing together), automatism (the running gag), character inconsistency (an inconsistent personality trait), surprise (the unexpected), and derision (poking fun at people and institutions).

Comic relief: Comic elements in a tragedy or serious play to relieve the tension, so that it will build more completely once the comic scene ends.

Complication: Change in direction of the dramatic action in a play.

Conflict: Opposition; antagonist and protagonist engaged in a struggle to triumph over one another.

Constructivism: Including in the setting only those elements that are necessary to the action of a play.

Conventions: Writing and theatrical practices, devices, or processes agreed upon and accepted by both theatre artist and audience to further the progression of a play.

Corrales: Open courtyards in northern Spain where plays were presented during the Renaissance period.

Counterweight system: A system of ropes and pulleys used to fly scenery in a proscenium theatre.

Cue: The final line or action that signals that it is time for an actor to begin the next action or speech.

Cue sheet: Written instructions giving information about prearranged signals for any changes in lighting, sound, scenery shifts, and so on.

Cycle plays: In the medieval period, a series of plays presented one after the other, though not necessarily related structurally, and dealing with Biblical subjects.

Cyclorama: Usually a circular curtain surrounding the sides and rear of the acting area in exterior scenes, providing the illusion of distance.

Denouement or falling action: The final portion of a play in which all the loose ends are tied up, and all the questions answered.

Deus ex machina: A machine or crane used to fly in the gods to address human problems in ancient Greek drama; in current usage, a derisive term applied to a playwright's having fate intervene in solving the protagonist's problems rather than having the character solve them.

Derision: Making fun of people or institutions for the purpose of social reform.

Dialogue: The conversation between or among characters in a play; the lines or speeches of the characters in a play.

Dimmer board: The panel containing switches to raise and lower the intensity of stage lighting.

Dionysus: The god of wine and debauchery in Greek mythology; hymns of praise called "dithyrambs" in his honor are at the root of Western theatre.

Director (or Artistic Director): The person responsible for interpreting a script, planning blocking and movement, and rehearsing the actors. The person generally oversees all the aspects of a production.

Dithyrambs: Hymns of praise to Dionysus, delivered by a chorus of fifty men.

Domestic tragedy: Sentimentalized tragedy about common people and involving in some way the protagonist's disregard of virtue.

Downstage: In a proscenium theatre, the area closest to the audience.

Drama: All written plays, regardless of their genre or form.

Dramatic action: Everything that occurs in a play and advances it toward a conclusion; the motivation and purpose of a play; the physical, spiritual, psychological, and emotional elements that hold a play together.

Dramatic time: The amount of time represented by a play; an hour onstage may represent any amount of time, although more time usually is represented as having passed than the actual two hours or so it takes to present a play.

Dramaturg: A relatively new position in America, though long-established in Europe. The dramaturg's duties vary from theatre to theatre, but may include historical research about a play, acquainting potential audiences with the writer and the period, and helping with the script's interpretation.

Dress rehearsal: The final stage of rehearsals when all the technical elements, costumes, and makeup are added to a production. The dress rehearsal should be as polished as the production before an audience.

Drolls: Comic excerpts from familiar plays, presented at fairs in England during the seventeenth century.

Dutchmanning (dutching): Applying a strip of fabric to scenery flats, those that are hinged together, to cover the cracks between them.

Eccyclema: A stage device in ancient Greece somewhat like a wheeled cart or platform in which "bodies" of fallen warriors could be brought on and taken offstage.

Ellipsoidal reflector: A type of spotlight that has a framing device. It allows no spill of light from one area to another.

Emotional memory: Remembering how one felt in a particular set of circumstances and then relating those emotions to similar circumstances in a play.

Empathy: Emotionally relating to or identifying with a character, a theme, or a situation in a play.

Ensemble acting: The concept that no one actor is more important than any other, and the effect of the total production is more important than any of its parts.

Environmental theatre or found space: The production of plays in any available space large enough to accommodate theatre artists and audience members. In environmental theatre, there was a mixing of audience and actor and blurred lines between acting and audience areas.

Epic theatre or theatre of alienation: A style of theatre, advocated by Bertolt Brecht, in which the audience is asked to identify with the overall social problem, rather than with individual characters. Generally, the style of the drama is episodic.

Epilogue: The concluding scene of a play, occurring some time after the major conflict has been resolved; in Greek tragedy, it usually involved a shift in mood or tone, often the inclusion of a *deux ex machina.*

Episodic structure: A series of loosely related events to make up a play.

Exaggeration: Humor through overstatement and intensification.

Exodus: In Greek tragedy, the departure of the chorus at the end of the play.

Exposition: Any background information necessary to the understanding of a play; it may be presented through dialogue, setting, and properties.

Expressionism: A style that presents the inner reality of the major character; the audience witnesses the workings of the character's mind.

External approach: Concerned with the technique of acting, or which outward signs of a particular emotion can be used to portray that emotion.

Falling action or denouement: The part of a story play that occurs after the climax. It shows the results of the climax.

Federal Theatre Project: A federal program of the 1930s. Like other Works Progress Administration projects, it was geared toward work within specific communities and to provide employment for out-of-work actors, playwrights, and other theatre artists.

Flashback: A theatrical convention in which the audience, through the eyes of a character in a play, is able to see scenes from the past before the time in which the play exists.

Flat: Scenery frame constructed of one-by-three boards, covered with canvas, painted, and used most often for interior or exterior walls of a building in a stage setting.

Floodlights: Nonfocusable lighting instruments used for general illumination.

Floor plan: A drawing of the setting as seen from above.

Fly space: The area behind the top of the arch of a proscenium stage.

Focal point: The area toward which the audience's attention is directed. This can be accomplished by actor placement, lighting, costuming, and so on, or through a combination of these elements.

Formalism: Using the physical appearance of the stage rather than a designed setting; using only what is absolutely necessary. For example, ladders represent houses in *Our Town*.

Fourth wall: The imaginary wall that exists between the actors in a representational play and the audience; through this "wall" the audience sees the action of the play.

French scene: Begins with the entrance and ends with the exit of an important character.

Fresnel: A type of spotlight that provides a circle or oval of light with a softened edge.

Gelatin or gel: Translucent plastic placed in front of a lighting instrument to add color to the lighted area.

General lighting: Lighting that provides visibility on the whole stage.

General manager: The person who oversees a production's budget and financial operation.

Genre: A way of classifying plays into types such as tragedy, comedy, farce, and so on.

Given circumstances: The background information provided about a character or the play as a whole. Actors take the given circumstances as a beginning in establishing a character.

Grand drape: The heavy front curtain in a proscenium theatre.

Greenroom: The waiting area for actors before a show or their entrance and at intermissions.

Hand props: Articles that are handled or carried by the actors.

Happenings: A type of unstructured theatre presentation, generally involving the audience, in which there was little planning; the purpose was to break down the separation of life and art.

Harlem Renaissance: A cultural reawakening centered in the black American area of Harlem (New York City) in the 1920s affecting all the arts with a great deal of experimentation in style and form.

Heroic tragedy: Popular during the Restoration period in England, heroic tragedy was written in rhymed couplets. It nearly always dealt with themes of love and honor.

High comedy: Humor through verbal wit that appeals to the intellect.

House: The auditorium or seating area; a "good" house refers to a responsive audience.

Immediacy: The quality of a work of art that makes it important or relevant to the time in which it is presented to the public.

Impressionism: A style in which the designer and director determine what they wish to emphasize most and apply this element to the setting; the style deals with the design exclusive of the script.

Improvisation or improvisational theatre: Building a scene or a play on the spur of the moment with little preplanning and no script.

Inciting incident: The point of a play at which the initial balance is upset and the plot begins to build.

Incongruity: Humor through showing differing or opposing elements together, such as tennis shoes worn with a formal gown.

Independent Theatre Movement: A movement that began in the late nineteenth century to counteract censorship of plays by opening private playhouses.

Instrument schedule: The lighting design plan showing the location and specifications of lighting instruments.

Interlude: A scene or presentation not related to the play and usually presented during intermissions. Also, in medieval England, a short morality play.

Intermezzi: A series of short scenes or plays, with singing and dancing, and presented between the acts of a neoclassic tragedy.

Internal approach: Seeking within oneself the emotions and experiences to portray a character in a play.

Kabuki theatre: Secular Japanese theatre involving female impersonation.

Lazzi: Stage business in *commedia dell'arte.*

Lenaia: The winter festival in Athens where comedies were presented.

Liturgical drama: A play presented in conjunction with a church service, such as the "tropes" or playlets presented in the Middle Ages throughout western Europe.

Low comedy: Humor that relies on physical actions.

Ludi romani: Roman games at which theatrical performances were given.

Managing director: The person responsible for financial matters in a non-profit theatre.

Mansion or sede: One of several specific locations in medieval theatre and used as the starting point for playlets that then moved to the **platea** or unlocalized playing area.

Mask: To conceal areas (such as backstage) and objects (such as lighting instruments) from the audience's view. The word also refers to face or head coverings used by actors to alter appearance.

Masque: A dramatic form presented in England during Cromwell's time and featuring spectacular staging and costumes. Written by Ben Jonson, masques told allegorical stories honoring well-known persons or occasions.

Mime: A short play, usually comic and often improvised; a particular favorite in ancient Roman theatre and one of the few types of theatre in which women appeared. The word currently refers to a performer who uses actions without words or props.

Mimetic instinct: The human need or desire to imitate; through the mimetic instinct we acquire much of our learning.

Minstrel shows: The minstrel show consisted of white men with blackened faces presenting comedy, music, and dance interspersed with dialect conversations and, finally, the "stump speech"—a lecture on a current topic, but filled with puns and malapropisms.

Miracle play (Saint play): A medieval drama that dealt with the lives of saints and martyrs, but could include topical scenes involving family troubles.

Monologue: A long speech delivered by a character in a play, either to the audience or to other characters.

Morality play: A form of medieval drama concerning moral instruction, particularly the attempt to save a person's soul. All the characters were allegorical, and the central figure usually was called Everyman. Such characters as Virtue and Vice fought over his soul.

Motivation: The reason for taking any action; why the protagonist in a play attempts to reach a certain goal.

Motivational base: Same as the inciting incident, the point at which the conflict is introduced.

Motivational unit: The occurrence of a new scene when something slightly alters the direction the protagonist takes in attempting to reach the goal or solution to the problem.

Musical: Any play that includes a substantial amount of singing and dancing, more recently as an integral part of the plot.

Mystery play: In medieval Europe, a play depicting episodes from the life of Christ.

Naturalism: A theatrical style that attempts to duplicate life, or, in effect, to transfer actual life to the stage.

Neoclassicism: A style popular during the Italian Renaissance, with a strict five-act format and a completely unified production.

New Comedy: The form of Greek comedy popular in the time of Alexander the Great and associated with the playwright Menander. It dealt with middle-class citizens and character types.

No or Noh theatre: A form of classical Japanese theatre that was temple-centered and used rigid production conventions.

Off-Broadway: Professional New York theatre outside the Broadway district, mostly in Greenwich Village. At its inception in the 1950s and into the 1960s, it was synonymous with experimental drama. Presently, however, it's more akin to Broadway in terms of union contracts and theatre capacities.

Off-Off-Broadway: New York theatre that usually is nonprofessional and generally experimental. It developed in the 1970s to combat the commercialism of Broadway and Off-Broadway theatre.

Offstage: Out of sight of the audience.

Old comedy: The form of Greek comedy which lasted from 454 to 404 B.C. and is characterized by its emphasis on an idea rather than on a cause-to-effect relationship of events. The plays have many episodes, which often seem unrelated to each other, but do build in comic intensity.

Orchestra: In Greek theatre, the area where the chorus appeared. In contemporary theatre, the seating area closest to the stage in a proscenium theatre.

Pace: The overall rate of speed in handling lines and business.

Pageant wagons: In medieval theatre, wheeled platforms on which plays were mounted and which usually moved from location to location.

Pantomime: A form of Roman entertainment in which dancers performed, accompanied by music. In eighteenth-century England, as presented by John Rich, pantomime featured dances and mimicry to musical accompaniment, presenting both comic and serious scenes with elaborate scenery and effects. In today's usage, *pantomime* is the same as *mime*—performing actions without words.

Paradoi: The space on either side of the orchestra and between the skene and seating area in the Greek theatre; used primarily for the chorus's entrances and exits.

Platea: The unlocalized or central acting area near the **mansions** in medieval theatre.

Plot: The progression of a story from the point of attack through the climax and denouement.

Point of attack: The place in a story where the writer decides to begin.

Poor Theatre: Phrase coined by Jerzy Grotowski to refer to a theatre that rids itself of nonessentials—that is, everything but the actor and the audience.

Postmodernism: A disregard for veracity in the presentation of cultural and historical pieces; a blending of styles, periods, forms, and so on.

Practical: Refers to something onstage that actually works, rather than simulating an object. For instance, a "practical" window in the set actually opens.

Presentational style: A broad category of theatrical style that is audience centered; the actors, director, and designer make open acknowledgment of the audience.

Preview: A public performance of a play before the official opening.

Producer or Producing organization: The person, group, or institution providing the financial backing for presenting a play.

Properties: Articles that can be moved or carried in the course of a play. Set properties include such objects as curtains and paintings; hand props include anything that the actors use or carry.

Proscenium or Proscenium arch: A picture-frame stage; the framing device that isolates the stage area and provides the focal point for the action. The audience views the action through an imaginary fourth wall.

Promptbook: The director's record of blocking, business, movement and technical cues, and any other information necessary for running the show. The stage manager uses a promptbook to "call" the production.

Protagonist: The major character in a play; generally, the protagonist tries to reach a certain goal and is opposed by the antagonist.

Purim plays: Religious plays celebrating Purim, which occurs around the middle of March or on the fourteenth of Adar in the Jewish calendar and depicting the story of Esther and Haman.

Raked stage: A stage that slopes upward from front to back.

Realism: A style that attempts to present life as it is, but selectively; not all details are presented—only those that are essential for the audience's understanding of the play and for the establishment of the mood.

Repertory company: A theatrical company that alternates a series or repertoire of plays.

Regional theatre: Professional, nonprofit theatre existing in various locations across the country; also called resident theatres.

Rehearsal: When the actors, under the supervision of the artistic director, ready a show for performance. The process begins with an interpretation of the script and individual characters, progressing to blocking followed by a period in which concentration is more completely on developing character and on line delivery. Then come run-throughs and finishing rehearsals. *See* **technical rehearsals** and **dress rehearsals.**

Restoration comedy: Beginning in 1660, when Charles II was restored to the English throne, there developed a particular type of comedy, marked by witty dialogue and addressing the foibles of the upper class. This form was known as a Comedy of Manners.

Representational style: A broad category of style that is stage-centered; the actors make no acknowledgment of the audience, but try to duplicate life.

Revolving stage: A circular portion of the stage floor that rotates, taking from view one setting and revealing another.

Rhythm: The flow of the lines; the speed with which the actors pick up their cues.

Rising action: The building or intensification of the struggle between the protagonist and the antagonist.

Ritual: A repeated pattern of behavior, which may have its basis in religion, pageantry, or individual behavior. It originally meant a controlled sequence of action to achieve a supernatural goal. Now it also refers to a type of play structure in which a pattern of action is repeated.

Role playing: Changing one's ways of behaving in different situations; modifying behavior to fit the situation.

Romantic comedy: A comedy whose humor lies in the complications the hero and heroine face in their love for each other.

Romanticism: A style characterized by freedom, gracefulness, and a belief in humankind's basic good.

Run-through: A rehearsal that includes the entire play from opening line to ending, ideally without any stops.

Rural Dionysia: A festival honoring Dionysus and held each year in December in ancient Greece.

Satyr play: A ribald form of comedy in ancient Greece and presented along with a playwright's three tragedies. A satyr was half goat and half human.

Satire: Gentle mockery for the purpose of reform.

Schematics: In regard to theatre makeup, outlines of the head with the face divided into areas, showing the color or type of makeup to apply to each area.

Scrims: Semitransparent cloths usually serving as backdrops; when lighted from the rear they are semitransparent and when lighted from the front they are opaque.

Sede: *See* **Mansion.**

Selective visibility: Providing focus through lighting.

Sentimental comedy: Characterized by false emotions and sentimentality over the misfortunes of others. The plays were referred to as comedies—not because they were funny, but because they ended happily.

Set dressing: Articles such as draperies or paintings that are attached to the walls of the set.

Set props: Articles that stand within the setting, including furniture, trees or bushes, and rocks.

Setting: The environment or physical background for a play; the visual symbol of a play.

Sightlines: The line of vision for the audience watching a theatrical production. A designer considers sightlines in relation to how well the audience can see all of the action from any part of the seating area.

Situation comedy: A comedy whose humor derives from placing the central characters in a comedy in unusual situations.

Skene: The scene house in ancient Greek theatre. Used at first for storage and then as a place for actors to change costumes, it became a background or "scenery" for the action.

Slice-of-life: Refers to a movement, extremely naturalistic, in which a playwright was to be a faithful recorder of life, transferring it directly to the stage as observed. As a "slice" of life, it should have no manufactured beginning or ending.

Soliloquy: A theatrical convention in which a character thinks aloud, revealing his or her innermost thoughts.

Specific lighting: Lighting for special effects, such as to suggest sunlight or to set the mood.

Spine or superobjective: The major goal of a character in a play.

Spotlights: Focusable lighting instruments customarily used for specific illumination.

Stage directions: Blocking, movement, and scene descriptions written into a published script.

Stage Left (or Left Stage): In a proscenium theatre, the area that is on the actors' left as they face an audience.

Stage manager: Second in command after the director. After the opening, this person calls the show.

Stage Right (or Right Stage): In a proscenium theatre, the area that is on the actors' right as they face an audience.

Stock characters: Character types in which certain traits, such as miserliness, are highly exaggerated.

Story play (or cause-to-effect play): A form of drama that has a plot and builds in intensity from an inciting incident to a turning point and climax.

Street theatre: Literally taking to the streets to bring theatre to the people, usually in support of a political or social cause.

Straight makeup: Makeup that accentuates an actor's natural features.

Striplight: A troughlike lighting instrument with lights a few inches apart, covered with lenses in the primary colors.

Subplot: A secondary or subordinate story or plotline accompanying the major thread of a play.

Subtext: The meaning behind the actions and spoken words in a play or script; the ideas, message, and motivation beneath the surface and often more meaningful than the text itself.

Summer stock: Theatre companies that perform only during the summer season. They include resort and tourist area theatres and outdoor theatres.

Surprise: Humor through the unexpected.

Surrealism: A movement begun in theatre in the 1920s and characterized by a blurring of lines between the conscious and the subconscious.

Symbol: One thing that stands for another. In the theatre the setting and lights, for instance, represent a background or environment for the action, while the actors symbolize the characters in the play.

Symbolism: A style that presents life in terms of allegory; it depicts subjective or internal reality, determined by the playwright.

Symmetrical balance: Giving either side of a setting exactly the same elements in the same relationship to each other.

Teasers: Short curtains that are used to mask the lighting instruments and fly space in a proscenium theatre.

Technical director: The person, usually in resident and educational theatres, who is responsible for overseeing all the technical aspects of a production and for carrying out the director's plan for the production.

Technical rehearsal: One of the finishing rehearsals in which all the technical aspects—lights, sound, scenery shifts, etc.—are added to a production.

Theatre of cruelty: A theory of theatre's purpose and execution developed by Antonin Artaud in which the goal was to confront the violent impulses in the subconscious mind through sensations rather than a plot.

Theatricalism: A treatment of a play in which audience members are constantly reminded that they are in a theatre; the fourth wall is broken down and the audience uses its imagination in the matter of setting.

Theatron: Literally "seeing place;" used in ancient Greek theatre to mean the audience area.

Thematic structure: The organization of a play unified around a particular idea or theme.

Thesis play: A subgenre of the well-made play; it attempted to teach a moral lesson.

Thespian: Synonym for *actor;* derived from the name Thespis, a man who is credited with being the first to step forward from the Greek chorus and deliver dialogue as an individual.

Thrust stage: A stage that juts into the seating area, with audience seating on three sides.

Timing: The use of pauses in delivering lines.

Tormentors: Curtains hung at either side of the stage to mask the backstage area.

Tragoedia: Hymns of praise to Dionysus sung by the ancient Greek dithyrambic chorus dressed as satyrs (half goats); goat songs.

Trope: A liturgical playlet that was a part of medieval church services in western Europe.

Turning point: The moment in a plot when the action can go no further without something irrevocable happening.

Unity: A harmony in the way all the elements of a play combine.

Unities: Neoclassic ideal stating that a play must observe the three unities of time, place, and action. That is, they should occur in a single day, at the same location, and should not mix genres.

Universality: The trait of having meaning for everyone in all places and times.

Upstage: The area closest to the back wall in a proscenium stage.

Upstaging: Actors drawing attention to themselves to the detriment of the production.

Vaudeville and variety shows: Presented as a series of unrelated acts in a single program. These could be dancing, singing, recitations, animal acts, and so on.

Wagon stage: A platform on casters that can be wheeled on and off the stage.

Well-made play: In current theatre refers to a play with a plot; historically, a play that presented a particular social problem for which the playwright offered a solution.

Willing suspension of disbelief: The audience's willingness to accept theatrical conventions and allow themselves to be transported into the world of the play.

Wings: Flats that stand independently and are placed a short distance apart from the front to the back of a stage; also the areas to the right and left of the playing area in a proscenium theatre.

Zanni: The comic servants in the *commedia dell'arte.*

Selected Bibliography

Chapters 1–2

Archer, William. *Play-Making: A Manual of Craftsmanship.* New York: Dodd, Mead & Company, 1928.

Aristotle, "The Poetics," *European Theories of the Drama.* Barrett H. Clark, ed., newly revised by Henry Popkin. New York: Crown Publishers, Inc., 1965.

Baker, George Pierce. *Dramatic Technique.* Boston: Houghton Mifflin Company, 1919.

Bentley, Eric. *The Life of the Drama.* New York: Atheneum, 1964.

———. In Search of Theatre. New York: Alfred A. Knopf, Inc., 1953.

———. *The Theatre of Commitment and Other Essays.* New York: Atheneum, 1967.

———. *The Theory of the Modern Stage: An Introduction to Theatre and Drama.* Baltimore: Penguin Books, Inc., 1968.

Driver, Tom F. *Romantic Quest and Modern Theory: History of the Modern Theatre.* New York: Delta Books, published by Dell Publishing Co., Inc., 1970.

Fergusson, Francis. *The Idea of a Theater.* Princeton, N.J.: Princeton University Press, 1949.

Gassner, John. *Directions in Modern Theatre and Drama.* New York: Holt, Rinehart and Winston, 1965.

Heffner, Hubert. *The Nature of Drama.* Boston: Houghton Mifflin Company, 1959.

Jones, Robert Edmund. *The Dramatic Imagination.* New York: Meredith Publishing Company, 1941.

Kerr, Walter. *The Theatre in Spite of Itself.* New York: Simon and Schuster, 1963.

Langner, Laurence. *The Play's the Thing.* New York: G. P. Putnam's Sons, 1960.

Lewis, Allan. *American Plays and Playwrights of the Contemporary Theatre.* New York: Crown Publishers, Inc., 1965.

Willet, John, ed. *Brechet on Theatre.* New York: Hill and Wang Inc., 1964.

Williams, Tennessee. *Where I Live: Selected Essays.* New York: New Directions, 1978.

Woolworth, George. *The Theater of Protest and Paradox: Developments in the Avant-Garde Drama.* 2nd ed. New York: New York University Press, 1971.

Chapters 3–7

Arnott, Peter D. *Public and Performance in the Greek Theatre.* New York: Routledge. 1989.

Artaud, Antonin. *The Theatre and Its Double.* Translated by Mary Richards. New York: Grove Press, 1958.

Barnet, Sylvan, Morton Berman, and William Burto, eds. *Eight Great Comedies.* New York: New American Library, 1959.

———. Morton Berman and William Burto. *The Genius of the Early English Theater.* New York: New American Library, 1962.

———. *The Genius of the Later English Theater.* New York: New American Library, 1962.

Bieber, Margarete. *The History of the Greek and Roman Theater.* 2nd ed. Princeton, N.J.: Princeton University Press, 1961.

Berthold, Margot, *A History of World Theatre.* New York: Frederick Ungar Publishing Co., Inc., 1972.

Bigsby, C. W. E. *Modern American Drama, 1945–1990.* Hampshire, England: Macmillan Publishers Ltd., 1992.

Bradby, David, and David Williams. *Directors' Theatre.* Hampshire, England: Macmillan Publishers Ltd., 1988.

Brandon, James R., ed. *The Cambridge Guide to Asian Theatre.* Cambridge, England: Cambridge University Press, 1993.

Brockett, Oscar G. *History of the Theatre.* Boston: Allyn and Bacon, Inc., 1968.

Cheney, Sheldon. *The Theatre: Three Thousand Years of Drama, Acting and Stagecraft.* Rev. ed. New York: Longmans, Green & Co., Inc., 1972.

Clurman, Harold. *The Fervent Years: The Story of the Group Theatre in the Thirties.* New York: Alfred A. Knopf, Inc., 1945.

Cohn, Ruby. *New American Dramatists, 1960–1990.* Hampshire, England: Macmillan Publishers Ltd., 1991.

Corrigan, Robert W., ed. *Theatre in the Twentieth Century.* New York: Grove Press, Inc., 1963.

Fowlie, Wallace. *Dionysus in Paris: A Guide to Contemporary French Theatre.* New York: Meridian, 1960.

French, Warren, ed. *Sam Shepard, Arthur Kopit, and the Off Broadway Theater.* Boston: Twayne Publishers, 1982.

Fuller, Edmund. *A Pageant of the Theatre.* New rev. ed. New York: Thomas Y. Crowell Co., 1965.

Gassner, John, ed. *A Treasury of the Theatre, Volume One, World Drama From Aeschylus to Ostrovsky,* Revised and expanded edition. New York: Simon and Schuster, 1967.

Gillespie, Patti P., and Kenneth M. Cameron. *Western Theatre: Revolution and Revival.* New York: Macmillan Publishing Company, 1984.

Grose, B. Donald, and O. Franklin Kenworthy. *A Mirror to Life: A History of Western Theatre.* New York: Holt, Rinehart and Winston, 1984.

Guicharnaud, Jacques. *Modern French Theatre from Giraudoux to Beckett.* New Haven, CT.: Yale University Press, 1961.

Harris, Andrew B. *Broadway Theatre.* New York: Routledge, 1994.

Hartnoll, Phyllis. *The Theatre. A Concise History.* Revised edition. New York: Thames and Hudson, Inc. 1985.

Hewitt, Barnard. *Theatre U.S.A., 1665–1957.* New York: McGraw-Hill Book Company, Inc., 1959.

Jacobsen, Josephine, and William R. Mueller. *Ionesco and Genet: Playwrights of Silence.* New York: Hill and Wang, 1968.

Laurenson, T. E. *The French Stage of the XVIIth Century.* Manchester: Manchester University Press, 1957.

Mantzius, Karl. *A History of Theatrical Art In Ancient and Modern Times, Vol. I, The Earliest Times.* New York: Peter Smith, 1937.

Macgowan, Kenneth, and William Melnitz. *The Living Stage: A History of World Theatre.* Englewood Cliffs, N.J.: Prentice-Hall, Inc., 1955.

Meserve, Walter J. *An Outline History of American Drama.* New York: Feedback Theatrebooks & Prospero Press, 1994.

Nagler, A. M. *The Medieval Religious Stage: Shapes and Phantoms.* New Haven, CT: Yale University Press, 1976.

Nicoll, Allardyce. *The Development of the Theatre. A Study of Theatrical Art from the Beginnings to the Present Day.* 5th ed. Revised. New York: Harcourt, Brace and World, Inc., 1966.

———. *History of English Drama, 1660–1900.* Cambridge: Cambridge University Press, 1955–1959.

———. *World Drama from Aeschylus to Anouilh.* Revised ed. London: Harrap. 1976.

Roberts, Vera Mowry. *On Stage: A History of Theatre,* 2nd ed. New York: Harper & Row, Publishers, 1962.

Wickham, Glynne. *A History of the Theatre,* 2nd edition. London: Phaidon Press Limited, 1992.

———. *The Medieval Theatre.* London: St. Martin's Press, 1974.

Chapter 8

Auster, Albert. *Actresses and Suffragists: Women in the American Theatre, 1890–1920.* New York: Praeger Publishers, 1984.

Backalenick, Irene. *East Side Story: Ten Years with the Jewish Repertory Theatre.* Lanham, MD: University Press of America, 1988.

Barlow, Judith E., ed. *Plays by American Women, 1900–1930.* New York: Applause Theatre Book Publishers, 1985.

Berson, Misha, ed. *Between Worlds: Contemporary Asian-American Plays.* New York: Theatre Communications Group, 1990.

Bigsby, C. W. E. *The Black American Writer, Vol. II: Poetry and Drama.* Deland, FL: Everett/Edwards, Inc., 1969.

———. *A critical introduction to twentieth-century American drama: Beyond Broadway, vol. 3.* New York: Cambridge University Press, 1985.

———. *The Second Black Renaissance: Essays in Black Literature.* Westport: Greenwood Press, 1980.

Broyles-Gonzáles, Yolanda. *El Teatro Campesino: Theater in the Chicano Movement.* Austin: University of Texas Press, 1994.

Cassady, Marsh. *Great Scenes From Women Playwrights.* Colorado Springs, CO: Meriwether Publications, Inc., 1995.

Chinoy, Helen Krich, and Linda Walsh Jenkins. *Women in American Theatre.* New York: Theatre Communications Groups, 1981 and 1987.

Citron, Stephen. *The Musical From the Inside Out.* Chicago: I. R. Dee, 1991–1992.

Clum, John M. *Acting Gay: Male Homosexuality in Modern Drama.* New York: Columbia University Press, 1994.

Cohen, Sarah Blacher, ed. *From Hester Street to Hollywood: The Jewish-American Stage and Screen.* Bloomington, IN: Indiana University Press, 1983.

Couch, William Jr. *New Black Playwrights: An Anthology.* Baton Rouge: Louisiana State University Press, 1968.

Curtin, Kaier. *We Call Them Bulgarians: The Emergence of Lesbians and Gay Men on the American Stage.* Boston: Alyson Publications, 1987.

de Jongh, Nicholas. *Not in Front of an Audience: Homosexuality on Stage.* New York: Routledge, 1992.

Dolan, Jill. *Presence and Desire: Essays on Gender, Sexuality, Performance.* Ann Arbor: The University of Michigan Press, 1993.

Donkin, Ellen, and Susan Clement, eds. *Upstaging Big Daddy: Directing Theater as if Gender and Race Matter.* Ann Arbor: The University of Michigan Press, 1993.

Dreher, Sarah. *Lesbian Stages: Plays by Sarah Dreher.* Norwich, VT: New Victoria Publishers, Inc., 1988.

Faderman, Lillian, ed. *Chloe Plus Olivia: An Anthology of Lesbian Literature From the Seventeenth Century to the Present.* New York: Viking, 1994.

France, Rachel, ed. *A Century of Plays by American Women.* New York: Richard Rosen Press, Inc., 1979.

Furtado, Ken, and Nancy Hellner. *Gay and Lesbian American Plays: An Annotated Bibliography.* Metuchen, NJ: The Scarecrow Press, Inc., 1993.

Gardner, Vivien, and Susan Rutherford, eds. *The New Woman and Her Sisters: Feminism and Theatre, 1850–1914.* Ann Arbor: The University of Michigan Press, 1992.

Geiogamah, Hanay. *New Native American Drama: Three Plays.* Norman, OK: University of Oklahoma Press, 1980.

Gilder, Rosamond. *Enter the Actress: The First Women in the Theatre.* Boston: Houghton Mifflin Company, 1931.

Goreau, Angeline. *Reconstructing Aphra: A Social Biography of Aphra Behn.* New York: The Dial Press, 1980.

Griffith, Francis, and Joseph Mersand. *Eight American Ethnic Plays.* New York: Charles Scribner's Sons, 1974.

Hamalian, Leo, and James V. Hatch, eds. *The Roots of African American Drama: An Anthology of Early Plays, 1858–1938.* Detroit: Wayne State University Press, 1991.

Hart, Lynda, and Peggy Phelan. *Acting Out: Feminist Performances.* Ann Arbor: The University of Michigan Press, 1993.

Hatch, James V., ed., and Ted Shine, consultant. *Black Theater, U.S.A.: Forty-Five Plays by Black Americans, 1847–1974.* New York: The Free Press, 1974.

Hay, Samuel A. *African American Theatre: An Historical and Critical Study.* New York: Cambridge University Press, 1994.

Helbing, Terry, ed. *Gay and Lesbian Plays Today.* Portsmouth, NH: Heinemann, 1993.

Hill, Errol, ed. *The Theater of Black Americans,* Vols 1 and 2. Englewood Cliffs, NJ: Prentice-Hall, Inc., 1980.

Hoffman, William M., ed. *Gay Plays: The First Collection.* New York: Avon Books, 1979.

Houston, Velina Hasu, ed. *The Politics of Life: Four Plays by Asian American Women.* Philadelphia: Temple University Press, 1993.

Hutner, Heidi. *Rereading Aphra Behn: History, Theory and Criticism.* Charlottesville, VA: University Press of Virginia, 1993.

Hwang, David Henry. *Broken Promises: Four Plays.* New York: Avon Books, 1983.

———. *M. Butterfly.* New York: New American Library, 1989.

Jones, Eugene H. *Native Americans as Shown on the Stage, 1753–1916.* Metuchen, NJ: The Scarecrow Press, Inc., 1988.

Jones, Therese. *Sharing the Delirium: Second Generation AIDS Plays and Performances.* Portsmouth, NH: Heinemann, 1994.

Kanellos, Nicholás, ed. *Hispanic Theatre in the United States.* Houston: Arte Publico Books, 1984.

Keyssar, Helene. *The Curtain and the Veil: Strategies in Black Drama.* New York: Burt Franklin & Co., Inc., 1981.

Kilgore, Emilie S., ed. *Contemporary Plays by Women.* New York: Prentice Hall Press, 1991.

King, Bruce. *Contemporary American Theatre.* New York: St. Martin's Press, 1991.

King, Jr., Woodie, ed. *New Plays for the Black Theatre.* Chicago: Third World Press, 1989.

Lerner, Alan Jay. *The Musical Theatre: A Celebration.* New York: McGraw-Hill Book Company, 1986

Lifson, David. *The Yiddish Theatre in America.* New York: Thomas Yoseloff, 1965.

Lipsky, Louis. *Tales of the Jewish Rialto: Reminiscences of Playwrights and Players in New York's Jewish Theatre in the Early 1900s.* New York: Thomas Yoseloff, 1962.

Lucas, Ian. *Impertinent Decorum: Gay Theatrical Manoeuvres.* New York: Cassell, 1994.

Mahone, Sydné, ed. *Moon Marked & Touched by Sun: Plays by African-American Women.* New York: Theatre Communications Group, 1994.

Mates, Julian. *The American Musical Stage Before 1800.* New Brunswick, NJ: Rutgers University Press, 1962.

McDermott, Kate, ed. *Places, Please!: The First Anthology of Lesbian Plays.* San Francisco: Spinsters/Aunt Lute, 1985.

McGovern, Dennis, and Deborah Grace Winer. *Sing Out, Louise!: 150 Stars of the Musical Theatre Remember 50 Years on Broadway.* New York: Schirmer Books, 1993.

Miller, James. *The Detroit Yiddish Theatre: 1920–1937.* Detroit: Wayne State University Press, 1967.

Mitchell, Lofton. *Black Drama: The Story of the American Negro in the Theatre.* NY: Hawthorne Books, 1967.

———. *Voices of the Black Theatre.* Clifton, NJ: James T. White & Company, 1975.

Moore, Honor. *The New Women's Theatre.* New York: Random House, 1977.

Osborn, M. Elizabeth, ed. *The Way We Live Now: American Plays & the AIDS Crisis.* New York: Theatre Communications Group, 1990.

Perkins, Kathy A., ed. *Black Female Playwrights: An Anthology of Plays before 1950.* Bloomington: Indiana University Press, 1989.

Prosky, Ida. *You Don't Need Four Women to Play Shakespeare.* Jefferson, NC: McFarland & Company, Inc., Publishers, 1992.

Rabkin, Gerald. "The Sound of a Voice: David Hwang," in Bruce King, *Contemporary American Theatre.* New York: St. Martin's Press, 1991.

Robinson, Marc. *The Other American Drama.* New York: Cambridge University Press, 1994.

Rogers, Katharine M., ed. *The Meridian Anthology of Restoration and Eighteenth-Century Plays by Women.* New York: Meridian, 1994.

Sampson, Henry T. *The Ghost Walks: A Chronological History of Blacks in Show Business, 1865–1910.* Metuchen, NJ: The Scarecrow Press, Inc., 1988.

Sanders, Leslie Catherine. *The Development of Black Theater in America: From Shadows to Selves.* Baton Rouge: Louisiana State University Press, 1987.

Scharine, Richard G. *From Class to Caste in American Drama: Political and Social Themes Since the 1930s.* New York: Greenwood Press, 1991.

Schofield, Mary Anne, and Cecilia Macheski, eds. *Curtain Calls: British and American Women and the Theater, 1660—1820.* Athens, OH: Ohio University Press, 1991.

Seller, Maxine Schwartz. *Ethnic Theatre in the United States,* Westport, CT: Greenwood Press, 1983.

Shewey, Don, ed. *Out Front: Contemporary Gay and Lesbian Plays.* New York: Grove Press, 1988.

Smith, Edward G. "Black Theatre," in Maxine Schwartz Seller, ed. *Ethnic Theatre in the United States.* Westport, CT: Greenwood Press, 1983.

Snyder, Rebecca, "See the Big Show: Spiderwoman Theater Doubling Back" in Lynda Hart and Peggy Phelan, eds., *Acting Out: Feminist Performances.* Ann Arbor: The University of Michigan Press, 1993.

Suskin, Steven. *Opening Night on Broadway: A Critical Quotebook of the Golden Era of the Musical, Oklahoma! (1943) to Fiddler on the Roof (1964).* New York: Schirmer Books, 1990.

Swaim, Joseph P. *The Broadway Musical: A Critical and Musical Survey.* New York: Oxford University Press, 1990.

Turner, Darwin T. *Black Drama in America: An Anthology,* 2nd ed. Washington: Howard University Press, 1994.

Uno, Roberta, ed. *Unbroken Thread: An Anthology of Plays by Asian American Women.* Amherst: The University of Massachusetts Press, 1993.

Wallace, Robert, ed. *Making Out: Plays by Gay Men.* Toronto: Coach House Press, 1992.

Watkins, Mel. *On the Real Side: Laughing, Lying and Signifying—The Underground Tradition of African-American Humor that Transformed American Culture From Slavery to Richard Pryor.* New York: Simon and Schuster, 1994.

Chapters 9–10

Busfield, Roger M., Jr. *The Playwright's Art.* New York: Harper & Brothers, 1958.

Cassady, Marsh. *Characters in Action: A Guide to Playwriting,* Lanham, MD: University Press of America, 1984.

———. *Characters in Action: Playwriting the Easy Way,* Colorado Springs, CO: Meriwether Publications, Inc., 1995.

———. *Playwriting Step by Step.* San Jose, CA: Resource Publications, Inc., 1985.

Cole, Toby, ed. *Playwrights on Playwriting: The Meaning and Making of Modern Drama from Ibsen to Ionesco.* New York: Hill and Wang, Inc., 1961.

Gassner, John. *Direction in Modern Theatre and Drama.* New York: Holt, Rinehart and Winston, 1965.

Heffner, Hubert. *The Nature of Drama.* Boston: Houghton Mifflin Company, 1959.

Jones, Robert Edmund. *The Dramatic Imagination.* New York: Meredith Publishing Company, 1941.

Kerr, Walter. *How Not to Write a Play.* New York: Simon and Schuster, 1955.

Langner, Laurence. *The Play's the Thing.* New York: G. P. Putnam's Sons, 1960.

Lawson, John Howard. *Theory and Technique of Playwriting.* New York: Hill and Wang, Inc., 1960.

Niggli, Josefina. *New Pointers on Playwriting.* Boston: The Writer, Inc., 1967.

Shroyer, Frederick B., and Louis G. Gardeman. *Types of Drama.* Glenview, IL: Scott, Foresman and Company, 1970.

Chapter 11

The American Theatre Planning Board, Inc. *Theatre Check List: A Guide to the Planning and Construction of Proscenium and Open Stage Theatres.* Middletown, CT: Wesleyan University Press, 1969.

Boyle, Walden P. *Central and Flexible Staging.* Berkeley: University of California Press, 1956.

Brown, Catherine R., William B. Fleissig, and William R. Morrish. *Building for the Arts: A Guidebook for the Planning and Design of Cultural Facilities.* Santa Fe, NM: Western States Arts Federation, 1984 and 1989.

Burdick, Elizabeth et al., eds. *Contemporary Scene Design U.S.A. New York: International Theatre Institute of the U.S., Inc.,* 1974.

Burris-Meyer, Harold, and Edward C. Cole. *Theatres and Auditoriums.* 2nd ed. New York: Reinhold Publishing Corporation, 1964.

Carlson, Marvin. *Places of Performance.* Ithaca, NY: Cornell University Press, 1989.

Cogswell, Margaret, ed. *The Ideal Theatre: Eight Concepts.* New York: The American Federation of Arts, 1962.

Izenour, George. *Theater Technology.* New York: McGraw-Hill Book Company, 1988.

Kaye, Deena, and James Lebrecht. *Sound and Music for the Theatre.* New York: Back Stage Books, 1992.

Kernan, Alvin B. *The Modern American Theatre.* Englewood Cliffs, N.J.: Prentice Hall, Inc., 1967.

Leacroft, Richard and Helen. *Theatre and Playhouse: An Illustrated Survey of Theatre Building from Ancient Greece to the Present Day.* London: Metheun London, Ltd., 1984.

Mielziner, Jo. *The Shapes of Our Theatre.* New York: Clarkson N. Potter, Inc., Publisher, 1970.

Tidiworth, Simon. *Theatres: An Architectural and Cultural History.* New York: Praeger Publishers, 1973.

Chapter 12

Archer, William. *Play-Making: A Manual of Craftsmanship.* New York: Dodd, Mead & Co., 1928.

Baker, George Pierce. *Dramatic Technique.* Boston: Houghton Mifflin Co., 1919.

Busfield, Roger M., Jr. *The Playwright's Art.* New York: Harper & Brothers, 1958.

Cassady, Marsh. *Characters in Action: A Guide to Playwriting,* Lanham, MD.: University Press of America, 1984.

———. *Characters in Action: Playwriting the Easy Way,* Colorado Springs, CO: Meriwether Publications, Inc., 1995.

———. *Playwriting Step by Step.* San Jose, CA: Resource Publications, Inc., 1985.

Chapman, Gerald. *Teaching Young Playwrights.* Portsmouth, NH: Heinemann, 1991.

Egri, Lajos. *The Art of Dramatic Writing.* New York: Simon and Schuster, 1946.

Ervine, St. John. *How to Write a Play.* New York: The Macmillan Co., 1928.

Frome, Shelly. *Playwriting: A Complete Guide to Creating Theater.* Jefferson, NC: McFarland & Company, Inc., Publishers, 1990.

George, Kathleen E. *Playwriting: The First Workshop.* Boston: Focal Press, 1994.

Grenbanier, Bernard. *Playwriting.* New York: Thomas Y. Crowell Co., 1961.

Hatton, Thomas J. *Playwriting for Amateurs.* Downers Grove, IL: Meriwether Publishing Ltd., 1981.

Howard, Louise, and Jeron Criswell. *How Your Play Can Crash Broadway.* New York: Howard and Criswell, 1939.

Hull, Raymond. *How to Write a Play.* Cincinnati: Writer's Digest Books, 1983.

Kerr, Walter. *How Not to Write a Play.* New York: Simon and Schuster, 1955.

Langner, Lawrence. *The Play's the Thing.* New York: G. P. Putnam's Sons, 1960.

Matthews, Brander, ed. *Papers on Playmaking.* New York: Hill and Wang, 1957.

Niggli, Josefina. *New Pointers on Playwriting.* Boston: The Writer, Inc., 1967.

Packard, William. *The Art of the Playwright.* New York: Paragon House Publishers, 1987.

Pike, Frank, and Thomas G. Dunn. *The Playwright's Handbook.* New York: New American Library, 1985.

Smiley, Sam. *Playwriting: The Structure of Action.* Englewood Cliffs, NJ: Prentice-Hall, Inc., 1971.

Straczynski, J. Michael. *The Complete Book of Scriptwriting.* Cincinnati: Writer's Digest Books, 1982.

Sweet, Jeffrey. *The Dramatist's Toolkit: The Craft of the Working Playwright.* Portsmouth, NH: Heinemann, 1993.

Williams, Tennessee. *Where I Live: Selected Essays.* New York: New Directions, 1978.

Chapter 13

Bates, Brian. *The Way of the Actor: A New Path to Personal Knowledge and Power.* London: Century, 1986.

Black, David. *The Magic of the Theater: Behind the Scenes with Today's Leading Actors.* New York: Macmillan Publishing Company, 1993.

Boleslavsky, Richard. *Acting: The First Six Lessons.* New York: Theatre Arts Books, 1933.

Burton, Hal. *Great Acting.* New York: Bonanza Books, 1967.

Cassady, Marsh. *Acting Games, Improvisations and Exercises.* Colorado Springs, CO: Meriwether Publishing Ltd., 1993.

———. *Acting Step by Step.* San Jose, CA: Resource Publications, Inc., 1988.

Chaikin, Joseph. *The Presence of the Actor.* New York: Atheneum, 1972.

Chekhov, Michael. *To the Actor on the Technique of Acting.* New York: Harper & Row, Publishers, 1953.

Cohen, Robert. *Acting Professionally: Raw Facts About Careers in Acting,* 4th ed. Mountain View, CA: Mayfield Publishing Company, 1990.

Cole, Toby, and Helen D. Chinoy, eds. *Actors on Acting: The Theories, Techniques, and Practices of the Great Actors of All Times as Told in Their Own Words.* New York: Crown Publishers, Inc., 1949.

Duerr, Edwin. *The Length and Depth of Acting.* New York: Holt, Rinehart and Winston, 1962.

Grotowski, Jerzy. *Towards a Poor Theatre.* New York: Simon and Schuster, 1968.

Jeffri, Joan, ed. *The Actor Speaks: Actors Discuss Their Experiences and Careers.* New York: Greenwood Press, 1994.

Kalter, Joanmarie, ed. "Geraldine Page," *Actors on Acting.* New York: Sterling Publishing, 1979.

McKim, Robert H. *Experiences in Visual Thinking.* Monterey, CA: Brooks/Cole Publishing Co., 1972.

O'Neill, Brian. *Acting As a Business: Strategies for Success.* Portsmouth, NH: Heinemann, 1993.

Redgrave, Michael. *The Actor's Ways and Means.* New York: Theatre Arts Books, 1953.

Schechner, Richard. *Environmental Theatre.* New York: Hawthorn Books, Inc., 1973.

Stanislavski, Constantin. *An Actor Prepares.* Trans. by Elizabeth Reynolds Hapgood. New York: Theatre Arts Books, 1936.

Chapter 14

Bradley, David, and David Williams. *Directors' Theatre.* London: Macmillan Publishers Ltd., 1988.

Clurman, Harold. *On Directing.* New York: The MacMillan Company, 1972.

Cole, Toby, and Helen Krich Chinoy, eds. *Directors on Directing.* Indianapolis: The Bobbs-Merrill Company, Inc., 1951.

Jones, Margo. *Theatre-in-the-Round.* New York: Holt, Rinehart and Winston, Inc., 1951.

Jones, Richard. *Great Directors at Work: Stanislavsky, Brecht, Kazan, Brook.* Berkeley: University of California Press, 1986.

Leiter, Samuel L. *The Great Stage Directors: 100 Distinguished Careers of the Theatre.* New York: Facts on File, Inc., 1994.

McCrindle, Joseph F., ed. *Behind the Scenes: Theatre and Film Reviews from the Transatlantic Review.* New York: Holt, Rinehart and Winston, 1971.

Chapter 15

Burdick, Elizabeth et al., eds. *Contemporary Scene Design U.S.A.* New York: International Theatre Institute of the United States, Inc., 1974.

Gassner, John. *Producing the Play,* 2nd ed. New York: Holt, Rinehart and Winston, 1953.

Gillette, A. S. *Stage Scenery: Its Construction and Rigging.* New York: Harper & Row, Publishers, 1959.

Hays, David. *Light on the Subject: Stage Lighting For Directors and Actors—and the Rest of Us.* New York: Limelight Editions, 1989.

Ingram, Rosemary, and Liz Covey. *The Costume Designers Handbook: A Complete Guide for Amateur and Professional Costume Designers,* Englewood Cliffs, NJ: Prentice Hall, 1983.

———. *The Costume Technicians Handbook: A Complete Guide for Amateur and Professional Costume Designers,* Portsmouth, NH: Heinemann Educational Books, Inc., 1992.

Izenour, George. *Theater Technology.* New York: McGraw-Hill Book Company, 1988.

Jackson, Sheila. *Costumes for the Stage.* New York: New Amsterdam, 1988, ©1987 by Sheila Jackson and published by arrangement with The Herbert Press Ltd., London.

Kaye, Deena, and James Lebrecht. *Sound and Music for the Theatre.* New York: Back Stage Books, 1992.

Larson, Orville K., ed. *Scene Design for Stage and Screen: Readings on the Aesthetics and Methodology of Scene Design for Drama, Opera, Musical Comedy, Ballet, Motion Pictures, Television and Arena Theatre.* East Lansing: Michigan State University Press, 1961.

Laver, James. *Costumes Through the Ages.* London: Thames and Hudson, 1963.

Oenslager, Donald. *Scenery Then and Now.* New York: W. W. Norton & Company, 1936.

Payne, Darwin Reid. *Computer Scenographics.* Carbondale, IL: Southern Illinois University Press, 1994.

Reid, Frances. *Designing for the Theatre.* London: A & C Black [Publishers] Limited, 1989.

Rowell, Kenneth. *Stage Design.* New York: Van Nostrand Reinhold Company, 1969.

Swinfield, Rosemarie. *Stage Makeup Step-by-Step.* Cincinnati: Betterway Books, 1994.

Chapter 16

Crawford, Cheryl. *One Naked Individual: My Fifty Years in the Theatre.* Indianapolis: The Bobbs-Merrill Company, Inc., 1977.

Farber, Donald C. *From Option to Opening (A Guide for the Off-Broadway Producer).* New York: Drama Book Specialists Publishers, 1968.

Field, Shelly. *Career Opportunities in Theater and the Performing Arts.* New York: Facts on File, 1992.

Gruver, Bert. Revised by Frank Hamilton. *The Stage Manager's Handbook.* New York Drama Book Publishers, 1952 and 1953; new material copyright 1972.

Langley, Stephen. *Theatre Management in America.* New York: Drama Book Specialists Publishers, 1974.

Lord, William H. *Stagecraft 1: A Complete Guide to Backstage Work.* 2nd ed. Colorado Springs, CO: Meriwether Publishing Ltd., 1991.

Sponberg, Arvid F. "Producing," *Broadway Talks: What Professionals Think About Commercial Theater in America.* New York: Greenwood Press, 1991.

Stern, Lawrence. *Stage Management.* 5th ed. Boston: Allyn and Bacon, 1995.

Wolf, Thomas. *Presenting Performances.* New York: ACA Books, 1991.

Ziegler, Joseph. *Regional Theatre: The Revolutionary Stage.* New York: Da Capo Press, 1973.

Acknowledgments

Edward Albee: Excerpt from *Who's Afraid of Virginia Woolf?* by Edward Albee. Reprinted by permission of Scribner, a Division of Simon and Schuster, Copyright © 1962 by Edward Albee.

William Alfred: Excerpt from *Hogan's Goat* by William Alfred, Copyright © 1966 by William Alfred, Copyright renewed 1994 by William Alfred. *CAUTION:* Professionals and amateurs are hereby warned that "HOGAN'S GOAT," being fully protected under the copyright laws of the United States of America, the British Commonwealth countries, including Canada, and the other countries of the Copyright Union, is subject to a royalty. All rights, including professional, amateur, motion picture, recitation, public reading, radio, television and cable broadcasting, and the rights of translation into foreign languages, are strictly reserved. Any inquiry regarding the availability of performance rights, or the purchase of individual copies of the authorized acting edition, must be directed to Samuel French Inc., 45 West 25th Street, NY, NY 10010, with other locations in Hollywood and Toronto, Canada.

Aristophanes: Excerpt from Aristophanes' *The Clouds,* translated by B. Bickley Rogers, from *Aristophanes, Volume 1,* Copyright © 1924 by Harvard University Press. Reprinted by permission of the publishers and the Loeb Classical Library.

John Beaufort: "New Chapter in Wilson Saga of Black Life" by John Beaufort. Copyright © March 30, 1988, *Christian Science Monitor,* Boston, Massachusetts.

Jane Chambers: Excerpt from *A Late Snow* by Jane Chambers, Copyright © 1970, reprinted by permission of Beth Allen Management, 402 Fifth Street, Greenport, NY 11944 (Phone: 516-477-2491 or 212-580-9999). *A Late Snow* is distributed by T 'n' T Classics, Inc., P.O. Box 1243, Ansonia Station, New York, NY 10023. For performance rights, contact Beth Allen Management.

Anton Chekhov: Excerpt from *Uncle Vanya* by Anton Chekhov, from *Plays by Anton Tchekoff,* translated from the Russian by Marian Fell. Copyright 1912 by Charles Scribner's Sons. Reprinted by permission of Scribner, a Division of Simon and Schuster.

Alice Childress: Excerpt from *Wine in the Wilderness* by Alice Childress, Copyright © 1969 by Dramatists Play Service, Inc. Used by permission of Flora Roberts, Inc., New York, NY.

Euripides: Excerpt from Euripides' *The Trojan Women* as translated by Richmond Lattimore, Copyright © 1947 from *Greek Plays in Modern Translation,* ed. Dudley Fitts, Dial Press. Reprinted by permission of Paul Benedict, Vice President/Trustee for the Estate of Richmond Lattimore. Bryn Mawr Trust Company, Bryn Mawr, Pennsylvania.

Nancy Franklin: Excerpt from "Camping Out" by Nancy Franklin, from *The New Yorker* © May 30, 1994.

Charles Fuller: Excerpt from *A Soldier's Play* by Charles Fuller, Copyright © 1981 by Charles Fuller. Reprinted by permission of Hill and Wang, a division of Farrar, Straus, and Giroux, Inc.

Herb Gardner: Excerpt from *Conversations with My Father* by Nancy Franklin. Copyright © 1994 by Herb Gardner. Reprinted by permission of Pantheon Books, a division of Random House, Inc.

James Goldman: Excerpt from *Lion in Winter* by James Goldman, Copyright © 1966 by James Goldman, Copyright © Renewed 1984. Reprinted by permission of Samuel French, Inc. *CAUTION:* Professionals and amateurs are hereby warned that "LION IN WINTER," being fully protected under the copyright laws of the United States of America, the British Commonwealth countries, including Canada, and the other countries of the Copyright Union, is subject to a royalty. All rights, including professional, amateur, motion picture, recitation, public reading, radio, television and cable broadcasting, and the rights of translation into foreign languages, are strictly reserved. Any inquiry regarding the availability of performance rights, or the purchase of individual copies of the authorized acting edition, must be directed to Samuel French Inc., 45 West 25th Street, NY, NY 10010, with other locations in Hollywood and Toronto, Canada.

Mel Gussow: Excerpt from "The Essential Ming Cho Lee" by Mel Gussow. Reprinted by permission from the April 1995 issue of *American Theatre,* published by Theatre Communications Group.

Lillian Hellman: Excerpt from *The Little Foxes* by Lillian Hellman, Copyright © 1939 and renewed 1967 by Lillian Hellman. Reprinted by permission of Random House, Inc.

David Henry Hwang: Excerpt from *M. Butterfly* by David Henry Hwang, Copyright © 1986, 1987, 1988 by David Henry Hwang. Used by permission of Dutton Signet, a division of Penguin USA.

Eugène Ionesco: Excerpt from *The Bald Soprano* by Eugène Ionesco, translated by Donald M. Allen, Copyright © 1958 by Grove Press, Inc. Used by permission of Grove/Atlantic, Inc.

John Lahr: Excerpt from "Sons and Mothers" by John H. Lahr, Copyright © 1994 by John H. Lahr. Reprinted by permission of Georges Borchardt,

Inc., for the author. The review "Sons and Mothers" first appeared in *The New Yorker.*

Terrence McNally: Excerpt from *Frankie and Johnny in the Clair de Lune* by Terrence McNally, as published by Dutton Signet, a division of Penguin Books USA in *Three Plays by Terrence McNally,* Copyright © 1986, 1988 by Terrence McNally. Reprinted by permission of the William Morris Agency, Inc., on behalf of the Author. All rights reserved. *CAUTION:* Professionals and amateurs are hereby warned that "FRANKIE AND JOHNNY IN THE CLAIR DE LUNE" is subject to a royalty. It is fully protected under the copyright laws of the United States of America and the Berne Convention, and of all countries covered by the International Copyright Union (including the Dominion of Canada and the rest of the British Commonwealth), and of all countries covered by the Pan-American Copyright Convention and the Universal Copyright Convention, and of all countries with which the United States has reciprocal copyright relations. All rights, including professional, amateur, motion picture, recitation, lecturing, public reading, radio broadcasting, television, video or sound recording, all other forms of mechanical or electronic reproduction, such as information storage and retrieval systems and photocopying, and the rights of translation into foreign languages, are strictly reserved. Particular emphasis is laid upon the matter of readings, permission for which must be secured from the Author's agent in writing. Inquiries concerning rights should be addressed to: Gilbert Parker, The William Morris Agency, Inc., 1325 Avenue of the Americas, New York, New York 10019. The play was originally produced by the Manhattan Theatre Club Stage II at City Center in New York City on June 1, 1987, directed by Paul Benedict, produced by Steven Baruch, Thomas Viertel, Richard Frankel and Jujamcyn Theatre/Margo Lion.

Eugene O'Neill: Excerpts from *Long Day's Journey into Night* by Eugene O'Neill, Copyright © 1955 by Carlotta Monterey O'Neill, 1987 by Yale University Press, reprinted by permission of Yale University Press.

Michael Phillips: "'No Time' Confusing Overload of Ideas" by Michael Phillips, Copyright © April 17, 1995, *San Diego Union-Tribune.* Reprinted by permission.

George Bernard Shaw: Excerpt from *Arms and the Man* by (George) Bernard Shaw, reprinted by permission of The Society of Authors (London) on behalf of the Estate of Bernard Shaw.

Martin Sherman: Excerpt from *Bent* by Martin Sherman. Copyright © 1975. Reprinted by permission of Nina Reznick on behalf of the Author.

Neil Simon: Excerpt from *Brighton Beach Memoirs* by Neil Simon, Copyright © 1984 by Neil Simon, and from *Broadway Bound* by Neil Simon, Copyright © 1987 by Neil Simon. Reprinted by permission of Random House, Inc.

These plays or portions thereof cannot be performed, recited, recorded, or broadcast in any media without a license from the Author. All such requests should be made to Samuel French, Inc., 45 West 25th St., New York, NY 10010.

Luis Valdez. Excerpt from *Zoot Suit* by Luis Valdez from *Zoot Suit and Other Plays by Luis Valdez,* Copyright © 1992 by Arte Publico Press. Reprinted by permission of Luis Valdez, El Teatro Campesino, San Juan Bautista, California.

August Wilson: Excerpt from *Joe Turner's Come and Gone* by August Wilson. Copyright © 1988 by August Wilson. Used by permission of Dutton Signet Library, a division of Penguin Books, USA.

Index

B

G

Q

R

S

T

415

Y

Z